To Vietnam With Love

A Travel Guide for the Connoisseur

To Vietnam With Love
Edited & with contributions by Kim Fay
Photography by Julie Fay Ashborn

Copyright ©2008 ThingsAsian Press

Credits and copyright notices for the individual essays in this collection are given starting on page 284.

To Asia With Love series created by Kim Fay
Cover and book design by Janet McKelpin/Dayspring Technologies, Inc.
Editing assistance provided by Robert Tompkins

Please be advised that restaurants, shops, businesses, and other establishments in this book have been written about over a period of time. The editor and publisher have made every effort to ensure the accuracy of the information included in this book at the time of publication, but prices and conditions may have changed, and the editor, publisher, and authors cannot assume and hereby disclaim liability for loss, damage, or inconvenience caused by errors, omissions, or changes in regard to information included in this book.

For information regarding permissions, write to:
ThingsAsian Press
3230 Scott Street
San Francisco, California 94123 USA
www.thingsasian.com
Printed in Singapore

ISBN-13: 978-1-934159-04-0
ISBN-10: 1-934159-04-2

Table of Contents

INTRODUCTION

Imagine that on the eve of your upcoming trip to Vietnam, you are invited to a party. At this party are dozens of guests, all of whom live in or have traveled extensively through the country. Among this eclectic and well-versed group of connoisseurs are authors of acclaimed guidebooks, popular newspaper columnists, veteran gourmets, and pioneering adventurers. As the evening passes, they tell you tales from their lives in these exotic places. They whisper the names of their favorite shops and restaurants; they divulge the secret hideaways where they sneak off to for an afternoon or a weekend to unwind. Some make you laugh out loud, and others seduce you with their poetry. Some are intent on educating, while others just want to entertain. Their recommendations are as unique as their personalities, but they are united in one thing ... their love of Vietnam. If you can envision being welcomed at such a party, then you can envision the experience that *To Vietnam With Love* aspires to give you.

Kim Fay
Series Editor, *To Asia With Love*

Every time I arrive back in Vietnam, I think about the opening line of A.S.J. Tessimond's poem "Where." *You are in love with a country where people laugh in the sun.* Despite Vietnam's many hardships throughout history, the people are as warm as the climate they inhabit. I believe that every person has a place in the world that is in harmony with something deep in her soul, and Vietnam is mine.

I fell in love with the country the moment I first arrived in Ho Chi Minh City in 1995. The buttery, tropical heat nearly made me swoon. I felt as if I were coming home. I lived there on and off for nearly four years, and I continue to return to visit friends and write about a culture that still, after all this time, captivates me.

The best thing about compiling this book was working with so many people who are in love with Vietnam as much as I am. Meeting people who love Vietnam feels like meeting fellow members of a secret society. Some I knew before I started the book; others I met along the way, and it has been such an inspiring way, developing camaraderie with the eclectic group of people who helped me create a book that is as seductive and diverse as Vietnam is.

In Vietnam you will find an abiding respect for tradition side by side with a breakneck charge into the future; grand wilderness areas and dynamic urban spaces; rusticity that has not been crafted for the tourist trade and glamour that has not been tarnished by pretension; and some of the best food on the planet. Exploring all of this in *To Vietnam With Love* are people from diverse backgrounds. Some are professional writers; all are passionate. You will read stories by English teachers, NGO volunteers, war veterans, an adoptee returning to his birth country, traveling boat makers, *Viet Kieu*, expatriates from countries as antipodal as Nepal and South Africa, and locals whose insights are invaluable.

There are beautiful symmetries in *To Vietnam With Love*, such as three essays that address the Vietnam-American War. One is by a man who cannot bring himself to tour war sites, one is by a veteran who returns to volunteer in the area where he once fought, and one is by the stepdaughter of a veteran who comes to help her stepfather heal. There are essays that take you to sad, forgotten places such as Ba Chuc, where a memorial honors more than 3,000 Vietnamese villagers who were massacred by the Khmer Rouge, and that take you on joyous journeys, including a motorcycle sidecar ride along perilous mountain roads. The book's contributors introduce you to a vast range of destinations and experiences, from a drive-in ice cream shop in Hanoi and hot springs in Hue, to ballroom dancing in Dalat and bird watching in Mui Ne. They also write eloquently about organizations created to help those in need.

One of the best things about these stories, written from so many different perspectives, is how they overlap, weaving in and out of one another in subtle ways. The resulting mosaic is a unique portrait of Vietnam, which encourages you to develop not only a relationship with the country, but also with the people who are writing about it.

If it seems that we've left out the obvious or essential, that's because we have. We trust your classic guidebooks to provide you with all the information you need to book flights, check into hotels, and find Bobby Chinn's restaurant in Hanoi or the War Remnants Museum in Ho Chi Minh City. Instead, we hope to inspire you to seek out our favorite places, discover a few of your own, and enjoy the journey just as much as the destination.

Kim Fay
Editor, *To Vietnam With Love*

How this book works

A good traveler has no fixed plans, and is not intent on arriving.
~Lao Tzu

*T*o *Vietnam With Love* is a unique guidebook with chapters organized by theme as opposed to destination. Of course, we don't want to be confusing, so within each themed chapter you will find the recommendations grouped by cities and regions. Geographically, the book moves from north to south, beginning in Hanoi, exploring the surrounding area, and then traveling down toward Ho Chi Minh City and the Mekong Delta.

Each recommendation consists of two parts: a personal essay and a fact file. Together, they are intended to inspire and inform. The essay tells a story while the fact file gives addresses, phone numbers, and other serviceable information. Because each contribution can stand alone, the book does not need to be read in order. As with an old-fashioned miscellany, you may open to any page and start reading. Thus every encounter with the book is turned into its own small armchair journey.

To facilitate locating the recommendations in the essays, the index is organized by place. As well, additional information and updates can be found online at WWW.TOASIAWITHLOVE.COM/VIETNAM. Keep in mind that *To Vietnam With Love* is selective and does not include all of the practical information you need for daily travel. Instead, reading it is like having a conversation with a friend who just returned from a trip. You should supplement that friend's stories with a comprehensive guidebook such as one published by Lonely Planet or Frommer's. That said, there are a few terms that you should be familiar with when reading these essays; these can be found on the following page.

Confucius said, "A journey of a thousand miles begins with a single step." We hope that this guide helps you put your best foot forward.

Key terms and practical information

American War: Known as the Vietnam War around the world, the conflict between the Vietnamese and Americans is known as the American War in Vietnam.

Cyclo (*xich lo*): A three-wheeled mode of transportation in which the passenger sits in a bucket seat, and the driver sits behind the passenger and pedals. As cars become more common in Vietnam, and regulations change to accommodate them, you will see fewer cyclos in the big cities.

Doi Moi: The "renovation" policies instigated by Vietnam's Communist government in 1986, which paved the way for liberalized economic and social reforms.

Metric system: Although we are an American publisher, we have used the metric system for all measurements. For easy conversion, go to: www.metric-conversions.org.

Saigon: Before 1975, Ho Chi Minh City was called Saigon. Saigon is still often used by both locals and travelers.

Tet: The Lunar New Year is also Vietnam's biggest annual holiday. Taking place over three days in late January or early February, *Tet* is an exciting time to visit, but it can also mean that shops, restaurants, and other services are closed.

Viet Kieu: A Vietnamese person who lives outside Vietnam.

VND: Vietnamese Dong is the local currency. In this book, all non-Vietnamese currency is in US dollars. Exchange rates can be found at: www.xe.com/ucc.

Xe om: Literally translated as a "motorcycle hug," this term can mean both a motorcycle taxi or a motorcycle taxi driver.

Moveable Feasts

A tasting menu of exotic flavors.

Every time I eat a meal in Vietnam, I feel as if I am participating in a conversation. As I sit on a diminutive plastic stool at a sidewalk café, my palate interpreting *banh cuon*'s silken rice paper wrapping and crisp minced pork filling, it is as if I am sharing a language with those around me. Eating in Vietnam is about more than just sustenance. It is about immersing yourself in history and culture, and bonding with every person who has ever savored the same dish you have. By simply telling a new Vietnamese acquaintance how much you love *pho* or *ca kho*, you will establish an instant rapport.

When I spent five weeks on the road to research *Communion: A Culinary Journey through Vietnam*, I was continually amazed by the attitude toward dining out, even though I had previously lived in Vietnam for four years. How often, in a Western country, does a restaurant become your second home—a place you frequent for gossip, relaxation, solace, friendship, *and* food? In her essay about Café 129, Tenley Mogk describes such an experience, which is not uncommon in Vietnam. This kind of attachment—to places and the people who run those places— shines through in all the essays in this chapter, from Adam Bray's contemplation on how Mui Ne's Forest Restaurant became a part of his life, to Jennifer Davoli's reminiscences from New York about her days and nights of eating in Hanoi. As for personal relationships with individual dishes, Nguyen Qui Duc and Christine Thuy-Anh Vu have crafted toothsome odes in their respective essays on *bun cha* and *bun rieu cua*.

Eclecticism is another attribute of this chapter. Stephen Engle waxes poetic about the fried stink bugs at Hanoi's Highway 4, while Thin Lei Win Elkin evaluates the distinctions of Nepalese cuisine at Chautari in Ho Chi Minh City. You will gain insights from locals, such as restaurateur To Hanh Trinh, whose oenophilic education sheds light on her country's relationship to the world of wine, and Professor Duong Lam Anh, who not

---

Fresh crab at the market in Nha Trang

only deconstructs the many types of *banh Hue*, but also offers suggestions on where to sample the best. In one case, a place is so special that two writers weigh in: Renee Friedman offers a personal perspective on ice cream institution Kem Trang Tien, while Elka Ray puts it in a historical context. And from my sister, whose photographs enhance this book, you will learn how even the pickiest eater can survive in Vietnam; her recipe for banana flower salad is a must-try.

Since I have dozens of favorite dishes and restaurants, it was difficult for me not to appropriate this chapter. But I managed to restrain myself and have included only one essay, on *ragu* in Dalat. As for my beloved clam rice (*com hen*) in Hue, I will allow you the adventure of tracking it down for yourself. In closing, however, I will recommend the Lang Bian Barbecue at Y Nhu Y in Dalat and the clam noodles at Phu Xuan in Ho Chi Minh City.

According to a Vietnamese proverb, "In food, as in death, we feel the essential brotherhood of man." Once you have eaten a meal in Vietnam, you will understand fully what this means.

HANOI

*Nguyen Qui Duc
obsesses about
bun cha in Hanoi*

I resent the fact that for seventeen years of my life, I did not know *bun cha* existed. I grew up in cities in central Vietnam. *Bun cha* is a product of the north. How many bowls of *bun cha* could I have eaten in seventeen years? How many bowls have I already missed? I did not even go to Paradise (read: eat my first bowl of *bun cha*) until I was thirty years old, when I returned to visit Vietnam after living abroad for several years.

It was my first trip to Hanoi, at the end of five weeks in my homeland. My companions were two American radio journalists who saw safety in established restaurants serving food that could pass for British (read: no spices or taste).

"He's going native again," my colleagues noted eight, ten times a day, as I charged through crowds and shops to satisfy an energetic, persistent, exuberant—okay, okay, out-of-control—hunger for Vietnamese fruits, spicy bowls of noodle soup, tapioca pudding with lotus seeds, and other culinary delights.

Being home after fifteen years was pure happiness; eating only Vietnamese food all the while was divine; and visiting Hanoi was a dream come true. But, as I soon discovered, few things can compare to eating *bun cha*. In Hanoi. On the streets.

One fateful day during that trip, I got my companions to "sidewalk" it with me. Actually, when I saw the tables and stools on that sidewalk, I just sat down. My companions didn't have a choice. "What're we eating?" one asked.

I had no idea. "Vietnamese food," I announced. "You'll like it."

I didn't know we'd stumbled upon a *bun cha* stand. Or rather, a *bun cha* squat. The stools were so low that you might as well be squatting. Imagine my face when the woman brought out the enormous plate overflowing with every kind of leaf and green. Then came the plate of white noodles. Then the bowl of broth—golden and clear, like the color of the finest cognac.

And then I could smell it. The aroma. The soft, sweet perfume of the grilled pork and meatballs. The whiff of Vietnamese seasoning sauce, *nuoc mam*, thinned and textured with just a drop of oil. All so inviting in that bowl of tawny broth. A feast I'd never before known. Right in front of me, ready for my pleasure.

I attacked the food. Devoured it. I made it all disappear inside me, faster than you can say "*bun cha*!"

In the years since, I've returned to Vietnam several times. The first thing I do in Hanoi is, well, you know. Can't help it! I have to have *bun cha*. Have to have it now! And hurry up, would ya,

NORTHERN VIETNAM

please? I want to go next door, eat another bowl. No, one isn't enough. Are you kidding? I haven't had one since my last trip to Hanoi. *Pleeease*! So, what's with this *bun cha*? All right. For you calmer, more rational souls, I'll concede, *bun cha* is just a noodle dish. It comes, as mentioned, in three components: the green (veggies), the white (noodles), and the golden (broth and meat).

The veggies. Let's see. Red leaf lettuce. Green leaf lettuce. Basil. Mint and cilantro. And one that's purple on one side and green on the other. Some type of shaved celery that's all beautifully curled up. There is also that triangular leaf which has a delightfully tangy lemon taste to it. Hey, I'm not a botanist, okay?

The noodles provide the white in this verdant environment. Noodles are noodles, but these are of medium thickness, and the whiteness attests to their freshness. Dated noodles turn a shade darker, and they stick together. At good *bun cha* places, the noodles are fresh and slide off each other easily.

The meat. The pièce de résistance. Ah. My English fails. Sweet, succulent, bite-size pieces of pork, grilled over a charcoal fire. Some meat is wrapped in *la lot*, large and crinkled pepper leaves with a delicate flavor. Some is seasoned with garlic, black pepper, and the slightest touch of chili sauce.

The broth. Just before you are served, the meat is dipped into the broth, which is made with a touch of fish sauce, thinned with a mixture of sweetened vinegar, water, and lime. It should be clear, with a fragile swirl

of oil from the grilled meat. No one ingredient should overwhelm another. A few slices of the thinnest freshly pickled papaya at the bottom of the broth provide a bittersweet taste.

The delight. Pick up a few strands of noodles, a few of the leaves, and dip them into the broth. Then gracefully pick up a slice of grilled pork and bring it all to your mouth. You should feel your tongue going all tangy and sweet at the same time. Relish the texture of the raw leaves, the softness of the noodles, the sweetness of the meat, and the lemony taste of the broth. At this point, say, "Ahhh." Follow that up with an "Uh-hmm." You've found Paradise.

Dac Kim

Dac Kim serves only *bun cha*. It tends to be really crowded at lunch, which starts at 11 a.m. Some evenings, it isn't open at all, or it closes early. One of the reasons I like the Dac Kim is the fact that the stools are actually the right height. There are three floors, so if the ground floor is all full, keep going upstairs. Don't feel uncomfortable if you have to share a table. This is acceptable, encouraged, and sometimes just plain unavoidable.

1 Hang Manh St.
Hoan Kiem District
Hanoi

Tong Duy Tan Street

This whole alley of restaurants This whole alley of restaurants and food stands located in the Old Quarter at the end of Hang Bong Street where five major roads converge is absolutely the place to visit, as there are many places serving Paradise. None of them has a name; just look for *bun cha* painted on pieces of plywood hanging outside. Squeeze your way through the bikes, motorcycles, customers, and "valet attendants." Sit under the verandah of the old French houses and try a bowl of *bun cha*. Talk to the old women if you can. Tong Duy Tan eateries have been around for a dozen years, but the women have been in Hanoi for many more—they have great stories to tell, and they all are skilled in making *bun cha*.

Christine Thuy-Anh Vu gets crabby over Hanoi's bun rieu cua

Certain cities never sleep, but Hanoi is not just a city that never sleeps. It is also one that never stops eating. Just take a walk through my West Lake neighborhood. With the clamor of shopkeepers waving you in to try their "famous" dish, schoolchildren running with sticky snacks in hand, and honking fast food delivery motorbikes whizzing past women selling banana fritters on the curb, you will know you have landed in the middle of a very dynamic eating culture. Around West Lake Palace,

bustling open markets and food stalls boast fresh finds from local fishmongers, who prepare them in the most mouth-watering fried, steamed, boiled, skewered, sautéed, toasted, and grilled versions.

Among these, one very light dish that should not be missed is *bun rieu cua*. This was my favorite as a kid, and while I was growing up in the States, there were many versions from cooks vying over the title of best "original" recipe. It is only one in a long list of Vietnam's famous noodle soup dishes, but it is perhaps the most widely eaten seafood noodle soup. The esteemed culinary writer, Bang Son, says that of all the *bun* noodle soups in Vietnam, the most popular must be *bun rieu cua*. But why?

When I sit down at one of my favorite *bun rieu cua* stalls, all I have to do is nod to the attendant, and moments later, out comes a giant, steaming bowl of savory noodle soup. As with many other Vietnamese dishes, every restaurant or food stall will have its own signature version, but all serving *bun rieu cua* have the basic essentials—clear tomato broth, rice vermicelli noodles, crispy-fried bean curd, and spongy crab dumplings.

The sweet and tangy broth can be made from a chicken stock and clear fish sauce, but some cooks also add pork bones, shrimp, and crab shells to make it more complex. Others spice it up by adding chilies or chili oil. The part that makes this soup extra special, though, is the crab mixture. In the old days, I have been told, *bun rieu cua* was made with shredded crab meat that you bought

Northern Vietnam

from a vendor and took home to prepare; now, with modern technology, crab meat can be sold pre-pulverized in a blender along with shrimp and eggs. From the blender, it looks like a culinary accident, but once the thick mixture is gently poured into the pot of broth, it cooks into a pink, full-flavored patty.

Fried shallots and finely minced onions are also either added to the dumplings before cooking or directly into the clear persimmon-colored broth. Chopped fresh lettuce, mint, and bean sprouts are served on the side. Some stalls, like the one in my neighborhood, will also serve it with a salty pork sausage, *gio*, that has a fine mixture of glass vermicelli and crunchy wood ear mushrooms. With a balance of textures and a unique combination of sweet, sour, spicy, and salty flavors, *bun rieu cua* is an incredibly tasty dish.

Often, kitchens are out in the open so the showmanship of the cooks becomes an attraction. An expert cook can entice with the flick of her skilled wrist and captivate watchers during the delicate execution of her specialty. When you order your *bun rieu cua*, she will grab a bowl, fill it with the delicate rice vermicelli, and with a large ladle, top it off with the boiling soup of tomatoes and crab dumplings from an enormous steel pot. Come when it's crowded, and you will get to see the real action, with the lines of bowls and the race to fill them before hungry diners even find their seats.

With this mouthwatering bowl of goodness placed in front of you and the din of the street making its way through the food stalls, the eating experience here is never short of diversion. While you slurp away and look beyond the steam, cab drivers queue along the lakefront with their minds on coffee and cigarettes, and plastic swan boats idly drift on the lake with their ice cream-snacking teenagers on dates. Really, the eating never stops in Hanoi, and you can mark your next hours exploring other treats—but instead, why not order just one more bowl of *bun rieu cua* for the road?

Understanding bun rieu cua

When trying different types of *bun rieu cua*, you will find that the consistency of the crab dumplings varies from very soft to firm. You will also notice from restaurant to restaurant that the dumplings range in color. Not to fear. Sometimes the dumplings are a little more pink or brown, depending on how many fried shallots are added or which part of the crab the meat comes from. The broth, however, should still be a clear, light-orange color. There is also a dish called *bun cua*, but don't get the two confused—they are completely different.

Finding *bun rieu cua*

Because my own West Lake haunts are a little tricky to find, I suggest the following alternatives, which also serve excellent *bun rieu cua*.

City center dining

This food stall is at a prominent

corner location, so it's quite easy to spot. It is your traditional street food stall with a fairly rundown look, but the soup is out of this world.

1 Thi Sach St.
Hoan Kiem District
Hanoi

Thanh Hong

This is perhaps one of the most successful *bun rieu cua* stalls in Hanoi. It is more upscale than the location on Thi Sach Street and even has its name elaborately etched on its porcelain bowls. The *bun rieu cua* is quite light, so don't feel like a glutton if you find yourself ordering a second or third bowl. Also, try the delectable pork sausage.

9b Hoa Ma St.
Hai Ba Trung District
Hanoi

To Hanh Trinh appreciates the fruits of the vine in Hanoi

I first heard the words *ruou vang*—wine—from my beloved grandfather when I was a little girl. My younger brother and I were lucky enough to live with my grandparents, so we were around whenever he enjoyed rice liquor with his meals. Back then, during the war of the 1960s and '70s, and even into the 1980s, wine was almost nonexistent in Vietnam. But on special occasions, we small children were given a little taste of fruit liquors. I still remember the flavors and smells of those orange and lemon elixirs.

From the stories I heard about wine in those days, my understanding was that it was a reddish liquid made from grapes in France. But some local traders faked it by mixing rice liquor with juice from the skin of the mangosteen to create a drink with the hue and tannin taste of red wine. It was not until the early 1990s, as Vietnam's *doi moi* policy gained momentum, and Vietnam increasingly opened its doors to foreign investors, that the country began to be transformed. Luckily, and with a bit of determination and confidence, I was among the first to work for a foreign corporation, and my job gave me the opportunity to travel to many other continents, opening my eyes to different and exciting aspects of life, including work, interior design, cuisine, and good wine.

While I can credit Vietnam's increasing prosperity and my travels for part of my wine education, Ray, my Australian husband, must also be acknowledged for my introduction to the world of wines—mostly New World wines, though. My apologies to the French! Ray still tells friends about our first date, which was a dinner at his house. Because of last-minute cancellations, it included only three people and four bottles of wine. The two Australians were stunned to watch me drinking as much wine as they were, and without a red face, which many

NORTHERN VIETNAM

Asians get after just a sip of alcohol. And I still found my way back home. That wine-soaked dinner—and a nearly two kilogram lobster that I hand-carried from Ho Chi Minh City for a Sunday brunch Ray hosted—won his heart. It also set the stage for our future. Little did we know that ten years later, I would end up being the co-owner of three high-end restaurants in Hanoi, overseeing a wine list of more than 100 labels from major wine-producing countries like France, Spain, and Italy, and such varied New World growers as South Africa, Chile, and New Zealand.

For most Westerners, this growing interest in wine may not seem significant, but if you knew where Vietnam was even five years ago when it came to wine, you would understand how exciting this is. Most Vietnamese have experienced wine only through traditional homemade brews. For locals to have access to fine wines is a fairly new experience, which can be attributed for the most part to Donald Berger, Managing Director of Vine Group. He has revolutionized Vietnam's wine scene. I think he deserves a medal for his efforts to introduce and educate the Vietnamese through monthly wine tastings and a wine club targeting Vietnamese clients.

I will always be grateful for Donald's raw passion for food and wine. He was the first professional wine expert to take the time to educate me, and my appreciation has grown substantially over the years. Before, while putting together my wine lists, I would ask, "Why do you buy that one? Why buy a $20 bottle and not the one for $5." Gradually, I learned about aroma, flavors, and color, and how to pair food

with wines, and I realized how unhappy I would be if I had to drink rice wine because that is what is naturally paired with Vietnamese food.

Now, wine is a part of my life, as are dinner parties, another relatively new concept here. I might gather with a group of friends—among them perhaps a music producer, a conductor, a songwriter—in a private dining room, call Cellier D'Asie wine distributor, and ask them to bring over some bottles for us to try. My vocabulary has new words, such as decanter and appellation, and recently I had a rustic wine cellar added to our home as a birthday present for my husband. I have even tasted a bottle of wine from 1966 that one of my friends bought for $10,000 at an auction in London. Such things are rare in the world in general, and to think that they are possible in Vietnam today makes them all the more thrilling. It is also why it is so much fun for locals *and* visitors to drink wine in Vietnam—there is a sense of adventure that does not exist in places that take wine for granted.

My grandfather on my father's side was my living inspiration, my hero in all respects: he was an amazing man who loved his country, risked his life for its freedom, and enjoyed life to its fullest. I remember he often told me, "You never know how long you will live. Enjoy what you love, and do it with passion."

It seems that when it comes to *ruou vang*, I am carrying on my grandfather's legacy, pursuing it with love and passion.

Whoever said, "Life is too short to drink bad wines," knew exactly what he was talking about.

Exploring Trinh's restaurants

Wild Lotus

55A Nguyen Du St.
Hai Ba Trung District
Hanoi
(84-4) 943-9342
wildlotus@ftp.vn

Wild Rice

6 Ngo Thi Nham St.
Hai Ba Trung District
Hanoi
(84-4) 943-8896
wildrice@fpt.vn

Moon River Retreat

Located on the Red River on the outskirts of Hanoi and showcasing Trinh's passion for interior design, this boutique inn also has a scenic restaurant.

Bac Cau 3
Ngoc Thuy Village
Long Bien District
Hanoi
(84-4) 871-1658
moonriverretreat@vnn.vn

Wine tasting in Hanoi

Vine Wine Boutique Bar & Café

Along with serving a great wine selection, Donald Berger's venue offers wine tasting dinners and other wine events.

1A Xuan Dieu St.
Tay Ho District
Hanoi

(84-4) 719-8000
www.vine-group.com

Local sipping

Vang Dalat

Editor's note: Trinh serves imported wines at her restaurants. For a taste of the local grape, keep an eye out for Dalat Red, produced by Vang Dalat, on menus throughout the country. While this wine has a way to go to meet international standards, it's a fun way to support Vietnam's fledgling viticulture.

www.dalatwine.com

www.novusvinum.com/features/dalat_wine.html

Tenley Mogk finds her anchor at a Hanoi café

Café 129 has been around since 1992, and I was introduced to it soon thereafter by an American professor of Vietnamese history. It was February, and he led his class, fifteen freezing college students, on bicycles up Mai Hac De Street toward warm, comforting cups of joe. Back then, the tall, narrow café offered six miniature tables, a menu of comfort food such as cheese omelets and French fries, blindingly strong coffee, and service without flair. Fifteen years later, it offers these same things, plus Mexican food. It was only just recently that the proprietors, an elderly couple with five adult daughters, slapped up a new coat of paint and reframed the photographs. Hanoi tears itself down, remodels, rebuilds, alters, and fills itself with cars and bars constantly, but Café 129 remains stubbornly, charismatically the same.

In the beginning, I studied Vietnamese vocabulary at the front table, looking up to catch a glimpse of an occasional water buffalo pulling a cart down the street—you don't see that much anymore. I'd cram lists of words into my head, silently mouthing each, seeking relief in my iced coffee when a particularly ridiculous group of vowels swarmed together. The best foreign-born Vietnamese speaker I knew hobbled in at noon on most days, sat at the table closest to the street with his back to it, and drank Lipton tea with buckets of sugar. He once produced two single-spaced, hand-written pages of Vietnamese swear words for me. Since my teachers refused to instruct me in this department, I guess because I'm female, I was until that point without street wit, a highly valuable commodity throughout the country.

Once I got a job, I'd come for a morning coffee and the paper, which I picked up from the newsstand across the street. On Sunday mornings, friends and I would show up for a sure hangover cure: French toast and avocado shakes. At the table closest to the pastry display case, I told a friend about my uncle's cancer and my imminent trip home to surprise him. My brother ate daily at 129 when he visited, and was instantly identified by the owners that June as

"Ever-perspiring Little Brother."

These days, I go to chat with the sisters. They tell me which 129 regulars have dropped in since my last visit, how tall the grandkids around the house are now, and their opinions of major world events—why can't Bill Clinton run for office again? I tell them where I've traveled since I last dropped by, the people I've come across doing HIV/AIDS work, and that I still haven't gotten married: matrimony is an unavoidable topic in Vietnam, and thus the best defense is a proactive offense.

When I'm not in Vietnam, I send the sisters postcards. When I've been gone for a long time, they ask where I've been and how my parents are doing. The sisters don't seem to age much, and that allows me to believe I haven't either. One of them is always there, primed to chat and to adamantly refuse my money. Friends and anchors they are. And the coffee is still eye-popping good.

Café 129

129 Mai Hac De St.
Hoan Kiem District
Hanoi
(84-8) 821-6342

Tenley adds a few words of advice:

All meals are served at the café. Breakfast and lunch are especially good. Service is on Vietnam time; if you're in a hurry, you're in the wrong place. This is a great place to try Vietnamese coffee with sweetened condensed milk. The ice is safe. Since this is a popular brunch spot for international undergrad and PhD students on Saturday and Sunday mornings from 10 a.m. to 2 p.m., you may not find a spot if you come during that time.

Renee Friedman cruises into a drive-in ice cream shop in Hanoi

In Hanoi, open running space is at a premium, so once a week I take my seven-year-old daughter not to the obvious choice, the park-like area around famous Hoan Kiem Lake, but to the American Club at 19-21 Hai Ba Trung Street, behind whose walls she plays soccer and runs around an unobstructed grassy patch with other foreign children seeking outdoor exercise. It isn't our back-home, great Canadian wilderness, but it is fun. The American Club is directly across the street from another ex-pat haunt, the Hanoi Cinémathèque, which shows alternative movies and is where we sometimes go for a Brooklyn egg cream after our workout: her working, me hanging out. But then we discovered "Kem Chaos," as we affectionately term our favorite ice cream place.

Situated a block away, on Trang Tien Street, one of the spokes of streets that radiate out from the Opera House, L'Espace, and many other tourist magnets, Kem Chaos is a *kem* (ice cream) outlet that is wholly, thoroughly, and absolutely Hanoian. When I was given vague directions to this place by a longstanding ex-pat, he also informed me that when the country's Communist government began to loosen its policies, this ice cream parlor was among the first to open its doors in Hanoi. Of course, people all over the city flocked to it for a rare treat before its Western counterparts arrived and places like Fanny's got a foothold.

One day we decide to forego our egg creams and search for this ice cream maverick. True to their French influence, cities in Vietnam have many, many passages, which from the street look uninviting, but that often open up onto whole other worlds. From the main street, it is difficult to determine just what lies past the entryway leading to Kem Chaos. What gives my daughter and me a strong clue is a small cluster of motorcycles and people milling around licking ice cream and dropping popsicle sticks, tissues, and related debris onto the already garbage-filled sidewalk, knowing that it will be swept up by the evening street cleaners.

Once we begin our tentative steps in, we encounter faux wrought-iron grating on walls entwined in lush plastic vines and peeling, Greek-theme-colored paint; the décor holds the promise of our favorite, tacky, Canadian West Coast gelato place. Surely, this one offers varieties of flavors ranging from pumpkin to wasabi to jackfruit, in deference to the tastes of its Asian customers. We couldn't be more mistaken. We soon realize that the similarity ends

NORTHERN VIETNAM

at the façade, and we embark on an ice cream journey unlike any other we have encountered. We dodge the numerous motorcycles driving in and out, and which in Hanoi have right of way over pedestrians.

When we reach the shop, the anticipated tables with chairs and people sitting coolly around them on stools are nowhere to be seen. Instead, we find a helter-skelter of motorcycles and people shouting to be heard above the cacophony of engine noise. Ice cream aficionados are either standing or leaning against their motorcycle seats. Since this wide space resembling an underground garage is enclosed under a roof and most customers don't turn off their engines, fumes waft through the air. In one part of the shop is a buzzing swarm of people haphazardly pushing their way forward to crowd around their queen bee—the ice cream counter.

The shoving is not aggressive, it is simply the way things are done, and we gently push our way to the front. In the area behind the counter is a shelf filled with tubs of ice cream—chocolate or green bean, but nothing too exotic. Cone after cone is filled and stored in a holder that is emptied as quickly as it is miraculously refilled. Reminiscent of *The Sorcerer's Apprentice* segment of Disney's *Fantasia*, workers magically and endlessly reappear from behind the scenes and replace dwindling ice cream tubs with full ones. There are rows of stacked unwrapped popsicles. When I look up I see outstretched, seemingly disembodied arms, Vietnamese currency in fist. In no order that I can discern, the money is removed from

each fist and replaced with either cone or popsicle and necessary change. The arms retreat and, like the tubs, are repeatedly replaced by others.

We take our cones and help ourselves to some flimsy tissues from a metal side counter, put out for wiping up the drips that this sticky-sweet, irresistibly delicious dairy concoction makes as it immediately begins to melt in the sweltering summer humidity. As my daughter and I begin to wind our way back through the mayhem, into the glaring sun and onto the touristed streets, we are delighted with our discovery and know that we will become regulars before our life here in Hanoi is through.

Kem Chaos

Kem Chaos is officially Kem Trang Tien, which Elka Ray writes about in the following essay. For location, please see Elka's accompanying fact file.

Elka Ray discovers old Hanoi in young rice ice cream

Around the turn of the millennium, I met an old friend in Hanoi. Looking glum, he announced that Kem Trang Tien—a state-owned ice cream shop near Hanoi's magnificent French-colonial Opera House—was closing down. Had the Opera House itself faced demolition he could not have been more outraged.

The rumor spread like melting *kem*,

with various Hanoian friends in their twenties and thirties bemoaning the imminent disappearance of a place filled with childhood memories. "My grandpa used to take me there," moaned one. "I took my kids there only last week," wailed another. For anyone old enough to recall the last war or what Vietnamese people call "the subsidized times" that followed, Kem Trang Tien represents bittersweet memories of days when they were so poor that an ice cream was an exceptional treat.

The rumor of Kem Trang Tien's demise proved to be just that; it remains unchanged to this day, its stark interior a sharp contrast to the art galleries and fancy boutiques that have sprung up nearby. Although some new flavors have been added—*kakao* (cocoa) and *oc que* (cinnamon)—the old ones are still served—*sua* (milk), *dau xanh* (green bean), and my favorite, *com* (young rice). The prices remain low: 2,500-3,000 VND, or less than 25 cents. Even the matrons behind the counter evoke Vietnam's pre-*doi moi* (renovation) days, back when all of the shops were state-owned and the customer was always wrong.

And yet Hanoians are as loyal as ever, still clogging Trang Tien Street with traffic as they perch on parked motorbikes and savor their *kem*, cheerfully ignoring the wardens who bellow into megaphones in an attempt to move them along. On steamy summer nights it seems that half the city stops by for *kem*, from pajama-clad grannies holding grubby tots to trendily dressed teens on dates.

In the past decade my Hanoian friends have become successful. They've studied and traveled overseas. They drive Mercedes cars and $6,000 motorbikes. Each time we meet they seem to have a new, more expensive mobile phone. Hanoi now boasts dozens of cafés that serve ice cream in pleasant, air-conditioned settings, and yet my friends still go to Kem Trang Tien and savor their *kem* surrounded by honking traffic, screaming cops, and other nostalgic Hanoians.

Kem Trang Tien
54 Trang Tien St.
Hoan Kiem District
Hanoi

Tips for ordering
Locals recommend ordering only one flavor per visit. Apparently, each flavor is a different price, and dealing with more than one flavor at a time is considered a hassle. Also, bring small bills for paying.

Jennifer Davoli eats her way through a day in Hanoi

This Saturday morning from my Manhattan apartment, I ordered a spinach cheese omelet, a toasted and buttered bagel, and a hazelnut coffee, light with cream. Each bite of this classic New York breakfast brought comfort and satisfaction,

NORTHERN VIETNAM

a nourishment to my spirit—that is, until my mind wandered to Hanoi.

A year ago today, while living in Vietnam, my morning meal would have brought the same inner joy … and then some. I made it a point to eat only among the locals, and living with a Vietnamese family my first four months, I soon discovered that eating in Hanoi awakens taste buds I didn't know existed. It combines flavors I never imagined, and it engages me in the culture. Grounding both body and mind in the present moment, a meal, in effect, embraces the spirit of Vietnam in an instant. Each bite reflects its people, its culture, its core. Each meal provides an experience in what is Vietnam.

To start the day, a classic bowl of *pho* is by far the most popular choice. In the entrance hall of the public kindergarten near my home, I join a crowd of early local commuters, filing in for a steaming broth containing barely boiled, flaky-thin beef slices surrounded by noodles. Seated at plastic tables half a meter off the ground with toy-like matching chairs, locals are served by the elderly woman who runs the stall. She offers a few fresh limes, chili sauce, and sprigs of basil for flavoring. I hunker down, chopsticks awkwardly held, and somehow manage to scoop up most of my soup. For once, I actually blend into the crowd. Conversation over *pho* is minimal, and a morning meal with the sun breaking through has both Hanoians and me captivated—a soothing start to the day.

Banh cuon, at a stand a few blocks south of Hoan Kiem Lake, is another

favorite breakfast choice for me. Offered on many street corners, this is a wet rice noodle sheet layered with minced pork, topped with dried onions, and dipped into *nuoc mam* (fish sauce): one of the best meals around for 80 cents. I usually share this pleasure with my friend Linh, while listening to her dramas of dating Vietnamese and American men.

As I move through the morning, finishing English lessons with my crew of five teenage boys, I take time to fill up on a little caffeine. I often sit at a quiet, plant-filled spot on the pedestrian walkway where I first began taking Vietnamese lessons. The owner places a glass containing a spoonful of condensed milk in front of me and then on top balances a drip can which releases black caffeinated liquid. Avoiding the clouds of heavy tobacco smoke from the older men reading local news indoors, I arduously study my Vietnamese flash cards in the outdoor area.

If I want my coffee with a pastry or fresh milk, there is only one place in town to go, despite it serving Westerners: Café 252, which was Catherine Deneuve's favorite while filming *Indochine*. This cafeteria-like shop packs in travelers for its one-of-a-kind banana bread and chocolate croissants. It emanates a fresh-baked aroma that has passersby on motos turning for a look. The homemade yogurt, presented in 80s-style, polka-dot glasses and served alongside bowls of seasonal fruits, is also a top menu item.

For lunch, I sometimes invite my

teen students to join me, using this as an opportunity to get to know them better. Not far from the Long Bien Market where many of them live are several stalls of *bun cha ca*, a fish and noodle stew with hints of mint: the healthiest meal around. We quickly slurp, digesting our meal with *cha da*, a cold herbal tea that balances out our perspiring bodies. The lady in charge here chatters away about her husband who passed away, her current boyfriend, and her daughter who doesn't like to listen. She also teases me about my own love life—or lack of one.

My typical lunch, however, is the all-time classic: *bun cha*. If you are only able to eat one thing in Hanoi, this must be it. Toward the end of my stay in Vietnam, I ate *bun cha* at least four times a week. These grilled pork patties are prepared over an open flame that crackles into a cloud of white smoke, enticing any nose within thirty meters. Floating in a broth of flavored fish sauce, garlic slivers, and chopped chili, the succulent patties are nibbled up along with cold noodles, fresh mint, cilantro, and leafy greens. At my *bun cha* joint, the son of the owner parks my bike in a hurry, flashes me a big smile, and pretends not to understand my Vietnamese. He's hawking locals with ferocity, as they pour into the competing stands for lunch hour. His flirtatious smile and friendly demeanor bring me back every time.

Some days I get a call from my friend Hanh to meet for *pho cuon*, another offer not to be passed up.

Riding on the back of her motorbike, I hug tightly as we cruise through the alleys around Truc Bach Lake, eagerly anticipating the meal to come. This dish, making my personal "Top 3," consists of fresh cilantro, boiled beef, and lettuce, rolled in a soft wet noodle, and dipped into fish sauce. Covered with sautéed garlic, spinach, and beef, the fried noodle snippets that are served with *pho cuon* are as addictive as McDonald's fries.

By the close of lunch hour, my teachers, boss, and everyone else in Hanoi insist on coffee, again, and then a nap. Post-lunch napping on motorcycles, benches, desks, or chairs is the norm. At the Vietnamese Institute of Anthropology where I teach afternoon classes, students share all sorts of fresh fruit: rambutan, longan, jackfruit, pineapple, mangosteen, or whatever else is in season at that time. As we dip grapefruit in chili-flavored salt, we chat about the weather, the office, the workday, or the culture of Vietnam. It's over this naptime fruit that I often learn my most insightful lessons.

After a day of teaching, around four, I head back toward home for a cup of *che*. Green mung bean mixed with coconut milk, fresh fruit, and/or jelly-like agar, *che* is the most varied dessert offered in Vietnam. Located in an unusually wide alley, my *che* place has narrow stairways leading to several floors of seating, and serves its *che* in glass mugs with a bowl of ice. With ice scooped into it, *che* becomes a cool sweet to relieve the tropical heat. Every Vietnamese seems to know about this secret spot and is willing to pay the extra 20 cents for its generous portions, and yet, as far as I know, not one Westerner, other than me, has ever ventured here.

By now it's nearly the dinner hour, and with it comes an entirely new set of options, but for now, I head home. As I rest, contemplating my evening dining options, a summer afternoon rain shower brings my appetizing day to a close.

Finding Jennifer's favorite Hanoi dining haunts

Breakfast

Pho café

This nameless shop is located in a pre-K school parking lot, which is converted to a restaurant in the morning. Look for the sign "Truong Mam Non Sao Sang."

44 Tran Hung Dao St. (north side between Hang Bai and Ngo Quyen Streets)
Hoan Kiem District

Bun oc café

Nguyen Quyen St., Alley 220
Hoan Kiem District

Banh cuon café

On the east side of Ba Trieu Street at To Hien Thanh Street.
Hai Ba Trung District

Coffee

Café Nhan

7A Tong Duy Tan Food St. (pedestrian walkway)
Hoan Kiem District

Café 252

252 Hang Bong St.
Huan Kiem District

Lunch

Bun Ca (for bun cha ca)

42 Hang Dao St. (at Hung Phuc St. near Long Bien Bridge)
Ba Dinh District (bordering Hoan Kiem District)

Bun Cha Hoang Anh (for bun cha)

47 Bui Thi Xuan St.
Hai Ba Trung District

Pho cuon café

25 Ngu Xa St. (near Truc Bach Lake)
Ba Dinh District

Snacks

Che café

This shop is located in a small, wide alley on the north side of Tran Hung Dao Street between Quang Trung and Da Tuong Streets.

72G Tran Hung Dao St.
House G in Alley 72
Hoan Kiem District

Stephen Engle tries not to let Hanoi drive him buggy

Have you ever driven a motorcycle down an open road, open-mouthed into a swarm of winged stink bugs? Me neither. But I can tell you what it might taste like, and even where you can taste such a thing. Tucked away down Hang Tre Street in old Hanoi, Highway 4 is *the* road kill café. It's where your meal meets the windshield.

A Vietnamese stink bug crunches under the teeth not unlike popcorn. But it's not corn, and you know it with each crispy-fried exoskeleton crunch. What you're eating is an unfortunate sap-sucking arthropod whose foul-smelling, predator-thwarting glandular emissions were no match for oil and a wok.

"Stink bugs are healthy," I was told by Markus Madeja, a native of Switzerland who started the restaurant in 2000 with his Vietnamese wife. "They're high in protein and low-fat. All bugs are low-fat."

And these were the best low-fat stink bugs I ever tasted—washed down swiftly with Markus' homemade snake liquor (two cobras, two kraits, and one grass snake) that, as the menu promised, coiled around my taste buds. I passed on the hooch juiced from gecko, seahorse, and starfish for reasons best described by the distiller: "Gecko increases blood pressure and is a real booster to the lower parts." Markus added with a grin, "And seahorse is the real natural Viagra."

If you need an extra buzz or spring in your step, try the crispy-battered bee larvae, crispy-fried crickets, or locusts roasted with lemon leaves. If lemon isn't your thing, then try crunchy-grilled scorpions or finely chopped sparrows with prawn crackers. Strange that they had run out of vegetables and tofu the day I was there.

To be fair, Highway 4 has a diversified menu with dishes from all corners of the animal kingdom: chicken grilled in a passion fruit sauce; banana flower salad with dried beef (highly recommended—we ordered two); and catfish spring rolls, "a Highway 4 specialty." What's more, you can even join cooking classes to, as the menu says, "produce an authentic taste back home."

Best to ask your local grocer when stink bugs are in season.

Highway 4

5 Hang Tre St.
Hoan Kiem District
(84-4) 926-0639
www.highway4.com

Beyond stink bugs

Editor's note: Along with exotic, powerfully flavored snake liquors, Highway 4 also offers more popular fruit liquors (plum, apricot, apple, mulberry, passion fruit, etc.), traditional blends (a range of liquors made with a selection of

NORTHERN VIETNAM

NORTHERN VIETNAM

traditional herbs), and plain Phu Loc liquor, which is the base for all the liquor varieties. All of these high-quality liquors are produced under the Son Tinh name, which is a registered brand belonging to Highway 4. As well, you will find many non-bug-oriented dishes on the menu, but keep in mind that these classic Vietnamese favorites are tailored for a Vietnamese clientele. This is not the place to get a sanitized, spring roll experience. But if you want a taste of authentic Vietnam, it's a great start.

Renee Friedman isn't chicken to get your goat in Hanoi

During my stay in Hanoi, I taught English to some relatives of a friend from back home. It started with four people, but as is the custom in Hanoi, the relatives brought a couple of friends who brought a couple of co-workers who brought a couple of relatives, and soon the class burgeoned to more than twenty people. In exchange for the free lessons, the students would often bring me some small gifts or take me out to sites of interest.

One man, Huyen, regularly offered to take me out for a meal in my "spare time." Initially, he chose places like Pepperoni's Pizza, but when he realized that I didn't relish the thought of eating cheap pizza,

he switched to venues that served food more typical of cuisine from the countryside. It became our routine: I would call his mobile phone in my "spare time," and he would come to get me on his motorcycle. I would hop on, an obvious foreigner with my helmet. If it was raining, he would bring the double-hooded plastic ponchos made especially for motorcycles, and we would ride off for an adventure in the foods of Vietnam.

We never made it to one popular tourist mecca, the snake village where one is served snake parts and snake wine. But we did get to establishments where the fare ranged anywhere from buffalo, eel, turtle, dog, and cat in various forms, to seafood like *cha ca* or *cha muc* (fish or squid pancakes), to the *really* unusual. I was taken to a restaurant on a reservoir where we fished for our own lunch. The water was filthy and rubbish-laden. When I tactfully commented on this, I was told, "The fish like garbage." Luckily, we were unlucky that day and had no bites.

On Chicken Street, as I termed it, technically the corner of Ly Van Phuc and Ngo Nguyen Thai Hoc, was a row of storefront barbeques, tables, and chairs. During hot nights, electric fans were placed outside to cool the customers. Each spot served chicken parts grilled on skewers. There was a choice of thigh, breast, wing, or claw/foot. The wings at approximately 15 cents each were the best value for your money. There were also potato slices on a stick and a bannock-like fried bread, spread with a thin layer of honey. As you order, the item, which is printed on individual papers, is ticked off. One friend managed to get eighteen ticks next to his *bia* (beer) column. At one place we visited, Anchor beer was flowing on tap and cucumber salad was gratis with each order. If chicken isn't your thing, kitty-corner across the street on Nguyen Thai Hoc is a *pho sao* (fried flat noodles with vegetables and broth) stand. Just saying *"khong mi chinh"*—hold the MSG—is enough to be duly rewarded with a savory platter.

Once we rode down a labyrinth of lanes and alleys so twisting I could never have found my way out, let alone back in again. I wondered at how Huyen could navigate so confidently. One alley was so narrow I feared my knees would scrape against the walls. Eventually we arrived at a place that served a multitude of frog dishes, and only frog dishes, from frogs brought in from the countryside. People were sitting in what appeared to be the living room of a private home, straw mats rolled out, cushions on the floor, and communal plates of food in the center with personal eating bowls for each person. Since the living room was fairly full, we were led up the stairs to what was obviously a bedroom, and as we joined another party that was already eating, we were brought the usual seven different varieties of frog—all delicious.

By far, the most memorable culinary adventure was when we hit an insect establishment. While I found the desiccated and fried grasshoppers crunchy and palatable, if somewhat bland, I could not manage the "house crickets," a euphemism for cockroach. We were served a heaping mound of them, looking very fat and juicy, on a platter. Despite my

open-mindedness about food and cultural differences, I could bring the roach to my lips, and even open my mouth, but try as I might, I couldn't make myself eat it.

Meanwhile, Huyen, unconsciously and unknowingly providing an imitation of my Jewish mother, admonished me, "Eat, eat, they're good for you!" Visions danced in my mind of my childhood in Brooklyn apartment buildings and my mother's perpetually full Roach Motels—cockroach traps. I thought of our tight budget and all the food we wasted then. Of course, I also thought of this country whose population was starving in the 1980s due to food shortages, and the resourcefulness of the populace in making anything that was remotely edible, edible.

It was to my great surprise when on our next outing Huyen took me to a place at a busy intersection only a few blocks from my house. It was a *bia hoi* (beer hall), famous in Hanoi for its beer on tap and succulent goat hot pots. I had passed it often and was always tempted to go in, but was reluctant because of what I presumed would be a language barrier. Like the frog establishment, there was a multitude of ways to eat goat in addition to *lau thit de*, the goat hot pot served to each group of diners with a mini gas burner and a boiling pot of broth on top. Flat rice noodles, bean sprouts, and greens accompanied the slices of goat, all of which we added to the broth in a specific sequence at Huyen's leisure. There were side dishes of crackers, pickled cucumber, and alternatively prepared goat bits. This place was bustling with Vietnamese customers

NORTHERN VIETNAM

from near and afar, making it an ideal immersion in local color and cuisine.

Getting some goat

This always-crowded place is right on Lang Ha Street, a few doors up from the National Cinema. If you can't speak Vietnamese, you can always point to the dishes of other patrons or basic words in a dictionary, and the helpful waiters will assist in any way they can. Beer flows freely. The low tables are surrounded by chairs the size of footstools. As you squat over your meal, the garbage just gets thrown either on the floor or into the street if you are seated at the sidewalk tables sandwiched between the curb and the parked motorcycles. There are restaurant "valets" who park your motorcycle on the sidewalk, chalk a number onto the seat, and provide you with a paper with the corresponding number. If, like me, you are not the beer-drinking type, you may grab one of the cans of soda or bottles of water already on the table; you get charged for ones you open.

Joe Springer-Miller whets his appetite on a Hanoi block

As I walk with my nieces and sister-in-law along Ly Thai To Street, across from the Sofitel Metropole Hanoi, I think about how much I love this little block. Whenever I'm not quite sure what I'm in the mood to eat in the evening, I head for the restaurants that fill this short stretch. Over the course of just a handful of places, strikingly different foods, atmospheres, and prices can be found.

On the corner at #59A is the famous Hanoi Press Club. Perhaps the first real venue for networking news or finding rare-in-Hanoi dining treats and sports viewing from home countries, the Press Club started in the mid-1990s and remains a great place to connect with others. Over the years it has expanded, and it now offers a popular restaurant, deli, bar, and The Terrace, which is somewhere between a bar and a club, and is absolutely hopping on Fridays with its DJs and live music.

Next, in the middle of the block at #59, we pass the well-known Club Opera, one of the best Vietnamese restaurants in the city, very traditional and featuring lovely, un-amplified classical Vietnamese music. Farther down at #57 is a nice outdoor venue called Au Lac Café. But for me, the real treasure is yet to come.

At the other end of the block on the far corner, with the same street number as Au Lac, is Diva Art Café. A few tables are inside, but most are spread around the corner outside, under a sheet roof and a huge mango tree that shades most of the restaurant. I love mango, and if you order something with mango in season, there may even be fruit from the tree above on your plate.

This gem features a typical Vietnamese travelers' menu with every dish you have ever seen anywhere in the country and at reasonable prices. The difference is that while many decent restaurants have this kind of variety, they just can't get the Western fare right. Not so at Diva Art Café. My nieces love the chicken parmesan, which goes great with the game of UNO that we like to play with their mom. Served with crisp steamed vegetables, mashed potatoes, and all my favorites, the dishes here never disappoint me. As for a sweet treat to cap my meal, I always go for the Orange Irish Coffee. This place is so friendly, and let's face it, it is canopied by a sprawling mango tree in the middle of one of the nicest areas of Hanoi. How can you go wrong?

Diva Art Café

Along with a wide array of food, there is jazz music outside on the weekends, and a pianist plays on most weeknights.

57 Ly Thai To St.
Hoan Kiem District
Hanoi
(84 4) 934-4088

Jennifer Davoli nibbles away during the dinner hour in Hanoi

While dinner options in Hanoi are diverse, most locals eat in their homes. Mothers, daughters-in-law, and live-in nannies are usually in charge of the production of meals. When I first come to Vietnam from New York, my own meals are often eaten with the Vietnamese family I live with, until I learn all that this city has to offer.

Fried rice may sound unexciting, but at 90 cents a plate at ABC, or just a bit more at the "upscale" Chien Beo, I rediscover the pleasure of this simple dish. I often go with my friend Tuan to "Fat Chien's," which is accurately named after the chubby owner. Heading north out of town, we ride on Tuan's chocolate-brown Vespa, and once there, we share *com rang*—fried rice—along with dishes of sweet, tender, marinated beef chunks known as *bo luc lac*. Big crowds, big tables, and a bustling clientele of wealthy Hanoians make this one of the few places in town where locals actually wait in line to eat. As a successful young Vietnamese who studied architecture and worked in the States for many years, Tuan can afford this splurge, though he's equally content at the simpler ABC, Chien Beo's polar opposite, where the rice is almost as good.

Closer to home, on rainy evenings, I head for *my xao*—fried noodles with tomato, spinach, and beef—served by the café owner who insists on marrying me off. Looking on while I awkwardly manage noodles with chopsticks, she explains that her brother, thirty years my senior, wouldn't make too bad a husband. The four young teens who serve, cook, and clean eagerly chat with me while we fawn over the adorable pair of mutts that appear to rule this roost.

You may be able to eat dog meat in Vietnam, but don't let anyone tell you that the Vietnamese don't love their pets. These two dogs, along with the teens, provide plenty of entertainment for everyone, as well as opportunities to practice my Vietnamese language skills. My meals, delicious in themselves, are just one part of the unforgettable evenings where I almost feel like a member of a Vietnamese family.

There is, however, no debate as far as I'm concerned on the best evening meal to be had in this country, and one that I indulge in to no end. *Lau*—hot pot—is not only a meal, but also a social and communal event that I miss most dearly now that I've returned to live in New York. Whenever the huge bowl of boiling broth is placed between us, all my Vietnamese friends kindly opt for the seafood, passing up chicken hearts and cow brain for my sake. Instead, we order clams, shrimp, fish patties, calamari, water spinach, taro, Chinese mushrooms, tofu strips, and wheat noodles for our seafood hot pot, known as *lau hai san*. Over a period of an hour, each element is dropped into the pot by the leading females at the table, boiled, and served, at which point each bite is dipped into side dishes of salted lime juice. I generally take a back seat in this process and let my friends Vi, Hanh, or Trang run the show. The eating goes on and on, along with accompanying beers or sodas as we all get lost in the Tao of *lau.*

Lau is a long meal where eating goes in stages—cooking is an essential part of the process, and drinks must accompany. Along with giving me nourishment, my *lau* dinners are often a time to share my thoughts as well as my struggles with my Vietnamese friends, and for them to offer guidance and insights. As we eat, I find myself reflecting on all I've learned during my time in Hanoi, including one of the city's greatest lessons: how well the Vietnamese use the ritual of eating to enjoy life in the present moment.

ABC

This is the sister restaurant of Restaurant 123, at 55 Pho Hue Street. ABC is a few blocks north between Tran Hung Dao and Ham Long Street. It serves a Western-friendly menu, but I'm telling you, the fried rice is fabulous.

Chien Beo/"Fat Chien's"

Known as a steakhouse, this restaurant serves terrific *bo luc lac* and steaks, as well as fried rice.

192 Nghi Tam St.
Tay Ho District
Hanoi
(84-4) 716-1461

Nguyen Hung (for my xao)

This restaurant also serves incredible *pho.*

27 Han Thuyen St. (just east of Lo Duc St.)
Hai Ba Trung District
Hanoi

Lau 4C (for hot pot)

4C Cam Chi St.
Ba Dinh District
Hanoi

HUE

Duong Lam Anh deconstructs the subtleties of banh Hue

Formerly the imperial capital of Vietnam, modern-day Hue is characterized by a unique mix of royal and common lifestyles. This combination can be found in various aspects of day-to-day life, and the cuisine is no exception. Because of the city's noble heritage, dishes are diverse and well known for their distinctive flavors. Among the foods that visitors should try is *banh Hue*. The umbrella term for a type of small, often bite-sized dishes, *banh Hue* comes in many different varieties, all made from the same, simple ingredients: regular rice, sticky rice, or cassava flour, plus shrimp and/or pork. The secret then lies in the way those ingredients are put together.

Even more interesting is that within each kind of *banh Hue* usually two versions exist. One is served at formal meals and the other on casual occasions. Often, the differences are so subtle that even some Hue locals do not notice. For example, *banh nam* and *banh la* are seemingly similar: sticky packets of steamed rice flour filled with ground shrimp and pork. But while *banh nam* is wrapped in banana leaves, the ultra-thin *banh la*

is wrapped in *la dong*, another type of leaf, which adds a special fragrance that the banana lacks. And *banh la* is always accompanied by *cha tom* patties, made from shrimp.

The same duality holds true for *banh bot loc*, whole shrimp and boiled pork inside a nearly translucent tube of cassava flour. The ones wrapped in banana leaves look neat and are used for formal meals, while the more modest ones without leaves are sold by street vendors as snacks. As well, *banh beo*, which is a disc of steamed rice paper batter topped with a mixture of minced shrimp and green onions, has two types: *banh beo dia* is displayed on plates, while the stickier *banh beo chen* is served in tiny bowls. I like *banh beo chen* because it is fun to eat. Children often compete with each other, counting the number of bowls they leave after a meal. Originally, to eat *banh beo*, diners used knives made of bamboo. Today, to suit the formal atmosphere in restaurants, chopsticks are provided instead. But if you buy *banh beo* from street vendors, chances are that you may still be given a bamboo knife and can eat the snack in the traditional way.

The next set of differences when it comes to *banh Hue* concerns the sauces. As you may already know, *nuoc mam* (fish sauce) is the staple ingredient for Vietnamese sauces. Fish sauce by itself is unique—many visitors find its distinctive smell unbearable—but how Vietnamese cooks use it to make so many different kinds of sauces is impressive. The key is in the amount of supplementary ingredients added. A squeeze of lime juice, some slices of green and/or red chili, a little bit of fresh garlic, a

CENTRAL VIETNAM

dash of sugar, and varying amounts of water, for example, can all bring about very different results. And the most interesting part for me? Making sauces must be learned by experience, not from recipes.

Each type of *banh Hue* should be served with a different kind of sauce. *Banh bot loc, banh nam,* and *banh la* go well with pure, salty fish sauce, plus some slices of green and red chili and nothing else. *Banh uot,* which is a sheet of steamed rice flour containing shrimp *(tom)* or grilled meat *(thit nuong)* and fresh herbs, must be dipped into a mixture of fish sauce, shredded chili, garlic, and lots of lime juice. Both *banh beo* and *banh it,* a pork-filled, sticky rice flour dumpling, taste best with fish sauce and other spices such as sugar, chili, some drops of lime juice, and especially shrimp paste.

Another important distinction of Hue cuisine is that it must be pleasing to the eye. Hue cooks believe that the appearance of the dish is by no means less important than its taste. Each dish is a combination of specific colors and shapes. Traditionally, *banh la* is cut up into rectangular shapes and placed neatly on a plate surrounding cubes of *cha tom,* though some cooks roll the *cha tom* inside the *banh la. Banh khoai* provides a good example of artisanship too. This is perhaps Hue's most famous *banh Hue* specialty, an omelet-style dish consisting of a rice flour "crepe" filled with pork, shrimp, and bean sprouts. When presented properly, it is its own work of art.

Because of Hue's imperial legacy, a history of emperors who ate dozens of different dishes at a single meal, don't expect an abundance of food when you order. You will receive just a little of each dish at a time. While this may seem unsatisfying to Western appetites at first, what it means is that you will always have room to try just one more of the many types of *banh Hue* offered around the city.

Sampling banh Hue

All types of *banh Hue* are sold at various places throughout Hue. On Nguyen Binh Khiem Street you should seek out Huong Cau (#4) and Ba Do (#7). The city's well-known Hang Me restaurant has moved to 45 Vo Thi Sau Street.

Banh khoai

Besides Lac Thien on Dinh Tien Hoang Street near Thuong Tu Gate, the famous *banh khoai* restaurant mentioned in some guidebooks, there is Quan 222 (or Ben Do Con) on Chi Lang Street, which isn't as well-known to tourists, but is my favorite.

Banh uot thit nuong

To try *banh uot thit nuong,* head north to the Kim Long area (about halfway to Thien Mu Pagoda). Huyen Anh Restaurant is at 52 Kim Long Street on the right side of the road.

More about banh Hue

This informal online guide has plenty of pictures to help you identify types of *banh Hue.*

http://dina-n-brian.com/Alice/Banhguide.htm

Michael Burr befriends a fellow photographer in Hue

If you find yourself in the old imperial capital of Hue on the central coast of Vietnam, be sure to stop in at Mandarin Café on the south side of the Perfume River.

When I was last in Hue, during the Tet holiday, I checked into my hotel in the Old City, grabbed a cyclo, and headed over to the Mandarin, anticipating a tasty lunch and a reunion with the owner, the affable Mr. Phan Cu. I met Cu on my first trip to the city in 2003, when he was referred to me by a fellow photographer, a *Viet Kieu* friend of mine in California. Cu is an accomplished photographer who has exhibited in Paris and Milan, and the walls of his café are lined with his images. Upon my arrival, I found the restaurant closed for the holiday, but fortunately Cu was there. He suggested we go elsewhere for lunch, so we jumped on his motorbike and went to a fantastic place on the banks of the river where we dined on fresh crab and other Hue delicacies.

After lunch we got back on the bike and headed out into the countryside. We drove down a dirt road bordered by rice fields and soon arrived at a small hamlet where the villagers were gathered around celebrating Tet by drinking, socializing, and playing a gambling game. I got many great shots that would not have been possible without Cu's help, since I *never*

would have been able to find this place on my own. After about an hour we started back into the city, stopping along the way by the river where I was again able to take more terrific photos of fishing boats, children playing, etc. Then it was back to the Mandarin for an ice cold Huda beer: the perfect ending to a perfect day.

Mandarin Café has a full menu of Asian and Western fare to suit all tastes, and you can browse through a number of albums of Cu's photography while enjoying breakfast, lunch, or dinner. I'm fond of the banana pancakes and the *banh khoai*, a savory rice-flour crepe. Prints, postcards, and calendars featuring Cu's work are available for sale. There is also a travel desk where you can book tours, including boat cruises to the pagodas and temples on the Perfume River. In short, Cu is a great resource, and Mandarin Café is a great place to enjoy a good meal, hang out, and meet other travelers from around the world. Do stop in and, if you're so inclined, say I sent you. Who knows? You may even find yourself on the road with Cu, in search of the perfect photo op.

Mandarin Café
24 Tran Cao Van St.
Hue
(84-54) 821-281

HOI AN

Alice Driver pledges her loyalty to a Hoi An restaurant

First I must explain that I am a foodie, a person who relishes everything from a delicious eggplant curry to crusty bread eaten on the side of the road. I don't just get excited about food, I dream and plan my days around meals just like Sancho Panza, Don Quixote's trusty sidekick. I wake up thinking, "What will I eat today?" and this thought motivates me right out of bed.

One of the great joys of traveling through Vietnam was the opportunity to try new dishes—dishes I had never eaten before in my life—every day. In Hanoi I sampled sweetened sticky rice with sesame and coconut milk; crispy shrimp sweet potato pancakes; bowls of steaming *pho* noodles garnished with ginger, lime, and fresh cilantro; and hot buns filled with sweet red bean paste. I was fascinated daily by the different jelly drinks sold on the side of the street; they included ingredients such as water chestnut, tapioca pearls, coconut milk, and syrup made of dragon fruit.

When my husband Isaac and I arrived in the town of Hoi An and settled down for a month, I set off to turn the city upside down in search

of good food. Isaac was working on a boat-building project in Dien Duong, and we spent our afternoons sharing lunch with the boat builder, Anh Lu, and his family. Some days they served us steamed fish covered with peanuts, greens, and hot peppers, and other days it was bits of pork, greens, rice, and fresh fruit. Always we were offered homemade rice alcohol, and once Anh Lu mixed the alcohol with fresh sheep blood and made a toast to our health.

One day while out walking near our hotel, Isaac and I found the Mermaid Restaurant. Outwardly, there was nothing to endear it to us, just a normal-looking restaurant facing the street. It didn't have any particularly exciting decorations or striking artwork, but tired and hot, we walked in for dinner. The restaurant was open to the street, and we watched children run by selling clay whistles and colorful postcards, women in conical hats hawking their daily wares, men selling pyramids of fuchsia and green dragon fruit, bicycles piled with two or three kids, and gaggles of tourists streaming by. As I sat and observed, I thought about how the Vietnamese have a sense of industriousness that is palpable.

We first ordered White Rose, a flower-shaped steamed dumpling filled with meat. One serving of this signature Hoi An dish included three small dumplings, which quickly disappeared. Next came a green mango and shrimp salad and two mango-lime smoothies. Green mango, peanuts, wedges of lime, Thai peppers, and ripe mango formed the salad, which was garnished with a sprig of fresh mint. It was an appetizing mix of spicy and sweet. In coming days, I would enjoy the equally tasty spicy beef salad. The smoothies brought me the most happiness because they arrived cold and were made of real fruit. How many times had I ordered a smoothie and been disappointed by a lukewarm drink tasting of fake fruit syrup? Too many! Isaac ordered a sugar and lime pancake for dessert, and liked it so much I hardly got a bite.

We returned to the restaurant many times during our month in Hoi An, and enjoyed the food, service, and staff. For those days when we were feeling homesick or craving something familiar, we ordered the blue cheese pizza or even, sometimes ... a hamburger. The waitresses at the restaurant came to know us by name, and before we left, they gave us a handmade paper lantern as a farewell gift. Although there were other good restaurants in Hoi An, we remained loyal to the Mermaid Restaurant, since we felt it offered the best combination of quality, price, and hospitality.

Mermaid Restaurant

I recommend the fresh spring rolls, eggplant, fish in oyster sauce, clay pot dishes, and fruit smoothies, but I was happy eating almost everything I tried on the menu.

02 Tran Phu St.
Hoi An
(84-510) 861-527
www.hoianhospitality.com

Alternative dining

Good Morning Vietnam

I highly recommend the chocolate mousse here. The other food is a bit overpriced, but the mousse is divine.

34 Le Loi St.
Hoi An
(84-510) 910-227

Hoi An Hai San

Owned by a Swedish man and his Vietnamese wife, this restaurant offers a delicious homemade passion fruit ice cream. The dinner menu is also excellent, but more expensive than at the Mermaid Restaurant.

64 Bach Dang St.
Hoi An
(84-510) 861-652

DALAT

Kim Fay infiltrates Dalat's secret world of ragu

I have been to Dalat, in the southern highlands of Vietnam, many times. It's my favorite destination in the country. Although I have a restaurant of choice there, the Maison Long Hoa, I could not say that there was a dish I associated with the city until my last visit. I was traveling through Vietnam working on a food book, and I had been corresponding with Antoine Sirot, an

SOUTHERN VIETNAM

infectiously enthusiastic gourmet and the general manager of the Sofitel Dalat Palace—the best hotel in all the world. In one of his emails, he wrote the following:

"A popular delicacy is *ragu*, spelled *ragout* in French. It is basically a long-cooking stew in a pot, mixing meat and vegetables, and flavored with herbs. This dish is traditionally served with French bread in a local restaurant and people dip slices in the stew, just like French peasants used to do in their countryside. It is very suitable to Dalat's cool temperatures, quite affordable and flexible: potatoes, white beans, peas, carrots, and mushrooms mixed with beef or sometimes pork."

The moment I read this, I began craving *ragu*. I just *had* to have it. When my sister Julie and I arrived in town, the first thing I did was ask the hotel's head of guest services, Linh, where we could eat the best *ragu* in town. Linh had been crafting an itinerary interwoven with appointments for my book. She managed to cram my *ragu* request into the agenda on Day Two.

As our scheduled time to try *ragu* came and passed, Linh began to stress out. We had been at least an hour late to every appointment so far, and I couldn't understand why she was so concerned that we were running behind for lunch, especially since Vietnam is not a country big on punctuality. As our car raced up to Doan Doan, a small café located on a side street just off the main town square, Linh practically booted us out and told us to call her when we were through.

The place was simple and clean, the way the best Vietnamese restaurants are. The lunch crowd had come and gone—it was after two—and we were

given a table at the front picture window. Beyond Julie, across the street, were two slender buildings separated by an alley. Down the alley, crowning an upslope of tile roofs like a coronet, was the Eiffel Tower, or rather a facsimile of the original, serving as the local telecommunications tower. The theme song from *Love Story* played softly over the stereo system, as if to make us feel at home, since we had already heard harp, piano, xylophone, and Filipino band versions of it throughout this trip.

The atmosphere was tranquil and the staff attentive but unobtrusive. As happens in dreams, when events occur out of sequence, but still make sense, two bowls of *ragu* were brought to our table before we had a chance to order. One was beef, the other vegetarian for Julie, who does not eat beef or pork. Both smelled warm, not just in temperature, but with the promise of a snug comfort, which was antidotal to the gloomy weather outside. A plate with thick slices of a fresh baguette was set on the table between us. We requested beer. We were in heaven.

We talked, quietly, mostly about the *ragu*. It was made with ingredients similar to those used in a stew, such as onions, potatoes, mushrooms, and peas, but the broth was lustrous, a silken consommé rather than a thick gravy. There was a buttery flavor that we were unable to determine. Later, cooking with the Dalat Palace's Chef Huong, we learned that it came from a combination of fish sauce and tomatoes, the latter peeled, seeded, and completely reduced so not a trace of their flesh remained. The bread in Dalat is different from bread in the rest of the country, lighter, as if to better absorb the broth. Julie finished all of her broth, even though she suspected (as she often did with "vegetarian" food in Vietnam) that it was meat-based.

I requested a menu to see how the restaurant described its *ragu*. I found steamed porcupine, wild boar, grilled anteater, and fried deer, but no *ragu*. Once we were back in the car and headed to our next appointment, I asked Linh about this, and she told me that *ragu* is rarely on menus. It takes too much time to prepare. You can't just saunter into a restaurant and ask for a bowl. You must order ahead of time so that it is prepared and waiting when you arrive.

This explained her concern about our being late. It also made me happy, I confess, in a smug way. I had discovered the secret world of *ragu*. It was a world the average traveler did not know about, but that I knew about because an insider told me. Now, I am an insider too.

Doan Doan

8 bis Nam Ky Khoi Nghia St.
Dalat
(84-63) 510-588

Rustic ragu

For a down-home *ragu* experience at a restaurant favored by locals, try Hoan Kiet. Order a bottle of local Dalat Red wine to complement your meal. Keep in mind that the staff does not speak English.

31 Hoang Dien St.
Dalat
(84-63) 826-921

Making ragu

You can learn how to make Dalat *ragu* by taking a lesson with Chef Huong at the Sofitel Dalat Palace hotel. Go to the cooking class essay on page 275 for more information.

Maison Long Hoa

Simply because I love this place, I must include it. The menu contains high-quality Vietnamese fare, and the ambience—with its warm lighting and classical music— always soothes me. I have spent many an evening here, and I have always left feeling a sense of calm, as if the world has slowed down just for a moment, so that life can be enjoyed to the fullest.

#6 Ba Thang Hai St.
Dalat
(84-63) 822-934

MUI NE

Adam Bray finds history, heart, and soul in Mui Ne

Although the Forest Restaurant looked like the ruins of some ancient Cham temple swallowed by the jungle, construction had just completed when I first arrived in Mui Ne. Its primitive brick

SOUTHERN VIETNAM

walls, fired in the kilns outside Phan Thiet, seemed to crumble where vines and native flora crept through. Streams of sunlight and rhythmic downpours alternated through the ceiling and into the central rainforest garden.

Half the staff lived in the fishing village while the others were ethnic Cham from Phan Rang. Many of my local friends were hired, and they asked me to tutor them in English so they could speak more easily with foreign customers. I was honored when the owner later invited me to be the restaurant's first guest, to thank me. When I climbed the stone stairway that opening night, passing the garden streams, I saw that the inner walls were decorated with Cham textiles and ceramics, as well as masks, hunting implements, and crafts made by highland minorities. The display rivaled any museum exhibit I'd seen in Vietnam.

The staff's black, toggle-clasp uniforms were decorated in the vibrant patterns of Vietnam's hill tribes. However, the warmth and enthusiasm with which I was treated was even more notable than the remarkable attire. My friends were always giddy when I met them at the restaurant—joking, teasing, and inundating me with questions— but they were even more so on that opening night. On many subsequent occasions, I have been invited to join the owner at his table and sample the latest dishes on the menu, and a few that aren't, like grilled snake and roasted dog. Nowhere else in Vietnam have I experienced such warm hospitality.

A later addition, which runs the length of the restaurant, is said to be Vietnam's only remaining example

of native bamboo water music. Forty bamboo chimes are played rhythmically by a system of ropes and pulleys, all driven by running water. The sound is mellow and hypnotic, like a cross between a marimba and a gurgling stream. The instrument was constructed by the country's last known master artisan, and it's one of several examples of hydro-powered technology at the restaurant.

I have always enjoyed the activities and special events at the Forest, whether it's Cham music and dancing, a weaving demonstration on a traditional loom (free woven gifts are presented to all guests), or a ceramics exhibit by ethnic minorities. I should note that in regard to music, the local waiters suffer some degree of discomfort for our benefit. Although exotic and melodious to our ears, many of the lively Cham tunes they play are locally used as funeral dirges. I lived at the base of a local cemetery for a while and heard many similar tunes every day as the parades of mourners passed by.

One of my favorite occasions at the restaurant is drinking *ruou can* with my friends. The ingredients and flavor of the wine vary according to which ethnic minority makes it. The batches sold here contain the husks of rice and other grains, and have a seductively sweet, chocolate-honey flavor. *Ruou can* is a social experience, requiring a group of friends who take turns drinking from long bamboo straws protruding from a hefty ceramic jar. Like most wine-drinking, it's accompanied by a light snack. My friends and I often enjoy salty, dried sting ray, dipped into sour tamarind and soy sauce. One warning—it's easy to underestimate the potency of *ruou can*, and it's all but guaranteed you'll come away from the experience at least a little tipsy.

As for the great food, the shrimp and banana spring rolls are a *must*. They've been so popular that many of the surrounding restaurants have tried to imitate them. The tangy beef salad with green mango is also one of my favorites. Lobsters, prawns, and fresh fish are all chosen live from a tank. The Forest is also the best on the beach as far as quality ice cream is concerned. To wrap up your meal, try the durian, soursop, or passion fruit flavors.

Staff members at the restaurant form a tightly knit group. I've enjoyed many birthday parties with them on the beach, camping trips in the nearby mountains, and late night runs for fruit salad or rice porridge. Most have left their homes in northern provinces and live at the restaurant, sending much of their pay back to their families. They sacrifice a great deal, even though it's not obvious to visitors. As a personal request, please be sure to tip your waiters well. Tips are increasingly expected in restaurants catering to foreign travelers in Vietnam and are often shared among all the serving staff.

Forest Restaurant

This was the first upscale restaurant serving Vietnamese cuisine in Mui Ne, and it continues to be a top restaurant in the area. It was built at a time when Mui Ne was in the early stages of development, although the town has quickly become one of the hottest beach destinations in the country. Even now the Forest Restaurant stands distinctly apart from the handful of ex-pat-run Italian restaurants, backpacker bars, travel cafés, and in-house resort eateries. Free hotel pick-up and drop-off is available. The restaurant accepts special requests for items not on the menu, but elaborate feasts require advance notice. Budget for about $10 per person for a good meal.

67 Nguyen Dinh Chieu St.
Central Mui Ne Beach
Phan Thiet
(84-62) 847-589
www.forestrestaurant.com

HO CHI MINH CITY

Thin Lei Win Elkin demystifies Nepalese cuisine in Ho Chi Minh City

We knew that Ho Chi Minh City was filled with terrific Indian restaurants, but a Nepalese place? We'd never encountered one. So when we heard that Andrew Nguyen, an American *Viet Kieu*, was planning a Nepalese restaurant in the center of town, we just had to go and check it out. We've been fans ever since that first visit in November 2006.

Chautari, meaning "resting place," is a gem, and not just because it serves appealing food. We've been

SOUTHERN VIETNAM

in Ho Chi Minh City long enough to have tried most restaurants that are deemed "good," but service is almost always a letdown, and we're not just talking about communication problems. It's either too blasé—trying to get the staff's attention is a struggle—or too eager to please—we like attentiveness, but not someone breathing down our necks when we're reading the menu. Few places in town get it just right. Chautari is one of them.

It helps that it is run by a family of foodies who are immensely proud of their traditions and cuisine. Their affection finds its way into the preparation of the food. The staff is attentive but unobtrusive, and Andrew and Agata, the young couple behind the restaurant, are always on hand to explain the finer details of Nepalese cuisine.

And just what is Nepalese cuisine? Is it like Indian, with numerous curries and breads, or like Chinese, with dumplings and stir fries? We found out that it incorporates both. But Agata says that although it may contain elements of other cuisines, the way it is prepared makes it truly Nepalese. "We put our own flavor in it," she explains, referring to her mother and uncles who take care of the kitchen.

To us, the warm red light that bathes the restaurant was already a plus, and so were the brick walls hung with traditional musical instruments and watercolor portraits of Kathmandu. You see, no matter how many chic eateries pop up in Saigon these days, it's always nice to find one that doesn't resort to neon lights. We found out later that Agata's father (a friendly, chatty Nepalese gentleman) was responsible for the decorations,

and that even the logo holds deep meaning. It incorporates the "eyes of truth," the mountains for which Nepal is known, and a gurkha knife. If you ever meet him, ask him to explain the meanings of the paintings and the logo: it makes for great conversation.

Overall, though, the best thing about Chautari is the food. The menu is satisfyingly big. There are Indian dishes, Chinese dishes, and true Nepalese delicacies—seventy in total. Order the refreshing house specialty, the Chautari mocktail with passion fruit and ginger, while you pore over the menu. Make sure to try one of the beef dishes, which caught our attention. The young couple charmingly and sheepishly admitted they are one of the few Nepalese restaurants serving beef, so with our interest piqued, we asked for *sukuti bhatamash sadheko* (dried beef with green soy bean salad). Apparently it's popular with the Japanese. Little wonder really, since the dried and imported beef, cut into thin strips, tastes like it's been fermented in wasabi sauce. A bit of an acquired taste, but my partner loved it.

If you're looking for a good starter, try the Himalayan vegetable fritters—fresh, green chunks of fried vegetables that are soft, sweet, and absolutely yummy, with a spicy dip of garlic, chili, and lime. Or ask for *momo*—Nepalese steamed dumplings—which look like the Chinese variety but have a slightly thicker skin. Another customer favorite is the *aloo* with *timbur*—baby potatoes cooked with special herbs found only in the Himalayas. This latter dish is an easy entry into Nepalese cuisine, but it wasn't as adventurous as we would have liked.

One specialty that is a must-try is

the *aloo ko pratha* (bread stuffed with mashed potato). It is crispy at the top with a thick skin, and with a soft, mushy, and utterly delicious potato inside. We could have eaten it as a meal on its own, while the sweet *sel roti* is syrupy and spongy and perfect for dessert.

We've been back to Chautari numerous times since our first visit, and the food and service have not changed, thankfully. What has changed, however, is our impression of Nepalese food, which despite its many influences, we now regard as its own distinctive cuisine.

Chautari

The restaurant is located smack in the center of Ho Chi Minh City, on a street known for the numerous restaurants it houses, including Italian, Japanese, French, Vietnamese, Indian, and even an American diner. Along with serving dinner, Chautari has launched a business set lunch, featuring thirty different delicacies.

15B4 Le Thanh Ton St.
District 1
Ho Chi Minh City
(84-8) 822-3017

Emily Huckson remains faithful in Ho Chi Minh City

Saigon is moving ahead so quickly! Everyone wants the best bar, the latest fashion, and newest restaurant. As fine as this is for most, I prefer to keep to my usual haunts, and the Mandarin is a tradition I would never want to give up. Even the quiet, tree-lined street where it's located—off busy, bustling Le Thanh Ton—feels Old World.

The Mandarin is housed in a handsome villa, with creaking wooden floors and massive wooden beams. While the quartet in the lobby takes you back to old Vietnam with classical music, you are led to a table that is draped in linen and laden with more eating accessories than you will ever need. The service is professional, timely, and friendly. The staff helps with appropriate suggestions, but leaves you to make the final decisions.

This atmosphere and service can make one feel very important, but the food here will excite you even more. Do not leave this establishment without having at least one plate of the Imperial Ribs. They are sticky, succulent, tender, juicy, aromatic, and absolutely the most delicious things I have ever encountered. A nice accompaniment to this is the lotus salad with a good mix of crunch, freshness, and tartness to balance out the sweet of the ribs. The salad comes with crisp shrimp chips to assist you in scooping up all the bits. Fresh spring rolls are among my favorite appetizers. These are a Vietnamese standby which you can purchase at almost any restaurant in Vietnam; however, you will *not* have tasted a real one until you have the Mandarin's version—soft rice paper with a generous amount of pork, shrimp, bean sprouts, carrots, and onions, accompanied by a tangy, smooth, unbelievable peanut sauce.

This is not a down-and-dirty place

to eat, so when the occasion marks it—and you want to experience what I think is the best Vietnamese food in Ho Chi Minh City—ditch the t-shirt, put on some long pants, and head for the Mandarin. Feel important. Be impressed.

Mandarin

11a Ngo Van Nam St.
District 1
Ho Chi Minh City
(84-8) 822-9783

Nicole Hankins navigates the world in Ho Chi Minh City

Living in Ho Chi Minh City is a delicate balance between seeking things that are reminiscent of home, and appreciating the simple, basic way of Vietnamese life that is so far from the world I knew for years in Southern California. One of the things I value most about this hybrid lifestyle is the diversity of ethnic restaurants, from Indian and Spanish, to French and Korean. Even Nepalese is on the map. They are quaint and cozy and offer authentic foods that haven't been "Americanized."

About once a week, I find myself at a charming Japanese place called K-Café. No more than twenty people would fill up this tiny joint, which serves the freshest sushi in town. Each customer walking in is celebrated by a chorus of waitresses shouting "Welcome!" in

Japanese, though with strong Vietnamese accents. Masking laughter, I smile back, bow through the small entrance, and find a seat at the sushi bar.

Another of my favorite eateries is a Mediterranean place called Skewers. It is a family-owned restaurant, and the waiters are as nice as can be. Both Tristan, a *Viet Kieu* who has returned from California, and his wife Lien, greet you with welcome smiles every time you walk through their doors. They know all their customers by name and serve up the best barbequed meats and vegetables. My personal favorite here is the mouth-watering-richness-to-die-for, appropriately named, "Death by Chocolate" dessert. One bite and you've gone to heaven!

There is also a lovely outdoor restaurant in District Three that serves up the best seafood cuisine from Nha Trang. Quan Ta is filled with ravenous and often loud patrons who don't seem to have eaten in months, judging from the amount of food on their tables. The fresh shrimp steamed in coconut juice, and raw fish sashimi-style, wrapped in rice paper and herbs, are house specialties, but the hot pot with its deliciously spicy broth, selection of seafood choices, and vegetables will delight all your senses.

In many ways, my Vietnamese roots are now well ingrained. Food is so much a part of the culture that a casual greeting to friends or family is, "Have you eaten yet?" All social gatherings are planned around meals. Even past midnight and into the wee hours, many street vendors are serving meals everywhere in the city. One of the best middle-of-the-night spots is No. 94. This place has been serving crab dishes for more than forty years. While the décor is not the most enticing—the plastic green bowls match the green chopsticks, chairs, and tables—the smell of the deep-fry at the entrance alone will lure you in. There is rarely an empty seat for more than ten minutes, even late into the night, probably because the crab spring rolls, crab legs in tamarind sauce, and crab vermicelli are guaranteed hangover cures!

K-Café

74/A4 Hai Ba Trung St.
District 1
Ho Chi Minh City
(84-8) 824-5355

No. 94 — Hang Cua

The story on this place is that the original restaurant was at #94 for many years, until the landlord saw how successful it was and did not renew the lease. The family moved its business two doors down but still kept the same name. To confuse matters further, the old landlord opened a restaurant on the original site using that name as well. Make sure to go to the correct one, which is the *second* "No. 94" on the right, when traveling on Dien Tien Hoang Street, a one-way street.

Dien Tien Hoang St.
District 1
Ho Chi Minh City

Quan Ta

There is a rumor that this institution lost its lease and will move. At the time of writing, it is located at the address below.

39 Nguyen Thi Dieu St.
District 3
Ho Chi Minh City

Skewers

9A Thai Van Lung St.
District 1
Ho Chi Minh City
(84-8) 822-4798
www.skewers-restaurant.com

GENERAL VIETNAM

Julie Fay Ashborn offers advice for picky eaters in Vietnam

If you knew me, it would seem crazy that I would choose Vietnam as my favorite destination and continue to travel back there. I hate the heat; I am a very picky eater, a sort-of vegetarian (no pork, no beef, and no chicken unless it is farm fresh and then white meat only); and every time I go there, I spend at least two days down for the count with some horrible stomach ailment.

But I love the Vietnamese people—they are warm and genuinely friendly. And despite my absurd food restrictions (and my sensitive stomach), I love the food. The Vietnamese seem to have incorporated the best flavors from the countries around them to create their own fresh cuisine. So, even if you are the pickiest eater in the world, there are plenty of delicious meals to be found. Here are my five favorite (mostly vegetarian-friendly) recommendations.

Banana flower salad — *Nom hoa chuoi*

This unique dish is a new discovery from my last trip through Vietnam. The purple, pendant-shaped banana flower/blossom is sliced thinly like an onion and then tossed with crispy shallots, chopped peanuts, a combination of sautéed fresh Thai basil and mint, and a savory/sweet *nuoc cham* dressing. I love making it at home for parties. If you aren't a fan of spicy food, definitely ask for this *mild*, because there can be a lot of chili in the dressing.

Stir-fried water spinach (morning glory) — *Rau muong xao toi*

Stir-fried with garlic and/or shallots, Vietnam's ever-present *rau muong* is a staple on most menus. It tastes very similar to sautéed spinach and is delicious.

Clay pot fish — *Ca kho to*

This is another new discovery that I had a chance to make in the numerous cooking classes I took during my last trip. As well, my sister has perfected the recipe, so I am able to enjoy it back home. Essentially, it is fish simmered in a caramel sauce in a traditional clay pot, which gives the dish a distinctive flavor. You can find it in restaurants throughout the country, but most commonly on the coast and in the south.

Miss Vy's fried eggplant

I have never been an eggplant fan. The typical eggplants that you find in America are dense and meaty, with a consistency I don't care for. But in Vietnam there is a small, round, white eggplant that is more delicate. I made a fried version of it at Miss Vy's cooking class at the Morning Glory, one of her Hoi An restaurants, where you can also order it. The eggplant is cut into thin slices halfway down on opposite sides, then boiled and pressed flat and lightly fried. It has a soy sauce dressing, and is sprinkled with fresh chopped garlic, chili, and sautéed spring onions.

Banh mi and *pho ma*

Translation: baguette with Laughing Cow cheese spread on it. This is a crucial meal, especially on a long trip when you are craving something familiar and safe, or when it feels like the exotic Vietnamese spices seem to be having a party in your stomach. You can find this sold at carts on street corners in even the most remote cities, and it can be a life saver.

Tip for vegetarians

I would avoid *pho* and the other noodle soups. Most soups are made with a beef or pork stock. I have also learned that when you say you don't eat meat this is often interpreted to refer only to beef. Many times I found pieces of pork in a spring roll that I was assured was vegetarian. When I spoke up, I was assured that pork is not meat. Finally, keep in mind that many dishes contain fish sauce or come with a dish of fish sauce-based *nuoc cham* on the side.

Do it yourself

For a list of recommended cooking classes, where you can make banana flower salad, clay pot fish, fried eggplant, and more, turn to page 274.

Recipe for Banana Flower Salad

Salad ingredients
- 2 banana flowers (thinly sliced)
- 2 Tbsp. (30 ml) peanut oil
- ¼ cup (60 ml) shallot (coarsely chopped)
- ½ cup (120 ml) roasted peanuts (chopped)
- ½ cup (120 ml) fresh mint (coarsely chopped)
- ½ cup (120 ml) fresh Thai basil (coarsely chopped)
- Juice of 2 limes

Dressing ingredients
- Juice of 4 limes
- 2 tsp. (10 ml) brown sugar
- 1 red Thai chili (chopped)
- 2 tsp. (10 ml) fish sauce
- 2 large cloves garlic (chopped)

Directions
1. Squeeze fresh lime juice into a large bowl of water. This will be used to prevent the banana flower slices from turning brown.

2. Peel back the first few dark purple layers of the banana flower. Slice the banana flower into thin rings, beginning at the point and slicing about three-quarters of the way down. They will look similar to onion rings. I recommend that you use a mandoline. Rub lime juice on the blade to help prevent browning.

3. Immediately soak the rings in the lime water until ready to use. Set aside.

4. Heat the peanut oil in a large skillet. Sauté the shallots until golden brown. Leave them in the oil and set aside to cool.

5. Once the oil is cool, mix in ¼ cup (60 ml) of the mint leaves and ¼ cup (60 ml) of the Thai basil.

6. Mix the dressing ingredients. For a milder dressing, use less chili. Heat lovers will definitely want to add more.

7. Remove the banana flower from the water and mix with the shallot/mint/basil mixture, chopped peanuts, and remainder of the fresh mint and basil.

8. Toss in the dressing and serve immediately.

This recipe serves four as a side salad or two as a main dish. If banana flowers are unavailable, a good substitute is peeled and shredded green papaya.

SEEING THE SIGHTS

Fresh perspectives on exploring must-see attractions.

Vietnam is not what I would call a sightseeing country. It does not have metropolises like Paris or Washington, D.C., stuffed with museums and monuments, or colossal attractions like the Pyramids or Great Wall of China. When visitors used to ask me what they should do in Ho Chi Minh City, of course I recommended the War Remnants Museum or Reunification Palace. But I emphasized hanging out. Sip a cup of coffee at a sidewalk stall or a gin and tonic on the roof of the Rex Hotel. Check out everyone cruising downtown on their motorbikes on a Sunday night. While I have enjoyed the sites Vietnam has to offer, I feel that it is foremost a country where you should go to just be there and experience it: the nostalgic French ambience of Hanoi, the intimacy of village life, the sweet relaxation of the beach towns.

Perhaps this is why most of the essays in this chapter find their anchors in personal encounters. When Jessy Needham and Simone Samuels make pilgrimages to Yen Tu Mountain and the Perfume Pagoda, respectively, their journeys are all the more meaningful because of interactions with their colleagues and students along the way. Skipping Sapa—where most travelers go for their *de rigueur* hill tribe experience—Iris Opdebeeck and Ray Waddington write about visiting lesser known villages, whose appeal lies in the hospitality that is integral to treks and homestays among Vietnam's ethnic minorities. Even when James Sullivan and Antoine Sirot describe the old French villas of Dalat, they are writing as much about lifestyle as they are about architecture.

I do not mean to undervalue Vietnam's many worthy attractions, such as mystical Halong Bay and the other-worldly emperors' tombs of Hue. Wherever you are, you will find interesting sites, from the obvious, like Hanoi's Ho Chi Minh Mausoleum, which I have written about for this chapter, to the city's lesser-visited Museum of Ethnology, whose galleries, according to art expert

Fish sellers in Hoi An

Christine Thuy-Anh Vu, are a must for any itinerary. Because perspective is everything, typical travel haunts get a twist from Dominic Hong Duc Golding, a Vietnamese adoptee who explores Hanoi and Hue in search of his identity, and James Sullivan, who perches atop a Ho Chi Minh City landmark to gaze down on the iconic architecture. Samantha Coomber makes it clear why you should hit the well-trod path to Hoi An, and better yet, how to find your way off it. She also takes you to remote Ha Tien, home to one of her favorite temples, while Lillian Forsyth guides you to the birthplace of unified Vietnam's first president on equally out-of-the-way Tiger Island. Adding his two cents to the mix, Asia travel specialist Nick Pulley reveals his top picks from his many years of in-country research.

Of course, no discussion of touring Vietnam is complete without including its conflicts, and on this subject, the essays in this chapter are especially poignant. Traveling to Ba Chuc, Vietnam's own Killing Fields from its clashes with Cambodia during the late 1970s, Samantha Coomber reflects on a country that has been able to move forward despite such tragedies. This same issue is at the core of Lorene Strand's visit to the Cu Chi Tunnels, as she attempts to help heal the emotional wounds of her stepfather, who served in the infantry there. Taking an alternative approach, Jan Polatschek tries to avoid the relics of war, but he only proves how important it is for travelers to face Vietnam's painful past. By understanding where Vietnam has come from, you will fully appreciate the generous spirit of the people who enrich every attraction you visit during your trip.

HANOI

XXXXXXXXXXXXXXXXXXXXXXXXXXXXXXXXXXXX
○○

Christine Thuy-Anh Vu explores ethnic cultures in Hanoi

Following the craze for Chinese contemporary art that took off in the late 1990s and flourished during the early 2000s, collectors have been scrambling in search of Asia's next hotspot. For some, Vietnam is that place, with Hanoi considered the ultimate art stop. In the midst of the Old Quarter, shops and galleries offer the best buys, while around the city center, artist studios, cultural bureaus, and museums present an insider's look at the arts for the inquisitive traveler or culture junkie. Although such sites are widely known and visited, there are still a few overlooked cultural destinations that are highly relevant to the local art scene. One such location is the Vietnam Museum of Ethnology.

During my most recent visit to the museum, Hung, a young artist friend, came along to check out a new exhibition. While striding up the broad spiral ramp, he explained that as part of his course, he and his classmates were required to live in a Hmong village for a month. Creating traditional art was not the purpose of this trip; their mission was to explore new environments, learn about ethnic crafts as a way to connect with Vietnam's diverse traditions, and practice the French-imported activity of painting outside—*en plein air.* If you check out the fascinating exhibits at the museum, you can imagine how such a trip would inspire young, artistic minds.

Representing all fifty-four of Vietnam's ethnic minorities, the museum's ambitious private collection surveys the rich legacy of each tribal culture through its elaborate costumes, textiles, handicrafts, tools, and major architectural accomplishments. You will also see video footage of traditional rituals, like that of the *lau then* ceremony from the Tay tribe. This particular performance honors the Emperor of Jade through an overnight recital of a 5,000-line poem committed to memory.

Since Hung and I regularly visit this museum, we skipped past the well-preserved artifacts and headed straight to the third-floor space committed to special and traveling exhibitions. Much to our surprise, the current exhibition took a personal look at the poignant stories of Vietnamese who lived through the hardships of the country's subsidy economy from 1975-1986. In the gallery, dilapidated interiors of homes were recreated to give the visitor a look into the abject poverty of this period. Some officially banned art and literature that was created during this time were also on display, which to us is amazing, since Vietnam is known for censorship. Although this may not seem that notable to those from Western countries, for a Vietnamese museum to take such

NORTHERN VIETNAM

care to present well-handled artifacts, along with thought-provoking curatorial work, is a step forward both socially and in regard to museum practices. It is an indication not only of advancement in the arts and its supporting institutions, but also of a more forward-thinking national governance.

Adding to the museum's unique programming is an incredible outdoor exhibition of ethnic architectural structures. While looking out the third-floor balcony, Hung and I could see a towering Bahnar communal house. It can be accessed by scaling a seemingly precarious ladder incised into long tree trunks propped against the house. Other homes, like the furnished Ede longhouse or Tay stilt-house, are also accessible to the public, and imposing structures, such as the Gia Rai tomb, make for a grave photo op.

The day we visited, it poured rain, as it often does at certain times of the year in Hanoi. If the same happens to you, never fear. Take shelter in a tribal home and snack on tasty peanut candy and tea offered by museum attendants. And if the day is cool and sunny, the museum may also host a water puppet show, yet one of the many programs to introduce you to the traditions of Vietnam.

Vietnam Museum of Ethnology

The museum has an Asian/Western restaurant on the grounds and is handicap accessible. Various performances and children's events are offered throughout the year.

Nguyen Van Huyen St.
Cau Giay District
Hanoi
(84-4) 756-2193
www.vme.org.vn

Round-trip tip

The museum is about twenty minutes outside the city center, and it can be difficult finding a way back without getting stuck with a bad cab and hefty return tab. I suggest using a reliable company like Hanoi Taxi (http://hanoitaxi.com.vn) for the roundtrip haul. Once you arrive at the museum, ask your driver to wait for you. If you take the cab from your hotel, have your concierge inform your driver. Take note that your cab driver will keep the meter on while you are taking your museum stroll. Not to worry: the cab fee should not exceed $15. Once you return home, you can pay for the metered roundtrip and give the driver a nice tip for waiting and saving you some hassle.

Gallery hopping

The Vietnam Fine Arts Museum is another fun destination if you're on an art quest. While its collection is heavily weighted in twentieth-century art, this museum's collection goes back as far as the eleventh century. In addition, it features a unique and extensive collection of wartime art from the 1960s and '70s.

66 Nguyen Thai Hoc St.
Ba Dinh District
Hanoi
(84-4) 823-3084/733-2131
www.vnfineartsmuseum.org.vn

Kim Fay travels through the afterlife in Hanoi

There we were, three days after 9/11, in Hanoi, stuck. Our minds were numb. Our flight home was cancelled. STAR TV played just one Eddie Murphy movie over and over and over. Why not distract ourselves by visiting Vietnam's waxen former president? At the front desk of our hotel, my sister and I asked for directions to the Ho Chi Minh Mausoleum. The kind clerk told us that it was closed, as it shuts down for a month or two every year so that Uncle Ho can be "touched up."

We decided to visit the Ba Dinh Square area anyway, to tour Ho Chi Minh's former home and the National Museum of Vietnamese History. When we reached the enormous park, we spotted a line of Vietnamese people near the Soviet-style colossus of the mausoleum. In my rudimentary Vietnamese, which is laughable at the best of times, I asked a guard if the site was open. It was, and he ushered us to the back of the line. The Vietnamese line. Strange, since I had been told there was a separate line for foreigners. As my sister and

I both have blue eyes, and I have blonde hair, this couldn't be a case of mistaken identity, but no one seemed to notice the obvious: we were out of place. Observing the far-off line of foreigners being led from the blazing heat into the mausoleum, we stood behind three countryside women who wore conical hats and black smocks and trousers.

We were busily fanning ourselves with our cheap paper fans, just like everyone else around us, when our turn finally came. Following the elderly women, we ascended the steps and entered a freezing room. Beneath us, on a platform in a kind of pit, lay Uncle Ho, looking like a giant candle. At each corner of the pit were guards, baby-faced young men who did not look capable of defending the revered revolutionary, despite their guns. As we moved slowly around the viewing gallery, behind the old women shuffling in their rubber sandals, we could hear one of them weeping. She sobbed as she gazed down at the man who had promised Vietnam so much: identity and freedom.

Lowering my eyes, I saw a smudge on the floor. Someone's foot was bleeding, and the blood was being smeared along behind the wound. I don't know why there was something so eerie about that sight, accompanied by the grief of the old woman. Perhaps because open grief is not something you see often in public in Vietnam. As my sister and I emerged back into the hot morning, we felt as if we had just come from another world. We had been

NORTHERN VIETNAM

inside the mausoleum for only a few minutes, but it seemed like a lifetime. It was as if we had taken a journey back in time, to that brief period when Vietnam was a place of great hope, before it became a country defined by war.

Ho Chi Minh Mausoleum
Ba Dinh Square
Ba Dinh District
Hanoi

Dominic Hong Duc Golding finds his true north in Hanoi

As I continued my rail journey north from Hue, the environment changed drastically above the seventeenth parallel. Gone was the warmth of the south, where I was then living, with its two seasons—wet and dry. Northern Vietnam has all four. By day we passed great gorges that looked like Chinese ink paintings, and bays filled with water crashing upon rocks. Fog covered the rice paddies where cows and buffalos emerged, followed by their owners. At night the atmosphere felt spooky as I gazed out at huts atop the water and boats with nets cast wide, all lit dimly by lanterns.

As a Vietnamese child adopted by Australians, all my life I grew up on stories of America's war in Vietnam. Now I was seeing The North as a real place and not just some dark specter of the Yellow Peril or invading Reds. Still, stopping in villages and seeing the lone conductor in his Communist uniform smoking under a single street lamp brought back images from old Cold War movies I'd seen.

In Hanoi, I took up residence in the Old Quarter. It was late fall—the best time to visit Hanoi, I'd say, as the burning summer has passed, but the coldest of the winter chill has not set in. I stuck around the lake, soaking up the crisp, cool vibe of Hanoian life. Like Ho Chi Minh City, Hanoi has its café culture, albeit male dominated, and plenty of places where young lovers hang out. It felt partly bohemian, partly French, and partly excessive, and I loved every bit of it. I found myself getting lost in the alleyways, greeted by the warm smells of the noodle stalls and stumbling upon small contemporary art galleries.

Among my cultural missions was a visit to the Ho Chi Minh Mausoleum. Standing in an open park of manicured lawns, it is a huge, rectangular, concrete structure. It made me feel vacant and cold. To see Uncle Ho preserved and entombed seemed so at odds to the photos of a thin, warm, smiling, grandpa-type figure, surrounded by children and comrades-in-arms. It was a sharp reminder of where I was, a country where the iconic worship of Stalin and Mao imposed so much on the Vietnamese people.

Next on my checklist was the National Museum of Vietnamese History, which became my place of worship. As a history buff, I was staggered at the scope of Vietnam's past. Vietnam had

Stone *and* Bronze Ages! So, there was indeed more to Vietnam than the three wars—the Japanese occupation during WWII, the French Indochina war of the 1950s, and American Conflict of the 1960s and '70s. Vietnam had its own sword and sandal epics, just like Rome, centuries of fighting the Chinese, Mongols, Siamese, and, of course, one another. In every room I walked into, I could see a blockbuster movie.

That old institution, the Temple of Literature, underscores the foundation of Hanoi for me. It is a place where art students flock to practice their illustrations, tourists come to admire the architecture, and I retreated to shut down my brain, sitting in the stone courtyard watching everything and thinking of nothing. Centuries ago, scholars studied here to become mandarins of the highest order, and it was here that I received the greatest validation of my *self*, seeing my original family name—Nguyen—inscribed on stone stelae dating as far back as the thirteenth century. As an adoptee who was called Nguyen Hong Duc in an orphanage, well, to see my name immortalized in Hanoi, man, that gave me the biggest buzz. I felt that I was finally learning to accept being Vietnamese.

The last thing to top my northern Vietnam cultural immersion was the Thang Long Water Puppet Theater. Water puppetry is a Vietnamese art form developed out of the flood plains by farmers wishing to tell folk stories. At the show I attended, there were seventeen puppet skits, all accompanied by a live musical group and fireworks. The reason I find this special is that as an Australian, it is rare for me to witness such traditional Vietnamese arts, since international art festivals find it incredibly hard to grant visas to Vietnamese artists. On a personal level, to see the puppets telling the stories held within the walls of the country's museums is to see one's own culture—my own culture—come to life.

I spent my last day walking around Hoan Kiem Lake and people-watching: Vietnamese crossing the little red bridge to the island pagoda dedicated to General Tran Hung Dao, Western families strolling with their kids dressed in *ao dai*, and photographers taking shots of young couples or locals fishing. Coming from living in Ho Chi Minh City, where it is hot, crazy, and stifling at times, I felt as if I crossed my own personal Checkpoint Charlie. Although Hanoi is steeped in tradition, it is also cool, trendy, and sophisticated, with a real cosmopolitan lifestyle. I felt liberated. I felt at home.

Ho Chi Minh Mausoleum

See the fact file in the previous essay.

National Museum of Vietnamese History

1 Trang Tien St.
Hoan Kiem District
Hanoi

Temple of Literature

Quoc Tu Giam St. and Van Mu St.
Quoc Tu Giam Park
Dong Da District
Hanoi

Thang Long Water Puppet Theater

Book early, as this theater fills up fast, and make sure to buy front row seats.

57B Dinh Tien Hoang St.
Hoan Kiem District
Hanoi
www.thanglongwaterpuppet.org

Suffusive Art Gallery

This tiny space is run by local artists selling contemporary pieces.

2B Bao Khanh Ln.
Hoan Kiem District
Hanoi
www.suffusiveart.com

CAO BANG

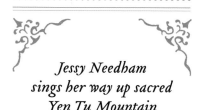

Jessy Needham sings her way up sacred Yen Tu Mountain

Each year, the provincial college in Bac Giang, where I was a teacher, sponsored a staff trip in honor of Women's Day in March. Many of the teachers invited their mothers instead of their husbands to join them, since the destination was a nearby pagoda. Vietnamese women are generally known as keepers of the faith, especially older women. Since most country teachers lived by modest means, travel was an infrequent luxury, and my colleagues were excited for our road trip. Along with bags full of offerings for the pagoda, we packed a picnic lunch and headed to Yen Tu Mountain, a Buddhist pilgrimage site in eastern Quang Ninh Province.

Yen Tu rises 1,060 meters above sea level and is the highest mountain in northeastern Vietnam. At the end of the thirteenth century, King Tran Nhan Tong abdicated the throne to his son and moved to Yen Tu to live a monastic life. He founded the Truc Lam (Bamboo Forest) Zen Buddhist sect, and 200 years later, during the Le Dynasty, the Dong Pagoda was built at the top of the mountain. There are several other pagodas built at various points on the mountain, but the Dong Pagoda is the most important.

The main purpose of visiting Yen Tu is simply to climb the mountain, enjoying nature along the way, and to pray at the pagoda at the top. In the past, visitors started their climb from the foot of the mountain, and slept on pagoda floors during the two-day journey. Considering the effort that goes into the climb, the now available cable car that carries pilgrims halfway up is a saving grace. As we piled into the cable car and slowly made our way diagonally over the tops of the trees, one of my friends commented, excitedly, "This must be what it's like to travel by plane!"

Emerging from the cable car station, we walked up a flight of stone steps to the first of a series of pagodas. We were surrounded by trees, several of which had labels boasting that they were *ancient*, 700 years old or older. Their leafless branches were stark gray against the clouds. The mist was so thick that we could not see the valley below us, and it felt as though we were floating on an island in the sky, dotted with ancient pagodas and monks' tombs. Our Sunday visit coincided with an annual three-month festival, and visitors swarmed around the pagoda, preparing platters of incense, paper money, beer, fruit, and flowers.

The English department teachers spread bamboo mats in the center of the courtyard and ate a picnic lunch of baguettes, pork sausage, sticky rice, peanuts, and watermelon. Unaware of the climb ahead of us, I reclined on the mats and enjoyed the convivial atmosphere of families and groups of teenagers relaxing together. Since I'm not a Buddhist, the spiritual aspect of the trip did not resonate with me as much as the opportunity to spend time with my colleagues and their families—to experience the closeness of relationships that make Vietnam a special place to live. As I helped cut up fruit for dessert, I felt like I was on a trip with my extended family, not just my co-workers.

After our meal, we began making our way up the steep stone staircase, passing young women carrying their high heels in one hand and wearing rented plastic slippers in order to avoid sprained ankles. There were a surprising number of little old ladies on an intense mission to get to the top. Women who normally might shuffle slowly across a busy traffic intersection in the city showed superhuman strength, hastening past us.

As we ascended, light rain began to fall, and the stairs became perilously slippery. I began to wonder whether it was a mistake to continue the climb. The steps were narrow and uneven, and did not have railings. My American friends and I often marveled at the lack of safety precautions in Vietnam. I had been in countless national parks and nature spots that would have been awash in railings, barriers, fences, and warning signs, had they been located in the United States. But there were no protections of that sort at Yen Tu—we were on our own, every woman for herself.

Despite my misgivings, I had passed the point of no return—we'd gone more than halfway up the stairs, and though we were exhausted, it seemed a better option to continue on than to turn around and impede the progress of our fellow pilgrims. Besides, I was entertaining myself by asking my friend to teach me the lyrics to my favorite pop song, *Giac Mo Tinh Yeu*, even though I couldn't remember anything past the first verse. It was also amusing to hear the comments people made when passing me along the way, speculating on my nationality and how the heck I came to be at Yen Tu. Unlike its better known sister, Chua Huong (Perfume Pagoda), Yen Tu does not see many foreign tourists.

Eventually nearing the top, we passed the tree-line, and the narrow staircase widened to a stone plateau, providing more room for everyone to spread out and avoid slipping and falling on each other. Vendors along the route offered young bamboo, forest mushrooms, and herbal medicine, freshly collected from the mountainside. I shuddered to think of the climb they had to endure each day, just to sell a few dried herbs to pilgrims.

The pagoda on the mountain peak was smaller than I expected, and people crammed into a tiny space between the surrounding boulders to pay homage to the images inside a small shrine. Despite the crowded conditions, dozens of people focused intently on their prayers, willing the spirits in the statues to hear them. My friends, so gaily singing pop songs a few minutes ago, were now closing their eyes and pressing their hands together in prayer, finding stillness in the middle of the crowd. I found it inspiring that so many people would climb all this way to see these humble structures, and I considered what an immense sacrifice it was for a king to give up his throne in order to spend his remaining days on this windswept, barren peak.

Yen Tu Mountain

The mountain is located in Quang Ninh Province, just over 100 kilometers east of Hanoi, northwest of Halong Bay. It is best reached by private motorbike or by arranging a car in Hanoi. Unless you want the experience of being one of a multitude of pilgrims, avoid the Yen Tu festival during the first three months of the lunar

year, or if you must go at this time, try to visit on a weekday when there are fewer people. Also, do lots of stretching before you head to the top—I didn't, and the next day my thighs hurt so much I could barely walk.

HA TAY

Simone Samuels makes a pilgrimage to the Perfume Pagoda

The agenda was to travel with my Vietnamese students to visit the Perfume Pagoda, known as Chua Huong to the locals. Whilst I had no idea what the day ahead would hold, I hoped to learn something of the customs that were involved in taking a spiritual pilgrimage. I was enthused the moment we left Hanoi, traveling southwest through Ha Tay Province and the traditional townships that exist on the outskirts of the city as they have done for centuries, with their backdrops of bright green rice paddy fields.

In the Huong Tich (Fragrant Traces) Mountains, we reached the Perfume Pagoda, which is actually a complex of pagodas and temples. My view of pastoral Vietnam was abruptly replaced by a bunch of women haggling at us through the bus windows. They were speaking fast and frantically, waving wads of red notes wildly, and insisting that we all purchase some. What sort of strange black market was this? And at a temple, of all places! A few of my students handed over 100,000 VND notes in exchange for the equivalent amount in red 200 VND notes. I later learned that these "lucky notes" would be used as part of the offering ritual at each of the temples we visited.

Once we bought our admission tickets and entered the complex, we arrived at a river, known as Yen Stream, where all pilgrimages begin. Thirty of us were ushered along and piled together into a small, metal boat. I must have looked as if I thought it would capsize because one student asked me, "Are you scared?" As we started to sail upstream, I couldn't believe we'd all managed to fit. Two weathered-looking Vietnamese women served as our front and rear oarswomen, steering us up the river, which was flanked by limestone karst formations and looming mountains.

We made our first stop at the Trinh Temple. Here I was to see, for the first time, the preparation of an offering plate. I was led by the hand to a special area, where my students showed me the loving and attentive process. I watched with curiosity as a huge plastic plate was filled with the many delights of life. Along with bundles of lucky red 200 VND notes, offerings included chicken and biscuits, fruit, small bottles of vodka, cigarettes, incense, flowers, and little notes with family names inscribed on them. This hamper of goodies reminded me of something you would give as a gift at Christmastime.

Next, the offering plate was taken into the temple and up to the shrine. It was passed to a monk who blessed it so that the ancestors might bring forth prosperity, health, and happiness for my students, who were praying by pressing their hands together and shaking them three times. Everyone participated in this ritual, and I began to see my normally raucous students in a contemplative light.

When we emerged from the temple and returned to the riverbank, the sun revealed itself. The first sun I'd seen in weeks—this truly was a spiritual journey. We returned to our overcrowded boat for a half-hour trip upstream. I admired the scenery, while my students continued their banter and passed around snacks and then the offering plate.

"Why are you eating the offering food?" I asked, shocked.

There were some chuckles, and then one student explained that by eating the blessed food, the good fortune would enter the living body and make the luck they'd prayed for happen. This all seemed so superstitious, but to everyone else it was normal, as they munched away happily on consecrated chicken and biscuits.

At our next stop, I found myself surrounded by a horde of people who crowded together to arrange offering plates and then force their way through the mob to present their plates at the altar for the God of the Mountain. It was so difficult to get to the front of the temple that some people had to hold the plates on their heads to carry them forward. I followed my group, jostled along as we approached the altar with another beautifully presented offering. I felt a little out of place and also like a bit of a fraud, since I didn't fully understand the prayer and offering practice, and I was not a participant, but rather an observer, in something that seemed so intimate.

From here we traveled on to the Huong Tich Grotto. In previous decades, the tens of thousands of pilgrims who visited this site would walk a few kilometers up the mountain. Now, it is possible to catch a cable car. Once we hopped out at the top, we had to walk a short distance to the cave entrance. Located down 120 steps deep in the mountain, the cave is known by many as the most picturesque in Vietnam. Everyone was excited, even those who made this pilgrimage each year, and the enthusiasm around me was infectious.

We walked single file down a precarious walkway into the mouth of the enormous cave, which revealed numerous stalagmites and stalactites, with several lit shrines dedicated to Buddha nestled among them. There were hundreds of people crammed inside with burning joss sticks and offering plates, making prayers solemnly at each shrine. One stalactite dripped droplets of water every few minutes, and people held their hands up expectantly, hoping for a holy drop to fall into their palms. It was a spectacle unlike any I had experienced before, and I was pleased to be there with locals. I was starting to feel more comfortable,

and I even said a prayer of my own with the encouragement of my friends.

Then came the day's highlight: a temple I am sure most Western tourists don't get the chance to visit. Upriver, we had to drive to another pier and then catch a motorized ferry across to get to Duc Thanh Ca Temple. It was much quieter than in the Perfume Pagoda complex, and the most rewarding part was watching the burnt-orange reflection of the sunset over the river. It was extremely relaxing as we soaked in the serenity: a local farmer oaring a boat downstream with his feet, cattle meandering through the fields, and children playing on the riverbank.

As we sat there drinking tea, I realized that this day was as much about camaraderie as it was about paying respect to one's ancestors. And after one last peaceful observation of my students praying at the altar, I felt somehow enlightened. I had a greater understanding not only of the beliefs that are so much a part of this country, but also of my students and colleagues—my Vietnamese friends.

Making the pilgrimage

The Perfume Pagoda is seventy-five kilometers southwest of Hanoi. Day trips can be easily organized at most travel agencies in Hanoi, but I recommend befriending a local to show you around and teach you the customs and traditions.

When to go

The pagoda serves as a pilgrimage destination for Vietnamese people, who visit during the first three months of the Lunar New Year. The Perfume Pagoda Festival begins on the sixth day of the new year (usually near the end of February or beginning of March) and finishes at the end of the third month. When I went, I was told that it was a really busy time to be visiting, but also the best, as it was in the midst of the festival season. One student told me that if it had been a weekend day, we would have been lucky to even get into the complex, due to the crowds.

The name game

The name of the last pagoda I visited, Duc Thanh Ca, was given to me by one of my students, but is not listed in any guides. I believe it is part of the Tuyet pagoda group, which is on the Tuyet Stream. From the Perfume Pagoda complex, make your way to Tuyet Stream and the ferry for the Tuyet pagodas. The pagoda with the gorgeous sunset is the first one you will encounter from the ferry landing on the other side.

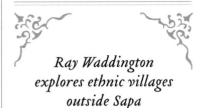

BAC HA

Ray Waddington explores ethnic villages outside Sapa

While there is certainly enough to keep a visitor satisfied in Hanoi, a popular side trip is a three-day, package tour to the Alpine-like town of Sapa. Tourism companies in Hanoi shuttle guides and visitors there every weekend in time for the Saturday market. You can book a trip at your hotel. That's what my travel companions did—it was then that we parted company.

I headed for the Vietnam Museum of Ethnology on the outskirts of Hanoi. I spent the whole day there learning about the fifty-four ethnic minority groups officially recognized by the government. I also picked up copies of *Ethnic Minorities in Vietnam* and *Mountains and Ethnic Minorities: North West Vietnam,* and headed back to my hotel for some speed-reading. The next evening I was in the Hanoi station waiting for the night train to Lao Cai to pull out. Once it did, I got a surprisingly good night's sleep on the hard, wooden seat that was my bed. Early the next morning, I stepped off the train

NORTHERN VIETNAM

into what seemed like the middle of nowhere and wondered what I had let myself in for. At least there was a small restaurant where I could get a hit of caffeine and get oriented.

Soon a young man approached and without asking where I was going, pointed to his motorbike and offered to take me to Sapa. When I told him my destination was instead Bac Ha, he was surprised. This was Saturday, and surely the only reason I could be in the area was to visit the famous market in Sapa like all the other foreigners. He informed me there were no buses to Bac Ha and offered to take me there. I knew better and offered him 10,000 VND to take me to the bus station. The bus ride to Bac Ha was only a couple of hours, giving me enough time after I arrived to choose from the few hotels available and check out camera angles for shooting the following day.

Before first light, I was walking around the local, little-known market, watching people arrive from the outlying, indigenous villages. The Dao, Nung, and Tay were represented, but the most striking photo opportunities were afforded by the Flower Hmong. Being less accustomed to tourism than their cousins in Sapa, they were quite curious about me. Buying some fruit broke the ice, and I was allowed to take all the photos I wanted.

The next day I walked to Hmong and Tay villages around Bac Ha. The residents were entirely unused to foreign visitors, and I was something of an attraction. I spent quite a bit of time in village schools where I was

saddened to see firsthand something I had only read about. The national education policy in Vietnam requires all teaching to use the Vietnamese language and the culturally Viet-centered national curriculum. This policy makes it harder for non-Vietnamese speaking, indigenous children to understand the material and leads to a high drop-out rate among them. In the long run it will also contribute to the loss of indigenous cultures.

By now Sapa would be largely free of its weekend tourists, so I headed there next. My plan was to eat, find a hotel, and then find a local guide to take me to the outlying villages. During the meal those plans were disrupted when a young Hmong girl asked if she could sit at my table. Her English was excellent for someone who was self-taught. I learned her name was Shu; she was fifteen years old and had never been to school, but wanted to and worked as a guide through one of the hotels in town. I admired her courage, motivation, and strength, and stayed at that hotel so she could be my guide. We spent the first night in a Hmong village; along the way we visited Shu's family in the village where she was born. The next night was in a Red Dao village before returning to Sapa.

Back in Hanoi, I ran into my former travel companions. They had not enjoyed their packaged, over-touristed Sapa experience. By getting away from the tourist crowds, mine had been a rewarding and fulfilling adventure from start to finish.

Exploring on your own

Northwest Vietnam is one of the best areas in Southeast Asia for visiting indigenous villages. The easiest option is to take a package tour by bus from Hanoi to Sapa. This is also the least rewarding way to go and is recommended only for those who have little time or who insist on having everything arranged for them. Instead, opt for independent travel, which is easy to arrange. There are both day and night trains from Hanoi to Lao Cai. From there it's a short ride on one of the frequent buses into Sapa; groups of four or more will find it cheaper and faster to take a taxi. Once in Sapa, finding a hotel is also easy, as there are dozens to choose from in a wide price range. For your guide, local, indigenous people are by far the best. You'll find them all over town, or your hotel can put you in touch with someone. If you are in the area on the weekend, you should consider staying in Bac Ha. Bac Ha is much smaller than Sapa, has fewer accommodation and guide choices, and has a Sunday market that is also smaller than Sapa's famous Saturday market, but it's so much more pleasant because it isn't overrun with tourists.

Background research

However you choose to explore this area, your best starting point is the Vietnam Museum of Ethnology in Hanoi (see Christine Thuy-Anh Vu's essay on page 51). A daylong visit affords a thorough introduction to the indigenous groups of Vietnam: their history, culture, and customs. While there, pick up a copy of *Mountains and Ethnic Minorities: North West Vietnam* by Tim Doling, and consider it required reading to get the most from your experience. Also pick up *Ethnic Minorities in Vietnam* by Dang Nghiem Van, Chu Thai Son, and Luu Hung, if you'd like more detail. Both books are published by Hanoi's *The Gioi* Publishers. Doling's book can also be ordered from ThingsAsian: http://store.thingsasian.com.

Playing it safe

However you travel, make sure that your guide's services include arranging all local stay permits that are required by local authorities for any overnight stops in indigenous villages or uncommon destinations. Without these permits, you put yourself and, more importantly, your hosts at risk.

HUE

Dominic Hong Duc Golding searches for his identity in Hue

The former imperial capital and a World Heritage listed city, Hue is a

CENTRAL VIETNAM

must-see for an adoptee from Vietnam, especially one who is looking for a past. As a transracial adoptee raised in Australia, growing up in a dominantly Anglo-Saxon environment, I wanted to find out more about my people's history, the way they must have lived long ago. With Hue once being the center of intellectualism and the ruling classes, I felt this was the place to begin.

The best way to make the trip to Hue from Ho Chi Minh City is by rail, traveling overnight in soft sleeper class and eating Vietnamese-style TV dinners of cold rice, bitter soup, and cold fish, while listening to the overhead cabin music consisting of revolutionary songs and ancient operas. For me Vietnam by rail is to travel slowly back in time: to chuff along the winding embankments, relaxing to the rhythm of the tracks and gazing out at the country's beaches and foggy mountain passes.

Although I had been living back in Ho Chi Minh City, this was the first time I was going north of the seventeenth parallel, the old dividing line between South and North. This railway journey for me was significant because for the first time I would be able to see this land of my ancestors not just culturally, but historically, in order to grasp the bigger picture. I had a few days in Hue, and once I arrived, I checked into my hotel. Refreshed, I made a booking for a local tour to the seven imperial temples and tombs, and then I headed back to the hotel for a little state-run TV.

The next morning, I was driven by minibus to the gates of our first temple, to be greeted by a sign: *Admission: 55,000 VND for foreigners, 22,000 VND for Vietnamese.* This would be the case at each destination. Ouch! But my desire to know my culture outweighed the restrictions of my wallet. And it was worth it.

All of the temples and tombs were beyond the splendor of Chinese epics like *Hero* or *Curse of the Golden Flower,* as they were real, and each place had its own characteristics and architectural style, a reflection on the individual tastes and beliefs of the emperor it represented. To stand among these ancient sites, in this place that is both geographically and spiritually the center of Vietnam, felt like being in the middle of a personal jigsaw puzzle and watching the pieces start to come together.

The last stop of the day was the massive Citadel fortress in the center of the city. I came here with two goals. First, I needed to learn more about the Tet Offensive, whose focal point was Hue. Second, I wanted to immerse myself in the lifestyle of the imperial era. My guide could not help with the first; as for the second, I found out how many concubines an emperor had. I was also shown the efforts to restore the grounds to its former glory, after it had been destroyed by bombs. Clearly, I was going to have to get my historical fix elsewhere.

I have read many books written by GIs about the battle of Hue and watched *Full Metal Jacket* as a teenager, but I needed to see the other side of the story, from the point of view of the "enemy," and I wanted to understand the battle that changed the course of the war for the Americans. I went to the Military History Museum the following day. The museum is split in two, with one building housing exhibits on French colonial atrocities, the other those of the American War. Schoolchildren were buzzing about as I carefully scrutinized the photos and documents full of slogans of glory and victory. I left with more questions than answers: Was the campaign a worthy sacrifice for either side? And to win a battle, does one need to destroy another's heritage?

My curiosity about Vietnam's imperial past was satisfied at the Museum of Royal Fine Arts. With its earthy tones and wooden structure, the museum felt both real and unreal, deathly quiet, with not a soul in sight. It seemed especially calm after visiting tombs and the Citadel teeming with tourists and schoolchildren. For a lover of Chinese antiques like me, the opportunity to view coins dating as far back as 1,200 AD and bronzes engraved with mythical animals, as well as to discover stories of emperors and empresses, treason and gunpowder, was a privilege. What was more significant is that while being dominated by the Chinese, the Vietnamese claimed cultural ownership, making their own distinctive mark by incorporating local arts and crafts.

As I sat in the DMZ Bar that night, nursing a beer and listening to Jefferson Airplane, I knew that coming to Hue had helped to heal the cultural vacuum for me. It felt good to be in a country where people know who they are, where they came from culturally, and why they fought the battles they had to fight. As an adoptee, I had lost everything: family, language, and culture. But in Hue I was slowly getting *me* back. Maybe not my language or my parents, but certainly my sense of place, of being. And a pride in saying that I am Vietnamese.

Booking a tour

Shop around—some operators may offer a really cheap tour, but that means you end up walking to all seven temples/tombs, as opposed to taking a minibus. To get started, check out tours offered by Mandarin Café, recommended by Michael Burr on page 35.

Van Xuan Guesthouse

I highly recommend staying at this guesthouse. It's run by a lovely, immensely helpful old couple. It is central to all the trendy craft shops, restaurants, and bars. Yes, it probably helps if you can speak Vietnamese, but it's not essential.

Riding the train

Definitely take the rail journey from Ho Chi Minh City to Hue. Get a sleeper cabin, which comes complete with talkative companions. If you can't speak Vietnamese, just nod, smile, and accept the sour fruit with chili/salt that is sure to be shared.

www.vr.com.vn

Museum of Royal Fine Arts

3 Le Truc St.
Hue

Military History Museum

23 Thang 8 St. (opposite Museum
of Royal Fine Arts)
Hue

LANG CAT

Iris Opdebeeck
sips local liquor in
Lang Cat village

On a trip from Hue to Hoi An, my husband Jan and I travel through the DMZ, following the Ho Chi Minh Trail, visiting Khe Sanh, and gazing out the windows of our car at the monochromatic green hills and coffee and pepper plantations. We even pass through a village where we are told that all the inhabitants have surnamed themselves Ho, after Uncle Ho, of course. After a short visit to Lao Bao city all the way up on the Lao border, we arrive at Lang Cat, a Bru/Van Kieu minority village where we are to spend the night in a stilt house homestay.

The village looks as if it has about thirty houses, each balanced on two-meter, wooden stilts. The structures are rectangular in shape, mostly with tin roofs, though some are topped with tile and some still with straw. The walls are made of wood panels

or bamboo mats and the floors of dried bamboo that bounces back a little and squeaks whenever you walk over it or even move. Of course, shoes are taboo and left downstairs. Some bigger houses have porches, and all have partitions for the kitchens, where everything is cooked on wood fires.

Looking as if they were randomly built, the houses come with lots of kids, chickens, pigs, and dogs ... but no inside toilets. I am terrified to go to the toilet in the bushes surrounding the houses, especially in the evening because of the fiercely barking dogs! Also, there are buffalos at the spot where you are supposed to pee—and no light at night, except for your own torch. Yep, this is the real thing: adventure.

The men here wear Western clothes, and the women wear Western t-shirts or blouses with wrap-around skirts of dark green or blue, with patterns woven in, similar to the Lao and even some Burmese. Some women wear scarves, others headbands. The kids are also wearing Western clothes, which are very dirty and even torn, making me think they must have been inherited from older siblings. A few older ladies still have blackened teeth and smoke pipes. During our visit, the younger kids play along the river while a woman fishes with a net attached around a wooden circle like a bag; she carries a small cane container on her back to collect the fish in. We also see bigger children coming back from the fields hauling nicely woven bamboo baskets as big as backpacks.

In the late afternoon, our local area

guide, Mr. Duy, calls for the "catering staff." A minivan carrying three or four women arrives with excellent Vietnamese food—more than enough for Jan and me; Mr. Duy; our tour company guide, Mr. Hien; and our hosts—along with cooking utensils, bowls, plates, and chopsticks. They also bring mats to sit on and most importantly, local wine. Protocol is followed. The head of the village is invited to join us, along with his wife, his children, and other family members, mostly men. We sit around the food on the floor and make small talk about Jan and me living in Vietnam. Well, it's the men who mostly do the talking, of course! The villagers are curious about where we are from, and we try to explain snow—a classic conversation topic—and where on the planet Belgium is. The men are able to figure it out, as they like European football and there is even a TV in the village.

After dinner, once the "table" is cleared, the local wine is served. The container looks like a terra cotta barrel, decorated with brown lacquer paint. It is filled with weeds that have been fermenting for a while ... who knows how long? Although the barrel is quite large, there isn't much "juice" to start with inside; in order to drink it, you have to add water. The wine is sipped through meter-long bamboo straws, usually three to five being used by various drinkers at a time. While it's quite a scene, getting drunk doesn't seem to be the goal, especially since the wine, with its slight taste of lychees, isn't too strong, and it's a hassle to get the fluid through your straw. You have to suck really hard sometimes.

One has to wait to be invited to drink because you can't drink alone. According to custom, the guests and the head of the village go first, then the guides, etc. But, and this I like a lot, the young girls of the village are also invited. They are around sixteen years old, and Jan and I think part of this tradition is that they must be virgins. (Jan has heard this from his Vietnamese colleagues.) The girls giggle throughout the evening but eventually grow bored, having checked us out completely and commented on everything about us from head to toe amongst themselves. At least, that's how it feels. Then again, we do the same with them as we smile and stare at each other. Our Vietnamese guides and some of the village men seem to tease the girls because they giggle, shyly, with their hands covering their mouths—I'm sure this is all part of some kind of custom. Finally, everyone is invited to sing.

As the night wears on, and we continue to suck on the straws, the wine begins to taste like water and takes on a sour flavor. Too many cigarettes have been consumed-—Marlboros exchanged for local smokes—and the conversation comes to a dead end. It's time to go to bed, and everybody leaves, except us. We sleep in the same room where we ate, inside mosquito nets brought by the women who served the food and are now bunking down on the verandah outside.

Ours isn't a long sleep, as we all rise and shine together with the chickens. We thank our host family again and again, shaking hands and pinching the babies' cheeks until, at last, we're off, heading back for the Ho Chi Minh Trail where we stop in the first Vietnamese village we encounter for a breakfast of *pho ga* (chicken noodle soup). In the café bathroom, a mirror confirms that we slept on bamboo floors and woke up too soon. Such is the price for authenticity ... a small price to pay, as far as we're concerned, for warm hospitality and a glimpse of a world untouched by tourism.

Heading for the border

We booked our homestay through a company called Eco Travel Vietnam, whose manager, Mr. Hien, also served as our driver and guide.

www.ecotravelvietnam.com

Understanding your destination

Keep in mind that despite having a TV, this village in general seems to be very poor, and certainly is less advantaged than some other minority villages I have visited in the north. I suspect it is because of the remoteness of the area on the Lao border. There is no industry in the region, and I did not notice a lot of rice paddies. I also imagine the area was heavily bombed during the war. And there is no tourism whatsoever;

we did not see a single tourist until we were back on the main roads to Hue.

Bru Ethnic Minority
www.cedarpointfoundation.org

HOI AN

Samantha Coomber divulges Hoi An's secret pleasures

When I first visited the historical town of Hoi An in 1998—one of the "must-see" places on any traveler's itinerary for Vietnam—I was guilty of clinically ticking off all the main attractions in my guidebook as I went along. Running around like a thing possessed, I self-satisfyingly declared I had "been there, done that," before whizzing off to the next stop, Hue. Yes, the centuries-old sights are well worth seeing, and by all means, get lost in a retail frenzy of ordering up a new wardrobe at the ubiquitous tailor shops (although you may find that you never actually end up wearing the stuff). And yes, Cua Dai Beach is a pleasant enough spot to recharge after all the frantic sightseeing up and down the Vietnamese coastline, although it's not *the* reason to come here in the first place. But people often miss the point about Hoi An. Vietnam's answer to Laos' Luang Prabang is predominately a chill-out zone; Hoi An is as much about human encounters and simple experiences as it is about ancient vestiges. Beyond the tourists, sights, and shopping, there are subtle layers, so take your time and smell the coffee (literally).

From the sixteenth to eighteenth centuries, the ancient riverside town of Hoi An, formerly known as Faifo, was a major Silk Road trading port in Vietnam's central provinces. That is, until the river started silting up. Today, Hoi An's delightful historic quarter is virtually intact, miraculously escaping the ravages of time and wars and still bearing visible evidence from its seafaring merchant visitors—from Japan, China, and Europe—who traded in precious goods and very often ended up settling.

Hoi An's main historical area of interest actually consists of just three main streets running parallel to the Thu Bon River—Tran Phu, Nguyen Thai Hoc, and Bach Dang—plus Le Loi, running vertical. Conveniently, most of Hoi An's thoughtfully preserved monuments and attractions, which are characterized by a rich architectural fusion, are concentrated within walking distance. A distinctly antiquated air permeates, with narrow streets dotted with traditional, two-story, wooden-fronted Chinese merchant houses and communal halls, temples, a Japanese bridge, and French colonial villas. No wonder, then, Hoi An was awarded UNESCO World Heritage status.

But remember: with its ancient sights, time-warp charm, fastest silk tailoring service in the East, to-die-for local cuisine, and decent beach, Hoi An is not surprisingly one of Vietnam's most popular tourist destinations. And as such, the place is likely to be overrun with visitors; after all, you would hardly expect a tourist magnet like Angkor Wat to be without crowds. Some travelers are disappointed with the highly evident, blatant pandering to travelers, while jaded ex-pats steer clear of the town, cynically categorizing it as a "Disney-fied" money trap. This is all just a fact of life; get over it—Hoi An has so much more to offer, and there *are* ways to avoid the hordes.

Let's put some things in perspective. Unlike at Angkor Wat, locals actually reside and work in this living, breathing museum—it's their community. And being Vietnamese (and thus, never one to miss a chance to earn a fast buck), enterprising residents have opened up art galleries, shoe and tailor shops, restaurants, etc., virtually every second door, squashed in amongst this lucrative history. But in fact, locals still value their cultural heritage, with traditional craft workshops and dance performances keeping their unique traditions alive. The recently introduced Full Moon Night (nothing, I might add, to do with suspicious substances), celebrated monthly on the fourteenth day of the Lunar calendar, bans motorized vehicles and electrical

CENTRAL VIETNAM

appliances; instead, it offers traditional cultural performances out in the streets, illuminated by silk lanterns.

And unlike many other places in Vietnam—or indeed the world— local authorities have done a fairly decent job in preserving the historic architecture, with building guidelines and bylaws monitoring renovations and new buildings (such as adhering to the same low-rise architectural style). Funds, from money *you* cough up for a ticket system, are ploughed back into upkeep. But rather than a squeaky new appearance, the historic quarter affords an organic, dilapidated charm: moss grows unchecked between the crumbling terra cotta roof tiles, and some houses have preserved their centuries-old, antiquities-packed, jumbled interiors down to the minutest detail.

Is it clear how much I love Hoi An? Living in Vietnam for many years, I am fortunate enough to return here again and again, *never* tiring of the place. I still revisit my favorite "touristy" haunts (Diep Dong Nguyen House, Trieu Chau Assembly Hall, Chua Ong Pagoda, and the wondrous, seventeenth-century Japanese Covered Bridge), but now, mellowed out, I also take advantage of the inherent café culture, sitting on the porch of an old French villa-converted-café and making a cup of *ca phe* stretch for hours, as I watch the world pass languidly by.

Sometimes I hire a bicycle and head off out of town in any direction, and within minutes I am plunged into a timeless rural scenario with an impossibly idyllic tableau of boy-on-

buffalo/lush-green-paddy-fields/ excitable-kids-shrieking, "Hello! Hello!" Or while others rush around in the mid-afternoon oven temperatures, I am found instead devouring bowls of ridiculously cheap, delicious local specialties such as *cau lao* (thick noodles, fresh greens, and roasted pork slivers) inside family-run restaurants. Or later on, steamed fish wrapped in banana leaf, in the wall-to-wall riverside restaurants strung along impossibly photogenic Bach Dang Street.

Perhaps hire a sampan from here and watch riverine life and sunsets unfurl, admire the yellow-hued French architecture along Phan Boi Chau Street, or explore slender back alleys, accompanied by the familiar *clackety-clack* of an army of hand looms. Stop to appreciate *yin yang* signs above facades of wooden slats, miniscule carp ponds in hidden courtyards, and glazed ceramic figurines on rooftops: such details for me are the real charm of Hoi An.

Getting there

Hoi An is situated in Vietnam's central provinces, thirty kilometers south of Danang City and just four from the South China Sea. Danang is the main gateway for Hoi An; visitors arrive at Danang International Airport or the railway station, or are dropped off in Danang by Open-Tour buses. To get to Hoi An, either pre-arrange transfers with your accommodation, or take a metered taxi, around $15 one way.

Tasty eats in Hoi An

Miss Ly Cafeteria

Recommended: *cau lao* and other Hoi An specialties

22 Nguyen Hue St.

Hong Phuc Restaurant

Recommended: Steamed fish in banana leaf

86 Bach Dang St.

Yellow River (Hoang Ha) Restaurant

Recommended: *cau lao* and other Hoi An specialties

38 Tran Phu St.

Chill out in Hoi An

Brothers Café

27 Phan Boi Chau St.

Hai Scout Café

98 Nguyen Thai Hoc St.
www.visithoian.com

Mango Rooms

111 Nguyen Thai Hoc St.

Places to stay in Hoi An

Hoi An Riverside Resort & Spa

Hoi An's Old World charm couldn't be better encapsulated than at this boutique hotel, set amongst Balinese-style gardens, along a quiet stretch of the river. Gorgeous traditional-style Japanese or Vietnamese rooms have timbered floors and private balconies right on the water, looking out onto paddy fields and duck pens.

175 Cua Dai Rd.
(84-510) 864-800
www.hoianriverresort.com

Life Heritage Resort Hoi An

This is an innovative, boutique-style, Dutch-run hotel that places emphasis on the aesthetics of the location. Housed in a mock French-colonial style mansion, set in tropical gardens alongside the river, it is a few minutes' stroll east of the historic quarter. Spacious studio guestrooms offer a Zen, minimalist approach; book a river-view room and watch sampans chug past from your private porch with sofa. Fabulous buffet breakfasts.

1 Pham Hong Thai Rd.
(84-510) 914-555
www.life-resorts.com

Phu Thinh II Hotel

This is a large budget/good-value hotel along the beach road, with a pool and pretty gardens. Some back rooms have balconies overlooking paddy fields. Rates include complimentary buffet breakfast in a rustic open-air restaurant overlooking an idyllic lotus pond.

488 Cua Dai Rd.
(84-510) 923-923
www.phuthinhhotels.com

SOUTHERN VIETNAM

When not to go

Hoi An's rainy season and surprisingly cooler temperatures come during October, November, and December, when the town can experience heavy rains and serious flooding.

Insider tip

If you do want to avoid the crowds, start really early when places first open up for the day, or straight after opening post-lunch, or see as much as you can during lunch when everyone else is otherwise preoccupied.

DALAT

James Sullivan travels back to Dalat's gracious beginnings

On my honeymoon in Dalat in 1994, I dutifully checked out the city's bal-lyhooed attractions with my wife—the waterfalls, the kitschy Valle d'Amour theme park, the stark, 1961-built market—and I loathed the place. But as soon as my wife led me into the quiet, bygone neighborhood where she'd lived for two years as a girl, in a dilapidated villa with a sturdy stone foundation and a roof so grand that

its eaves covered the long, wooden verandah that ran along the broadest façade, I began to yearn to know more about the city's castaway homes.

Throughout Vietnam, the architectural legacies of French tenure are abundant. But where Saigon's colonial architecture is smothered by agglomerations of ground floor shops and dispiriting hack-jobs that accommodate new construction, Dalat is relatively pristine. Hundreds of colonial-era villas, built by *colons* homesick for the Landes, Savoy, Brittany, and Normandy, still speckle the city's pine-clad hills, moldering, forlorn, and uncelebrated by tourist authorities who don't seem to under-stand there's gold in their hills.

Recently, I finally had the opportunity to explore the city's architectural heritage. With Antoine Sirot, general manager of the 1922-built Sofitel Dalat Palace hotel, I motored in a restored, two-tone, gold and black, 1952 Citroen Traction up Tran Hung Dao Street, known in the colonial era as Avenue Paul Doumer, past the most magisterial homes in the city. Just a few years my senior, with longish blond hair that curls at the nape, Sirot seems like a man from another century. He writes with a fountain pen, and from the first, one suspects him of cuff links. For each of these homes, he had something to share—an anecdote, a descriptor, a provenance. He distinguished the Norman villas (wood detailing) from the Savoyarde (wood up top, stone on the ground floor), the Corsican (all stone) from the Landaise (one long sloped roof, one shorter sloped roof). The co-lonial architect, Paul Veysseyre, lived in #16, where Sirot himself lived for two years after coming to Dalat in 2003. Recently, Sirot moved to #27, a yellow villa in the Landaise style, that was once the home of the general director of a rubber plantation.

"When I was renovating, a man knocked on my door one day," Sirot recalled. "He told me he used to come to this house, his godmother's house, when he was a kid. His godmother used to ask him to wear *patinettes*, small pads made of wool and flannel that older people asked us kids to wear so we wouldn't scuff up the wood. When we walked in *patinettes*, we were—" Here, Sirot demonstrated the action, arms rocking from the steering wheel, "—like cross country skiers."

On Hung Vuong Street, we stopped at Veysseyre's Benedictine Monastery, with a rough, salmon stucco chapel whose façade was touched with intermittent stonework and a medieval door framed by a Gothic arch. "Very Disney," said Sirot, marveling at Veysseyre's sense of adventure and courage. In Dalat, far from the judgmental regard of established peers, architects like Veysseyre dared to be different.

One example of the city's historic villas that is accessible to travelers is the old Bellevue Quarter along Le Lai Street. Here the Six Senses resort group has revived a collection of seventeen villas, nearly all designed by Paul Veysseyre, as the Evason Ana Mandara Villas and Six Senses Spa at Dalat. Set among towering pines and yuccas that put you in mind of a prehistoric landscape, the villas com-

mand high ground above the Cam Ly River. They boast prominent turrets, long, sweeping verandahs, and grand stonework foundations that are like plinths to Veysseyre's monuments.

Inside, banks of windows light up rooms of fatigued, wooden floors and beams of boxy, tropical hardwoods. The entrance to one dining room describes a giant half moon in the wall. The décor, from villa to villa, is subdued, with khaki-colored draperies and brass fixtures complementing colonial-inspired wood furnishings. In the gloaming, with the light filtering through the pines and slanting through the windows, you wonder whether it's time to just sit down and write that novel after all.

After wandering around Dalat for several days, I'd been lulled by the buildings into some imagination of Vietnam's antebellum past as prelapsarian. This nostalgia for the trappings of colonialism is at large all over Vietnam, promulgated not only by savvy Western marketers but by the Vietnamese themselves who've keyed into the Western traveler's penchant for iron filigree, quoins, and brass-bladed Marelli fans, and, in response, have gussied up landmark hotels like the Morin in Hue into even grander colonial confections.

In cerebral circles, these nostalgic yearnings are lightly sneered upon as politically incorrect, as *Indo-chic*. And of course, the critics are right. Beyond the architecture, the baguettes and berets, the legacy of the French in Vietnam is sordid. Their vaunted *mission civilisatrice* was a fiction, trumped up to expiate the guilt of colonizers who were here to

SOUTHERN VIETNAM

make money and live large. In Dalat, especially, a policy of apartheid elevated the *colon* and degraded the Vietnamese and the highlanders. Most visitors understand this, and most, be they French or American, still tend to travel through the country with varying degrees of penitence.

The historians remind us that these sumptuously revived colonial salons and chambers are not an accurate echo of a glamorous colonial era, that these so-called "antiquarian effects" are part of a mythology, not an actual past. But it doesn't matter. In Dalat, it doesn't take much imagination to understand that the French were enthralled by the possibility of a fantasy up here on this 1,500-meter-high plateau that had been uninhabited by the Vietnamese when physician Alexandre Yersin first explored the area in 1893.

As I dined alone one evening in Le Rabelais restaurant at the Dalat Palace, a pianist was playing Satie on a baby grand as I started dinner. While I dined, one of my candles drooled wax off the stem of a silver candelabra onto a starched white tablecloth. Waiters hovered near my table, delivering prawns, fish, squid, and scallops skewered by lemongrass; sautéed Dalat vegetables; and red wine from South Africa. As my silverware was changed between courses, I looked from the bronze-framed panels of this elegant salon to the chandeliers and four-meter drapes restrained by golden tasseled cords.

You can get all of this on the continent, of course, but in Paris you're de-prived of the juxtaposition of opulence and the rawness of the developing world that's made evident by a power failure that plunges the rest of the city in darkness while the Palace's generators churn on. In the same way that summer is never so glorious as in the wake of a hard winter, the refinements of Dalat's colonial architecture are all the more alluring for this setting in the highlands of Vietnam.

Sofitel Dalat Palace

12 Tran Phu St.
Dalat
(84-63) 825-444
www.sofitel.com

Evason Ana Mandara Villas and Six Senses Spa at Dalat

Le Lai St.
Dalat
(84-63) 555-888
www.sixsenses.com

The inside scoop

To find out more about life inside the villas, as well as a walking tour, continue to the following essay by Antoine Sirot.

Antoine Sirot recalls daily life in the French villas of Dalat

Upon first arriving in Dalat, I was much surprised by what I found:

French, 1930s-beach-style resort architecture spread around a lake among pine trees. But wait a minute, I was 1,500 meters above sea level, and the people here wore conical hats! Geographically and culturally, this was quite a bit different from what I remember of the beach resort I used to go to as a child, where my family had a villa: Le Touquet on the French coast of La Manche/English Channel. But although there is no sea here, the local gardens scattered with evergreens felt very familiar to me.

While you can find older, early twentieth-century homes, similar to the ones in Hanoi, the Art Deco style of the 1930s and '40s is dominant in Dalat. While the exterior of each home often reflects the original owner's regional origin in France, all the houses' indoor layouts are similar to one another, though different from the ones I knew back home when it comes to the basement: in Vietnam, the "boyerie" was the sleeping quarters for the "boys," an English name used by the French to qualify their young male servants. This room was close to the kitchen, also in the basement, where female maids would do the cooking on charcoal-fired stoves.

For most kitchens in Vietnam, the gas stove came in the 1980s. That's why you can notice more than one chimney on the rooftops of these old villas; one was linked to the stove and one to a wood-fired hot water boiler all the way down in the basement. The garage for the cars was also in the basement or in a side building, often with a workshop and a small room for the Indian drivers, originating usually from Pondicherry, a French trading post in India. Perhaps the Indians were considered better skilled at driving cars, or was it that the French did not trust the locals, famous for enjoying rice wine and opium?

On the ground floor, Dalat villas are not much different from their French counterparts. The main room, which was the dining room, had the best view and was located generally close to the entry hall. In the past, the French would spend three to four hours per meal here, not lingering in a living room as in today's houses. The dining room was linked to the pantry, which would be linked to the basement kitchen by a narrow stairway for the "boys" to bring the various dishes.

Accommodations were quite simple, a master bedroom on the ground floor with an en suite bathroom, and children's or guestrooms on the upper floor with one shared bathroom. Toilets were in a separate closet accessible to all without entering the privacy of the bedrooms. The size of the villas might look massive to today's Westerners, but in those days, they had to accommodate an entire family with many children and also some eight to fifteen staff.

While these villas feel a bit scattered all over the city, all areas of Dalat once followed an exhaustive city planning and zoning program. Each zone was dedicated to a particular usage; for example, administration, trading, and living quarters for French; living quarters for high

Vietnamese society; and living quarters for farmers. The living quarters dedicated to the French were divided into three categories: A, B, and C. The A type was for villas built on a piece of land that was a minimum of 1,000 square meters, with a mandatory 40 percent authorized construction area, leaving 60 percent for a garden. Very few villas have kept their gardens, as the land surrounding has been sold and new construction added.

The only street that still has the former atmosphere in a significant way is Tran Hung Dao, which was included in the Sofitel Dalat Palace hotel's venture to keep it from being ruined by new building. Today, the government is very conscious of the uniqueness of this street and imposes some regulations on the present owners to keep this authentic feel. It has the best concentration of villas in the city and is a good starting point for a stroll through Dalat's architectural past.

Touring the villas

Depending on availability, special guests of the Sofitel Dalat Palace may enjoy a slide show and lecture on the city's villas, followed by a tour around town, sometimes in the hotel's vintage Citroen. For independent touring, you may walk to Tran Hung Dao Street from the hotel by exiting out the back door and heading to your left, away from the "Eiffel Tower." Plan for a couple of hours in order to take your time and enjoy the atmosphere of this

historic boulevard. Please remember that these houses are privately owned, and their residents should not be disturbed.

Villa #21

This is the home of the former Governor General of *Cochinchine*, the southern part of Vietnam, who wanted to own the largest villa on this street and had it built in a classic style of southern France. The building in fact reflects a more overdone, "nouveau riche" style than a purely straightforward interpretation.

Villa #27

I refurbished this villa entirely in 2004, and it is now my home. It was built in 1937 for the former director of the area's largest rubber plantation, which belonged to the Michelin Corporation. Before moving to this villa, I lived in #16, which was the villa of the most important architect of Dalat, Paul Veysseyre, who lived in the city from 1937 to 1951. He designed the city's two Art Deco palaces, Palace II and Palace III, as well as some 350 villas in the city.

PHAN THIET

Adam Bray takes you on a walking tour of Phan Thiet

Associated by the Vietnamese with the production of *nuoc mam* and dragon fruit (originally imported by the French from South America), Phan Thiet is often dismissed by travelers as a resort town with a nice golf course. In truth, I'm happy that the capital city of Binh Thuan Province has been overlooked by visitors in favor of nearby Mui Ne Beach. Easily reached from my home in Mui Ne, Phan Thiet has been my quiet getaway from crowds of tourists, both foreign and domestic.

My favorite time to explore Phan Thiet is early morning, and the best place to start is the central market. Beginning in Mui Ne, head west on Nguyen Dinh Chieu/Thu Khoa Huan Streets, straight through Phan Thiet and across Le Hong Phong Bridge, which is suspended across the Ca Ty River. The other side of the river affords the best view, looking back, of the Phan Thiet Water Tower. This elegant symbol of the province is incorporated into numerous local emblems. It was designed in the 1930s by Prince Suphanouvong of Laos who was the chief engineer of the Nha Trang Public Works Bureau under the French Indochina government. Continue past the square on Nguyen Tri Phuong/Tran Phu Street, around the roundabout, stopping at the city market for breakfast. My top picks here are *banh xeo* (crispy seafood crepe), *cha gio* (fried spring roll), *sinh to sau rieng* (durian shake), and *che buoi* (pomelo pudding). Prices are very cheap because the market isn't a common stop for foreigners.

Once you've eaten and browsed through the market, head back to the river on Nguyen Hue Street, and take a left on Trung Noi Street, passing Duc Thanh Bridge, to arrive at the Ho Chi Minh Museum and Duc Thanh School. In 1910 Ho Chi Minh taught at the school for a year, before leaving to pursue more revolutionary endeavors. The school was abandoned but later rebuilt in his honor, along with a new museum on the site of his former home. The museum contains some of his personal effects, dioramas from the revolutionary period, and some local natural history displays and wildlife specimens. This museum is not yet on the tourist circuit and for that reason offers a unique view of Ho Chi Minh's very humble past, without the overwhelming propaganda found in other national museums intended for foreign visitors. That's not to say there isn't propaganda present, but that message is intended for local visitors and so foreigners won't come away feeling like they've been preached at.

Wandering back along the riverfront, you'll pass vendors selling candied fruits, dried squid, and peanut brittle, and eventually come to the Tran Hung Dao Bridge. From here the Ca Ty River flows into Phan Thiet's harbor, with its brightly colored fishing fleet and small lighthouse beyond. I've watched all the major festivals and parades culminate in this area, including celebrations for Nghinh Ong and the Mid-Autumn Festival; Phan Thiet is nationally recognized for both. The riverfront is especially beautiful during evening festivities when there are elaborate fireworks shows.

Passing Tran Hung Dao Street, the road becomes Trung Trac and leads to the seaport. This area is always crowded with restaurant owners shoving each other to get to the best seafood right off the boat. Other vessels also dock here to buy supplies for far-off islands and oil rigs. After turning right on Ngu Ong Street, you can visit the Van Thuy Tu Temple dedicated to whale worship. The ancient religion is believed to originate in the Cham and Khmer cultures. Built in 1762, the temple contains skeletons of more than 100 whales, including one more than twenty-two meters long.

Back at Tran Hung Dao Bridge, you'll arrive at a park by the same name on the opposite side of the river. Tran Hung Dao was a revered Vietnamese military leader who led armies to defeat three Mongol invasions during the thirteenth century. Statues of the general and other great historical leaders guard the park, which is also overlooked by palatial capital buildings.

Continuing up the street you'll pass the sizable Duc Thanh Bookstore. Bookstores are Vietnam's best-kept

shopping secret, as they often double as gift shops. You can find Cham textiles, ceramics, lanterns, chimes, maps, dictionaries, and more—all for rock-bottom prices. And no haggling is involved because the prices are set.

Farther up Tran Hung Dao Street and to the right, Nguyen Tat Thanh is a grand boulevard divided by immaculately kept gardens. On the left you'll pass the provincial performing arts center. I've spent many evenings here for concerts, traditional operas, and patriotic spectacles. I once parked my motorbike under some trees near the center, only to realize that four of the trunks belonged to elephants. I discovered that there was a circus in town and there would be Chinese acrobats, fire dancers, and magic shows that night. Events are rarely advertised more than twenty-four hours in advance, so it always pays to swing by in person and see if there is a show that evening. Ticket scalpers are the norm, and while they may have some good seats, they don't necessarily offer the best ones—and they'll be expensive. Even with tickets in hand, you should arrive very early. Although seats are numbered, there are never enough, as it's common practice to let small children in without tickets.

Behind the center is a welcoming café and Phan Thiet's famous "Banh Xeo Street" (Tuyen Quang Street), lined with restaurants. Phan Thiet is a city of cafés, and there are numerous distinctive choices in the city center, many with gardens, waterfalls, and fish ponds. The hot afternoon is a great time to stop in one, as most shops and restaurants are otherwise closed for the customary "afternoon nap."

At the end of Nguyen Tat Thanh Street, you will finally arrive at Doi Duong Beach, lined with inexpensive cafés full of young Vietnamese lovers sitting in the shade of pine trees. East of the beach, you can play a round at the Ocean Dunes Golf Resort. Designed by Nick Faldo, it was ranked among the "Best 500 Holes in the World" by *Golf Magazine*. As for me, I head to the west end where I often enjoy a delicious and relatively cheap lunch of seafood hot pot. The seafood restaurants on Doi Duong Beach are also some of the few restaurants in the city that are open for lunch. After a big meal, I find that the recliners at the beach cafés are a perfect place for a nap, lulled by the crashing waves.

Getting from Mui Ne to Phan Thiet

There is a shuttle bus between Mui Ne and Phan Thiet for less than $1. Another option is a motorbike, at $5-$7 per day. Most travelers will drive west on Nguyen Dinh Chieu/Thu Khoa Huan Street into Phan Thiet from their accommodations in Mui Ne. I've made the drive to and from town more than 2,500 times (really, I've counted), and I never grow tired of the coastal scenery, which includes the ancient Thap Poshanu Cham Towers, rainforest covered mountains, two river systems, cashew farms, and immense sand dunes.

Getting around Phan Thiet

Unlike in other cities in Vietnam, *xich lo* (cyclos) and taxis are hard to come by in Phan Thiet, so a tour around town is usually by motorbike and on foot. Once you arrive at the central market, you can leave your motorbike with a parking lot attendant for 1,000 VND and spend the day walking the town.

Dining details

Breakfast at the central market should be less than $1 (4,000-7,000 VND). Coffee with milk will also be in that range at any given café, depending upon how extravagant the place is. Seafood hot pot on the beach will start around $3, plus drinks. Please use sound judgment when ordering your lunch. If you see sea turtles in the seafood tank, don't order them. Better yet, move on to the next restaurant.

HO CHI MINH CITY

James Sullivan perches high above Ho Chi Minh City

On my first night in the Caravelle Hotel, I parted the curtains draping my room's windows, and eighteen

SOUTHERN VIETNAM

floors up, gazed out over Lam Son Square, the cinematic heart of Ho Chi Minh City. Looking up Dong Khoi Street, toward the twin spires of Notre Dame Cathedral, I caught sight of an arresting image that I hadn't read about in any of the guidebooks, but is seared into our collective memory of the war: the elevator shaft.

Together with *The Girl in the Picture*, *The Burning Monk*, and *The Viet Cong Execution*, *The Last Helicopter* ranks as one of the most iconic photos of the Vietnam War. For many, this image barely warrants description, but for the forgetful or the young, picture this: A helicopter precariously perched on the stub of a penthouse elevator shaft, a pilot leaning over to lend a hand, and a line of Vietnamese evacuees bunched up on the treads of a steep stairway. No other photo captures the desperation of those finals days in Saigon as powerfully. But its poignancy is more than a function of the evacuees' anguish, for in that image, in the suspect stability of that helicopter and that haphazard attempt to get people *out*, is the humiliation of a superpower for whom things had gone wrong, so terribly wrong over the previous decade.

Even today, newspapers still incorrectly identify the Hubert Van Es image as a photo of the US Embassy. It wasn't, though embassy employees did live in the apartment building. Nor was it the last helicopter to lift people out of the city; it was the last to lift evacuees off that particular perch. In fact, the shaft is located at 22 Ly Tu Trong Street, known during the war as Gia Long Street, in a building whose dominant tenant today is a construction company.

On subsequent trips to Ho Chi Minh City, I made a parlor game of what other legacies of the conflict could be glimpsed from the rooftop bar of the Caravelle Hotel, itself a wartime venue that comes into the present as a fabled prop in the infrastructure of a tragedy. CBS, ABC, and for a time, NBC, all ran their bureaus out of it. Otherwise, correspondents once heeded the after-hours summons of the same rooftop bar that I now frequented. Michael Herr, author of *Dispatches*—not only the best book about the Vietnam War, but also one of the most stunning tours de force in all of American literature—wrote this about being up there:

"In the early evenings we'd do exactly what correspondents did in those terrible stories that would circulate in 1964 and 1965, we'd stand on the roof of the Caravelle Hotel having drinks and watch the air strikes across the river, so close that a good telephoto lens would pick up the markings on the planes. There were dozens of us up there, like aristocrats viewing Borodino from the heights."

With a bit of informed reconnaissance, many colonial and wartime landmarks are still visible from this perch. There are the obvious landmarks, of course, that make the grade in so many recollections of Saigon: the Notre Dame Cathedral, whose towers could be seen far from the city as passenger ships wended their way up the Saigon River in the colonial era; the Continental Hotel, opened in 1880 by a French appliance salesmen; and the Municipal Theatre, with its broken mansard roofs and remarkable arched façade.

But the city's lesser known venues are somehow more evocative for being half-forgotten. Take the Eden Building, for example, located diagonally across the square from the Caravelle. On the ground floor is the Givral Patisserie where Graham Greene's Phuong stopped for her "elevenses," or afternoon tea, in *The Quiet American*. Further back in time, when the French author of *The Lover*, Marguerite Duras, was a *colon*, her mother played piano in a theater located in this same building. During the war, the AP bureau was located on the fourth floor. Otherwise, the Eden was home to "families, business operators, foreign journalists, spies and who knows who else," according to Richard Pyle, an AP correspondent who worked in Saigon during the war. To look at the Eden's drab, uninspiring façade today, you'd almost think the building was borne out of a Soviet inspiration. Not the case. I've seen at least one reference to the building in a pamphlet published in 1942, and students of architecture can likely pick out more than a few Art Deco details on the exterior.

In the early days of the war, the US military briefed the press on the events of the day on the ground floor of the Rex Hotel, a conference known derisively then and now as "the Five O'Clock Follies." But the Follies didn't dawdle at the Rex for all of the war;

they were shunted 150 meters away to a building on the corner of Lam Son Square and Dong Khoi Street, where the attractive new Artex Building now stands. Here's Richard Pyle on how he survived the Follies' location: "A single grenade tossed from a passing Honda motorbike could have taken out a sizeable part of the Saigon press corps and the only reason it never happened might be that the Cong believed the Western media were really helping rather than hurting their cause."

From the Caravelle, you can also see Gia Long Palace, the pearl-gray colonial French monument from which President Ngo Dinh Diem and his brother fled on the fateful night of their assassination in 1963. There's the roof of the Sûreté Building farther up Dong Khoi Street, built in 1917 as the headquarters of the colonial French police. There's also Dong Khoi Street itself, laid out by the French as a Far East version of the Rue de Rivoli in Paris. Initially, the French referred to this thoroughfare, from the Saigon River to the Cathedral, as Street 16. Later, it acquired a name that's achieved the most legendary appellation—rue Catinat. When Graham Greene lived in Saigon, and when the *colons* sipped their *citron presse* in the afternoon on the terrace of the Continental Hotel, it was on rue Catinat; as well, after the French ceded Vietnam to the Vietnamese in 1955, legionnaires marched down this boulevard. And during the wild and woolly days of the Vietnam War, the street was known as Tu Do (Freedom) Street and home to countless go-go bars. After 1975, the name changed yet again to Dong Khoi (General Uprising).

After living in Vietnam from 1992 to 1994 and now again since the summer of 2005, I keep telling myself that there's so much more to Vietnam than the legacy of the war. And there is. But the war's no less fascinating for all that, especially when so much is laid out before you still from the roof of one of its most significant monuments.

Caravelle Hotel

19 Lam Son Square
District 1
Ho Chi Minh City
(84-8) 823-4999
www.caravellehotel.com

Cu Chi

Lorene Strand learns about "the other side" in Cu Chi

Dedicated to Sergeant Brian A. Jones, 25th Infantry, 3/4 Cavalry, B Troop, "MacKenzie's Raiders" Cu Chi 1967

I had never met one, but I knew I had to. I knew that meeting a Viet

Minh soldier who had served in Cu Chi during the American War would somehow bring peace to my stepfather and my family. It was a journey my stepfather could not make—there are too many ghosts in Cu Chi, and there was too much death—but it was a journey I could make for him.

It seemed ironic to go to Cu Chi for peace. The name of this place has haunted my family. It was the reason for my stepfather's blackouts, the bottles of medicine, the trips to the hospital. All could be summoned by the name of a rural area located approximately seventy-five kilometers northwest of Ho Chi Minh City. My stepfather served in the 25th Infantry Division in Cu Chi and was one of the lucky ones: he came home.

When I first visited Cu Chi, it was a shock. Adults and children were clambering down into the tunnels where the Viet Cong soldiers once lived, laughing, joking, smiling, and snapping photos; everyone seemed oblivious to the death that had occurred here, the intense fighting, the carpet bombings, the destruction. Cu Chi is surreal. There is a "war is fun" mentality. I was expecting a memorial, but found an entrepreneurial playground: a small outdoor market selling lighters purportedly belonging to former soldiers, Cu Chi Tunnel t-shirts, and other assorted bits and baubles, along with a firing range where you can squeeze off rounds from an AK-47 or M16 rifle at a dollar a pop.

Now I have come to Cu Chi again, traveling down a dusty dirt road with the son of a former soldier who I met at a restaurant near Pham Ngu Lao Street in Ho Chi Minh City. Like me, the son speaks lovingly of his father and the sacrifices his family made for his country. Eventually we stop in front of a whitewashed, two-room house, and a gaunt man steps off the porch and smiles at us. As we shake hands, I look at his deeply lined face and cavernous eyes, and sense the same pain I sometimes see in my stepfather's expression. I know I have found my stepfather's kindred spirit.

On this ordinary, non-descript Saturday afternoon, we sit down together in the shade of a banana tree, sipping green tea and eating dragon fruit, and he begins to tell me about his life. He was born into a large family of Viet Minh farmers from Cu Chi. In 1964, at the age of seventeen, he joined the Viet Minh Army. His older brother had already joined the infantry, but had been killed. He too wanted to be in the infantry like his brother; however, his health was not strong, and so he agreed to train as a medic. He was given rudimentary instruction at a makeshift classroom in the jungle with 200 other students and was subsequently assigned to active duty assisting a doctor in the jungle for a few weeks, which completed his training.

From 1966 to 1969, his job was to follow the guerrilla forces and serve as their medic; approximately 60 percent of the men in his unit were killed. Medicine was always a problem. There was never enough. Sometimes the couriers would go into Saigon and buy medicine from the American shops to supplement shortages. Then, in 1969, he huddled with five guerrilla fighters while waiting in the tunnels of Cu Chi for two helicopter gunships to pass. When it became quiet, he went above ground to make sure all was clear. Wearing a camouflage poncho, he climbed up a nearby rubber tree. Without warning the gunship swooped in close enough for him to clearly see the flight crew. The gunner aimed and fired, hitting him in the leg. The big gunship turned and the other gunner fired. He was again hit in the leg. The impact sent him tumbling to the ground.

Now he was running as best he could, his injured leg useless; more shots were fired, hitting him in the back, and he could run no more. The gunship dropped a grenade, alerting the US infantry where he was. As he lay there waiting to be captured as a prisoner of war, one thought kept him conscious: "I must keep going for the country, keep going for the country, keep going for the country." As a recruit they had all been told, "Americans are trying to steal our country!"

"I wanted my country to be free," he explains to me.

From the tunnels of Cu Chi he was taken to the American hospital in Bien Hoa, where his wounds healed. He then spent the next three years as a prisoner of war on Phu Quoc Island, until he was sent to Hanoi on a prisoner exchange. Following independence in 1975, he became a party overseer at a ration factory. Every month, citizens came for their rations, and just like during the war, there was never enough food. In 1985 he retired

MEKONG DELTA

and now receives $30 every month from the government for his war wounds, and $5 a month for his oldest son, who suffers from the effects of Agent Orange. Together with his wife, he sells *pho* every morning in a small lean-to next to their house. From this they earn approximately $32, which helps to supplement his income. But he says, "Now my job is to enjoy life." The land that once composed the Iron Triangle is silent now. Gone are the American military bases. Many once familiar landmarks have been removed or cut down. Nature has taken over the craters that pock the ground from the carpet bombings. The land is healing, as I believe my journey to Cu Chi will help my stepfather heal, with my discovery of how much a Viet Minh soldier and a U.S. infantryman share: former warriors seeking an inner peace.

Getting to Cu Chi

Many places on Pham Ngu Lao Street in Ho Chi Minh City offer tours to the Cu Chi Tunnels. Always reliable is Sinh Café, which has been around for years.

246-248 De Tham St.
District 1
Ho Chi Minh City
(84-8) 836-7338/837-6833
www.sinhcafe.com

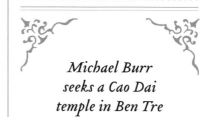

BEN TRE

Michael Burr seeks a Cao Dai temple in Ben Tre

I travel to Vietnam for the third time in April of 2005, for the thirtieth anniversary of the end of the war. There is a reunion of veterans, correspondents, photojournalists, and others who spent time in the country during the war years. After a week or so in Ho Chi Minh City, attending events, parties, and dinners, I set out for my first trip to the Mekong Delta. I board a boat for the first leg of the journey: Saigon to My Tho. We arrive about midday and, after checking into my hotel, I wander around the town shooting pictures until sunset.

The next day, after an unsuccessful negotiation to hire a car to take me to Ben Tre, I decide to strike out on my own. I'm photographing Cao Dai temples for a possible book project, and there are two in Ben Tre, a smaller town across the river. As I take a cyclo from the hotel to the Rach Mieu ferry landing and board for the crossing, I'm not sure how I'm going to get there, as it's about ten kilometers from the landing on the opposite bank. But as I'm standing at the rail shooting, a voice behind me says, "Hi, how are you doing?" I turn around to find a smiling *Viet Kieu* from Connecticut. He and his wife are here visiting her relatives. They have rented a van and driver, and they offer me a ride into town, which I gratefully accept. Leaving the ferry, we turn off the main road. I don't think too much about it as I'm having a good time, chatting in my rudimentary Vietnamese, eating rambutan, and enjoying the scenery. After about thirty minutes we pull into a driveway of sorts, everybody gets out, and the van is shut off. We have reached our destination—the middle of nowhere. I politely ask about getting into town. Apparently, there has been a misunderstanding, but not to worry, the couple arranges for a *xe om* (motorbike driver) to take me. We set off down a series of dirt roads. But the *xe om*, concerned for my well-being, wants me to wear a helmet, so we stop by his house where I have to meet his family.

Here's my dilemma. Cao Dai has four services a day: 6 a.m., noon, 6 p.m., and midnight. My plan was to hit one temple for a noon service and the other for a 6 p.m. I started out at 9 a.m. and now it's 10:30, so I'm starting to feel pressure. But even though I have no idea where the temples are located, I figure this guy must know where he's going, and surely it can't be more than fifteen minutes to town.

We reach a T-intersection with a paved road. Choices are left or right. My guy turns left. Ten minutes later I'm back at the ferry crossing! I'm flipping out but maintain my cool (can't lose face), and I tell the moto guy *khong duoc* (not okay) and that I want to go to

Ben Tre town. He finally understands, and even though he was paid by the *Viet Kieu*, he pops me for another 20,000 VND (just over $1) for the "extra" trip.

He drops me in front of what is supposed to be, according to my guidebook, the Ben Tre Province Tourist Office. It turns out to be a school. There's another office a few blocks away ... except that it's closed—it's Saturday. At this point, I'm hot, tired, frustrated, and about to give up as it's nearing noon, when a young Vietnamese man pulls up on a motorbike and asks, "May I help you, sir?" I ask him the whereabouts of the nearer Cao Dai temple. He doesn't seem to know. Another man walks up and they engage in animated conversation. After a few minutes they have a "Eureka!" moment, the first guy offers to take me there, and we jump on his bike for a wild ride to the temple where I arrive for the noon service with five minutes to spare, just in time for a special ceremony honoring an elderly Cao Dai priestess.

After the ceremony and some shooting around the compound, one of the elders takes me by the arm and leads me down the road to another temple complex where I get more great shots. As we walk back, I'm getting weary. I've been going on water and fruit since I started out this morning, and it's now 2:30. The elders arrange for another driver to take me back into town, and I bid them a fond farewell. After a hearty lunch of *com chien tom* (shrimp fried rice) and a couple Beer 33, I'm feeling much better and (wisely) decide not to try to find the other temple, which is apparently some distance from town. I spend the balance of the afternoon

MEKONG DELTA

wandering around Ben Tre shooting the riverfront, market, kids leaving school, etc., before getting a motorbike back to the ferry landing.

As the sun sets and I cross the river, I reflect on the events of the day. What a trip! A few moments of frustration and anxiety to be sure, but overall a fantastic little adventure. Amazing what can happen when you just let things flow. This is exactly why I travel solo (or at most with one or two like-minded individuals); *never* go on organized tours; always head for out-of-the-way places; and seek out the unusual. Makes for a better travel experience ... and terrific photos.

Getting to My Tho and Ben Tre

A pleasant, popular destination on a branch of the Mekong River, My Tho can easily be reached by road or river from Ho Chi Minh City. For my boat trip, I used Delta Adventure Tours. From My Tho, you can reach Ben Tre by ferry and bus, minibus, or motorbike driver. Gift shopping tip: Ben Tre is famous for its coconut candy.

267 De Tham St.
District 1
Ho Chi Minh City
(84-8) 920-2112
www.deltaadventuretours.com

Chuong Duong Hotel

In my opinion, this is *the* place to stay in My Tho. Every room has a river view, and the restaurant is quite good as well.

#10, 30 Thang 4 St. (30/4 St.)
My Tho
Tien Giang Province
(84-73) 870-875/870-876

Dong Khoi Hotel

I had a great meal here after "The Adventure." It's reported to be the best hotel in Ben Tre, as well.

16 Hai Ba Truong St.
Ben Tre
Ben Tre Province
(84-75) 822-240/632

LONG XUYEN

Lillian Forsyth pedals across a Mekong Delta island

Day four of the Lunar New Year means a return to work and everyday life, after three days of eating, drinking, talking, and visiting. For me the Tet holiday also included a message on day two from a student at about six in the morning, asking if I wanted to visit his house on Tiger Island (Ong Ho). Of course I said yes, and by eight my bike and I were on a ferryboat.

Tiger Island, in My Hoa Commune, is a small island in the middle of the Hau River, which runs past Long Xuyen, where I am a volunteer English teacher. It is the birthplace of Ton Duc Thang: Uncle Ton as he is fondly known by the Vietnamese people. Vice-president for Uncle Ho, Ton Duc Thang became the second president of North Vietnam and the first leader of reunified Vietnam.

The ferry to Tiger Island leaves from the main market in Long Xuyen, at the end of Nguyen Hue Street. The ferry takes about ten minutes, but it was like going back in time fifty years or so. The bustle of Long Xuyen, such as it is, was lost in that short passage across the water. My student, An, met me on the other side with his bicycle, his cousin sitting on the back. We took the one narrow (although paved) road down the center of the island. We rode past small, bamboo-pole huts, fields of soybeans, children, dogs, chickens, ducks, oxen, and rice paddies. The remarkable green that I have tried to describe in writing before (and failed miserably) was all around us. We were swimming in a sea of vibrant green, peppered with distant specks of conical hats bobbing up and down in the fields.

After about half an hour of riding in the early morning humidity, we bumped down the dirt road that led to An's home. An lives in a traditional countryside structure, with the floor and three of the walls made of wide wooden planks. The front of the house is open to the air, with a railing across it to serve as a sort of balcony. He has a large family, fairly typical for rural Vietnamese: three older sisters, two of whom are married, and a younger brother. His sisters were all visiting for the Tet holidays, as well as their hus-

bands and children, so the house was full of people, all of whom seemed slightly terrified of me, the foreigner, sitting on a stool in the front of the house. One of the babies even started crying when I tried to talk to her. This is fairly standard baby behavior upon seeing *nguoi la*, a stranger.

Once lunch with An and one of his friends from high school was over, we went for a bike ride around the island. Tiger Island, although it is just minutes from Long Xuyen, is much less "developed." In order to use the Internet, for example, An must leave the island. Almost all of the population are farmers, and although there are a lot of people, and the roads are lined with houses, it still has a quiet and peaceful atmosphere that is more countryside than city.

It took us about thirty minutes to make it from An's house on the far side of the island back to Uncle Ton Duc Thang's temple. An, his cousin, and I walked around the temple and associated gardens and then visited the Ton Duc Thang Museum. The museum, like many others in Vietnam, is a collection of documents and artifacts that chart Uncle Ton's revolutionary activities and struggles. It always makes me feel a little bit uncomfortable when I look at the exhibits about "The Struggle Against the Americans, 1954-1975." There are usually pictures of American soldiers being slaughtered by Vietnamese, or of Americans torturing innocent Vietnamese civilians. An didn't seem to bat an eye at this, and I didn't ask about it, but sometimes I wonder

MEKONG DELTA

what my students have learned about Americans, particularly in their history classes, and how that affects the way they perceive me.

After we finished at the temple, we wanted to pick *man* fruit, which is what the Vietnamese call rose apples. But the garden across the street had already sold all of its fruit. Though there are many other gardens around the island where you can pick fruit and relax in the shade, we stopped instead for a quick coffee break. Then I made the trip back to Long Xuyen where I took a much-needed nap.

Seeing the "real" Vietnamese countryside is something that not many foreigners have the chance to do. I have been lucky to visit it on several occasions because of my students, but the excursions usually require long rides on hot buses, walking long distances, and sleeping in rather difficult conditions. Tiger Island is unique in that it is within twenty minutes of a "major" city (such as Long Xuyen is), but is a part of Vietnam that few tourists access.

Getting to Tiger Island

Take the O Moi ferry at the end of Nguyen Hue Street in central Long Xuyen. Tickets are 1,000 VND for a bicycle, 2,000 VND for a motorbike, and 500 VND for a person on foot.

Ton Duc Thang Museum

Once you reach Tiger Island, take the only road in sight for about one kilometer until you pass under a gate that is framed by two tiger statues. The temple and museum are on the right, and Ton Duc Thang's childhood home on the left.

Eating and drinking

There are numerous coffee shops around the museum and along the main road. Any one should do for a cup of coffee. As well, there is a mango orchard on the main road past the museum; if you just continue straight, it's on the left side at "To TQ12, To 490/12 (#490/12 on Highway 12)." The fruit orchards (*vuon*) may have fruit available for picking, depending on what time of year you go.

Renting bicycles

Ask your hotel in Long Xuyen where to rent bicycles. It should cost less than $1 per day.

HA TIEN

Samantha Coomber encounters the end of the world in Ha Tien

Ha Tien is at the end of the world—well, it feels like that. It is in fact tucked away in the far northwestern corner of the Mekong Delta. And thus, it's a godforsaken place to get to, which is probably why few Western tourists make it there. Travel choices include horrendously long bus rides from, er, anywhere, or alternatively, the "scenic" but woefully more taxing option, which this crazy writer has tried twice and vowed never again. I'm referring to hiring a motorbike driver from Chau Doc and for about six hours or so hanging on for dear life on the back of the bike, traveling along a dirt road running parallel to a canal marking the Cambodian border. How adventurous, you utter, except that my first trip was in driving rain and on the second, though sunny, the route was partially submerged under monsoonal floodwater. I also tried to cadge a lift off the tugboats that sail westwards along the canal, which the guidebooks shamefully romanticize, feebly making arrangements with "salty sea captains" in Chau Doc, but I digress.

And after all that effort to get to Ha Tien, I can't specifically say *why* you should come here. First impressions are that it is merely a sleepy seaside port town straddling an estuary and small lake, a jumping off point for the "subject to availability" Xa Xia border crossing to Cambodia. There ain't that much catering to Western tourists, the few that actually get here (which is perhaps an attraction in itself), and hardly any significant "sights" as such. Yet I adore the place, one that has left a lasting impression on me after years of travels around Vietnam.

The only reason I ended up here was to update travel guidebooks, otherwise I may never have bothered. But accidentally, I stumbled upon a dilapidated charm, an endearing end-of-the-road outpost slightly frayed around the edges, and beyond it, astounding natural scenery of jungle-clad mountains, mangrove swamps, caves, and surreal coastal seascapes. I was captivated right from the moment I really *did* reach the end of the (canal) road, when it merged with a now visible coastline and swaying coconut palms. Since I was half dead and drenched from the motorbike ride, I especially appreciated the sight. Ha Tien is also of personal significance, as it was here, in an unassuming noodle restaurant back in 2001, that I witnessed the 9/11 tragedy unfurl on TV.

Fishing—and all that smells fishy— is the dominant livelihood here, reinforced by wafts of salty sea air and fish sauce (*nuoc mam)* production hitting the nostrils. Brightly painted fishing trawlers come and go with the day's catch, and within the harbor vicinity, fishermen squat repairing vast nets. Along unpaved streets, octopus, squid, and orange carpets of shrimp are laid out to dry on bamboo racks in the unrelenting heat. But it *is* possible to escape this fishy scenario: Ha Tien is encompassed by sweeping paddy fields that blur into the Cambodian countryside, and a coastline dotted with hidden coves.

Some of my most memorable experiences in Vietnam have been in places less frequented or hailed. Out of seemingly nowhere, a gem is unearthed, inducing an overwhelming feeling of contentment—very often, secluded temples and pagodas. Here is no exception. Although Ha

Tien is home to numerous pagodas, my favorite is the little-visited Mac Cuu Temple, honoring Ha Tien's most revered resident. Entered through an exquisite archway framed with frangipani blossoms leading to a walled compound, Mac Cuu Temple is administered by a few locals and guarded by the customary Asian gatekeeper, a territorial hound. Mac Cuu originated from China, fleeing the aftermath of the Ming Dynasty in the seventeenth century, which explains the unmistakable Chinese influence. Later, he was enlisted by Vietnamese royals to set up a coastal principality and port, where Ha Tien now stands.

Despite the passage of time, this serene temple is remarkably little changed. Dark wood pillars prop up an ancient roof of curved, red, terra cotta tiles. In the dim light, the cluttered interior is refreshingly cool from the midday temperatures, although the oxygen is sucked dry by constantly burning incense. With the place all to myself, the profound sense of history and serenity is accentuated. I come alone with no guide, and somehow it isn't necessary, even though I am curious to learn about the temple's namesake. I can visualize Mac Cuu all those centuries ago, strutting along terra cotta floors in swishing fine silks and neatly braided pigtails.

Seems Mac Cuu was on to a good thing, even when he expired. His place of worship and final resting place are constructed in an incredibly scenic position. To the back of the temple, up steps carved into a small hill, the view is stunning: the town hemmed in with swathes of coconut trees stretching down to the sparkling bay. When he died in 1735, Mac Cuu was laid to rest at the top of this hill. Guarded by two stone swordsmen in full regalia, he lies in a semi-circular brick tomb bearing *yin* and *yang* symbols and finely carved figures of a blue dragon and white tiger.

I would like to think that the dashing statuettes were made in his image; although massive sheathed swords are grasped firmly in their fists, their mustachioed faces seem to exude benevolence. Gazing long enough, I even notice faint smiles. Some of his relatives share this spot. Their tombs not quite so grand, but scattered over the sun-baked hillside, they are still intriguing to visit.

I remain for what seems like an eternity, totally mesmerized by the moment (and view) and unable to leave. Did I know Mr. Mac Cuu in another lifetime? I feel I belong here, drawn to this spot with an inexplicable pull. Maybe that's the real reason Ha Tien lies forever etched in my memory.

Getting to Ha Tien

There are buses (express and local) from Ho Chi Minh City's Mien Tay Bus Station that claim to take seven hours, but good luck! Otherwise, you can catch buses from other points in the Mekong Delta, such as Chau Doc or Long Xuyen. If you fly to Rach Gia, it's 100 kilometers north to Ha Tien by local bus, taxi, or motorbike. You can also arrive by passenger ferry from Phu Quoc Island, which lies opposite, to either Rach Gia, or Ba Hon, which is only nineteen kilometers from Ha Tien. Or you can motorbike the canal route from Chau Doc, but beware of flooding during the rainy season (May to November). From the newly opened Xa Xia Border Crossing (ten kilometers away), you can enter/exit from Cambodia. This crossing is good news for travelers, except that it may entirely change Ha Tien's current sleepy status, so get here as soon as you can.

BA CHUC

Samantha Coomber reflects on life and death in Ba Chuc

Ba Chuc. The name means nothing to the hordes of tourists snaking their way along the popular coastal towns of Vietnam. Come to think of it, Ba Chuc doesn't register with many Vietnamese either; they remain blissfully ignorant of its past. But near the Cambodian border in the southwest corner of the country are Vietnam's very own Killing Fields. Many history buffs may recognize the name of My Lai, but Ba Chuc is of equally tragic proportions.

Carrying me since dawn from Chau Doc, the somewhat precarious motorbike I had hired to take me to Ba Chuc grinds to a halt about five kilometers short of our destination. Its last gasp doesn't sound too healthy, and large black rain clouds loom ominously on the horizon. If I were superstitious, I would conclude that someone doesn't want me to make this journey, so that Ba Chuc's gruesome secret could stay exactly that.

My driver and I are on a dirt track running parallel to the Vinh Te Canal. A stone's throw on the other side lies Cambodia. During the late seventies, members of the Khmer Rouge regularly sneaked across the border and murdered Vietnamese civilians. In April 1978 they massacred more than three thousand inhabitants of the small village of Ba Chuc.

In the distance, hauntingly beautiful limestone hills—which accompanied most of our journey—paint an exquisite backdrop. The occasional tugboat chugs alongside us at a snail's pace, but, as it turns out, a pace quicker than ours. My driver kicks the offending machine a few times and shakes his head. Sensing my impatience, he states the obvious, "It's broken, we get it fixed."

"Where?" I ask, looking around doubtfully at the sparse dwellings strung along the practically deserted track. But I should have realized by now that in Vietnam you needn't worry about these things. For wherever you find yourself, there is always someone eking out a living fixing or mending something.

Although most guidebooks cover this

area in the Mekong Delta chapter, it's a world away from the full-on bustle of the frequently visited cities of Can Tho or My Tho. The locals even appear different, the Khmer-Cambodian roots easily recognizable by the darker skin and red-and-white checked headgear. We approach a group of them, and they try unsuccessfully to start our contraption. We're then led to a makeshift roadside stall doubling as a garage and invited to partake of some green tea. I'm on a tight schedule, and this is not part of the itinerary. But then precious little about traveling off the beaten path in Vietnam ever is. So I go with the flow.

"You can go with this boy," my driver blurts out, pointing to the unsuspecting son of the local mechanic. "He will take you to Ba Chuc and bring you back here afterwards."

Handed over like a parcel, I am bundled onto the back of a motorbike of a total stranger. He doesn't speak a word of English and I speak about five of Vietnamese—which I exhaust by the time we set out in a cloud of dust. In another country, the thought of going off with a strange young man in the middle of nowhere without a common language would be complete madness. But like I said, this is Vietnam. I put my faith in this harmless youth, along with all the other Vietnamese who have yet to violate my trust.

No sooner do we head out when another obstacle rears its head. The rudimentary wooden bridge spanning the river has been washed away by recent heavy rains, so locals are using a makeshift ferry instead. Waiting

for the boat, the full sense of my isolation and uncertainty suddenly hits home. With my designer sunglasses and camera, I am very out of place among the weary old women, farmers, and traders. But the young man standing by my side turns out to be a comfort—impromptu guide, protector, and companion all rolled into one, and worth his weight in gold.

As we land on the other side of the swollen river, threatening thunderclouds overhead suggest bad karma. At first sight, Ba Chuc is an unassuming village. People go about their daily business, children play, bicycles roll past laden with fresh produce—the usual street scenes—nothing out of the ordinary. The normality of it all assumes an almost eerie quality.

Then I see it. A solid concrete memorial surrounded by a sea of innocent-looking rice fields. Young boys run noisily around the vicinity. On closer inspection, the edifice is a large hexagonal glass case. Nothing could have prepared me for the sight about to greet me. Inside are thousands of bleached white skulls meticulously stacked on three levels. If this wasn't grim enough, they are also neatly labeled and sorted into various age groups, each group represented by a crude sign. The most poignant is the pile of tiny remains representing the years "0-2", a final tragic resting place of babies and toddlers who happened to be in the wrong place at the wrong time. Old people, "65-80", did not escape either.

I walk around the aptly named "Skull Pagoda" in somewhat of a stupefied daze. How can the living children laugh and smile with this right under their very noses? By now, spots of rain gently bounce off my face, or maybe they are tears. Quite frankly, I can't tell. In front, on a small makeshift shrine, spirals of incense coil across a simple condolence book. But what on earth do you write? What can you write?

Nearby, the small, unassuming Tam Buu temple documents that sad day's atrocities by way of black and white snapshots pinned on a board. In graphic detail they show how the villagers met their deaths in the fields. The photographs need no captions. Somehow, the temple feels miraculously peaceful and forgiving; the gentle monks who worship here perhaps hope these images serve as a permanent reminder to the sheer futility of it all. I am dumbstruck, but even if I could speak, no one around me would understand my words. It doesn't matter, as my face says everything I cannot.

Life, of course, goes on. The village women are now out in force for morning market, gossiping and joking. In all probability, many are related to the victims of that tragic April day. If anything humbles you about this noble country, it is that its past, while painfully remembered, is not dwelt on.

Yes, life goes on. Back at the "garage," I find my original driver sprawled out fast asleep in the shade, nicely funded by my hard-earned cash. The bike is now fixed and ready to go. Before departing for the coastal town of Ha Tien—our final destination—I pay my impromptu driver as much VND as I can. He is happy with this unexpected windfall. Right place at the right time?

As for me, the inconvenience of a broken bike and a delay seems pretty meaningless. For the next four hours I hang on for dear life to the back of a motorbike cruising along a route that closely resembles a quagmire. The horizontal rain is unrelenting; I am cold, fed-up, and smarting from the heavy backpack cutting into my shoulders. But do you hear me utter one word of complaint? I think not.

Getting to Ba Chuc

Using Chau Doc in southwest Vietnam as your base, you can hire a motorcycle for your own uncomfortable ride to Ba Chuc. As well, numerous tour companies include Ba Chuc in package tours of the region. For the latter, inquire at Sinh Café (see fact file on page 84).

GENERAL VIETNAM

Jan Polatschek
comes to terms with the
American War

My dear readers,
You must be wondering, "Jan has

traveled the length of Vietnam. He has extolled the physical beauty of the country and the wonderful people he has met. But nowhere in his letters has he mentioned the unmentionable." Stand by.

My recent tour outside of Ho Chi Minh City made a stop at the Cu Chi Tunnels. These tunnels formed a network of military strongholds that housed up to 16,000 Viet Minh for months at a time during the war. Only 6,000 survived the relentless bombing; some put the figure at much less. Thousands of civilians also died in the vicinity. At Cu Chi, tourists are encouraged to crawl around the tunnels and then visit the adjacent museum. I politely refused. Instead, I sat at the nearby café. I really cannot explain my reasoning; I cannot account for my emotions. Sometimes, I just decline.

I chose not to see *Sophie's Choice* and *The Pianist.* I expect I will never visit the Holocaust Memorial Museum in Washington, D.C. The most powerful image I need is the name Lisabetha Tausigova that I found carved into the wall of the Pinkus Synagogue in Prague. My grandmother's mother's name is forever engraved in black lettering on a white stone wall amongst the thousands of Czechoslovakia's "disappeared" Jewish citizens.

As for the Vietnam War, I have read many books and seen the movies. What is saddest for me now is to remember Henry Caballero, my young student at Haaren High School in New York. Henry's name appeared in a newspaper one day along with others killed in action in 1972. Henry is also on a wall.

When I decided to visit Vietnam, I did so with a bit of apprehension. I am an American of that certain age. Perhaps I would be treated with hostility. So, I flew from Bangkok to Ho Chi Minh City thinking that I would see the sights but decline to see the obvious reminders of the terror of the American War. Now, how foolish can I be? How naïve?

If I visit London, do I avoid Nelson's Column in Trafalgar Square? Heroic Admiral Horatio Nelson is credited with defeating England's enemies at sea. Defeating, of course, is the sinking of ships and the drowning of enemy sailors. When I arrive in Paris, do I not climb the Arc de Triomphe de l'Étoile, that grand memorial to Napoleon's avarice and brutality? And the Arch of Titus in Rome? It was erected to celebrate and illustrate the defeat of the Israeli Army and the razing and pillaging of The Temple of Jerusalem 2,000 years ago. How can I travel the length of Vietnam and hope to avoid the monuments to more recent events? Well, I tried.

I skipped the War Remnants Museum in Ho Chi Minh with its depictions of French and American atrocities. I nixed the DMZ tour, with the Vinh Moc Tunnels and the Khe Sanh Combat Base. The Rockpile? No. But on that very day of touring when I avoided the Cu Chi Tunnels, the young guide quite dispassionately pointed out the locations of bomb craters and bullet-ridden walls, and in a town, the very spot of *The Girl in the Picture.*

One of my drivers told me he had

been an enlisted man in the South Vietnamese Navy. When the Communist government took control in 1975, he was sent away to a "reeducation camp" for "only three years." Other higher-ranking soldiers and officers were "reeducated" for more than a decade. One young man told me that his parents were Viet Cong and that he himself was born in the jungle. Another driver proudly showed me a bullet hole in his belly. He was forced, at gunpoint, to fight the Khmer Rouge in Cambodia. He went to war with his buddy. He showed me a picture of them together. His buddy didn't make it home.

I visited the ruins of the ancient Cham Temples at My Son. They are in ruins because the North Vietnamese army used them as hideouts, and the American bombers did what they had to do. The awesome caves at Marble Mountain? A Viet Cong hospital. Hai Van Pass, that splendid mountain region along Highway 1? At the very top is a bunker built by the French and later used by the Americans. Halong Bay? It is at the western end of the infamous Gulf of Tonkin. And Hanoi? So many gracious old buildings bombed away.

As I made my way up the country on my happy, peaceful, safe, and delightful tour of Vietnam, writing my cheerful letters, I tried to imagine those of you who had been here before me. I do want you to know, Mike R., Bob K., David A., and Henry Caballero, wherever you may be, I want you all to know that every day I was thinking about you and your service here. And I also want you to know that

I was always welcomed with genuine hospitality, and yes, affection.

I am going to close my letter with one poignant story.

The most emotional moment of the trip came unexpectedly on my very first day in Ho Chi Minh City. I wandered over to the Municipal Theater, a typically elegant, French-style building with white exterior, a red mansard roof, and music-oriented carvings on the walls. Gardens and fountains surrounded the building. Several young couples posed for formal wedding pictures amongst the trees and flowers. Groups of children in uniforms swarmed in and out of the building....

Then it happens. On the steps in front of the theater stand twenty Western men, posing for a group photo. They all look to be of that certain age, some a little older than me, some a little younger. A couple of them have gray beards; one has a long gray ponytail. Several wear American flag ties. I know who they are. Have you guessed yet? I approach the group of American men who served in Vietnam more than thirty years ago. I turn on my best New Yawk accent. "Hey guys. What's happenin'?"

These enthusiastic, smiling veterans are representatives of American charity groups that are distributing scholarship money to needy Vietnamese children, some of whom are the children of sons and daughters left behind by American servicemen. The Vietnamese government originally shunned these Amerasians and their mothers, even though some were handicapped. These kids need all the assistance they can get. Many Americans, including these soldiers who fought here, are helping on a full-time basis.

The men are from Texas, Oklahoma, and Nebraska. We joke about how Oklahoma is a suburb of Texas and how Miami is a suburb of New York. But they are totally serious as they explain the motivation for their new, altruistic mission in Vietnam. My own emotions start to take hold, and I nearly break down as our conversation draws to a close. After all that this country has been through, and all these men have experienced, it is especially moving to hear one former serviceman, awkwardly, but with his marvelously genuine Midwestern sincerity, say, "We do this for love."

The Vietnam Experience

The following website provides a good listing of Vietnam veterans' charities. You can also read more about the Veterans Viet Nam Restoration Project on page 235.

www.vietnamexp.com

Nick Pulley gets serious about the business of traveling in Vietnam

After twelve years in the travel business, I've had my fair share of weird, wonderful, and downright impossible requests. "Where can we find a great five-star hotel close to lo-cal restaurants where we can eat and drink to our hearts' content and have change from $5?" Or, "Where can we trek through countryside and villages, practically untouched by the outside world ... oh, and be within one day's travel of an airport?" Or, my personal favorite, "Where is it hot, cheap, and deserted of crowds in mid-August?"

As the owner of an Asia specialist travel business, my aim is to find answers to these questions while never losing sight of my company's ultimate mission: to provide unique experiences for my clients.

One of the more pleasant aspects of my research is to throw away the guidebooks and travel through a country with local contacts and friends I've made during my stays, allowing them to take me to the destinations they enjoy, introduce me to the foods they love, and show me the "local way" to travel. Often, their choices are fascinating, but not suitable for my Western clientele—cockroach soup anyone? Other times, I'm handsomely rewarded, as I'm led to a lesser-known attraction, beach, or local eatery in a popular destination, but overlooked in all the books.

While I might not have the answers to some of my customers' strangest requests, the questions mentioned above didn't have me wracking my brains too much. There *are* destinations in Vietnam where you can stay in a luxury hotel while eating like a king for next to nothing; places where you can land at a domestic airport and, within a day, be trekking in the wilderness; and beaches where you won't be jostling for space to sunbathe. Wherever you travel, my advice is always to engage with the locals. They open doors, allowing you to interact with the community, and you will often find their hospitality incredible. When was the last time *you* invited someone off the street, introduced them to your extended family, and refused to let them leave until they had shared your supper with you? It could only happen in Vietnam.

Nick's Top Picks for Your Next Visit

Pu Luong Nature Reserve

For a great trekking option, this reserve, just a three-hour drive southwest of Hanoi, is one of my top recommendations. This richly forested area offers stunning scenery and panoramic views of magnificent rice terraces, not to mention some of the most abundant flora and fauna in the country. Many rare species, including the endangered Clouded Leopard, inhabit the forest, and if you are lucky, you might catch a glimpse. Cycling and trekking routes are numerous, ranging from gentle to strenuous.

Cua Dai Beach

With Thai beaches overrun during the high season, I always advise heading farther east. Vietnam has more than 3,000 kilometers of coastline and a fair number of great beaches to offer. Cua Dai Beach, just minutes from Hoi An, and the stretch of sand running north toward China

Beach and Marble Mountain, both offer visitors plenty of space, good weather, and freshly caught seafood. Hire a bike or moped and take the back road that runs parallel with the sea—all that's left to do is select your patch of paradise for the day.

Hoi An

Unquestionably my favorite destination in the world right now. Ask anyone in the country where to eat the best Vietnamese food and the majority will tell you Hoi An—it's simply fantastic. There's a restaurant to suit every budget, ($5 included), and Hoi An is home to some of Vietnam's finest hotels. My picks in both categories are Mango Rooms (go for the fresh spring rolls in a chocolate and peanut sauce) and the Ancient House (check into their poolside "special rooms").

Mango Rooms

111 Nguyen Thai Hoc St.
Hoi An
(84-510) 910-839

Ancient House

61 Cua Dai Rd.
Hoi An
(84-510) 923-377
www.ancienthouseresort.com

Secret Gardens

Where to hide away from the touring masses.

Those who have never traveled to Vietnam might wonder why it's necessary to know where to hide away from crowds. After all, isn't this a country of tranquil rice fields and serene natural attractions such as Halong Bay? But for those of us who have lived there, all wondering ceased within days of setting up house.

Vietnam hums with energy, manifest in the lawnmower retching of motorbikes no matter how remote you think you are, and the crowing of a.m./p.m.-challenged roosters no matter how metropolitan a lane you live on. Then there are all those people. More than eighty-five million of them, mostly crowded into the urban areas where travelers tend to focus their trips. While all this energy is intoxicating, escaping it can save your sanity. And there is something about tranquility, when juxtaposed with such exuberance, that makes finding solitude all the more pleasurable. This is clearly demonstrated in Lillian Forsyth's essay on a remote beach in Tra Vinh, where her getaway is made all the sweeter by the long, hot, and crowded van ride she must make in order to reach her destination.

I am particularly grateful to the writers in this chapter who have generously revealed their favorite hideaways. To do so is to entrust, as well as to offer a valuable gift: hidden places not easily unearthed during a three-week junket. These recommendations will also immerse you in local culture. Take, for example, Simone Samuel's favorite Hanoi havens, which range from a local pagoda to a hair salon. For me, these places encapsulate Vietnam's many dimensions. The country is past and present, spiritual and corporeal, all at the same time. Plus, I am as rejuvenated from meditating in quiet temple courtyards as I am from having my hair washed and catching up on neighborhood gossip at a local salon.

Another classic retreat is the coffee shop. While not always calm, coffee shops manage, even during their frantic peak hours, to offer respite. Most people I know, both locals and foreigners,

Vegetable gardens in Dalat

have a café whose honor they would fight to the death to defend. A love song to her favorite coffeehouse, Marianne Smallwood's essay makes it easy to understand why *ca phe sua da* drinkers are so territorial about, enamored with, and loyal to their java joints.

Because I now live back in the States and am a visitor, rather than a resident, when I am in Vietnam, I appreciate the new discoveries this chapter brought me. As I read and edited each piece, I dreamed of my return and how I would take advantage of the recommendations: an art cinema in Hanoi, tranquil guesthouses in Hoi An, quiet beaches in Mui Ne, and local churches in Ho Chi Minh City and the Mekong Delta. The next time I'm in Hanoi, I'm going to follow Simone Samuel's lead and paddle a swan boat into the privacy of West Lake, and if I ever find myself back in fast-paced Nha Trang, I will surely take Tom Chard's advice on nearby beach and mountain retreats.

I'm also looking forward to visiting Phu Quoc Island, where Mark Barnett has created a sanctuary within a sanctuary in his Cassia Cottage Inn. Once there, I know exactly what I'll do: drift in the warm sea, laze in a sun-kissed hammock, dine on freshly caught seafood, and reflect on where to escape next. To a flower garden in Dalat, perhaps, or a swanky resort on China Beach? Fortunately, there's no need to stress out over it. No matter where I travel in Vietnam, there's sure to be a quiet corner I can call my own.

HANOI

XXXXXXXXXXXXXXXXXXXXXXXXXXXXXXXXX
ooooooooooooooooooooooooooooooooo

Simone Samuels swans about Hanoi's West Lake

What better way to spend a hot, clear, sunny day than in a swan boat with a picnic and my lover? He had wanted to take me out on a romantic date for a long time, so we headed for West Lake and set sail.

We filled our pack with snacks and treats: cute petits fours, croissants, and pastries bought from a bakery on the lake, as well as cheese and crackers and some freshly cut green mango. And we just had to top it off with a bottle of Vietnam's finest red wine—Vang Dalat. We then made a beeline for the ticket booth where we were a little confused until we figured out that the literally translated "trample boat" referred to the paddle boats shaped like giant swans. In our small avian vessel, we each had a set of pedals, and there was a little steering wheel to turn with. It was really quite simple and not at all laborious. Once we had sailed out far enough that the men fishing on the banks of the lake resembled ants, we enjoyed our little picnic in solitude; there was not a sound and only calm reflections all around us.

It was quite hilarious and fun, and especially great was that we could experience complete seclusion in the middle of the city. Nobody seemed to care how far we went or how long we were gone. As a result, we got sunburned, and then we somehow broke the pedal on one side of the boat. We grew hot and sweaty from the exertion of pedaling with just one pedal, and our convertible roof kept folding down, leaving us in the glaring sun. Despite all this, it was a treat to be out on the lake, to enjoy the sunshine and each other's company, to get a little tipsy, and to have the opportunity to make out like teenagers where we could not be seen!

After we eventually made it back safely to shore and out of the swan, a three-scoop ice cream sundae completed the experience. My idea of a perfect date.

Swanning about

Paddle swan boats can be hired during the day and also in the early evening from a little booth on West Lake's (Ho Tay's) busy Thanh Nien Street. The cost is 40,000 VND for an hour. We paid for one hour initially, then paid the difference for the extra hour and a half when we got back to shore. We bought the delicious pastries and cakes from the Nguyen Son Bakery across from the boat ticket booth at 9A Thanh Nien Street, and sat on the roof of the bakery's café to enjoy an ice cream sundae afterwards.

Todd Berliner focuses on the cinematic side of Hanoi

Withdrawal from good movie theaters is not, I can only assume, as torturous as withdrawal from narcotics, but it's unpleasant. I was teaching film studies at Vietnam's National Film School in Hanoi, and among the many transitions I was suffering—along with the absence of potable tap water and Ziploc bags—was movie theater withdrawal. Hanoi has a rich history of art and music, but unlike other major capital cities such as Paris or San Francisco (which I think of as my nation's capital), it is not known for its cinemas. In fact, for a filmgoer in a big Asian city, it's practically a wasteland.

My wife, the memoirist and novelist Dana Sachs, who loves me almost as devotedly as she loves Hanoi (we and our two children moved to Hanoi for a year because she willed it), tenderly urged me to visit Hanoi Cinémathèque, an arthouse theater that digitally projects movies on a medium-sized screen, run by Gerry Herman, an American expatriate. As a film studies professor, I balked at the digital corruption of the 35mm image and delayed visiting the Cinémathèque for several weeks. It turned out, however, that I would spend a great deal more time at Gerry's cinema than I did working at Vietnam's National Film School. I practically became its mascot.

Gerry too, I quickly learned, bemoaned image degradation, but because of the practical impossibility of obtaining 35mm prints of the movies he wanted to show, he focused his energy and money on maximizing the audio-visual fidelity of his movie theater dream and on making it the loveliest hot spot for watching movies in Hanoi, the place to be for every cinephile in the city.

Everyone who knows Gerry knows that Hanoi Cinémathèque is his folly, an authentic labor of love designed not to make money but to indulge his fantasy of having his very own movie theater to screen his favorite movies for the population of Hanoi. He built a Parisian-style café outside the theater; it is designed largely to fund his folly and serves drinks, noshes, and meals. As well, it hosts events such as Indian Day, sponsored by the owner of two Indian restaurants in town, which screened some of the best Bollywood movies I have seen, and the events of the Brooklyn Club, to which I was invited partly because my mother was born in Flatbush but mostly because I'm Jewish.

If you've spent any time in Vietnamese movie theaters—with their dilapidated structures, fluorescent lights, and industrial-looking, mildewed walls—then Gerry's cinema is an astonishing sight: ninety relaxing seats in ten neat rows, each with a perfect sightline to a first rate screen; curtained doors; and the color and lighting of a boudoir. The design, classic and comfortable, makes you want to hang out.

Ah, but what of the movies themselves? The Cinémathèque mixes films from Hollywood's studio era, art films, and documentaries—films that would never receive commercial distribution in Hanoi. It also screens Vietnamese films that Gerry—who has helped preserve, restore, and subtitle Vietnamese films—feels did not receive proper exhibition in Vietnam. He organizes the screenings based on his tastes, whims, and the demands of his audience. During the time I spent in Hanoi, Gerry ran a series of cowboy classics; a documentary series; Ernest Lubitch, Fritz Lang, and Louis Malle retrospectives; a series of children's movies (programmed by me, my wife, and our kids); a Brazilian festival; an Australian classics series; a James Dean weekend; and maybe thirty other specialized programs. It's an eclectic mix, but Gerry's passion for movies ensures that the programs are either richly entertaining, arthouse-crowd pleasing, or artistically, and occasionally, politically provocative.

And, the popcorn is free.

Hanoi Cinémathèque & Café

Since the owner abjures signs, off-the-street traffic, websites, and advertising, you cannot find the Hanoi Cinémathèque unless you know where it is. At 22A Hai Ba Trung Street, you will see a sign not for a cinema or café but for Hotel des Artistes. Head under the sign and follow the dank alley to the end. You won't think you're heading to an oasis, but you are.

22A Hai Ba Trung St.
Hoan Kiem District
Hanoi
(84-4) 936-2648

Cinema paradiso

The Cinémathèque runs two movies almost every day, and on the weekends sometimes three or four. Vietnamese translation of the films is offered on complimentary headsets. It operates as a membership club. Membership, which you can obtain at the theater, costs about $6. Once a member, you'll receive weekly email schedules.

MegaStar Cineplex

During the time we lived in Hanoi, a new multiplex cinema appeared, run by the Asian conglomerate MegaStar. You go to Hanoi's MegaStar Cineplex when you must see a blockbuster and see it in a big theater, on a big screen, in 35mm—in short, when you must, if just for two hours, leave Vietnam for Hollywood.

Vincom City Towers
191 Ba Trieu St.
Hai Ba Trung District
Hanoi

Samantha Coomber steeps herself in tea and history in Hanoi

One of the great things I like about traveling around Vietnam is that, relatively speaking, it is still amazingly good value, often cheaper than other destinations in the region. So after surviving on a budget, you can occasionally afford to splash out on little luxuries, such as spa treatments, champagne brunches, and ... English-style Afternoon Tea, a particular love of mine since I'm English.

Maybe you are not in the habit of "doing" Afternoon Tea and had probably never thought of it in Vietnam, but here it is not only affordable, it can be enjoyed in the height of luxury. Just think how much it would cost back home—and not half as enchanting! Besides, time spent being pampered in a *quiet* sanctuary allows a welcome break from Vietnam's full-on mayhem and heat. It also makes a special way to celebrate a birthday on the road or to provide a surprise treat for a loved one.

The best place for Afternoon Tea in Hanoi is most definitely the Sofitel Metropole Hanoi. As well as an impressive example of French colonial architecture—with its classic white façade and chandelier-lit lobby—the former Grand Hotel Metropole Palace is drenched in local history. Restored to its century-old charm, this was once the elegant epicenter for colonial society and one of Southeast Asia's greatest hotels: Vietnam's very own Raffles.

Heaving with anecdotes, the guest list includes Noel Coward, Somerset Maugham, Charlie Chaplin (honeymooning here in the 1930s after his secret wedding to Paulette Goddard in Shanghai), and Jane Fonda, during her infamous "Hanoi Jane" broadcasts in 1972. English writer Graham Greene on assignment for *Paris Match* in

the 1950s, covering the Franco-Viet Minh War—wrote some of *The Quiet American* here; the Graham Greene Suite and namesake cocktail honor his stay. And now it's your turn to add to the guest list, or at the very least, savor the surprisingly inexpensive Afternoon Tea at Le Club Bar.

Le Club Bar oozes colonial atmosphere with whirring ceiling fans, dark timbered floors, and rattan chairs, blended with Oriental touches of lacquer paintings and tropical blooms, and encased by French windows. Resembling something from a period film set, the room has an air of refinement so palpable you can cut it with your butter knife. Afternoon Tea is an institution here, recalling the French Indochina days. So take your seats, throw a white linen napkin across your lap, and before you know it, one of the staff kitted out in traditional *ao dai* brings out an old-fashioned pastry stand full of teatime treats such as crêpes, scones, homemade jams, and finger sandwiches. Pots of piping hot tea such as Earl Grey, Darjeeling, and chamomile are regularly topped up. For those after a complete blowout, Le Club Bar also offers a totally sinful afternoon Chocolate Buffet which features more than twenty rich chocolate treats from France and Belgium.

This is an enjoyable way to spend the afternoon in Hanoi, especially during northern Vietnam's gloomy, drizzly winter days. History permeates: Le Club Bar is now where the old conference rooms once stood and where Ho Chi Minh held private meetings in 1946 with the commander of Indochina and president of Vietnam's Communist party. And with a contemporary clientele including Fidel Castro, H.R.H. Prince of Monaco, Mick Jagger, and Angelina Jolie on an adoption run, you never know who you might bump into at teatime.

Sofitel Metropole Hanoi

Afternoon Tea and the Chocolate Buffet at Le Club Bar are available daily from 3-5:30 p.m. Afternoon Tea: $12 per person, Chocolate Buffet: $10 per person

15 Ngo Quyen St.
Hoan Kiem District
Hanoi
(84-4) 826-6919

Marianne Smallwood catches a Hanoi-style caffeine buzz

Driving down Nguyen Du Street, I pull up to Café Mai and hand my shiny blue bicycle over to a red-uniformed youth who smiles and whisks it away to join the mass of motorbikes parked on the sidewalk. It's July in Hanoi and hot; a refuge is needed from the stickiness and heat that lingers even at night. Customers on the first floor gaze casually out onto the sidewalk, empty coffee glasses littering their small tables. Fish swim lazily around a tank in the middle of the room. Teenagers in Café Mai uniforms bustle around a bar crowded with containers of

coffee, condensed milk, and unlabeled plastic jars holding the secret to why Café Mai is known for some of the best coffee in Hanoi. During my time in Hanoi, I have had countless cups of coffee in dozens of cafés—none have affected me as lingeringly as Café Mai. From a blend of ground coffee beans, chocolate, and sugar, the rich aroma wafts throughout the café and down the street.

As usual, I skip the first floor and climb the narrow stairs to the second level, sidestepping a young girl carrying a full tray of glasses. The three-story café is packed on this stuffy afternoon. Luckily, my usual table is open, sandwiched between three other tables bordering the rail that overlooks the street. I settle in and peruse the menu, although I already know what I'll order. Café Mai offers juices, hot chocolate, and even tea, but I opt for the coffee every time. During my last visit, I was buzzed 'til 10 p.m. from a cup of *ca phe sua nong*, hot coffee with sweetened condensed milk. This time I order an equally buzz-inducing *ca phe sua da*, the customary drink of Vietnam, which is consumed as often and easily as water. *Ca phe sua da* translates to "coffee with milk and ice"; the *sua* usually refers to sweetened condensed milk, an ingredient that is ever-present in Vietnam and a downfall to the health conscious.

The young girl who takes my order returns in just a few minutes, glass in hand. Filled three-quarters to the top, it has a small layer of condensed milk resting at the bottom, with dark coffee and ice composing the rest of the mix. I

NORTHERN VIETNAM

stir, turning the drink a creamy caramel brown. I sip. Far more than any coffee I've ever had, Café Mai's variety is smooth and rich, an entirely whole coffee with enough sweetness to almost render it a dessert. The aftertaste leaves a chocolaty overtone that remains as long as the time between your last and next sip. This isn't your run-of-the-mill coffee pumped full of amaretto or hazelnut syrup; the flavor is founded in the coffee itself, and from as much sweetened condensed milk as you can handle. I've brought friends and visitors here and have repeatedly watched the widened eyes, unprompted exclamations, and eager second gulps.

And this coffee is strong. The first time I visited Café Mai, I downed three cups with a friend of mine while proclaiming immunity to caffeine, since I had worked in a coffee shop for three years in high school. I was wired until 2 a.m. that night. After tasting Vietnamese coffee, chain blends will seem like water. During a recent trip to Kuala Lumpur, I rushed to the nearest Starbucks for a creature comfort from a company yet to penetrate Hanoi. I left, having finished my overpriced latte, feeling decidedly unsatisfied. Vietnamese coffee—and Café Mai's in particular—is unbeatable.

I drink the rest of my coffee, idly study my Vietnamese lesson (concentrating can be difficult in the stifling heat of a Hanoi summer), and look around me. Men smoke cigarettes and chat, absent-mindedly stirring their glasses. A Westerner pores over notes and an academic journal. Couples quietly drink and murmur. Boisterous young adults laugh. I order a second cup. A third would be foolish—I'd like to make it through the rest of the day without vibrating out of my shoes. I nurse this one slowly, take in the French-style architecture of the building across the street, squint into the sun, and enjoy the slight breeze that rustles the beaded curtain by the railing. I smile. I'm in Hanoi, drinking a sublime cup of coffee on a lazy Saturday afternoon. At this moment, things couldn't get better.

Café Mai

From Hoan Kiem Lake, head south on Ba Trieu Street until you reach the Ba Trieu/Nguyen Du Street intersection. Take an immediate right (west) on Nguyen Du and continue down the block. On the right you'll see a large neon sign atop the building and many motorbikes parked in front. You can't miss it.

52 Nguyen Du St.
Hai Ba Trung District
Hanoi

Branching out

On Le Van Huu Street, #79 is a newer, larger, and brighter version of Café Mai, while #96 is a retail location from which to purchase coffee. What better souvenir to bring back for friends?

When to go

Anytime, depending on the mood you're in. The cafe is open from 7 a.m. until 10 p.m.

What to order

Make sure to try Vietnam's star beverage: *ca phe sua da*. The cost is about $1.

Making the most of it

Order at least two drinks and stay for as long as you can, whether you're a traveler or living in the city. Hanoi's coffee culture isn't slurp-and-go, but is characterized by sipping, talking, and observing. Grab a friend or a book and settle in. Ground-floor views allow for great people-watching at street level.

Simone Samuels seeks out Hanoi's quiet corners

Sometimes, I like to go around Hanoi at midnight, just so I can experience the city with empty streets, when it is eerily silent. At this time, it is always hard to believe that in just five hours there will be the sounds of countless motorbikes, car horns, construction, dogs barking, roosters crowing, people shouting—all manner of everyday din that becomes commonplace background noise when you have lived here for a while. But I have also found some *daytime* reprieves, where I can enjoy anywhere from a few hours to a full day of complete calm and restoration.

First, I stroll down the street and find my nearest temple or pagoda. There is never one too far away in Hanoi, and they can usually be recognized by a high yellow wall and a colorful gate of Eastern architectural design. The one closest to my house is only open twice a month, during the half and full moons on the lunar calendar. I recognize these dates by the ladies selling flowers, incense, and lucky money at the temple's front gate. I have never felt unwelcome in this sanctuary, and it's nice to mingle with the locals as they say their prayers, offer flowers, and burn incense. The brown-robed nuns usually just smile sweetly at me, but once a young nun led me around the temple and showed me how to pray with three shakes of the hands and make my offerings; as well, she encouraged me to make a small donation toward the upkeep of the temple. With its reflection pond and colorful flowers, the garden on a sunny day is the perfect place to sit and enjoy solitude.

If it's not the right time to visit my local pagoda, I like to head to the Temple of Literature, which is open every day. This 900-year-old shrine, also Vietnam's first university for Confucian scholars, is a quiet oasis among the city's madness. Despite its location in the heart of Hanoi, where it is surrounded by four busy roads, it is relatively quiet within the inner walls. There are several courtyards, pools, and gardens in the complex, providing the perfect setting to contemplate life. First, I like to rub the heads of the

NORTHERN VIETNAM

stone tortoises so I can be blessed, then I soak up the Chinese-influenced *feng shui* design before going to the pavilion at the very back of the complex. Whenever I visit, I climb the stairs within and look out over the tiled rooftops and down onto the turmoil below, from which I feel entirely separated within the refuge of the pagoda.

It's difficult to leave the serenity and enter the chaos once more, but a reprieve is not far. Tucked on a side street about ten minutes away on foot is the best place for pampering. Vu Doo Salon is on a surprisingly quiet street and is perfect for passing a stress-free afternoon. Sunbeams shine through the quaint front room where Senior Stylist Vu works wonders with the hair of Westerners. I love sitting in the comfy chairs and flipping through the up-to-date European magazines while sipping a coffee as my hair dye sets. And if Vu knows hair, then his assistants know head massage. It's worth coming here simply for a hair wash, which involves a divine half hour of your head being massaged by expert hands. I always feel special afterwards when my hair is dried by two boys at a time—very superstar-esque!

If my hair is already taken care of and I'm just after a pedicure and/or a facial, then I'll have to travel farther from the Temple of Literature and into the Old Quarter near Hoan Kiem Lake. Here is the Hi Salon, where one of the young staff works diligently and precisely on my nails and then face. Anyone who has had a facial knows how indulgent it feels to have your face rubbed, temples massaged, and

skin nourished with delicious smelling creams for an hour—it's always difficult not to fall asleep as the soft music lulls me while expert hands stroke my face, temples, and neck.

After all this heavenly treatment, I'm usually starting to feel like I have escaped Hanoi's madness, if only for the day. But that doesn't mean I don't feel deserving of just one more treat. On the way home, it's difficult to resist stopping in for an hour-long foot massage from a professional who expertly and efficiently kneads, rubs, and squeezes my feet, gently massages my head and shoulders, and manipulates my back. While all that is happening, I am lying on a reclining chair with hot packs on my knees and neck, and a cup of green tea to sip. Sigh! After this I can go home, rejuvenated and well and truly ready to face anything—including the constant traffic and noise.

Hi Salon
23c Hang Hanh St.
Hoan Kiem District
Hanoi
(84-4) 828-8599
Facial: $8-$19
Pedicures and manicures: $5 each

Hong Mau Don
5 Le Duan St.
Ba Dinh District
(84-4) 733-3139
Foot massage: 60,000 VND

Simone's Local Temple
Ngo (Alley) 209, Doi Can St.
Ba Dinh District
Hanoi

Temple of Literature
Quoc Tu Giam St. and Van Mu St.
Quoc Tu Giam Park
Dong Da District
Hanoi

Vu Doo Hair
& Beauty Salon
32c Cao Ba Quat St.
Ba Dinh District
Hanoi
(84-4) 733-8329
trieuvu78@hotmail.com
Haircuts: from $10

HUE

Jessy Needham
crosses a bridge over
Hue's untroubled waters

Of all the cities in Vietnam, the one most suited to bicycling is Hue. The Perfume River sets the pace, languidly flowing through the heart of the former imperial capital on its way to the South China Sea. Not only does Hue have less traffic than the crowded metropolises in the north and south of the country, but people are in less of a hurry. More time is spent on everything here: a walk along the riverbanks, a slow boat ride, or an evening at a café with friends.

When visiting Hue, I always look forward to following my favorite bike route, up the riverfront avenue of Le Loi, across Trang Tien Bridge, and into the walled Old City. I bypass the military staging ground at the front, preferring instead to head deeper into the grounds. To one side are the staples of any Vietnamese town—cafés, motorbike repair shops, and magazine stands—and to the other are the lily pad-filled moat and restored red-and-yellow gates of the nineteenth-century Nguyen dynasty palace.

The beauty of the citadel is that even though you might feel lost within it, it is small enough to ensure you never truly are. Even if you get momentarily disoriented in the maze of narrow streets, the surrounding walls serve as both guideposts and a helpful boundary. In the half hour it takes to explore the winding streets, you may discover the small island pagoda in the center of the complex, or perhaps you will encounter women in small boats fishing morning glory from ponds. Take time to admire Hue houses, which often feature gardens of bougainvillea and milk flowers. If you find yourself all alone in a small lane, enjoy the breeze and a serenity rarely felt in busy, crowded Vietnam.

The flat countryside surrounding the city also beckons the cyclist, especially the country roads to the northeast of town. My favorite destination is

CENTRAL VIETNAM

the Thanh Toan Bridge, over the Nhu Y River. Because there is not much shade along the road, I usually pull on long nylon gloves, like the Vietnamese girls wear, to protect my arms from the sun. Along the way are dozens of family temples, covered in bright, colorful tiles that shine in the sun, unlike the austere, red-brick pagodas of the north. Many residents in and around Hue have family members living abroad, and the money sent back is put to use building these enormous—some might argue ostentatious—monuments to ancestral lines. These temples and tombs are easy to spot as you wind along roads through vast rice fields dotted with white cranes standing sentinel alongside water buffaloes.

One legend has it that the covered Thanh Toan Bridge was built in the eighteenth century by a wealthy Vietnamese woman who wanted a son. She hoped to do a good deed for her village, bringing good fortune and thus increasing the odds that she would bear a boy. What I like best about the bridge is how out of place the intricately carved, tile-roofed wooden structure seems in the Vietnamese countryside. There is another covered bridge in Hoi An which fits into the overall aesthetic of the old trading port, but the Thanh Toan Bridge stands alone in the middle of an everyday village, an unexpected treasure on a simple country road.

Visiting the bridge on your own increases the chance that you may have it almost all to yourself, which is ideal. A local fellow might be napping, baseball cap covering his face, and occasionally a motorbike might pass

on the adjacent concrete bridge, but the covered bridge is for foot traffic only. Once, my friends and I met three young boys carrying fishing rods. They stopped to check out our digital video camera. At the far end, a very old woman with a mouthful of red betel nut juice offered us a sample and inquired when I planned on getting married. On another visit, I came upon a group of Vietnamese students who had brought their American teacher for a picnic. They were laughing in delight as their teacher submitted to having his fortune read by an enterprising fortune teller who had set up shop on the bridge.

I often remain until the sun starts to set, even though I know the return bike ride will be along an unlit road, full of bugs that all want to fly directly into my mouth. But swallowing a few gnats is a small price to pay in order to spend a day watching the Vietnamese countryside go by from the Thanh Toan Bridge.

Renting bikes

Although bikes are easily rented throughout Hue, I recommend Phuong Nam Café with its friendly proprietors. The café is just opposite the Festival Village Hotel.

38 Tran Cao Van St.
Hue

Thanh Toan Bridge

The bridge is located about ten kilometers to the east of Hue. Going south on Ba Trieu Street, take a left turn onto Truong Chinh Street. Follow this street out of town and through several villages until you reach the bridge. All of the motorbike guides in town know it, but I think traveling by bicycle allows for a more contemplative experience.

Thanh Toan Village
Thuy Thanh Commune
Huong Thuy District

Kim Fay drifts along Hue's peaceful Perfume River

It's one of those travel miracles. For the past two days, it's been dumping rain, but this morning, the morning of our boat trip up the Perfume River to the tombs of the Vietnamese emperors, the sky is a soft, milky blue. My sister Julie, my best friend Huong, and I pedal our bikes out the front gates of La Residence Hotel & Spa. Our journey is short—we turn left and immediately left again, down the lane that flanks the wall of the hotel's property. At the end is a quiet moorage of brightly colored boats.

Such boats are typical sights on the waters between Vietnam's former imperial capital of Hue and the tombs, but they are usually large and ferrying groups of tourists. Ours is petite, and it's just for the three of us. We were directed to it by a cyclo driver, who is the cousin of a cousin, or something like that, of the boat's owner. (Isn't that always the case?) Yesterday,

when we made our booking—through Huong, in Vietnamese, since the owner speaks not a word of English— we were asked if we wanted lunch on board (yes!), and if we wanted to bring our bikes (definitely yes!).

Now, as the owner's wife strongarms our bicycles onto the boat, our names and hotel are recorded on a document that is left with an official-looking man occupying a small wooden booth. We are even given a receipt, which impresses Huong. Inside the boat's cabin, whose windows are all open, a thin woven mat has been spread over the stunningly clean wooden floor. The entire boat is spotless and exhibits neither the moldy odor nor spongy texture that usually comes with river living.

As the boat cruises up the river, we sit back and enjoy the cool breeze, while the owner's wife tends the baby, who is hanging from a hammock in the alfresco cubby of a kitchen between the cabin and the pilothouse. We haven't made it very far when a police boat sidles up. This is the kind of thing that can throw a tourist into a panic, especially since it's impossible to tell what's going on—only that the owner and his wife grow solemn-faced and the police are no jollier, and the exchange of words that accompanies an exchange of papers is funereal. In fact, this is a routine episode. The police are simply checking to make sure that all documentation is in order, since paperwork is its own form of religion in Vietnam.

With the formalities out of the way, we putter on, witnessing a lifestyle as varied and dynamic as any found on land. Along the shores, boats lie heavy in the water, occupied by workers dredging silt up from the riverbed. Laundry and birdcages hang from the sterns of sampan-like vessels. In the distance, a tipsy floating "school bus" transports a cluster of children, uniformed in white shirts and blue pants, from one side of the river to the other. Occasionally, we pass a tour barge filled with tourists like a train car bloated with cattle.

A sprawling, abandoned estate, the tomb of Emperor Minh Mang is hot, calm, and poetic with its silken dragonflies. Everyone seems to be rushing through it, but we are so entranced that the boat owner finally comes looking for us ... after two hours. Back on the water, our simple meal awaits: beef and starfruit soup, beef sautéed with starfruit, caramelized fish, and oddly, since we didn't request it, French fries. The food is lukewarm, because we took so long, but it's satisfying, and impressive given the size and basic nature of the kitchen. As we finish eating, the owner's wife emerges with a sack filled with postcards and kimonos. Yet another formality, but who are we to complain? The entire boat ride, including our meals, costs only $12. We pay another $10 for a kimono, wishing we could just offer the money and leave the gown.

At our next landing spot, we have to clamber up a mud bank with our bikes and walk through a settlement with three old women watching an old man hack at a tree with a machete. It's already late in the afternoon, but

we've absorbed the rhythm of the river, and we bike slowly along the dirt lane, through the steamy greenery, past isolated stone relics, to a main road where we weave around sleek, sleeping cows in order to reach the Tu Duc temple complex. It is a shock to our systems: food stands, tour buses, and tourists everywhere. We take a rapid, obligatory look around and then pedal in retreat, slowing again when we reach fields of lemongrass.

As our boat travels back, the sun casts its flushed light over the water. Sunburned and tired from the heat, Julie, Huong, and I sit in the narrow bow to catch as much of the breeze as possible. The boats we pass seem different now, with the day's industry done. Locals sit out on their decks in sling-back chairs and hammocks, waving to us as we wave back. Two boys leap from the side of a boat, squealing with laughter, as if it's their favorite ride at a water park. Making good time, a tour boat cruises by, and the passengers stare out at us, draped over one another, cans of Huda beer in hand, laughing, relaxed, and content. It has been one of those perfect days, a day in which the journey is the destination.

Smooth sailing

If you are facing the front entrance of La Residence Hotel & Spa, at 5 Le Loi Street, you will see a lane on the right side, running along the property's east wall. Follow that lane to its end, where there is a small selection of boats. The owner of our boat, Le Van Can, lives onboard with his wife and (at that time) three children. Le and his wife do not speak English.

Le Van Can, TTH 0026
Ben Thuyen so 5 Le Loi
Hue
(84-54) 832 144

090-338-1602 (mobile phone for in-country) or 84-90-338-1602 (from abroad)

James Sullivan takes up residence in historic Hue

After moving into the garden house on Han Thuyen Street in Hue, my wife asked me to clean the altar of the home's former residents. It was January, Tet was coming, and the entire nation was in the midst of its annual, oblational scrub down.

Following Vietnamese custom, I washed the cinder pots and polished the brass candlesticks, dusted the wooden hutch and filled bowls with fruit and watermelon seeds, all under the gaze of the altar's principal beneficiary, a mandarin whose pencil-sketch portrait reigned from the altar top. This altar didn't memorialize anyone in the families of either the current or previous owners, but rather Nguyen Van Phung, the mandarin who built the place in 1942.

A few days after I'd finished cleaning, our landlord stopped by to offer

a memorial bottle of wine. "Who was Nguyen Van Phung?" I asked, intrigued after laboring for a good hour on behalf of his soul.

In hushed tones, Mr. Ung told a story of Phung's grandfather, Nguyen Van Tuong, an imperial regent who had dethroned King Duc Duc after a three-day reign in 1883; murdered his successor, shortly thereafter; murdered the next king; and prompted the exile of yet the next king. Tuong was dastardly, and his legacy distasteful, but by the time Phung reached maturity, he had reclaimed the family's honor. Flanking the altar, two vertical boards embossed with gilt Chinese characters detail well wishes from villagers in the north, with whom Phung had worked as an administrator.

Then there was another surprise from Mr. Ung: "Mr. Phung's grandson is a radio reporter in America. His name is Nguyen Qui Duc."

That night, I ordered Duc's memoir, *Where the Ashes Are*, and asked my mother to carry it to Hue on her next visit. Though she had twenty-four hours in the air to finish the story, she hadn't, but she'd read enough to talk about it and whet my appetite.

"Duc writes about a big tree in his grandfather's garden," she said one morning. "A longan tree."

"This longan," I said, gesturing at the immense tree that shaded our house and garden.

"And this porch," my mother went on. "He did his lessons out here with his grandfather, and his grandfather's temperament was ..."

I stopped her then. It was all too

CENTRAL VIETNAM

fascinating, but I wanted the story fresh, not secondhand.

It was spring when my mother visited, and in the late afternoons, we traveled across town with her two young grandchildren to swim in the pool at La Residence Hotel & Spa, once a part of the imperial governor's residence. When my wife and I married in Hue in 1994, we'd toured this hotel as a candidate venue for our wedding night, but back then, it was a government guesthouse and smacked of what I came to regard as "director's décor"—uninspiring wooden furnishings, pink tablecloths, fluorescent light, and too many dragons. Instead, we chose an equally uninspiring place farther downriver.

In the meantime, the 1930-built mansion had been rehabbed and expanded, and now ranked as the city's finest hotel and one of the most atmospheric properties in all Vietnam. The hotel's bowed façade, long horizontal lines, and nautical flourishes were hallmarks of the Streamline Moderne school. Inspired by styles popular in the 1920s and 1950s, the interior was made over as an Art Deco delight. The hotel was like something off South Beach in Miami. Going there nearly every afternoon was an indulgence; we couldn't stop. We'd sit on the pool deck, in the shade of a towering silk-cotton tree, and gaze out over the Perfume River at the landmark Flag Tower Bastion, the Trang Tien Bridge, and the Hue Citadel. In season, the longan and milk fruit trees would bear bumper crops, and kapok from the silk-cotton tree would coast on the breeze overhead like confetti.

We couldn't believe our luck, especially during those months when it was still freezing at our home in New England.

One afternoon, my mother finished the book on the pool deck, and I immediately started in. In the first scene, Duc writes about returning to Hue with his family in 1968, on the eve of the Tet Offensive that would forever color the way Americans viewed the war. Duc's father (the son of my home's Mr. Phung) was a high-ranking South Vietnamese official. That first night of Tet, while his family rested in the suite on the second floor of a government guesthouse, the Viet Cong stole into the city, infiltrating select sites all over town, including said accommodation.

Wait, I thought, looking up from the book to La Residence. This is the government guesthouse.

I left the pool and walked into the hotel, looking for Duc's landmarks: the second-floor suite where his family stayed, and the cellar where the family was held by its captors. The suite, under the cupola, is now La Suite du Resident. The cellar I couldn't find, unless Duc was referring to the ground floor.

Like my mother, I finished Duc's book on the pool deck. It was late in the afternoon. My three-year-old and five-year-old children were jumping into the pool repeatedly, kids on a mission. I thought about the parallel boards that frame the altar in the house on Han Thuyen Street. The last four characters express a desire to prevent Phung's automobile from carrying him away from the village when his time as an administrator was through. "We want to hold you back," was how my landlord translated it to me. As the hotel's façade glowed in the ambient light shed by lamps in the garden, that feeling of wanting nothing to change, of the richness of life in a place where so much seemed borne of a storybook, was something that I had come to know well.

La Residence Hotel & Spa

5 Le Loi St.
Hue
(84-54) 837-475
www.la-residence-hue.com

Where the Ashes Are: The Odyssey of a Vietnamese Family

If you would like to purchase a copy of this book by Nguyen Qui Duc, inquire at your local used bookshop or go to www.abebooks.com, a website selling used books from booksellers around the world. In the meantime, you can read Duc's essay on *bun cha* on page 13 in the "Moveable Feasts" chapter.

All in the family

Duc's father was the highest-ranking South Vietnamese official captured by Hanoi during the war. His captors spirited him to the north where he languished in a prison camp for some eleven years before release, a story that he later retold in a memoir of his own, *Anh Sang va Bong Toi (Light and Darkness)*. The book has not been translated.

Duong Lam Anh has a hot time bathing outside Hue

Once in a while in the summer, I go out for a hot bath. You may wonder why I go out when this can easily be done at home. What I'm talking about is a steaming hot bath at My An Hot Spring Resort outside Hue, about halfway to Thuan An Beach. Of course, you should go only if you can tolerate the heat and the smell. The smell comes from sulfur, the mineral abundant in the water that makes it so good for your health, and it offends those who are not used to its distinctive odor. I warn you, it lingers stubbornly even days after your bath. But it will disappear after two or three visits. No miracle at all—it's just because you get used to the stink and don't notice it anymore. And don't worry if the water looks opaque. It is also because of the sulfur.

At the resort there are two hot pools. If you are new to this experience and like your space, I don't recommend jumping into the small pool unless you want to get boiled in close quarters. The water in this very small pool is *really* hot! It's so hot that first-timers are required to have their blood pressure checked before they take the plunge. But don't let the small pool discourage you from visiting the hot springs altogether. The other pool is more spacious and its water less scalding.

CENTRAL VIETNAM

Later, you can stretch out on one of the beds beside the pool if you wish and chat with fellow visitors, do some kind of meditation, or simply enjoy the quiet of the large, shady garden. There is also a restaurant nearby, since the hot baths often make one thirsty and hungry. Recently, another pool was added for those who prefer a swim in cold water.

Before My An was built, locals in the area noticed the healing effects of the water springing up from under the ground. They thought there might be a volcano burning deep down beneath them. Research was conducted by scientists, and it was concluded that the water here was beneficial. The city council decided to get involved, and it encouraged a local hotel group to invest and develop the property into the pleasant retreat that it is today.

My An Hot Spring Resort

After a day visiting the imperial city and royal tombs, a dip in hot water is a nice way to relax. If you want, you can stay in one of the resort's charming, traditionally built houses. Also, for privacy, you can have a bath indoors with hot mineral water piped right to your room. The resort is not too far from the city center and accessible by motorbike (around twenty minutes). From Truong Tien Bridge on Le Loi Boulevard at Hue's city center, go east. Cross Dap Da Dam into Nguyen Sinh Cung Street. Keep following that street until you see the resort on the right, about four kilometers away.

Phu Duong Commune
Phu Vang District
Hue
(84-54) 869-704

An odorless alternative

If you can't stand the smell of sulfur and don't mind traveling farther from the city center, there is another hot spring for you. The water at Thanh Tan Hot Spring has no sulfur in it. The grounds are a large park with lots of trees and flowers. You can take a dip in the natural stream or swim and play in the pools. This hot spring is around twenty kilometers from the city and is easily reachable by motorbike. From Truong Tien Bridge at the city center on Tran Hung Dao Street, head west until you see the railway tracks and Bach Tho Bridge. Do not cross the railway tracks; take the right just before them. Follow that street until you see An Lo Bridge. Cross the bridge and then turn left. That road will lead you right to the resort.

Phong Son Commune
Phong Dien District
Hue
(08-54) 553-192/553-225

Bridging gaps

Truong Tien Bridge is often called Trang Tien Bridge in guidebooks. The former is correct. Truong means "place" and Tien means "money." In the past there used to be a place nearby where coins were made and thus the origin of the bridge's name.

HOI AN

Joe Springer-Miller enjoys a balcony view over Hoi An

As I sit sipping iced coffee on my narrow balcony at Minh A Guesthouse, overlooking the start of the market day, I think there is no place in Hoi An where you can feel as in touch with the history and workings of Vietnamese life as this old home. Draped in morning glory and wisteria, facing the open street portion of the busy Central Market, this balcony is one of the town's great secrets. I watch the many women who have already set their baskets of mangosteens and lemongrass on the sides of the narrow street; others arrive throughout the morning, or carry their goods up and down the stretch that leads to the water's edge. Cars don't fit, but a few motorcycles and bicycles try to make their way through the pedestrians.

The owner of this little gem of a guesthouse is Nguyen Pham Choi. Along with her husband and family, she rents out rooms and maintains the historic property, which is more like a finely crafted piece of antique furniture than a building. The youngest daughter says the family is unsure of the home's history between the time it was built in 1837 and the time the family purchased it in 2000. They don't know who built it, back when Hoi An was inhabited by numerous Japanese and Chinese residents, but it resembles the old travelers' inns I stayed in when I lived in Japan. If you have ever visited the polished and well-maintained *ryokan* in Japanese cities, you can imagine the design of this similar although more worn home. The 400-year-old *ryokan* of Kyoto can cost thousands of dollars a night, but these simpler rooms in Hoi An are available at backpacker prices.

Make no mistake, the style is basic. Rooms are modest and fan-cooled, their ceilings supported by round posts and beams, like those you would find in a Chinese temple, lacquered black. Worn wood dominates the lightly furnished rooms, which also include shuttered windows, mosquito nets, and the sole luxury of refrigerators. Bathrooms outside the bedrooms are simple, modern, and clean. I have been quite comfortable through several stays, and it's well worth it if you can get one of two rooms with balconies, especially the front room overlooking the market.

I stayed in this same front room on my favorite visit to Hoi An, during September for the Harvest Moon Festival. The streets were not only alive, but also seemingly growing—boys in Chinese dragon costumes stretched up, piling three and four atop one another, shoulder upon shoulder, in order for the top boys to reach through the gaping mouths of their outfits to collect small bills and coins from those on the

CENTRAL VIETNAM

balconies above. The dragons looked like Jack's beanstalk vines sprouting up from the street.

As soon as I handed a little money to a small boy, smiling within the gaping dragon's mouth, the dragon would tumble to the street. At one point I ran out of small bills and said I was sorry to a little guy; he smiled and gave me a piece of hard candy by way of the dragon's mouth. As the evening rolled on, my travel companion and I roamed the streets, bright and loud with sparklers and groups wheeling massive drums about. All was accompanied by chants and lights and reflections in the river.

Hoi An sometimes feels so international it's hard to tell if you are on a Greek isle, in a historic Chinese district, or here in Vietnam. Later today, after I leave my balcony perch, I will wander the narrow alleys again and go buy that painting I've been agonizing over—there is always a painting to agonize over in Hoi An. But for now, while a broom salesman calls his wares and the street below fills with the commerce of a busy day, my morning *ca phe sua da* and the quiet of this perch are all I need.

Minh A Guesthouse

In addition to running the hotel, the proprietors also sell some materials and tools for making fishing nets as a side business on the bottom floor of the guesthouse.

2 Nguyen Thai Hoc St.
Hoi An
(84-510) 861-368 (limited English)

Alice Driver settles into a home away from home in Hoi An

My husband Isaac and I had just arrived in Hoi An and were wandering the blazing hot streets wearing two towering backpacks. We had been traveling for a month during Isaac's two-month project studying the Vietnamese bamboo coracle boat. We began in Hanoi, taking a week of intensive language classes so that we would be able to communicate on a basic level with rural families who did not speak English. Then we visited Halong Bay, stopped in Ninh Binh, took a fifteen-hour bus ride from there to Danang, visited China Beach, and finally landed in Hoi An. Along the way we had been staying in cheap hostels, and by the time we arrived in Hoi An, we were craving creature comforts. We visited several hotels in our disheveled, sweaty state, but it was not until we reached the lush courtyard of Ha An Hotel that we were inspired to put down our backpacks and investigate.

Women dressed in pink and turquoise silk *ao dai* greeted us, offering us seats and glasses of lemonade. We wiped the sweat from our brows and clutched our cold drinks happily. As we sat in the reception area of the two-story white hotel, surrounded by potted plants, decorative porcelain, and clay vases filled with water and fresh flower petals, I looked out at the two hammocks in the courtyard, the flowering hibiscus and the coconut trees, and hoped the hotel would not be too expensive. It was so nice that I almost felt guilty sitting there; after a month of backpacking, I clung to the mentality that diehard travelers should endure cold showers and grow as a result of their hardships.

The receptionist informed us that this was a family-owned hotel and offered to show us the accommodations. We were ushered into an immaculate white room with dark wood furniture and fresh red hibiscus decorating the bedspread, bathroom, and shower. These rooms were $35 and the ones with balconies were $45, she told us. In a place where we could have rented a room for $3-$10, an asking price of $35 was a small fortune. However, when we explained that we would be in the area for a month while my husband worked with Anh Lu, a bamboo coracle builder who lived to the north in Dien Duong, the receptionist offered to cut us a deal. Since Internet, bicycles, and breakfast, as well as a remarkably friendly staff, were included, we decided to stay.

The buffet breakfast was nothing short of a feast. I woke up each morning to a table of fresh tropical fruits, cereal, yogurt, juices, traditional Vietnamese dishes, and coffee. There were also omelets and pancakes made to order. And on the mornings when we woke up at 3 a.m. to go fishing in a coracle with Anh That, a fisherman my husband befriended in China Beach, the staff packed us a breakfast to go.

What I most enjoyed about the hotel was the staff's willingness to put up with my husband and me as we practiced our basic Vietnamese. I also appreciated the attention to detail. Each day the staff left baskets of ripe mangoes, pears, and other seasonal fruit in our room. Fresh flowers decorated our bedside table and were placed throughout the lobby. As guests we were given bikes, and could pedal around town exploring the markets. We also rented motorbikes to get to and from Anh Lu's house, and we were allowed to park them in front of the hotel.

As the month passed, Isaac and I spent our days working and exploring. A Vietnamese coracle can be built from start to finish in about fifteen days, and during our time there Isaac helped Anh Lu work on two. Since I am not a wood-worker or boat builder by trade, I passed some afternoons helping teach English and playing games at the Hoi An Street Children Center. I also toured the countryside. One of my best memories is a day spent on a motorbike on dirt roads, looking out on the brilliant green of rice paddies and following another motorbike that had two live pigs tied to the back—every time the bike hit a rock, the pigs would squeal!

Because Hoi An is a lively town— hectic with tourists scrambling in and out of tailor shops, cooking classes, and historic sites—and because our days were filled with activity, a place like the lovely Ha An was all the more valuable. It served not just as a hotel, but also as a sanctuary at the end of our busy days.

Ha An Hotel

Rooms include private bathrooms, air conditioning, and cable TV. There is also a restaurant located on the premises, but the food is overpriced; guests would be much better off exploring local restaurants.

06-08 Phan Boi Chau Rd.
Hoi An
(84-510) 863-126/914-496
http://haanhotel.com

Karma Waters Restaurant

Vegetarians and vegans should visit this restaurant at nearby Cua Dai Beach. Paul Tarrant, the co-owner, is a boat enthusiast and also runs a business building models of Chinese junks. Tarrant has several boats in the water next to the restaurant, including a bamboo coracle.

47 Cua Dai St.
Hoi An
(84-510) 927-632
www.karmawaters.com

Traditional boat building

To read more about Alice and Isaac's adventures with Vietnamese coracles, go to page 202.

Joe Springer–Miller reflects on the high life in Hoi An

If you are going to splurge just once during your trip through Vietnam, and I mean splurge big, The Nam Hai in Hoi An has got to be the place to do it. I confess, I have been to a few nice places in Mexico and Phuket, but never anything like this. With its sense of space, unique lines, and reflective qualities—both figuratively and literally—The Nam Hai is a work of art.

My brother's family is accustomed to the very best when traveling, and a resort such as this one in Vietnam finally made a visit to little brother Joe more appealing. When I entered the grounds with them, I was struck first by the view of water: tiers of water from one marble pool to the next until they finally descended into the ocean. It made me realize how magical the ocean must have seemed to the ancients with its seeming infinity drop-off at the horizon. The marble was wet with color, reflecting the hues of the sky, ocean, and even my family ... everything reflected.

We hopped into golf carts and headed to our villa, past white walls whose strategically placed window openings were laced with black bamboo bars. As one wall sprang out behind another with surprising irregularity, it felt a little like being in a prison you want to break your way into, not out of. Although our accommodation was labeled as a three-bedroom, it was actually five structures, each bedroom free-standing, along with a large communal building, and a building for the two butlers and kitchen. As soon as we arrived, we slumped into luxurious sofas on the patios and just absorbed the view.

The layout was a series of rectangles, rimmed by the endless flow of four-sided infinity pools, one after another across the development. We jumped into our private pool, amazed by the overall effect of these perfectly balanced marble edges brimming with water: an atmosphere bright with the tropical tones of ocean, sky, and coconut trees. We were living in a dreamy, melting landscape where flowing water carried the brilliant reflection of nature. After tossing my nieces into the pool and chasing crabs on the beach, we all tried out our own bath facilities: an indoor rain shower as well as an outdoor, open air, but very private, garden rain shower. Below the bed sections were living rooms tiered down to full glass doors opening to an outdoor lounge area, infinity pool, coconut trees, Cua Dai Beach, and the South China Sea. What a view!

I have to admit, I generally prefer to travel as a backpacker, making friends with strangers from all over the world at shared tables in small guesthouses, and with the families that run the guesthouses. That isn't going to happen at The Nam Hai. The excellent service is unobtrusive, and the great sense of space gives incredible privacy, keeping travelers apart. Still, I'm glad I did it once. It was a memorable

place to be with my family for a week, and a luxurious base from which to explore Hoi An. It's good to feel like a king once in a while ... and so hard to go back to the real world afterward.

The Nam Hai

Hamlet 1
Dien Duong Village
Dien Ban District
Quang Nam Province
Hoi An
(84 510) 940-000
www.thenamhai.com

NHA TRANG

Tom Chard ascends a quiet mountain outside rowdy Nha Trang

Nha Trang is famous for being an over-developed beachside party town. And rightly so. It's a place that seems dedicated to paving paradise to put up a parking lot. But despite the government's zany high-rise development policies, Nha Trang Bay is one of the most magnificent bays in the world and provides some of the best seafood Vietnam has to offer. Nha Trang attracts thousands of Vietnamese visitors every year from Saigon, Hanoi, and Danang, as well as many international package tourists to its upscale resorts. Unfortunately, for the average backpacker, it provides little more than a binge-drinking, sunbathing sojourn en route.

I won't bore you with the infinite joys of riding a motorbike away from the party and into the Nha Trang countryside, but I guarantee that it is the best way to see Khanh Hoa Province, as well as find some peace and quiet. You will experience a stunning panorama, with no glass to separate you from the colors, smells, and noises that make Vietnam so overwhelmingly wonderful. There is a hidden world available to the independent traveler, full of some of the most beautiful sights and friendliest people in the world. Just inland from Nha Trang, you will find rainforests, hill tribes, wildlife, dams, picturesque mountains, and waterfalls.

The best motorbike ride available to those wanting a scenic day trip is to Hon Ba Mountain. A capable driver can travel from the beach at Nha Trang to one and one-half kilometers above sea level in two hours, including time to stop for photos, coffee, or beer. A jacket or sweatshirt is advisable, as it can get quite cold as you near the top of the mountain. To get on your way, pick up a local map for directions to Suoi Tien village, a cheesy tourist trap with a concrete waterfall.

To reach Suoi Tien, ride inland out of town on Yersin Street, which turns into Highway One. Once you take the turnoff to Suoi Tien, turn left immediately, and go through the township. When you get as far as you can on this road, you will be at a

boom gate. Here you will take a left onto a big new road. If you want to be sure you're headed in the right direction, you can stop at any time and ask locals the way. After you've tried pronouncing Hon Ba using a few different tones, someone should figure out what you're saying and be able to direct you without too much hassle. Don't get frustrated if you have difficulty communicating. Remember many people out here don't speak Vietnamese, as most are members of the Ede ethnic minority.

Once you hit the big new road marked Hon Ba, stay on it. It takes you all the way to the top. At the base of the mountain at the "19 km to go" marker, there is a rustic café. This is the last place you can buy anything. It has a minimal menu; you can order Coke, coffee, water, or beer. As far as food goes, you can eat either one whole chicken or one whole catfish, which the staff will kill to order. A walk to the bottom of the café's grounds is well worth the effort, since you will come across a small waterfall with turquoise-colored rapids. You might also purchase a takeout box of *com* (rice with chicken) for around 10,000 VND (less than $1) for a picnic lunch beside one of the waterfalls on the way.

During the monsoonal months of October to December, the new road may be closed due to landslides, but in general it is in great condition. Your ascent will only be hampered by your desire to stop frequently to take in the view. The journey, as opposed to the destination, is the highlight of this trip. The peak is almost always in the clouds, foggy and cold, but on a clear day you can see from Nha Trang to Cam Ranh Airport.

At the top of the mountain, the road comes to an abrupt stop, and you will see a locked wooden structure. This is a re-creation of the house that Alexandre Yersin was said to have lived in. A scientist and prodigy of Louis Pasteur, Yersin is honored in Vietnam for his work at the Pasteur Institute in Nha Trang and the Medical School of Hanoi, as well as for developing Dalat as a health retreat. Although there's nothing much else up here, this is a good spot to enjoy a nip of Scotch or coffee from your thermos. As well, there are some interesting wildflowers around the house, and you can venture into the forest for a short stroll.

The descent takes half the time, and you can put your bike into neutral and coast all the way without the engine running, allowing you to enjoy the sound of the birds, the rustling wind, and ... some of the only true silence you will experience in Vietnam.

Hiring a motorcycle

You can hire a motorbike in Nha Trang for $3-$10 a day, depending on the type of motorbike desired. If you rent for a few days, you have more bargaining power. Even a 100cc Honda step-through is enough for two people to do the trip to Hon Ba. An automatic clutch bike such as a Yamaha Nouvo is best for beginners. Vespa and Attila-style scooters are unsuitable for country riding as they have very small wheels, which are dangerous when combined with potholes, water, and rocks.

Motorcycle attitude

First, you need to be confident when riding a motorbike. Observe the random, anarchic, and downright dangerous way in which locals drive. You need to be very, very defensive. Drive slowly, and always expect the unexpected.

Use your head (and hide your arms)

Vietnamese law states that people only need to wear a helmet and possess a license when riding on the highway. I leave this to the rider's discretion; however, I feel that a helmet is always a good idea. Also, it is advisable that both driver and passenger wear a long-sleeved shirt, jacket, and long pants, and the driver should wear gloves to block the sun on the back of his hands. You should take at least half a liter of water each, as well as a road map and some snack foods. Sunglasses are a must to protect your eyes from wind, dust, and insects. Cover up well with sun lotion because the wind chill factor also stops you from noticing your skin frying. I recommend filling the tank before you set off, since the petrol gauges on rental motorbikes aren't always reliable.

oh, yeah!

CENTRAL VIETNAM

When to ride

When you ride a motorbike for several hours in hot weather, you will get very dehydrated as your perspiration evaporates if you don't have a windbreak for your upper torso. A good idea is to start early in the morning and have a long lunch and siesta during the worst heat of the day.

Legal limits

In Khanh Hoa Province, traffic police very rarely flag down tourists. If they do, you could flash your library card and nobody would be the wiser.

Tom Chard hits the beach—minus the hordes—in Nha Trang

Ba Dai means "long beach" in Vietnamese. While this name provides an appropriate physical description, it could also be used to express how far this beach is from the crowds of Nha Trang Bay—a long way.

Among the best beaches in Vietnam, it has a spectacular ocean shoreline, which on a clear day reaches as far as the eye can see. It is superior to the beach at Nha Trang in every way. Here you will find few people and water free of plastic bags. Unlike the city's bay, it has no sewage outlets or rivers feeding into it, so the water is clean and disease-free. The water also gets deeper more gradually, so there are no "dumper" waves, making it much better for children and inexperienced swimmers. In addition, the white sand is fine, the water always crystal clear, and there are no noisy and dangerous speedboats or jet skis to worry about. The only activity on offer is renting inflated tractor tire tubes to drift around in.

The north end of the beach is the main point of access and has several family-owned seafood shacks. They are temporary bamboo structures that are dismantled before each monsoon season. They provide huts for shade and fresh seafood ordered by the kilo. Only squid and prawns are available, but they are fresh, and usually barbequed over clay pots. You can get your vendor to cook for you, or you can have the small charcoal barbecue put on your table so you can cook to your preference. The squid can be ordered plain or in fish sauce and green chili. Prawns can be barbequed or steamed in coconut juice. Cold beer, soft drinks, and quail eggs for snacking are also available. Dipping sauces, salad, and all necessary cutlery and utensils are provided. The prices are very reasonable, roughly equivalent to the seafood market, but shop around. Go to a few huts and compare the seafood quality and price until you find a place you like.

This is by far the best place for lazing in the country, as each hut is equipped with large deck chairs for taking naps, sunbathing, or just enjoying the peace and quiet at this almost deserted beach. If you prefer to sit by yourself, simply walk up the shore half a kilometer and throw your towel on the sand. There are no hawkers to pester you, even at the height of the tourist season.

Getting there

This beach is not signposted and is known only to locals. It is about halfway between Nha Trang and the US-built airport at Cam Ranh. If coming from Nha Trang, it is a thirty-minute ride on the airport road, a perfectly paved new road hugging the mountains along the coast. Head out of town over Binh Tan Bridge. Turn right immediately after crossing the bridge and follow this road, which takes you around the coast and to the beach, and eventually the airport. The views are spectacular, especially at dusk. As you come down from the mountains, you will see a large roundabout before the road straightens out for kilometers all the way to the airport. Turn left at this roundabout down a small sandy path. This will take you to the beach. Motorbike parking is available for 2,000 VND.

Playing it safe

It is not advisable to leave your belongings on the beach unattended. If you're dining at one of the seafood shacks, the owners will keep an eye on your possessions if you ask.

DALAT

Jessy Needham stops to smell the roses in Dalat

The sun was high in the clear blue sky as my friend Quang drove his motorbike out of sleepy downtown Dalat and high up into the surrounding hills. He wanted to surprise me, and wouldn't tell me where we were headed. Jaded after my last visit to the legendary "City of Flowers," where I had seen a man in a bear costume posing for photos with tourists at Da Tan La waterfall, I was losing faith in the city's storied natural beauty and did not have high hopes for our destination.

We turned into a small, unassuming parking lot, easy to miss on the road out of town. To my astonishment, walking through the gate was like walking into a storybook garden, with flowerbeds overflowing with blossoms. I was surrounded by bright pink, white, and red rose bushes higher than my waist, and I was unable to walk by without burying my nose in their petals to inhale their aroma. Unlike in the "Valley of Love," a well-known Dalat nature spot, there was not a gnome statue in sight.

SOUTHERN VIETNAM

The flowers reminded me of home. Pale blue hydrangeas, heavy on their thick stems, were the same flowers my friend used in her wedding bouquet. I saw white azaleas and thought of my mother, an avid gardener, thousands of kilometers away. I felt the familiar pangs of sentimentality I often had while living so far from my family, wishing I could share my experiences in Vietnam with them. I decided that if my mom couldn't be there to share these floral wonders with me, I would bring them to her in photos, and I began snapping pictures of every flower in sight. A huge, hot pink rose had a bee hovering in its center. Hundreds of bright, round, purple blossoms reminded me of thistles, although less spiky. Here was an odd lavender flower that I'd never seen before, comprised of thin, delicate petals; there were dozens of wildflowers in periwinkle blue and mustard yellow.

Despite the presence of a modest guesthouse on the grounds, there were hardly any other visitors at the gardens. Staff members at the greenhouse at the back were napping as we browsed the orchids, aloe plants, and bonsai trees for sale. Quang and I sat on a shady bench and gratefully heard not motorbikes or construction, but birdsong. My faith in the "City of Flowers" was renewed, and I knew that on any future visits to Dalat, I would avoid the waterfalls and gnome statues and head straight for the Minh Tam Flower Gardens to enjoy my own secret hideaway.

Minh Tam Flower Gardens (Vuon Hoa Minh Tam)

The gardens are a short drive from downtown Dalat. There is a small entrance fee. It's possible to stay at the inexpensive guesthouse located on the grounds.

20A Khe Sanh Rd.
Dalat
(84-63) 822-447

MUI NE

Dominic Hong Duc Golding connects with humanity in Mui Ne

It had been eight months since I first arrived in Ho Chi Minh City. I was working as an English instructor, and on top of the job stress, I was emotionally tired, for I felt I was being constantly challenged to act—and be—Vietnamese. As a Vietnamese adoptee returning to my birthplace, it was as if I were being pressured to live up to something I couldn't, and that I had to constantly justify myself, because I looked Vietnamese but didn't speak the language. I needed a break. Here in Vietnam, everyone escapes to the beaches. So I went down my map of the country in search of one.

For the Saigonese, the choice is usually Vung Tau, but I had been there, and once was enough. I swear the people are a little mad. It is a place where people now escape to, but where so many people once escaped from during hard times.

Nha Trang is nice, but from my past experience there, I felt it was way too touristy in an acid junkie way.

I'd been told that Hoi An was commercial. Even though it had World Heritage status, I was in no mood to haggle every five steps I took.

And Danang was known to be overrated—America's old China Beach was now the private playground of the resorts anyway.

Then there was Mui Ne. Everyone, including my students, continued to rave about this small fishing town outside Phan Thiet. It was low season, and since Mui Ne was only two and a half hours by bus from Ho Chi Minh City, I booked a weekend trip that included a jeep tour on the second day.

The bus ride was uneventful, and the Minh Tam Resort basic. Sure, I could have chosen a multi-star accommodation like Dynasty or Coco Beach, but I was after a simple bed-and-breakfast experience, nothing too flashy. The outdoor restaurant-bar faced directly to the sea, and I had a choice of the "private" beach or the pool. My room was really clean, had a fridge, TV, and large bathroom—I was happy.

I headed out for lunch, just a short ride away on the beach, and enjoyed a massive plate of battered, fresh calamari and a cold Tiger Beer. Since it was such a nice day, I ordered two more beers and some soft-shelled crab too. Later, during the evening meal, I was invited to join a table with a family of South Koreans and some hotel workers who didn't mind drinking with guests—the more the merrier. And God, the sunset was glorious and calm.

During a night ride around Mui Ne, I could see that the bars were pretty much dead. I found my evening to be not about going out and getting drunk in some trendy beach club, but instead, I shared rice wine while chatting with male hotel staff about life, and some dessert—che—with female staff as they talked about their aspirations.

The next morning came with a free breakfast. Woo hoo! As for my jeep tour, it should have taken four hours but was done in an hour and a half. Sure, I visited all the things listed in the "tour" brochure, like the sand dunes, fishing port, market, and ... a creek? Hmm. I guess my guide was a bit lazy. Returning to the hotel, I had quite a few hours before heading back to Ho Chi Minh City.

So, what did I do with the rest of the morning? I walked the whole length of the beach. I watched the local fishermen pull in their catch, kids playing soccer, a little girl staring in wonder into a bowl of tiny sea creatures her parents caught, and a lone tourist reading a book, making the most of an empty beach and the sun. Observing the trawlers, I noticed the eyes painted onto the fronts of the boats, unlike on the vessels that cruise up the Mekong

SOUTHERN VIETNAM

River. With fascination, I watched families untangling a net while gossiping, and people rowing small circular cane boats loaded with fish.

With my last two hours I had a long lunch with the South Korean family and the staff. Our meal consisted of deep-fried local fish (*ca chieu*), prawns, and mixed seafood congee (*chao*), made with mussels fetched off the beach that morning. Lying on a beach chair overlooking the South China Sea, I thought about the small joys I experienced the previous evening and that morning, hanging out with the hotel workers and guests, and interacting with locals. It was so different from my life in Ho Chi Minh City, where I felt like an outsider. Here, I was welcome without prejudice, and I was reminded how small towns often offer the biggest rewards: connection and humanity.

Booking a tour

Travel agents in the major cities usually outsource to local tour operators, so what you read in an office in Ho Chi Minh City might not be what you get at your destination. My advice is to book a bus, rail, or plane ticket to wherever you want to go. Check into a hotel, and *then* shop around for local tours. That way you are dealing directly with the locals, and you can ask the questions that need to be asked.

Minh Tam Resort

What this resort lacks in amenities, it makes up for with its quiet, peaceful setting and warm service.

Rooms are around $22 per night. If you go during the off-season, call the hotel and see if they have any special rates. You can often get a discount by dealing directly with the property rather than going through a tour company.

KM 15, Ham Tien
Mui Ne
Phan Thiet
(84-62) 847-831

HO CHI MINH CITY

Elka Ray finds a strange new world in Ho Chi Minh City

When I first moved to Ho Chi Minh City in 1995, I rented a small, dark room in District Five, the city's Chinese quarter. Located over a smoky restaurant, the room smelled of rancid grease, which no amount of incense could mask. Whenever a truck rattled past, the whole building would shake, causing specks of blue paint to fall from the ceiling like dandruff. But I was a student and the rent was cheap, plus I commended myself on having found somewhere "authentic"—a room in a real Vietnamese neighborhood, where I could experience the local culture up close.

At that time, I'd have shuddered at the very notion of a new urban development like Phu My Hung in Saigon South. Rows of identical houses, stark high-rises, gated compounds, a neat grid of streets devoid of itinerant vendors and loiterers—I would have written it all off as lacking culture and character. A decade later, fresh air, orderly streets, and spacious sidewalks seemed a lot more appealing, and last year my husband and I bought an apartment in the dreaded "burbs."

Although the development has numerous international educational facilities and healthcare, it's the leisure amenities—parks, playgrounds, and swimming pools—that drew us to Phu My Hung, along with a hankering for cleaner air and less noise. It certainly is quiet, although not as lifeless as I'd feared, with construction sites visible in every direction and new businesses opening every week. On my daily stroll to buy bread from the local gourmet shop, I pass a bakery; a handful of restaurants offering Vietnamese, Korean, Japanese, and Western food; a bubble tea shop; a Lotteria fast food joint; and a travel agent, as well as shops selling everything from lingerie to life-sized carved marble lions. Most intriguing of all is the Korean-owned pet shop, which sells, along with a number of miniature puppies, dog strollers and fluffy white wedding gowns for pooches. I imagine my neighbor is a regular customer, as her maid has the daily task of wheeling a pair of large white poodles with dyed orange ears around our neighborhood in a baby carriage. And I thought Phu My Hung would be boring!

Of course, it's not just the pets that are pampered, as the residents are a well-off lot; each driveway has a shiny Mercedes or SUV. Korean and Taiwanese ex-pats and wealthy Vietnamese form the bulk of those who live here, with some Western ex-pats thrown in. While some complexes feature pre-made duplexes and fourplexes in standard, cookie-cutter styles, other streets are lined with villas that testify to their owners' big budgets, wild imaginations, and sometimes questionable taste. My favorites include an English cottage complete with climbing roses and white picket fence, a glass-fronted box with a moat, and a massive building that resembles a Tibetan monastery.

For the moment Phu My Hung feels luxuriously empty, but as Ho Chi Minh City's middle class continues to expand, more and more people will be able to afford homes in the suburbs. Before Saigon South turns into just another crowded neighborhood, come out and take a leisurely walk, and experience a jolt of culture shock, as well as the future of Vietnam. You'll find a whole new country, complete with empty lawns, uniformed security guards, and poodles in tutus.

Phu My Hung

A metered taxi from District One to Phu My Hung in Saigon South costs about 60,000-80,000 VND ($4-$6) and takes fifteen to twenty-five minutes, depending on traffic.
www.saigonsouth.com

SOUTHERN VIETNAM

Lorene Strand walks the walk in Ho Chi Minh City

I don't profess to know what it was like in Vietnam during the war. That's not my story to tell. I only know the aftermath of that time, when my stepfather returned home. But I imagine Vietnam now to be similar in some ways to how it was when he was there in 1967—water buffalo still working the rice paddies, women in their conical hats, and motor scooters everywhere, some transporting families of four, some with live ducks or chickens strapped across their gas tanks on their way to the markets.

I had long wanted to live and work in Vietnam, to study the language and to develop a cultural understanding of a country that had so greatly impacted my family. I eventually moved to Ho Chi Minh City in 2006. Surprisingly, it was fairly easy to adjust, though there were a few challenges. As a "Western-sized" woman, it was nearly impossible to find size ten clothing or size eight shoes. However, popcorn, Western DVDs, and *The New York Times* were readily available, and eventually, life without a washer, dryer, refrigerator, or any appliances for that matter, came to seem normal to me. But it wasn't until I attended a service at the Notre Dame Cathedral that I felt spiritually fulfilled and truly at home in Vietnam.

While the cathedral might seem out of place in this Communist country and predominately Buddhist society, a small Christian minority does exist, quietly walking the walk of faith. Locally known as Nha Tho Duc Ba, and officially as Saigon Notre Dame Cathedral Basilica by the Vatican, the cathedral has an interesting history. Situated at the center of District One, its twin Romanesque towers and iron spires stand sixty meters tall, and have graced Cong Xa Paris (Paris Square) since the church's inauguration in 1880.

Modeled after Notre Dame de Paris, the Romanesque-Gothic structure was designed by J. Bourad, a French architect of the colonial period. Monsieur Bourad oversaw the cathedral's construction, importing the vi brant bricks from Marseille and the square glass tiles from the Chartres area. Bishop Isadore Colombert laid the first brick in October 1877, and the last brick was set on Easter Sunday, 1880. The total cost was 2.5 million francs, and it was the largest French construction project in Indochina at the time.

Today, as you approach the cathedral entrance, the sweet smell of sandalwood incense greets you. Votive prayer candles emit a soft glow as you enter the sanctuary, and fluorescent lighting illuminates the altar as you slip into a pew. The locally made stained glass tiles, which replaced those damaged during WWII, offer colorful renditions of beloved Saints, the Virgin Mary, and Jesus, and the three-aisle design reflects the building's three-arch façade. Resonating throughout the sanctuary, as it has for more than a century, the choral singing is hauntingly beautiful. The sermon is given in Vietnamese, followed by an abbreviated sermon in English.

The day I first entered the cathedral was not unlike the foggy Seattle morning I boarded my flight to come to Vietnam. I could feel a spiritual presence in the fog as my plane took off. And as my plane landed in Ho Chi Minh City on the other side of the world, my first glimpse of my new home emerged through the cloudbanks, revealing the same presence that was to guide me through the doors of Notre Dame Cathedral that hazy Sunday morning.

Sunday services
The following are officially sanctioned places of worship in Ho Chi Minh City, offering services in Vietnamese and/or English.

Notre Dame Cathedral

In front of the cathedral, a statue of the Virgin Mary graces a small square. Adjacent is the grand Saigon Post Office, and a park where you will find groups of friends gathered for chess games, children playing, and lovers rendezvousing on benches beneath the shade trees.

59-61 Ly Tu Trong St.
District 1
Sunday Mass: 9:30 a.m.

The Saigon Church
(Hoi Than Tin Lanh)

Located near busy Pham Ngu Lau Street, The Saigon Church

is an oasis of tranquility. The traditional architecture of this whitewashed church is surrounded by a rod-iron fence and quaint garden.

155 Tran Hung Dao St.
District 1
Sunday worship service: 8:30 a.m.

New Life Fellowship International Church

The only international church in Ho Chi Minh City. Services are in English.
http://nlfvietnam.com

MEKONG DELTA

Tyler Watts explores ritual and real life in southern churches

As wisps of incense linger in the air and a slow melodic chant begins, you might assume that you have entered a pagoda or temple. But the quiet man at the front of the room is no monk. Rather, robed in vestments and whispering prayers as clusters of worshipers rush in to find a place to kneel before mass, he is a priest in one of the many Catholic churches speckling the land of Vietnam.

Here, Catholic churches are a marriage of Vietnamese and Western cultures, a testament to how the Vietnamese adapted a new religion to suit their lives. Above those praying, a crucifix looms, even though the interior architecture could easily be confused for that of a temple. The saints and figures that adorn the walls resemble the people of Vietnam: an ethnic minority meeting with Jesus, a Vietnamese man being healed. Throughout the country you can find this mixture of dominantly French church buildings blended with Vietnamese traditions. Even the mass itself is a marriage of ancient Western liturgy with the tonal Vietnamese language. Prayers are transformed into songs as the worship service rises and falls with each word, creating an interplay of meaning and aural beauty.

Equally as impressive as the cathedrals and chapels, with spires cresting the horizon of the landscape, are the people that enter their doors and fill their courtyards. Within the walls of these buildings one escapes Vietnam-the-tourist-destination. In these churches you encounter a spectrum of people. There are young children who cling to their parents, alongside old men who struggle to walk to the front altar and yet never miss a single mass. There are farmers with work-weary hands and businesswomen in pastel-colored pantsuits. This is where people from all classes and ages assemble, united by one thing: a faith that knows no social or cultural barriers.

Finding a church

It isn't difficult in Vietnam to find a church to worship in, share an experience in, or simply observe from a distance. Within the Mekong Delta there are a number of churches that are more than 100 years old or have some special quality about them. Below are a few of the churches that are located near major roadways, and thus, easy to access.

Bo Ot Church

One of the oldest in the region, built in 1886, this church provides an example of the typical French Gothic architecture found throughout Vietnam.

National Highway 91 (between Long Xuyen and Can Tho)
Thot Not Town
Can Tho Province

Nang Gu Church

This church stands alongside the highway between Long Xuyen and Chau Doc and dominates the landscape around it. It was also built in the late nineteenth century in the familiar French Gothic style.

National Highway 91
Chau Thanh Town
An Giang Province

Long Xuyen Cathedral

This cathedral is the seat of the Long Xuyen diocese. Begun in the 1950s, it was finished in the 1970s. Though not the most at-tractive or historic of churches, it is one of the more accessible parishes, within easy walking distance from the town center. Look for the large bell tower.

National Highway 91 (Tran Huong Dao St.)
Long Xuyen City
An Giang Province

Churches farther north

Fellow contributor Duong Lam Anh has a great listing of his favorite churches (with pho-tographs) in Hue and Dalat on his blog: http://duonglamanh. typepad.com. Click on the index for English entries and then click on "Church Tour."

TRA VINH

Lillian Forsyth interprets "crowded is happy" in Tra Vinh

This weekend I went with my friend Ms. Oanh, a bakery owner, and a bunch of her friends and relatives to the beach in Tra Vinh Province. It was a classic Vietnamese travel marathon.

The trip began at ten on Saturday night when I rode my bicycle through the deserted streets of Long Xuyen, where I volunteered as an English teacher, to the bakery. Although this was the appointed departure time, I waited with Ha and Huong from the bakery for about an hour and a half until everyone arrived, and then we all piled into the fifteen-passenger van that Ms. Oanh had rented for this excursion.

It was fairly uncomfortable, with three of us in the back seat and poor Huong vomiting every four seconds in the front, all the while holding her five-year-old daughter on her lap. The idea was to sleep on the mini-bus. Ha! As if that would happen. Although this was a private van, apparently deafen-ingly loud pop music was included in the price—all night long. Not to mention the trip took us through Dong Thap Province, which is notorious for its horrible road conditions. We were bouncing around like pinballs until I thought my brain was going to blast out of my ears. I didn't sleep at all. The first stop was Cao Lanh, where Ms. Oanh lives. We picked her up, along with her husband and a few of her relatives. With twenty people, the van now exceeded its limit. Comfortable.

Perhaps this is the time to introduce the concept of *vui*. The word *vui* in Vietnamese means "happy," "fun," or "funny," depending upon how you translate it and the context in which you use it. The Vietnamese use it a lot, in expressions such as *Tet co vui khong?* (Was your Tet holiday fun?) The correct response to this question is always the word *vui*, which means, "Yes, of

SOUTHERN ISLANDS

course, it was great." The word is also used together in expressions that don't seem to go with *vui* at all, for example, *An cho vui?* (Eat for fun?), or *Dong vui?* (Crowded is happy?) In any case, the response is always *vui* to agree that yes, whatever is going on is probably the best thing you've ever done in your life.

So, we were in the van, it was pretty *dong vui*, and we sped away to our next stop: Tra Vinh city. Here we picked up two more people. That's right. Fortunately, they were small. Our third stop was the market in Tra Vinh at about 4:30 a.m. I stayed in the van while a few people went out for what seemed like an eternity to buy seafood and various other items. We finally got back on the road at about six, and reached the beach a little after that. Suddenly, all of the sleepless, ear-pounding, brain-rattling, *dong vui* ride was worth it. The beach was breathtaking, with white sands, scatterings of conch shells, and clean water with gentle waves as far as the eye could see.

We went swimming right away, and after about an hour got out and took a break to enjoy the cool weather (that's right!) and have a delicious meal of various seafood: shrimp, crab, squid, and boiled fish, all wrapped with fresh vegetables in rice paper and dipped into fish sauce. Simple, yet distinctive. We took pictures of the landscape (everyone loves when I bring my camera along, and I willingly give up the photographer role to anyone and everyone), and then went in for another swim. Following swimming, there was a hearty sand war among the younger kids (with a little participation from me,

Ngoc, and Ha, as well).

After showering, relaxing, and packing up, it wasn't even noon. We traveled to Nghia's house. He works at the bakery and lives about a twenty-minute walk from the beach, lucky dog. His place was set in the fresh air with lots of shade, and we had a meal of rice soup and more shrimp and salad. Then, after an all too short nap, we got back into the van and began our *nong vui* (hot and happy), *dong vui* (damn crowded), and exceptionally long drive back to Long Xuyen.

Hitting the beach

My trip was based out of Long Xuyen on the southern tip of Vietnam. To be honest, I don't know the name of the beach town we visited, but if you head for Ba Dong, you're going in the right direction, and you're sure to find a friendly little shoreline to call your own.

PHU QUOC

Mark Barnett creates his own Phu Quoc retreat

As an American coming of age in the 1960s, Vietnam was complicated in my life, whether I went or not. Because of this, moving here in the early 1990s took a leap of faith, a tumble from the corporate ladder, and a surrender to serendipity.

When I arrived, bicycles ruled the streets. The moldering socialism, austere citizens, naive local business practices, and inefficiency were delightful. I planned to change the global spice trade and signed off on it with the government. In the beginning, I struggled with Singapore traders and surveyed "New Economic Zones," those former war zones resettled by farmer/soldiers. Then my staff came to me with a story about an island off the coast, lightly populated by pepper growers and fishermen.

Although briefly occupied by Cambodia in 1975, Phu Quoc had been overlooked by the American War. Its population used to be ethnic Chinese mingled with Khmer, but by the time I arrived, there were Vietnamese military stationed at local army and naval bases, along with laborers who had come to work in the farming and fishing industries. Many islanders had income from relatives abroad, since numerous fishermen had fled to America in the 1980s. Otherwise, nothing much had happened here in decades. The fragrant pepper was taken off the island by small ships from a picturesque port, and a thrice-weekly prop plane landed if the weather was good.

It appealed. It was perfect. It was Shangri-La without religion.

I got account number 0012 at the Agriculture Bank and traded most of the pepper on the island. I bought an abandoned coconut plantation on a quiet beach, with no road or electric lines. It was a retreat. There was an old mango tree, rotten with termites. My wife and I pruned, repaired, fertilized, cut forty years of brush, and terraced the slope. It sounded practical to a dreamer. A teak sailboat. A vanilla plantation. At dawn we'd row out to the fishing boats to buy their catch.

Outside our three-bedroom brick villa, I engraved "Cassia Cottage-PRIVATE" on a sign at the beach. We declined interviews with *Lonely Planet* and *Frommer's*—we are mentioned in there only as "a local spice planter living on the beach." I planned a quiet retirement.

Then, somehow, we became a diplomat's retreat, installed an electric fan, and added cottages, a swimming pool, and an ice cream shop—using our own vanilla and cassia. Pressured by staff and travel agents to bring in more guests, we made a website and took down the "PRIVATE" signs.

We had found our own island. We changed the local farm economy. The island changed around us. Phu Quoc now has six flights a day, and high speed ferries. But most of the island is still as it was. There are only two paved road sections. Farms hide in lanes winding through the forest. A dozen little fishing ports exist on fish sauce production, a few cigarette boats, and sunshine. The remote farmers' houses still have no doors. We walk in the quiet places with our friends.

SOUTHERN ISLANDS

We all need a place where friends can talk, lovers can think, children can be easy. We try to recreate that for our guests, who may come from the EU or USA. But I miss the old days and remember when life was simpler. Now we have eighteen rooms spread around the gardens. The old mango in the coconut grove is bearing healthy fruit. People in resort-wear stroll the beachfront looking for an authentic Vietnamese experience. Despite on-going progress, Phu Quoc is still that.

The boosters and speculators say the island will become another Singapore one day. But for me, Phu Quoc will always be another Vietnam. A forgotten spot in a sheltered and shallow sea. A frontier outpost of an emerging nation, itself taxiing to the runway, integrating into a changing world. There will be an international airport soon. But our island is still ours. And Cassia Cottage is now a place where we save the old pace, but serve it up with vanilla ice cream and air-conditioned rooms.

Cassia Cottage

Along with offering our barefoot bed-and-breakfast on the beach (air-conditioned rooms from $45-$125), we have eight tables scattered around our garden beneath a stone wall at the seafront. We specialize in grilled fish, using local and Mediterranean spices. The wine list runs from sangria to chateaux vintages, with an emphasis on Italy and Chile.

Ba Keo Beach
Phu Quoc Island
(84-77) 848-395
www.cassiacottage.com

More about Phu Quoc

Phu Quoc Island is located in southwest Vietnam on the Gulf of Thailand. The following website offers basics about traveling to Phu Quoc by ferry or Vietnam Airlines, descriptions of island attractions, festival information, and more.

www.phuquoc.info

Alternative Lodging

If we're full up, Bo Resort has French style and charm: a true resort with a cultured host, a simple but delicious kitchen, gorgeous gardens, and eighteen basic but charming bungalows ($25-$65). There is a fine beach, no neighbors, and the company of a few kindred spirits. It is located eight kilometers north of the airport and worth the drive.

www.boresort.com

Dining Out

Everyone needs to go out for a change, and I like Vuon Tao (Apple Garden) for the fried fish. Your hotel manager can help you find it—it's about five kilometers south of Duong Dong town down a road away from the beach. Very cheap and very simple.

GENERAL VIETNAM

Hanoi's Hoan Kiem Lake

RETAIL THERAPY

An insiders' primer to boutiques and markets.

From New York to Paris to Hong Kong, one of the great travel activities is shopping. Some people globetrot solely to acquire, and I must admit, I have found myself on a buying frenzy in more than one jewelry-laden, handicraft-sodden foreign locale. But if shopping is your only goal, Vietnam is not the place for you. While the country has its signature treasures, countless markets, and unique villages dedicated to single products, and while its repertoire of brand name stores is growing, it is not (yet) a diehard shopper's mecca. Not surprisingly, I received the fewest essays on this subject. But those I did get capture what is best about shopping in Vietnam: the experience.

Approaching the subject from different angles, Duong Lam Anh (a local) and Renee Friedman (an ex-pat) explore what shopping says about your character, stamina, acumen, and involvement in day-to-day life. Once you get the gist of it, you are then invited to Hanoi's Old Quarter to hunt for ceramics, jewelry, clothing, and even reproductions of old propaganda posters. Slip off to the Hai Ba Trung District with Preyanka Clark Prakash, and you'll discover a purse shop that's putting Vietnamese fashion on the map. Or take a wander around town with Jennifer Davoli, and find out where to track down clothing to fit your Western body.

The first thing you'll learn is that it's all about the tailor when it comes to clothes in Vietnam. Not just for travelers or the wealthy, tailors can be found in even the poorest areas. They are an intrinsic part of life here, and I don't have a Vietnamese girlfriend who isn't without a favorite. Nowhere is the cult of the tailor more evident than in Hoi An, a city whose photogenic, historic streets are crammed with tailor shops. To attempt to describe the quantity is impossible because you have to see it to believe it, storefront upon storefront of mannequins, fabrics, and sample dresses, suits, etc. You can also buy silk lanterns, paintings, and other pretty items here, but it's the custom

clothing that people are seduced by, losing all sense of prudence in the process—the last time I visited, I left with more cotton skirts (different colors, but all the same style) than a person can reasonably wear in a lifetime.

Outside of Hoi An and Hanoi, Ho Chi Minh City has nice shopping along Dong Khoi Street and the surrounding neighborhood. You will find numerous embroidery and knick-knack shops, plus newer boutiques haute enough to grab the attention of glossy travel magazines. As for the other main travel destinations, Sapa is known for its ethnic handicrafts, but Hue, Nha Trang, and Dalat do not have notable shopping scenes. All cities and towns do have markets, though, which are a must-see subculture, as Michael Burr makes clear in his essay about Ton That Dam Market in Ho Chi Minh City.

For a few final tips, check the fact files in other chapters: in Adam Bray's piece on Phan Thiet (page 77) he mentions that most state-run bookstores yield great souvenirs, and in the "Paying it Forward" chapter, shopping becomes a good deed at places like Vietnam Quilts, Mai Handicrafts, and Mai Tam Creations. Whether you're buying for a cause or simply to treat yourself to a memento, Vietnam—though still earning its chops as a shopping capital—offers distinctive treasures, if you know where, and how, to shop.

HANOI

Renee Friedman masters Vietnamese shopping techniques

By being in a Vietnamese workplace, I was spared the ordeal of shopping on my own in Hanoi. The big things were taken care of for me—mobile phone, DSL, maid, fridge, space heater, and even my daughter's dance classes. On the occasion of a purchase, I was simply taken to a business, shop, or street dedicated to the object of my desire. No one-stop shopping here.

In the Old Quarter, for example, the most tourist-frequented area of Hanoi, there are thirty-six different streets, each named for what is sold on it. Thus there is shoe street with the latest leather spikes copied from European designs; flower street where you turn the corner and are bombarded with brightly colored bouquets; and Hang Gai, the renowned silk street. However, when riding home from downtown, I would pass the less exotic thoroughfares like House Paint Street, Men's Dark Trousers Street, or Sheet Metal Street. I suppose this makes things simple. You go to the street that carries what you need and patronize whichever shop you or your friends have an

established relationship with. Forget the Yellow Pages. They are not available to consult and would probably not be of any use anyway. People take care of business according to who they know.

My co-workers insisted that I tell them first before any purchases were made, so I could be advised of price. Because even Vietnamese get taken advantage of if unaware of standard prices—*Viet Kieu* most of all—it is crucial to ask and be informed of going rates for just about everything before embarking on a shopping excursion. It is also the custom to reveal what you paid after the transaction is finished. My Quebecois friend has been married to a Vietnamese woman for fifteen years, and he told me he took her back to Montreal for a visit. Upon her return to Vietnam, the first thing she was queried about was the cost of products in Canada. The same goes for my husband; returning to our neighborhood with anything from blankets to beef in hand, he was often hailed with shouts of *bao nhieu*—how much? Once, I purchased a small vial of Tiger Balm outside a restaurant. After entering and being seated, the waiter came over to inquire not about my order but about how much I'd paid.

If I came to work with a new outfit, I was immediately asked the price and would either receive approving nods—if I hadn't been too ripped off—or be informed that I'd paid too much. I was told not to go too easy on the vendors when bargaining for just about anything, since they would merely view me as a "chicken," someone whose throat could be slit and bled dry, so to speak. I did my best, but never on my own did I get a great deal, nor did I expect to.

Despite Vietnam's commercial bent for selling only one thing in one place, my most prized possessions were often made serendipitously and purchased decidedly out of place, like when I collided with a pair of incredible shoes in the corner of a grocery I entered to buy toothpaste. Or an inexpensive, cheerful little print I got from a street vendor while waiting at a bus stop. I thought I'd buy it as a treat for my daughter, and I still smile every time I look at it.

While living in Vietnam, I often wondered how a country so chock full of people with such a talent for commerce and an intrinsic entrepreneurial nature managed to keep that spirit alive under Communism. Perhaps it was merely considered yet another of the many challenges of doing business. And perhaps that is the best way for a traveler to approach shopping in Vietnam, where the caveat "buyer beware" reigns supreme, but where the adventures and treasures to be had far outweigh the hassles you will encounter in your attempts to haggle for the perfect souvenir ... or vial of Tiger Balm.

Chris Mitchell promotes the art of propaganda in Hanoi

I hate shopping. So in theory Hanoi's Old Quarter would seem to be my nemesis: a maze of narrow shop houses that sell virtually everything you can imagine—silk, clothing, jewelry, housewares—and in which female travelers are guaranteed to become positively giddy at the purchasing possibilities.

In reality, the Old Quarter is one of my favorite places in the world. I've been back to Vietnam's capital city four times in the last five years because I never tire of wandering around the neighborhood's busy, crowded, constricted streets. My own fascination with these streets is not so much the shopping—although even I have to admit that the lacquerware, silks, and lanterns are quite beautifully presented—but the way in which the Old Quarter is a living, breathing part of Vietnam's history that continues to evolve right before my eyes.

For centuries, each tiny street has been dedicated to a specific craft, like shoemaking or metalwork or even masonry for tombstones. Most of them carry on with their local specialties, even as Hanoi grows as a tourist destination. What I love about the Old Quarter is that it has accommodated the influx of travelers like me during the last decade, with trinket shops and some fantastic restaurants, such as the colonially grand Green Tangerine, but at the same time its inhabitants continue with daily life much as they always have.

Life in this scenic section of town takes place on the pavement—it's here that business is conducted, friends are greeted, and families gather to eat together, sitting on the small plastic stools that are customary in Vietnam. Though not as plentiful as in years past, vendors wearing the iconic conical hats and carrying impossibly large loads balanced on their shoulders still weave in and out of the continual flow of motorbikes. For me, just walking aimlessly down the street is to be part of this kaleidoscope of noise and color that is the daily rhythm of life in Hanoi—picturesque, fascinating, noisy, and polluted too.

Despite my stated hatred of shopping, there is one store in the Old Quarter that I always visit, and that I spend hours browsing in each time. Hanoi Gallery sells hundreds of original propaganda posters and reprints from the American War. Step into the shop and you step into a time capsule of exhortations to patriotism and defeating the enemy, all under the watchful eye of Uncle Ho.

There's an initial kitsch value to browsing amongst the posters, which are stacked fifty deep and separated by cover sheets, but when flicking through them, a deeper, more sobering picture emerges of the Vietnamese struggle for survival and independence. The old lady who runs the shop might well have lived through both the French and American conflicts in Vietnam. I wonder what she thinks of all these backpackers crowding into her shop to buy these posters whose calls to arms and collective living were once taken so seriously.

Many artistic styles are at work; you will find blocky, Soviet graphic influences alongside almost impressionistic efforts. Many of these images are striking, regardless of their historical significance, and as they only cost a few dollars each, you can buy several. Ho Chi Minh crops up frequently, not surprising for the man credited as the father of the nation and who led Vietnam through the American War, although he did not live to see its independence. My favorite picture of Uncle Ho, as he's affectionately and respectfully known to the Vietnamese, is a portrait made entirely with Vietnamese stamps.

My repeat visits to Hanoi have led me to read up on Vietnamese history and culture—not just about the war, but also what has happened since its conclusion, and how the country has continued to open and transform itself. Because of this growing interest, my apartment at home is decorated with several Hanoi Gallery posters, which not only reflect Vietnam's fascinating past, but also provide proof that even for those who hate shopping, the Old Quarter still has something to offer.

Hanoi Gallery
17 Nha Chung St.
Hoan Kiem District
Hanoi

Green Tangerine
48 Hang Be St.
Hoan Kiem District
Hanoi

NORTHERN VIETNAM

Jennifer Davoli outwits Hanoi's hot, sweaty summer weather

As spring melts away and the countdown to summer begins, my anxiety about the upcoming heat reaches its peak, and I contemplate my daily survival. Sweating in early April, panicking at the thought of May, and considering an all-out escape for June, I've recognized that the heat in Hanoi is something I truly fear. Each day of this past month I challenged myself to one more "wear" of my jeans, attempting to culturally adapt to the Vietnamese norm of wearing them all summer. But my pores screamed for air, and my mind told me to get some new clothes.

To prepare for the coming heat, one Friday night I went out shopping with Yen. Yen does my eyebrows, has flawless skin and a deep, sexy voice, and can speak a sweet-sounding English, but chats away to me in Vietnamese, rarely slowing down to check my comprehension. She gives me an incredible chance to practice the language, and she understands Western and Eastern worlds—via both Western and Eastern boyfriends!

Yen took me to Vincom City Towers, a trendy, unaffordable shopping center where most locals hang out to be seen, but buy little. When she showed up at my house, I immedi-

ately felt the need to change, which was almost as common as my mispronouncing Vietnamese words. Over the course of my year in Vietnam, I had discovered that the loose, cotton Gap tops I wore were too plain and unfitting for the young age I appeared to be, the H&M polyester pants and tees unbearable in the heat, and my Ann Taylor sweater tops too formal for day-to-day work. But with Yen's sense of style now in charge, I was sure to find suitable replacements.

I found nothing. Nothing, that is, that fit.

Ah, to fit; to fit in; to fit in tees. Cute tees—that is, hip tees—worn with jeans: a classic Vietnamese outfit. The problem: my bones. There was more than one occasion when I explained, in my choppy Vietnamese, "I'm not fat, just big-boned," and I meant it. People in the United States drink fresh milk, in varying forms, whereas in Vietnam it's mother's milk as an infant and a spoonful of the condensed sweet stuff with coffee as an adult.

Shopping with Yen, though, I understood that I'd somehow managed during the past twelve months to delude myself. So accustomed to the petite size of every body frame around me, I'd developed the perception that I too looked like everyone else, oblivious to the fact that I was in no way, shape, or form the size of a Vietnamese woman—anyone a size greater than an American six is off the charts. Women in Vietnam are truly small, and fitting myself into the clothes sold here, a truly impossible feat.

In desperation, the next day, I headed to a more Westernized boutique, in the hope that things would, literally, fall into place. I tried on fifteen tops that I could not breathe in, only to verify that my shoulders were indeed broad, my chest hearty, and my tummy far from flat. My ego crumbled, and I reconsidered my perspective: H&M polyester wasn't sooooo bad.

But I couldn't convince myself, especially since I no longer cared for my old Western style of dressing. Since my arrival in Hanoi, the younger Vietnamese had had a strong positive influence on my fashion sense, freeing me from preppy, pushing me toward punk. Some young women were incredibly hip; it didn't hurt that a few wore big black shades while riding on cute white-and-pink Italian Vespas. The young men looked like they were right out of MTV: spiked, gelled-up hair, and bright, floral button-downs with jewelry to boot. They were unafraid of fashion and spending time on their appearances.

But style was not the main issue right now. I wasn't as worried about style as I was about heat. And so I took myself on my bike, against all local warnings, to the infamous Cho Hom, an open-air fabric market where one *must* bargain for all sales. Bargaining as an ex-pat, my Vietnamese friends informed me, was not to be done alone here no matter what your fluency in Vietnamese. Because of my busy schedule, however, I was forced to fight for cotton and linen, sans advocate. I haggled hard and successfully, exiting with enough material to make four blouses, a pair of linen pants, and a cute black linen dress.

The tailoring process involved three tailors, in three different locations. The first, well known in the ex-pat crowd, had me wait an hour for my fitting and two weeks for my pickup, and charged high prices. But because of his friendliness and the high recommendations, I put my immediate heat panic aside and ordered a top and a dress. That evening, a rail-thin ex-pat fluent in Vietnamese recommended a local shop with better prices. Arriving with some doubt as to how my curves would be handled, I realized how much more comfortable I was in an authentic Vietnamese setting, as well as how much more reasonable prices could be. In just two days, I had two tops and new material for another; still, it should be noted that it took three additional fitting sessions to get the tops to hang just right—all this in a non-air conditioned space. A final, third shop did my pants. Divorced from her husband and supporting her family, the owner had done some work for me earlier in the year, with prices that were sensible and service that was fast. The only problem was that she too had a misperception of my size. The pants looked hip, but the bottom tugged tight.

The following weekend, on my next visit with Yen to Vincom Towers, I donned a new tailored top with my new snug pants and made my way into the shopping center, purely for show. Going out with Yen, a model by any standard, proved to test the strength of my self-esteem, considering the new self-awareness I had recently gained about my body. Fortunately, a little MAC lipstick

NORTHERN VIETNAM

NORTHERN VIETNAM

and FACE eyeshadow can raise the confidence level quickly.

Yen wowed, big-eyed, "Oi! You look pretty," and I responded in classic Vietnamese, "No, I'm not pretty. I'm ugly." This, another "style" of the Vietnamese, somehow made me feel better. You see, for a moment I did fit in, since I knew what exactly to say. And if Yen thought I looked good, well then, I must have looked all right. For an instant, forgetting heat, body, and appearance in Vietnam, I kicked back, and smiled. Fabric cost: $15. Sewing cost: $40. A bargain for finally fitting, and fitting in.

Vincom City Towers

191 Ba Trieu St.
Hai Ba Trung District
Hanoi
www.vincom.com.vn

Tan Hung Tailor

Many Westerners use this tailor, since he's accustomed to Western body sizes and shapes. Keep in mind the longer wait times, both in the store and while having clothes made. Also, prices are higher.

17 Hang Be St.
Hoan Kiem District
Hanoi

Hang Nga Tailor

If you need anything fixed or simply taken out, this family-owned shop is as friendly and quick as it gets. Beware of having anything taken in though, as everything I had done seemed to run a little tighter than I wanted.

45 Mai Hac De St. (a block south of Cho Hom market)
Hai Ba District
Hanoi

Nguyen Style

The tailor here is Vu Thai Ha (first name: Ha). If you can speak a little Vietnamese or make a Vietnamese friend who can translate, this is your best deal—she's very kind, as are her two helpers. The street this shop is on is small and difficult to find, but the search is worth it.

01 Pham Su Manh St.
Hoan Kiem District
Hanoi
(84-4) 255-829

Cho Hom

In this famous open-air market, you can buy fabrics for tailoring much cheaper than in the Old Quarter. It runs nearly an entire block between Tran Xuan Soan and Le Van Huu Streets. You can also shop for silks on the well-known Hang Bong Street, not far from Hoan Kiem Lake.

Simone Samuels goes boutique shopping with the girls in Hanoi

"Which ring do you like best? This one ... or this one?"

"That one! Which pendant do you

think suits me—the big one or small one?"

"Ummm ... the small one."

"Maybe I'll take both!"

"Oh God, get us out of here before I spend all my money!"

This is the dialogue that the assistant at my favorite silver jewelry shop overheard as she silently popped our newly chosen wares into small, individual jewelry pouches, before she handed our new, shiny silver jewelry to us. My two girlfriends and I are such regulars that we get instant discounts, without even having to barter. The silversmith is always in the shop, and whenever I find something that doesn't quite fit or isn't exactly what I need, she's happy to remind me that she'll copy anything or adjust per my request.

On this particular day, Huong Jewellery Shop was our last stop in an afternoon of full-on shopping, which was launched with late lunch at Puku, where I'd totally lucked out with vegetarian lasagna—the last piece left in the glass counter cabinet. I'd washed down the delicious, creamy, vegetably goodness with a big glass of refreshingly acerbic passion fruit juice, without a doubt the best from any café in Hanoi. After we had a girly catch-up on the couches in our home away from home, we ducked out of the narrow alley and meandered down Hang Trong Street, casually window shopping.

When we reached my favorite little boutique, I dragged my friends in. Oh, how I just love the clothes and accessories at Kana. The colorful cotton fabrics and East-meets-West designs

are so cute and really affordable. There's always a half-price rack that I delve into, rummaging for a bargain, and when I find something that's not in my size, I know I can get measured and pick what I want up in two day's time ... and that it will fit just right. On this occasion, I walked out—yet again—with a new, Vietnamese-style, handmade top in a feminine floral fabric; my friends fell in love with a handbag and some cute hand-crafted earrings. The friendly staff joked that they'd see me next week.

We continued to enjoy the sunny Hanoi afternoon, that time of day when the city always seems at its best, by walking down Hang Gai Street until we reached the end and another favorite shop for designer clothes, Ma Ena Xanh. The fashionable and funky boutique always tempts me, and on this day I managed to find a pair of pants right off the rack. Couldn't resist their snug fit and just-me style, so I completely splurged and bought them on a whim. My girlfriends seemed to have a little more self-control. But I attempted to rationalize such purchases by arguing that I could not afford boutique clothes at home.

After we finished clothes shopping, we took the pleasant stroll down Hang Dao toward Huong Jewellery, which we affectionately and simply refer to as "the silver shop." Cheap clothing shops are crammed in along both sides of the street, and they're generally hives of activity. We did not even bother browsing, because even though the clothes are cheap, they are ready-made only in local sizes and don't fit Westerners. For me, as I've discovered after many disappointing shopping ventures, it's worth it to pay a little more at the boutique stores so as not to feel frustrated or depressed when the one-size-fits-all top or an XXL-size skirt doesn't even come close to fitting.

Size, however, is rarely a problem when it comes to jewelry, and the trays of tempting, shiny rings, earrings, pendants, broaches, and bracelets are always enticing. We seem to select things here in a frenzy and flurry, as if we are afraid we'll miss our chance if we don't choose quickly. On this occasion, after the decision-making was done, we were tired. We had all spent more money than we'd planned, so we decided to enjoy a cool, refreshing, cheap-at-2,000-VND-per-glass, fresh draught beer on plastic stools in perfect people-watching positions ... until the night market began at six, and I had to hold back my friends from buying cheap shoes which sadly (or luckily) didn't come big enough for my feet.

Huong Jewellery Shop

62 Hang Ngang St.
Hoan Kiem District
Hanoi

Kana

41 Hang Trong St.
Hoan Kiem District
Hanoi
www.shiva.com.vn/web/kana

Ma Ena Xanh

40 Hang Gai St.
Hoan Kiem District
Hanoi

Puku

50 Hang Trong St.
Hoan Kiem District
Hanoi

Bia Hoi Junction

At the convergence of Luong Ngoc Quyen, Dinh Liet, and Ta Hien Streets in the Old Quarter, there are numerous stalls selling cheap *bia hoi* (fresh draught beer) at the roadside. It's a good idea to keep track of the beers you drink, or to pay as you go, to avoid problems with the tab when you're ready to leave.

Night Market

Every Friday, Saturday, and Sunday night sees Hang Dao Street converted into a pedestrian-only night market. Mostly for sale are cheap clothes, cheap shoes, fake designer sunglasses, and other small souvenir items.

Preyanka Clark Prakash sees glamour in being a Hanoi bag lady

I remember my first addictive encounter with Ipa-Nima handbags.

I was sixteen and shopping for a purse for my junior prom at the United Nations International School of Hanoi. I walked into the fantastical aviary of beaded and brocade delights, and moving from shelf to shelf, rack to rack, I coaxed each colorful specimen into the palm of my hand until finally I found the one I wanted. It was made of silk taffeta, both pink and purple, and emblazoned with gold brocade. But what made it irresistible was its whimsical fringe. It looked as if it could take flight at any moment. I clutched it and walked to the counter, ready to pay whatever was required to take it home, until my friend tapped me ever so gently on the shoulder and whispered, "Do you really think that's going to go with your black dress?"

I snapped out of my trance and sulked as I returned the extraordinary purse to its perch. Though I had lost interest in my original mission, I managed to find the store's sole black-beaded clutch, hanging forlornly between embroidered velvet, neon feathers, and glittering tulle. I put aside my then-vegan aversion to the bone handle and purchased it before the other multicolored temptations drove me mad.

But my reluctant adoption—the black crow among Ipa-Nima's peacocks—took glorious flight on the May night of my prom. Its beads shone brilliantly beneath the disco ball, and it put every ghastly polyester and vinyl creation carried by my peers to shame. I'll be forever convinced that its dark charm and nothing else won me the best-dressed award that night.

Over the years, Ipa-Nima has gone from a small store of playful creations, all the creative offspring of former Hong Kong litigator, Christina Yu, to a worldwide fashion sensation, a label featured in top magazines such as *Vogue* and *InStyle*, and sported by everyone from Princess Victoria of Sweden to actress Cate Blanchett. Naturally, prices have been raised to suit the brand's status.

Thankfully though, while Ipa-Nima may have put Hanoi's handbag scene on the fashion map, it certainly isn't the only place to find a distinctly Hanoian purse. In the Old Quarter, Hang Gai, Ly Quoc Su, and Nha Tho Streets are lined with small boutiques that sell handbags ranging from the simple and elegant to the intricate and ornate. The prices are still rather expensive by Vietnamese standards, but the quality is consistent.

Another more adventurous way to find the perfect handbag is to visit the Van Phuc Silk Village, the source of the many different kinds of silks used to make the purses sold in Hanoi and elsewhere in Vietnam. Whether you browse Ipa-Nima, stroll through the shops on Hang Gai Street, or venture out of town to the Silk Village, you're sure to find a handbag that you'll want to clutch as tightly—and happily—as the one I did when I was sixteen.

Ipa-Nima
34 Han Thuyen St.
Hai Ba Trung District
Hanoi
www.ipa-nima.com

Van Phuc Silk Village

Located about fifteen kilometers southwest of Hanoi, Van Phuc has been producing silk for centuries. Today, though it's heavily touristed, it still offers an interesting glimpse into a long-standing tradition—as well as a look at the Vietnamese custom of entire villages manufacturing a single product.

Kathrine Hee Nielsen frequents her favorite Hanoi ceramics shop

As I leave my house this beautiful, damp, Hanoi winter morning, the bicycle guy on the corner gives me a little nod. He is my favorite person in the city. When I go to work, he sits quietly, leaning against the trunk of a tree, observing traffic, and waiting for customers in need of a quick bicycle tune-up. A good eight hours later, when I cross the street to return, he gives another nod to welcome me. It makes me feel at home, and this morning his friendly gesture sets me in a sparkling mood while I make my way up the street. I pass three *xe om* drivers hanging out on the corner and politely say no to their offers of a ride. My destination is only a few minutes' walk away.

I cross the rails where kids are playing and pass the area where the bulb and lamp shops are. The next street can only be described as a niche street. Here you can get a new seat cover for your moto if it needs sprucing up. Different designs are neatly displayed, hanging from the ceilings in the front of the shops. The route is narrow and there's no sidewalk, so every now and then I have to jump to avoid being hit by a motorbike. Sometimes it feels like I'm the character in a computer game, trying to avoid all the dangers in order to get to the hidden treasure.

At the end of this road, women with baskets filled with lush fruits are squatting in front of the entrance of Hang Da Market. One of them offers me a strawberry, and the taste of summer fills my mouth, but this is not what I'm here for today. Still, I make a note to buy some on the way out.

The market is quite dark and smelly, and you'll probably see a few rats while inside. And the food section is not for squeamish souls. I pass the butchers' area where flies gather around the freshly chopped meat. I haven't quite gotten used to the pigs' feet, but I'm sure I'll get there at some point. The butchers' section turns into a seafood section. In the plastic basins around my feet, fish are swimming around waiting to become the day's dinner. If you look closely, though, you'll find some of them aren't fish, but snakes. There are also turtles and toads in a net. And frogs stripped of their skin. I glance to the vegetable section. The colors are striking, and the smell is a lot better than where the pigs' feet are.

Finally, I reach my favorite shop, and its keeper and her daughter smile at me. They know me already and let me look around before approaching me—that's one of the reasons this is my favorite stall. The market has a whole ceramics section, and if I wanted to, I could easily shop around a bit, but in Vietnam I've come to value the opportunity to browse without having a shop assistant breathing down my neck all the time. It's bliss.

The tables, shelves, and floor are covered with ceramics. Though the stall isn't big, somehow it seems you can get any item you can think of, in any shape, size, or color. Yes, I know, most people go out to the village of Bat Trang to buy their pottery, but I find the prices and the variety much better here. It's all made in Bat Trang, of course, and here you won't get to see how the pottery is made, but you'll have the benefit of shopping in peace without a bunch of tourist buses to accompany you.

They both look young, the shopkeeper and her daughter, but the daughter has told me that she's eighteen. She eagerly points to the squared, black dinner plates I bought the last time. I smile back and tell her that I'm looking for something else today. I want to pick up a present for a friend back home. I consider buying a beige tea set. The pot has a bamboo handle, and the matching cups fit perfectly into my hand. Although they're beautiful, I had something more "Vietnamese" in mind. My eye catches a basket on the floor. It is filled with soup spoons neatly decorated with ornaments and figures.

The shopkeeper is quick to spot my interest and points to a red plastic stool, offering me a seat. I sit down with the basket on my knees and look through a variety of spoons. I suspect they're hand-painted, since no two seem exactly alike. After thorough consideration, I opt for eight different spoons in the same greenish shade, but with different motifs; one has a dragon, another has a tiny goldfish painted on it, some have lotus flowers, and others a pattern. I hand my choices to the shopkeeper's daughter, and she wraps them neatly in old newspapers and puts them in a mini basket that serves as a bag. I pay the mum, and once again I leave this market a satisfied shopper—but not before stopping for some strawberries on my way out.

Hang Da Market

The market is located on Hang Da Street in the Old Quarter. If you enter from Hang Da, turn right. My favorite stall is the second one on the right.

Bonus tip for the ladies

On the other side of the market is Duong Thanh Street. Walking toward Phung Hung Street, you'll find a tiny nail shop on your left hand side a few houses out from the market. It'll set you back less than $5 to have your nails painted in the most decorative patterns you can imagine. None of the staff speaks English, but there are quite a few books with nail designs, and pointing while smiling will do the trick.

Bat Trang Ceramic Village

Popular on the tourist circuit, Bat Trang is located about ten kilometers southeast of Hanoi. Along with shopping, you can watch craftspeople prepare the clay; shape, carve, and glaze items; and put them into the kiln.

HUE

Duong Lam Anh gets more than he bargained for in Hue

Frankly speaking, I just can't bargain. I'm very bad at remembering numbers; I cannot do calculations in my head. (I always need a pen and paper.) I almost never go to the market, as I am truly afraid of having to negotiate. All I can do is inquire, with a blushing face, "Is that the real price?" I know before I ask, however, what the answer will be: "Of course it is." More often than not, I end up paying a higher price than my sister does for the same items. Anyway, I prefer shopping in a quiet supermarket or a store with fixed price goods. People there walk along the aisles looking for what they want, reading price tags, putting items in carts, lining up at checkout counters, paying,

and leaving. All in order and silence.

For most of my life, the purpose of bargaining was a mystery to me. Until one day ....

I went to a lecture by an American professor. After speaking about how he liked that Vietnamese banknotes are decorated with pictures of interesting places all over the country, he observed the way Vietnamese people buy and sell things in the market—he called it "life." He found life in this process that was so agonizing to me, and I found his thought fascinating.

I began to observe my mother. She is old, and her weak legs prevent her from going to the market every day for food as she used to, and I know, deep in her heart, she really misses it. She has a keen memory and is good at buying things. Her ability to do calculations in her mind, despite her old age, is admirable. But she cannot go out a lot these days (except when necessary and when we are free to carry her on our motorbikes), and so she buys almost everything from home—fresh fruits, veggies, flowers, spices, even breakfast in the morning and snacks in the afternoon.

Street vendors drop by my house daily, bringing their wares. I notice that they sell to the neighbors too, but very quickly—just a few exchanges, and then they leave. But they stay longer at my house. Also, here in Vietnam, people believe that the first person who buys an item each day may bring good or bad luck to the seller, and that is why sellers usually choose a particular person to be their first buyer. The vendors in my neighborhood always select my mother.

They come to sell things, but they also talk with her. By bargaining and chatting, my mother does more than make small talk. She develops good relationships with the vendors. She questions the higher price of an item, and the seller explains the reason why; she decides not to buy it and explains why, and through this process, whole stories unfold. She and the vendors are not just transacting; they are sharing their living experiences. Their conversations drift to traffic, economy, politics—almost everything that has to do with day-to-day life. I now see that my mother is kept informed of the news that way.

Sometimes, my mother bargains not just to reduce the price; she makes sure she is getting value for her money. Every now and then, she is willing to buy something at a higher price if it is really good quality, and she feels that it's worth it. My mother is rather picky about foods. She always wants to be the first person to choose from a selection, and she is prepared to pay more for that. But the most interesting thing is that she buys in a way that both she and the seller feel satisfied. Gradually, I came to the realization that, for my mother, this routine affair is entertaining for her, and she feels sad on the days that the street vendors do not drop by.

That professor is right. Life is all there in bargaining. But despite learning this, I still hate bargaining because I don't feel comfortable doing it. I still enjoy buying things from

a shop where prices are announced loud and clear, where people buy and sell things in silence—no haggling, no joking, not even any loud talking. Still, I understand the importance of bargaining, and I realize why Vietnam's big markets like Dong Ba, Dong Xuan, and Ben Thanh cannot be replaced with closed, air-conditioned supermarkets. Put simply: to shut them down would be to shut down Vietnamese life itself.

Hoi An

Joanna Blundell falls into a shopping frenzy in Hoi An

I am a woman who loves to shop. I can shop for anything, but I especially like buying clothes, music, books, and, as I've recently discovered, silk lanterns. This odd revelation came upon me while I was traveling through Hoi An, tucked halfway up the S-shaped curve of Vietnam. I first learned about it during a trip to Fiji, from a girl whose face lit up as she described to me the wondrous shopping mecca of this ancient village. She said I could get all sorts of dresses, shirts, and pants tailored to my specifications, and, more importantly, they were unbelievably cheap. After months of anticipation, I was certainly not disappointed when I finally arrived.

Hoi An used to be an important international port, until the mouth of the Thu Bon river silted up in the late nineteenth century, cutting it off from the sea. Before that, an exotic mix of Chinese, Japanese, French, Dutch, and Portuguese merchants gathered there to trade fine silks, paper, and porcelain, as well as foodstuffs and Oriental medicines. While I had not come to trade, I did plan to participate in the frenzied consumerism that is a hallmark of the town. People now come to buy artwork, faux antiques, lamps, and handbags. Mostly, though, they come to buy clothes. There are countless tailor shops, all displaying fabric from floor to ceiling and littered with well-fingered copies of *Vogue* and *Elle*.

On the morning of my arrival, I encountered a young girl on the bridge that spans the Thu Bon River and leads into town. She mentioned that she had a dress stall in the market. Would I like to come and have a look? Since I had come to shop and shop some more, I agreed, though I warned her that I would just be browsing. I quickly realized that there is no such thing as "just browsing" in Hoi An. Before I could pause to collect my thoughts, I was standing with arms stretched wide, being outfitted for a blouse and a top.

With my appetite whetted, I went to bed early to prepare myself for my big day of shopping. As I tried to sleep, my mind filled with images

of various fabrics and fashions and cuts. How much to get made? Where to get it made? What to get for my friends? Could they send me their measurements in time?

Making my way toward town the next day, I lumbered down to the muddy silt on the river's edge where an old Vietnamese woman sat on a flat wooden boat, madly gesticulating at me. The early morning sun played brightly on the water as we bargained awkwardly, holding out notes and pointing to numbers. We agreed on a price and she grinned, exposing teeth stained from years of chewing betel nut. I clambered in and she punted the boat across the brown waters.

I hurried through to the Old Quarter, where the streets were quiet and still. For an hour I walked around, trying to clear my head of my fevered dreams. I strolled past countless art galleries. Every corner seemed to reveal a treasure. There are still vestiges of the presence of international tradesmen from hundreds of years ago. I stumbled across numerous Chinese assembly halls and a bridge built by the Japanese in the sixteenth century, which arches prettily over a ribbon of water. The most obvious influence is that of the colonial French, who rebuilt great swaths of the city after its virtual destruction during the Tay Son rebellion of the 1700s. Wandering through the quiet streets I was charmed by Hoi An's narrow buildings, which seemed to have been frozen in time. Muted yellows, blues, and reds, washed onto the rough plaster walls, contrasted with the dark wooden shop fronts and captured the sun's hot rays. Many buildings had balconies of wood or finely wrought iron, some draped in greenery. I joined the locals along the pavement, crouching on a tiny plastic chair as I drank freshly percolated coffee served with condensed milk.

Fortified with caffeine and sugar, I ventured forth to one of the larger tailor shops I had seen the previous day. It had been recommended in guidebooks, and besides, there were gorgeous winter coats in its front display. I wandered in and was greeted warmly; I was their first customer of the day. Despite the sticky heat, I was soon wrapped up in a long coat, issuing details on how I wanted my own made. A few hours later, I had my coat as well as a suit and some blouses ordered, and my first fitting appointment scheduled for later that afternoon. I decided to move on. A waiter at our hotel, in defiance of his boss who had a tailor shop, had covertly recommended my next destination. Here I ordered a skirt and matching top in one of the many Chinese silks on offer.

That is pretty much how I spent all my time in Hoi An, intensive days of appointments and fittings from early morning until sometimes ten in the evening, interspersed only with quick coffees and drop-offs at the hotel. I am truly in awe of my own shopping capabilities. The result was a beautiful new wardrobe of tailored, one-of-a-kind clothes: suits, dresses, coats, trousers, and shoes. Such

treasures, along with a few of Hoi An's signature silk lanterns, made the prospect of returning to an English winter seem almost appealing. And those five days were fantastic fun, a budget backpacker's version of *Lifestyles of the Rich and Famous.*

Editor's recommendations for shopping in Hoi An

Trinh 95

Along with my sister and best Vietnamese girlfriend Huong, I plundered this shop. Among the three of us, we had ten skirts made (feminine cotton skirts with embroidered patterns along the hem), as well as numerous other items. The fabric quality was good, something that's not always the case, especially when you're getting a bargain that seems too good to be true.

95 Phan Chu Trinh St.
(84-510) 862-457

Quang Trung

The woman who runs this purse shop is genuinely hospitable. Her designs are unique, and everything we bought from her has lasted, unlike items from some other places.

2C Nhi Trung St.
(84-510) 910-616

Lac Thu

As my sister wrote in her journal, this shawl and scarf shop is "touchy feely, quite pushy, but good prices." The sales staff doesn't have much awareness of personal space, but they offered great bulk deals when we bought shawls for nearly every friend and family member back home.

115 Nguyen Thai Hoc St.
(84-510) 910-876

HO CHI MINH CITY

Michael Burr focuses on country life in Ho Chi Minh City

One of my top spots for taking in local color is the Ton That Dam street market in central Ho Chi Minh City. I happened on this market during one of my "wanders," and it's become one of my favorite places to shoot. I've found the people very warm, friendly, and receptive—a bonus for a professional photographer. One of the great things about shooting digital is that you can show the subject his/her photo on the camera monitor. This invariably invokes peals of laughter as others crowd around to look and poke fun at the subject. It's a real icebreaker, and then I always get lots of volunteers to have *their* picture taken. It's fun, and I come away with great shots.

What I like most about Ton That Dam is that it's a little bit of the countryside in the heart of Vietnam's largest metropolis, and it's a great alternative to the heavily touristed Ben Thanh Market. No cars or trucks are allowed on Ton That Dam Street, but there is plenty of motorbike and bicycle traffic so ... watch out! Here you can find all manner of things for sale: clothing, medicine, liquor, cigarettes, books, magazines, CDs/DVDs (pirated, of course), hardware, pots, pans, and other household items, and, of course, comestibles. The fresh food vendors are my favorite attraction, as their wares make for interesting subject matter.

A cornucopia of everything that is grown and consumed in Vietnam is here, from ordinary fresh fruits and vegetables, such as bananas, carrots, and broccoli, to the exotic: durian, mangosteen, and rambutan, my personal favorite. The stalls are literally overflowing with produce, a testament to Vietnam's increasing prosperity. You will find them lining the center of the street, usually tended by women of all ages. Like most other enterprises in Vietnam, these are family affairs, so it is not uncommon to encounter three generations working side-by-side.

A riot of colors and shapes greets the eye at every turn, much of it arranged as if just waiting for the arrival of a photographer. In front of you is a vast array of exotic fruits, and when you turn around, there is a rice stall displaying more varieties than you ever thought existed.

I stopped counting at thirty. A little farther down is the meat, poultry, and seafood section. If this is your first experience of an Asian market, you will no doubt be shocked. Big shanks of pork and beef are hanging from hooks under the canopies. The tables are covered with the usual cuts of muscle meat, along with all types of internal bits: tripe, liver, kidney, intestine, heart, tongue, etc. There are also whole pig heads, plus severed ears and feet. In front of the stalls are baskets full of bones with scant flesh still on them.

At the poultry stands are whole chickens and ducks, as well as butchered birds with all their internal organs and cut-off feet on display. And in the seafood stalls, there is a large variety of whole and cut fish, along with squid, octopus, and crab. Near your feet you will see large aluminum pans filled with live fish in water, oxygenated by air pumped in through a plastic hose. Oops! Almost forgot to mention: there is no refrigeration, and everything is covered with flies. The best it gets is a few blocks of ice placed on top of the seafood or poultry. As for combating the flies, there is a dedicated "fly chaser" at many stalls. Her equipment consists of a plastic bag taped to one end of a stick, which is waved over the meat/poultry/fish to chase the aerial invaders away. Reasonably effective.

The market is always busy, but the best times to visit are in the early morning or late afternoon. Many Vietnamese are accustomed to buying fresh ingredients for nearly every meal, so this is when most people are shopping. Plus it's a little bit cooler. Between ten and three, the sun is high in the sky, and the market can be brutally hot, especially for the uninitiated. Mornings and afternoons are the best times for photography, as well, though you will need a flash to shoot under the canopies. The place is also quite fascinating at night, since there is a lot of activity at the food stalls, and most of the illumination is stark and theatrical, provided by bare incandescent bulbs and fluorescent lamps.

Ton That Dam Market

Ton That Dam is a short street that intersects Ham Nghi Boulevard, one of Ho Chi Minh City's main thoroughfares in District One. The market is between Ham Nghi and Huynh Thuc Khang Street.

INTO THE WILD

Outdoor experiences for adventurous travelers.

In my experience, Vietnam is not a place where travelers often wander far from the beaten path. I think the country is a bit to blame. It has such a manageable, serpentine shape, enticing you oh so comfortably from Hanoi to Ho Chi Minh City. Along the way, you will likely flow through the old imperial capital of Hue, the World Heritage town of Hoi An, the beach city of Nha Trang, and the hill town of Dalat. Sure, if you have some extra time in your three-week itinerary, you might make a side trip to Sapa or Halong Bay in the north, or overnight in the Mekong Delta in the south. In general, though, the route—which feels custom-made for travel—seldom veers.

I'm not a critic of this approach, since I think that Vietnam's tried-and-true destinations have great appeal, with their exceptional food, historical attractions, and, of course, the country's greatest treasure—the people. I also suspect that many travelers don't realize how accessible Vietnam's wilderness areas are. When Paul Young writes about hiking Fansipan Mountain, the highest peak in Indochina, he is a describing a destination only a few kilometers from the tourist hub of Sapa. In this same region, Iris Opdebeeck explores unspoiled natural beauty as she treks among the outlying hill tribe villages. For those whose tight schedules don't have room for such excursions, Simone Samuels illustrates how easy it is to slip away from Hanoi for just a day with a motorcycle ride to Ba Vi Mountain.

Given that Vietnam has more than eighty national parks, it's easy to find a wilderness area to fit into your itinerary. In Halong Bay, Jeff Greenwald visits a langur conservation project on Cat Ba Island. Outside Hue, Emily Huckson takes a day trip to the mystical caves at Phong Nha-Ke Bang National Park. Near Dalat and Phan Thiet, respectively, Richard Craik and Marc Moynot discover excellent birding. And north of Nha Trang, Alice Driver mixes relaxation with adventure at the Jungle Beach Resort. If you're looking for a less than

conventional experience, you can follow Marc's lead and hang glide over the Dalat Plateau, or check out Adam Bray's suggestion to sled the dramatic white sand dunes of Mui Ne. Other extreme escapes include Jessy Needham's adventure into the desolate Cao Bang region on the Chinese Border, and Jon Hoff's attempts to understand the oddities of the Con Dao Islands off the country's southern tip.

It's also important to keep in mind that "wild" can describe your mode of transportation as well as your destination. Adventure junkies will be inspired by Graham Roemmele's tour of mountainous northwest Vietnam on a Russian-made Minsk motorcycle. He is in good company, since the country has numerous ex-pat motorcycling clubs, including one with a twist, which is described by Hal Phillips, who travels from Phan Thiet to Dalat in the sidecar of a Ural M-72. Not everyone (including me), though, is up for the perils of developing-country back roads. But that's not a problem in Vietnam. You can dip your toe into the wilderness experience with a leisurely day trip or go whole hog on a weeklong motorcycle expedition. When it comes to getting back to nature, where and how is entirely up to you.

CAT BA ISLAND

Jeff Greenwald stalks the elusive langur of Cat Ba Island

"There are no guarantees," says Rosi, "that you will see even one langur the whole time you are on Cat Ba Island."

Sure, I nod, I understand, I get it—but I don't get it. True, it was a full four months before Cat Ba Langur Conservation Project director, Rosi Stenke, saw her first langur. But Sally Keith, a British volunteer, saw a group of seven her first *day*. And Seacology executive director, Duane Silverstein, saw one on a three-day visit. I'm convinced that I will too, Rosi's caveat to the contrary notwithstanding.

Rosi, Sally, Mr. Hung (Rosi's assistant), and I meet at the national park headquarters at 6 a.m. and throttle off on 110cc scooters to the harbor at Phu Long, on the island's northwest shore. There we meet Mr. Tranh, another of Rosi's three first-rank langur guardians. Tranh's shrimp and fish farm will be the starting point for the day's trek into langur territory. We climb aboard his noisy wooden motorboat. Navigating narrow, shallow channels that are impassible at low tide, it takes a long hour to reach his remote farm.

Many of the 366 islands in the Cat Ba archipelago were formerly connected by mangrove swamps, but shrimp and fish farming changed that. We'll be visiting several sites on nearby Dong Cong Island, possible haunts of the three female langurs that were marooned on Dong Cong when the mangroves were cut to build seafood farms. As part of her job, Sally (who holds a master's degree in primate conservation from Oxford) will be returning to Dong Cong alone, for weeks at a time. She'll habituate the langurs to her presence, find out where they sleep, and help create a strategy for moving them back among the breeding groups on Cat Ba Island.

Farms separated by long, narrow mud dams link Tranh's compound with Dong Cong. We set off on foot, followed by barking dogs. Mr. Hung cuts us walking sticks, and we begin the precarious journey across the dikes. On either side lies deep, muddy water. The tide is still high, and the dams are broken in several places. We sink to our shins in wet, stinky mud, which tries with all its might to suck the sneakers off our feet. One break is patched with mud-covered planks; they're as slippery as greased glass. I move very slowly. One false step and I'll be in the soup: binoculars, notebooks, camera, and all.

There are at least three areas called Frog Valley on Dong Cong, all separated by ridges; the elusive langurs might be in any of them. Part of the day's plan is to give newcomer Sally Keith (and me) a taste of jungle walking. As we leave the dike and begin our first ascent, Rosi hands us each a pair of leather gardening gloves. The limestone rocks—ancient coral reefs uplifted by seismic activity—bristle with points and edges so sharp they can be used to cut meat.

We reach a low perch overlooking the first Frog Valley, and spend fifteen minutes scanning for signs of activity. Nothing. Off to the next. The valleys are separated by rocky notches, which we reach by thrashing through dry undergrowth, squishing between stray mangroves, tripping over long roots, and climbing up calcified reefs. When we reach the overlook between the second and third valleys, Rosi sheds her daypack. This, she announces, is our best bet for seeing langurs.

It's difficult to find a perch. There are hundreds of stones, and not one of them has anything resembling a suitable sitting surface. Unless you have climbed over this limestone karst, wearing leather gloves and watching your sneakers being shredded, you can have no idea how sharp they really are. Visualize being a swami and sitting on a bed of nails. Better still, visualize sitting on a bed of nails without possessing the mind-over-matter of a swami.

Time passes. Fifteen minutes; an hour; two; three. There are loads of butterflies. Most of them have brilliant blue wings dotted with white specks. (There are no frogs; I guess it's too early.) There are ants, lizards, and starlings. There are wasps the size of single-engine aircraft. I'm convinced that if we had been looking for any of these things they would

of course be absent, and the jungle would be teeming with langurs.

At one point, there's hope. A hoarse call is heard from the jungle, near the top of a relatively nearby cliff. "Shhhh!" exclaims Rosi. "Langurs!" But it is a troupe of rhesus macaques, half a dozen that we can see, commanding the high ground. Though it's a treat to see any primate in the wild, this sighting contains a kernel of disappointment. The presence of these other monkeys makes it very unlikely that the three female langurs are nearby.

We continue to wait.

This, Rosi informs me, is what field research is all about: long hours sitting in the jungle, waiting to see something, or waiting to see something *do* something. "And always keeping your eyes and ears open," says Rosi. There's more: brushing off red ants, waving away mosquitoes, listening to the birds, watching butterflies. It's not bad, really. But one does hope to see something.

Three o'clock—the final window during which the primates might be active—comes and goes without a sign of the langurs.

"I'm about ready," I say, "to declare this a langur-free zone."

Rosi agrees; we have to return to Tranh's in time for an early dinner. Regretfully, we make our way back through the jungle, over the rocks, across the muddy dams. It's the first clear day I've seen in Vietnam, and the surrounding islets glow in the afternoon light.

"Where are you?" Rosi asks the invisible langurs, somewhere in the nearby jungle. "Are you up there, studying *us*?" More than once, she and her researchers have spent an entire day in an apparently fruitless search for the animals, only to pack up and find the langurs resting in trees less than twenty meters away, watching *them*. "Like television," she adds, dryly.

As I writer, I crave such a flourish. How sweet it would be to end this story with a last-minute langur sighting: a golden head popping through the tree cover; a tail hanging from a high perch; a Busby Berkeley number with the langurs in top hats.

But there are only three langurs on Dong Cong: females, not gregarious males. The island may be small, but there are a lot of places to hide. My only hope, dear reader, is that if you ever visit Dong Cong in search of Cat Ba langurs, your success will be all the more sweet for my failure. But don't bet the farm on seeing anything. Bring plenty of water, insect repellent, and a Dostoevsky novel.

Cat Ba Langur Conservation Project

The conservation website also includes information about traveling to Cat Ba Island, which is located southwest of Halong Bay in northern Vietnam.

www.catbalangur.org

Saving the langur

The Seacology Foundation is helping to pay for the work I witnessed on Cat Ba Island. Check out the or-

ganization's website to learn more and donate to the preservation of the endangered langur. On this site you can also find an additional essay about the situation of the endangered langur. Click on *news*, then *archived*, and then the links to my pieces in April 2006.

www.seacology.org

Success at last

On my final afternoon, on a peninsula in Cat Ba Bay with Rosi and Mr. Hung, I finally spotted a langur. We saw six in all, including a female holding a bright orange baby across her shoulder. True, they were too far away to photograph; it was kind of like seeing the Rolling Stones from the bleachers at Candlestick Park. But I'm not complaining.

CAO BANG

Jessy Needham encounters riches in impoverished Cao Bang

I wanted my first Tet in Vietnam to be memorable, so after several days spent visiting colleagues and students, drinking innumerable cups of tea, and attempting pleasantries in my rudimentary Vietnamese, I decided to spend the rest of the Lunar New Year holidays in Cao Bang, a province in the northeast of Vietnam. I took a bus north from Hanoi on a steep, winding, sometimes unpaved, and always perilous road that led into the mountains along the Chinese border.

It's difficult to get to Cao Bang, and when you do, the rewards are less obvious than in a touristy mountain town like Sapa. It does not have a market full of colorfully dressed villagers selling textiles, but it does have a remoteness that can appeal to a traveler seeking to discover what life is like in a harsh mountain climate. As well, there are a couple major attractions, including the Nguom Ngao cave and Ban Gioc waterfall, located on the Vietnam-China border.

Determined to make it to the falls and cave on my own (instead of renting a car and driver), I decided that the trip would involve taking a bus from Cao Bang town to the closest village and then locating a *xe om* to carry me the rest of the way. My experiences traveling in Vietnamese cities like Hanoi, Hue, and Dalat had led me to believe that *xe om* were readily available, just waiting around for passengers on every street corner. My excursion would soon teach me otherwise.

The bus route ended in Trung Khanh, a small town that was as close to the middle of nowhere as I had ever been. The market held about ten stalls, all empty. There were no people in the streets, and buildings seemed deserted. Most

worryingly, there were no *xe om* parked near the bus stop. I approached a few men who had congregated near a tea stand and asked for a ride. They laughed when I told them where I was headed.

"That's ten kilometers away," one said, "and it's freezing."

"Well, how much?" I asked.

"80,000 dong."

When I tried to bargain, they laughed again. It was clearly not on anyone's agenda to visit the Chinese border that day. Refusing to return to Cao Bang town in defeat, I sheepishly agreed to their price.

As we set off, I was glad that I had made the extra effort to get to this part of Vietnam. Houses were few and far between, and those that lined the road seemed straight out of the medieval era, made of stone and earth. White satellite dishes perched on the roofs were their only link to the twenty-first century. How strange that an area without access to running water and with limited electricity should have satellite TV. I imagined a giant truck full of satellite dishes lumbering down the road, stopping in every minority village and distributing its wares to every household. The satellite dishes presented a strange contrast to the large bamboo water wheels set up in the rivers in the valley, technology from a previous era. Although the road was paved, we passed only a few other people. Everyone on motorbikes was bundled up against the chill—men in dark windbreakers, shoulders hunched against the wind, and women with scarves tied around their heads so only their eyes could be seen.

As a volunteer English teacher, I lived in a rural area sixty kilometers north of Hanoi, and I thought I knew what Vietnamese poverty looked like. But I was unprepared for the lack of development I encountered in Cao Bang. Geography and climate limit the rice harvest to one per year, as opposed to the fertile southern delta, which can have up to three annual harvests. During the 1980s, rice had to be shipped from the south to the north to prevent famine, and this area of Vietnam continues to borrow power from the south because water levels are too low to provide a consistent source of hydro-electric energy. In January, the fields in Cao Bang were barren mud waiting for the planting season to begin again. Mist enshrouded the limestone mountains. I imagined how much the cold weather added to the difficulties of daily life.

My *xe om* driver stopped in at a friend's house to say hello. We sat on the cement floor, holding cups of tea in our hands for warmth. I longed to have the language skills to ask questions of my hosts—how big their families were, what type of crops they farmed. Surely they were just as curious about the crazy foreigner who was visiting the mountains in the middle of winter. My inability to communicate meant I had to make assumptions based only on what I saw—people politely smiling at their guests despite the bleakness of their surroundings. I vowed to return during the summer months when the rains re-plenished the streams and the rice was newly planted. Perhaps the poverty would not seem so overwhelming when surrounded by photogenic green fields.

My *xe om* driver and I spent the afternoon at Ban Gioc Waterfall and Nguom Ngao Cave. The waterfall, unfortunately, doesn't have much water in January, but I found the Chinese hotel and shopping complex on the other side of the riverbank an interesting illustration of the differences in economic growth between the two countries. It seemed unfair to ask my *xe om* driver to wait for hours while I enjoyed Nguom Ngao alone, so he came along for the adventure of exploring a cave using only flashlights. We followed a guide for an hour through the caverns, squeezing through narrow passages and admiring the rock formations, glittering in the light of our flashlight beams.

The adventure continued when I arrived back in Trung Khanh to discover that the last bus for Cao Bang had left for the day, and there were no guesthouses in town. All day I had been observing the lack of resources available to people in this remote area and feeling grateful that I had more creature comforts in my life, but ironically I now found myself in a situation where I had even fewer resources than the people around me. The local mechanic offered me a place to stay the night, but I balked at the prospect of camping out at a stranger's house. Feeling desperate, I went looking for another *xe om* who might drive me back down the mountain to Cao Bang.

Eventually, a local English teacher

took pity on me and drove me in the gathering dark. I was amazed that he felt it was his duty to get me back to town, and I felt guilty about abusing his generosity in order to get to my warm shower and comfortable hotel bed. Cao Bang may not have been as picturesque as other places I've visited, but my experiences there made a deeper impression on me, and challenged me to come to terms with my identity as a traveler who, despite being wealthier than any of the people I met, could still be enriched by the kindness of strangers.

Cao Bang

Cao Bang town, in the province of the same name, is about 270 kilometers north of Hanoi following National Highway 3. There are direct buses from Hanoi. It is a six- to ten-hour ride.

Ban Gioc Waterfall and Nguom Ngao Cave

Due to the waterfall's sensitive location on the Vietnam-China border, visiting requires a permit from the local authority, which your hotel in Cao Bang can arrange.

Trung Khanh District
Cao Bang Province

Pac Bo Cave

Another major area attraction is Pac Bo Cave, where Ho Chi Minh hid out upon his return to Vietnam in 1941 after thirty years abroad. The site is considered the birth-

place of the country's revolutionary movement, so it is little wonder that Lenin Stream runs past the cave beneath Karl Marx Peak. You can read more about the cave at the Vietnam Tourism website (www. vietnamtourism.com).

Trung Hoa Commune
Ha Quang District
Cao Bang Province

BA VI NATIONAL PARK

Simone Samuels gets the heck out of Hanoi to Ba Vi Mountain

We were feeling restless. The city was getting to us, as was the daily work grind, and we really needed to get away, if just for a day. My partner and I calculated and realized that we had not left Hanoi for more than six months. When we told our friends—some longtime Hanoi ex-pats—they were appalled.

"We're getting you out of here," they insisted. "This Sunday, we'll ride with you to the countryside. You'll love it."

We met at The Kitchen at West Lake for a hearty and delicious breakfast, and by 10 a.m., the four of us departed Hanoi on two motorbikes and headed west to Ba Vi National Park. What a treat it was from the very beginning. We were only half an hour into the trip, and already we could see fields of rice and the workings of Vietnamese agricultural life. We were following the signs to Son Tay, and the road led us through simple towns and rural villages. There were waves from small, excited children and high-pitched shouts of "Hello! Hello!" as we whooshed past their homes—I will never tire of this aspect of Vietnam. I also caught glimpses of some funny sights as we zoomed along, including a small boy riding a cow and a man tying a live buffalo to his motorbike.

After about an hour and a half of riding—more than halfway into our journey—we decided to rest our sore bottoms and take a small break. We pulled to the roadside in a scenic area and paused to observe rice being harvested. We had come at just the right time in the season; a week later and the fields would have been in the process of slash and burn. Now, we were able to view the fronds of rice being cut and then carried to a combine. We witnessed this scene over and over the whole way to the park; some of the hard-working farmers even waved at us as we drove past.

Around lunchtime we reached the foothills of Ba Vi Mountain, where we stopped for a simple, cheap lunch before we began our ascent to the top. The road was winding, and as the gradual incline became steeper, the view spread out over the Red River Delta. By the time we reached the top, we were level with the clouds, and the surroundings were tranquil. At the peak, we climbed off the motorbikes and began a walk up many steps through the jungle-like forest to the Mountain God Temple. The walk up was quite steep, and it took about forty-five minutes to complete the climb, but it was serene and peaceful, and the temperature at this altitude had dropped to a comfortable level. There were many local pilgrims also doing the walk, and they chatted with us as we trekked.

After we'd viewed the temple, we rested at the top and took in the view out over the clouds and beyond, where luscious mountainside greenery filled our view. We then walked back down the track to the motorbikes and began our way down the mountain. The descent was by far the most memorable part of the day. We switched off our motorbike engines and coasted in neutral—it was the closest I have felt to flying with my own wings. Riding pillion, I tilted my head back, held my arms out, and felt the wind rushing over me. It was completely quiet as we glided around the bends.

We took a different, shorter route back to Hanoi, and it was such a jolt when we reached the city outskirts, returning abruptly to the traffic ruckus. I felt the day was over too soon, before I had time to really digest the quiet and calm of the countryside and park. But it was such an easy day trip, and there would be no excuse for not making the time to return soon.

Getting to Ba Vi National Park

Ba Vi National Park is approximately fifty kilometers west of

Hanoi. There are various scenic back routes to reach it, but the most direct is by way of the straight-shot Highway 32 to Son Tay. Just before Son Tay, you will take a left—if you hit the center of town, you've gone too far. Follow this road for less than one kilometer, and then turn right onto the 87A, which will lead you to the mountain. The admission fee to the park is about 20,000 VND (less than $2) per couple. There is a minimal charge for vehicles. The food from the restaurant in the park is basic but cheap. Though not the best you'll find in Vietnam, it does the trick, and there is cold beer.

The Kitchen

No. 9 Xuan Dieu St.
Tay Ho District
Hanoi

SAPA

Iris Opdebeeck treks among hill tribe villages outside Sapa

I have seen the sudden changes in Sapa, from my first visit when it was a small, quiet mountain village, to my last, when it had grown into a seriously touristy place with lots of hotels, guesthouses, and restaurants. But I still like the atmosphere. Within a forest setting of bamboo and pine, the town is surrounded by hills with huge rice terraces that flow all the way down to the valley. Sometimes, it's cloudy and misty, or the rain comes, a downpour that must scare even the gods. At other times, the sun is burning, or the weather reminds me of a perfect spring day. Occasionally, it seems as if you can experience all four seasons in a single Sapa afternoon.

As with most people who travel here, my husband Jan and I come to visit hill tribe markets or hike in the vicinity. Trekking is becoming more and more popular; we made our first five-day trek to the villages around Sapa in 1999. Returning six years later, after we had moved to Vietnam, we took a three-day trip to the Ta Van and Ban Ho villages; this is a not-too-difficult trek, except when it starts raining. The path is full of small rocks, and you just slip down—caution and good shoes are key. It is a great way to see how the minority hill tribes really live: their houses, schools, tools, children, livestock, etc.

There is some controversy (even in my own heart) about these treks. The risk is that indigenous culture will eventually and inevitably be damaged by tourism. And there are other issues to consider. Because you stay in a village house, owned by one of the community members, it might create some sort of jealousy. One person is making Western dollars by opening up his house, while another is working hard to build a shack for his family. One time I had an interesting discussion with one of the guides that made me wonder if guides favor one family over another, since they are the ones who decide where you stay (read: where the money goes). And there are the children. Our maternal/paternal instincts are to give sweets to the kids, but the result is that they start begging.

So, please, only enter these areas with an ethical local guide, and choose eco-friendly tour operators. I am down on my knees begging: please be a responsible adult because these treks are *so* great. For many people, like my sister and some friends I sent up there, to stay at the houses in the villages is a once-in-a-lifetime experience. Everyone was more than excited when they reported back. For myself, I will *never* in my entire life forget the feelings I had the first time I did a trek.

Leaving Sapa on the main road, after our guide registered us at a police booth, we soon took a path straight down into the valley, along the rice terraces, which were perfectly shaped along the hillside and dappled with big dark rocks, bushes, and trees. The view gazes over the surrounding hills and down into the river, and depending on when you visit during the rice season, the terraces define the atmosphere. This particular time, in March, the paddies were empty of rice but filled with rainwater and leftover plantings from

the previous harvest, which the buffalos made part of their daily meals. Mirrored in the water, the white and gray from the heavy clouds, along with the misty sky, made our trip feel a bit mysterious, adding to the sense of adventure. Clouds and sunshine came and went throughout the day, and the scenery changed with every new climb, descent, and turn.

Sometimes we had to cross the water by using rocks, or walk along the ridges of a bamboo forest as we entered a village of the Hmong, Dzay, Tay, or Red Dao, with their sophisticated, red headdresses. It is still a mystery to me how they fold them so ingeniously and manage to keep them on their heads. Walking through villages, you will see young boys playing soccer and girls taking care of younger siblings. Some of them will come to look at you with big curious eyes, or just the opposite, run away because they are too shy. Local ladies who want to sell some of their handicrafts will surely follow you. You've been warned!

The trek we took went through the villages of Ta Van and Ban Ho, which belong to the Dzay and Tay minorities. In the evening, the guide used the kitchen of our hosts to prepare a fabulous northern Vietnamese meal. Every time I have been up there, the food was just perfect. During Tet holidays in February it was over the top. The host family took their dinner with us, and rice wine was brought to the table for *chuc mung nam moi*—Happy New Year—toasts. It's a harsh drink, but it goes really well with the food. (There is also bottled water,

NORTHERN VIETNAM

and usually soft drinks and even beer available, as well.) After dinner we warmed our feet around the kitchen fire and talked about the experiences of the day.

There is something very special about the combination of hiking through incredible natural surroundings and witnessing the traditional culture of the hill tribe people. Having lived in Vietnam, visiting Sapa and trekking in the area is one of my personal top-three experiences in the country.

Trekking around Sapa

For our treks, we used Handspan Adventure Travel, which has offices in Hanoi and Ho Chi Minh City.

www.handspan.com

Bunking down

Every time I have done a trekking homestay around Sapa, each house was clean, and there was a separate, concrete squat toilet as well as a place where you could get water to wash your face and wake your sleepy self in the morning. The only thing I recommend bringing is your own sheets. The very best—silk sleeping bags, lightweight, in all colors and sizes, and cheap—can be found in the silk shops of Hanoi or Ho Chi Minh City.

A good night's sleep

In Sapa, we enjoyed our stay at Auberge Dang Trung Hotel, a simple, atmosphere-laden,

French-style complex dating back to the town's colonial days.

7 Muong Hoa St.
Sapa Town
Lao Cai Province
(84-20) 871-243
www.sapanowadays.com

FANSIPAN MOUNTAIN

Paul Young climbs to Vietnam's highest point

Along with my three hiking companions, I was sitting quietly, playing cards and resting after hours of non-stop hiking up the side of Fansipan Mountain. My leg was wounded but not seriously, so I could still walk, despite the throbbing pain emanating from both of my callused feet. But was too late to turn back now—we had already come halfway and were determined to finish what we had started.

Through an unsettling, cloudy haze, I saw an alignment of charred trees, so different from the greener, more vibrant vegetation near our base camp. My companions and I gazed curiously at the black, scalded trunks. After dealing another round, one of us finally got up the courage to ask our guides, "Are the trees from ... the war?"

The guides all looked at one another, said something in Vietnamese, and then started to chuckle. "I think from fire," said one of them, peering over his round glasses that were held together with tape.

We burst out laughing. Apparently, we weren't on the run from the Viet Cong—my feet hurt only because I was stupid enough to wear sandals up a 3,143-meter climb—and forest fires, not just bombs, can destroy foliage on misty mountaintops in Vietnam.

After recovering from embarrassment, we all enjoyed an early supper around the campfire, prepared by our Vietnamese hiking guides. Shortly after the meal, one of the guides went off scavenging for something in a stream nearby. Only a few minutes later he came back with a skewer full of frogs, ready for cooking for our bedtime snack.

The next morning, after breakfast—yet another zesty meal—I stuffed my poncho into my brand-new backpack, which I had proudly purchased for less than $5 at a market in the hill tribe village of Sapa a day before our climb. After struggling to zip up the bulging bag, I threw it over my shoulder and was ready, full of confidence to take on the mountain. Suddenly there was a loud *pop pop pop* as I tightened the straps. The bag was already beginning to rip.

"This part, more difficult than the first part," said one of the guides. "About four hours to the peak." With a movement of his hand, he explained the difference. He stretched his arm out, extended his fingers fully, and then raised his hand from a flat platform-like position to a near ninety-degree angle pointing upwards toward the sky. His wrist let out a subtle *cracking* noise when his hand could bend no further.

As we walked away that morning, the plateau and reasonably flat area of our campsite gradually disappeared. It started to rain. The leisurely hike turned moderate climb had suddenly mutated into a full-fledged, gut-wrenching expedition, where no one equipped with faulty footwear and discounted backpacks had boldly dared to go before—toward the peak of Fansipan Mountain.

"Come on, man! You can make it! Give me your hand!"

Someone was shouting at me. I thought I had blacked out for a second. I lifted my head up from a puddle, and the mud slopped off of my face.

I snapped back to reality and saw a blurred hand reaching out to pull me up from the muck. The rain continued to pour down on my soaked, ripped poncho. I lifted my hand up and grabbed the arm. I stood up and managed to step onto a section of the trail that wasn't covered in mud to regain my balance. I wiped the soupy dirt from my eyes and re-fastened the strap on my dilapidated, worn-out sandals. With 2,000 meters remaining, and the air beginning to thin with each breath, I picked my bag out of the puddle and heaved it over my shoulder. Suddenly, the right arm strap ripped completely off and the bag splashed back to the ground.

With no chairlifts or helicopters in

sight to whisk us to the top, a few of us waited for the rest of the group to catch up. Luckily, when one of the guides arrived, he was able to apply first aid to my wounded backpack by tying the strap back into position with a combination of rope and tape.

Once everything was repaired, we all continued up the slippery, inclined trail toward the peak, which seemed to be unattainable at the pace we were moving. I fell on my backside more often than someone attempting to snowboard for the first time after drinking a few bottles of whiskey. The others were also showing signs of exhaustion, but we kept moving relentlessly toward the top, determined not to let the mountain get the better of us. After hours of blood, sweat, and near tears from intense climbing, eventually the end was approaching. Our view of the sky opened up increasingly with every step forward we made.

We had been climbing for approximately nine hours over the course of two days, and now, more than 3,000 vertical meters later, we finally reached the summit of Fansipan. Gathering together on a giant rock—tired and muddy, but triumphant—our group posed for a photo to commemorate our conquering the tallest mountain in Indochina.

Getting your bearings

Fansipan Mountain, AKA "The Roof of Indochina," is located in the Lao Cai Province in northwest Vietnam, nine kilometers southwest of Sapa in the Hoang Lien Mountain Range.

Hiring a guide

Once you get to Sapa, where hikes up Fansipan begin, there are many hotels and guesthouses ranging in quality. You can hire your guides for the Fansipan trek from many of the town's lodgings or tour agencies. Guides range from $100-$150 per person, depending on how many nights you spend on the mountain. The cost per person can be reduced if you travel with a group. Your guides will provide you with tents and cooked meals during the journey. Multi-day climbs can be arranged, depending how fast you want to hike. Reaching the peak of Fansipan and coming back down to Sapa can be done in two days (with one overnight), but some people may wish to extend the trek to three days because it can be quite strenuous. Word to the wise: If you like the convenience of a package tour, you can arrange multi-day Fansipan tours with an agent in Hanoi; however, it will be *much* more expensive and is not recommended.

Accommodation costs

Budget hotels and guesthouses in Sapa cost around $7-$25 per night. There is also a high-end option: Victoria Sapa Resort.

www.victoriahotels-asia.com

When to go

Sapa's weather is monsoonal with a hot, rainy season and a warm, dry season. Because of the area's elevation, it can get quite cool, even in the summer months. You should take appropriate mountain gear: proper hiking shoes, backpack, raincoat, sunscreen, and some warm clothes.

Northwest Highlands

XXXXXXXXXXXXXXXXXXXXXXXXXXXXXXXXX
ooooooooooooooooooooooooooooooooo

Graham Roemmele motors full throttle in northern Vietnam

I slammed down on the kick-start and my decaying bike roared to life. Thick clouds of oily blue smoke filled the gas station, leaving the pump attendant gagging. Mr. Dang, the friendly but nervous owner of the fume-spewing, Russian-made Minsks that my two comrades and I had hired, yelled after us, instructing us to remember to mix oil and gas together, emphasizing 5 percent oil. I nodded at him, and then with an offensive roar, maneuvered into the busy streets of Hanoi. In my mirror I saw Mr. Dang perform a little ritual that looked more like a prayer than a blessing.

Dean, Jason, and I planned to drive a 1,200-kilometer loop around northwest Vietnam. We had set aside six days to cover the distance, taking in the cities of Son La, Dien Bien Phu, and Sapa. The

trip would lead us into Vietnam's highest mountain region, and through lush valleys tended by hill tribe farmers. We would cruise along the borders of Laos and China and scramble over mountain passes 1,900 meters high.

According to our rudimentary map, leaving Hanoi appeared straightforward. It proved anything but. After riding around crumbling tower blocks and rubbish dumps on Hanoi's outskirts, we finally found the highway to the northwest. The traffic eased, whilst mountains loomed ahead and the scenery turned a thousand shades of green. The swarming motorbikes of Hanoi vanished, replaced by packs of students on bicycles, waving at us like mad hatters.

Following a full first day of incredible but hair-raising driving, we awoke in the town of Son La. We had already driven 320 butt-chafing kilometers, and the thought of climbing back on the bikes both thrilled and appalled me. As Son La disappeared in the rearview mirror, we dodged potholes around the contours of the hills. Descending into a tranquil valley, we stopped to look at an old waterwheel. Nearby a group of women in the river started to shriek and laugh, and we suddenly realized they were bathing butt-naked: the highlight of our day.

Twenty minutes later my Minsk was screaming beneath me and blasting clouds of dust into my comrades' faces. We were scrambling up a dangerous and rocky section of dirt road, and the bikes were struggling to make the steep grade. Suddenly, Comrade Dean's bike, the Red Baron, packed up. A few slack-jawed locals came to help us, but only ended up prodding the engine like it was the monolith from *2001: A Space Odyssey*.

After coasting back down the road and pulling Dean along to the nearest *xe may* (repair shop), we drank a well-deserved beer while the efficient mechanic repaired the Red Baron. Once again it spluttered into life, farting a cloud of fumes. This wasn't to be its last trip to the grease monkey, however. The Red Baron was always a few kilometers away from the scrap yard. We continued, making up for lost time by barely stopping in Dien Bien Phu. Pressing on, we passed through a luminous valley, where whole clouds of green butterflies filled the air. It was an undeniably beautiful sight, but damned painful when they bounced off my face.

By the morning of day four, Sapa was just a couple of hours away, but Vietnam's highest road at an elevation of 1,900 meters, the Tram Ton Pass, separated us from our destination. Whilst soaking up the incredible scenery and crisp air, we had to overtake the odd truck, each time frighteningly passing blindly through clouds of filthy soot belching out of its screaming engine. As we finally reached the top, we paused to look back at the most spectacular and treacherous road any of us had ever seen.

In Sapa, after pushing Dean and the Baron along to a *xe may* for the third time, we relaxed in a bar facing Fansipan, Vietnam's tallest mountain. An ancient-looking hill tribe lady came to sell us an attractive handmade blanket. Minutes later another hill tribe lady came to sell us hats, and

after her, another to sell us shirts. We got out of the bar only to realize that the town had been descended upon by scores of Hmong hill tribe people. As we wandered around in awe of the strange sight, a nineteen-year-old Hmong girl asked us, "Hey guys, whatcha up to? Fancy shooting some pool?" We joined her and a friend in a bar to watch them steadily kick everyone's ass on the table. Bored of winning, they took us to the night market to down some shots of nasty rice whiskey, whilst we drunkenly danced around in circles, making a racket with our new Hmong instruments that had just cost Jason $20.

The next day, at the gas station preparing to leave, we watched the pump attendant slop ladles full of oil into the petrol tanks of the other customers' Minsks. Ignoring Mr. Dang's wise words in Hanoi about mixing the oil and gas together, we stupidly let her do the same for us, assuming it would be fine. Two hundred meters down the road, the Red Baron seized up. It was a bad start to our last day's 370-kilometer ride back to Hanoi. After solving that problem, we rumbled through the countryside passing town after town without stopping.

Riding ahead of the others, I came to a railway bridge and crossed the tracks, careful not to jam a wheel between the ties. Intrepid Dean, however, opted to ride between the rails, James Bond style. He flew head over heels when the Baron's front wheel wedged against the track. Although the bike was not too damaged, Dean was understandably shaken up.

As a stormy night began to creep up on us, so did Hanoi. Stopping to regroup, Jason and I waited for Dean a full ten minutes before anxiously turning back and finding him at the side of the road. He had hit a pothole hidden under a puddle. A few grazes aside, he was largely unhurt and had been lucky not to be mowed down by passing trucks, which are driven like bastard, drunken kings of the road. The Red Baron had not fared so well. The steering was askew, the gear lever bent double, and the left foot peg was history, but the robust Minsk wasn't heading to the scrap yard yet. We traded bikes and I accepted the burden of the Baron for the last leg of the trip.

In the dark and drizzle, starved and knackered, we limped through Hanoi's chaotic streets, turning heads with our disheveled appearance. Just minutes from the hotel, Dean lost his concentration and drove my pristine Minsk into the gutter for his third accident of the day. As we triumphantly hobbled off the bikes for the last time, one thing was for sure. We had all returned feeling more alive than when we left— except for the poor old Red Baron.

Minsking around Vietnam

Everything you need to know about motorcycling in Vietnam can be found on two excellent websites.

www.minskclubvietnam.com

www.exploreindochina.com

Hiring a Minsk

Most travel agents can arrange Minsks for you—ask around. We hired our bikes from the travel agent in our hotel a day before we hit the road, which proved handy as my bike was gushing oil and needed to be fixed. It was also nice to practice driving around the boulevards encircling Hoan Kiem Lake. We paid $7 a day and left no deposit other than our yellow departure slips and some luggage at the guesthouse. You need your passport to check into the hotels along the way, so don't leave it as a deposit. Mr. Dang showed us how to mix the oil and gas for the two-stroke engine and a few other things, such as how to change the spark plug. You should ask for the same instructions. We also asked for helmets, which we received, although they were of little more use than wearing an ice-cream tub on your head in the event of an accident. Bringing your own helmet is a wise idea because the drive is extremely rural. For obtaining helmets in Hanoi and Ho Chi Minh City, see the fact file of Marianne Smallwood's essay on page 220.

Pit stops

The repairs on the Red Baron cost little more than a couple of dollars at a time. There was a xe may (repair shop) in nearly every village along the way, and we had no trouble fixing the Baron up. We saved the old parts that were replaced, and after some

NORTHERN VIETNAM

fast talking when we returned the bikes, the damage costs were waived in lieu of the cash Dean had already spent on the repairs.

On the road

It's hard to anticipate the schedule of the journey due to breakdowns, weather, sightseeing, etc. We stayed overnight in Son La, Tuan Giao, Lai Chau, and Sapa. There are several hotels in these and the other major towns on this route and also a few in the minor towns. We paid no more than $12 a night for all three of us and had no bother finding rooms. Ask your hotel to park your bike in the lobby because Minsks don't have keys.

HUE

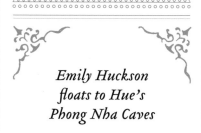

Emily Huckson floats to Hue's Phong Nha Caves

In the back of my mind—and for a very long time—I had been thinking about something a good friend told me: that I would really love to get my butt to the Phong Nha Caves up near Hue. This friend was a fellow ex-pat living in Saigon, with a similar spirit of adventure that I have, and so finally, last summer, I

took his advice to investigate the caves of Phong Nha-Ke Bang National Park.

Hue itself offers a great glimpse of Vietnam's past imperial grandeur, but for me, I had been there, done that, and was only interested in seeing the old Ho Chi Minh Trail and the incredible caves that had been recommended. After arriving in Hue, I booked a day tour, which left at 6 a.m.

Your impressions on a journey are never concluded by just the place; the people you meet, the way you are treated, and the surprises that unfold along the way—all are part and parcel of the overall experience. Take, for example, the *Viet Kieu* who befriended me on the bus. He was born in the very area that we were going to visit. Since his English was more than adequate, I was able to ask him as many stupid questions as I could. And I did. I learned so much more from him— about the ethnic tribes that lived in the area; about the area's situation during the war; about the attitudes of people in the middle of the war, and I do mean *the middle*—that it made this trip a total wonder for me. I so appreciated this information that I barely listened to the broken English of our guide. Once we arrived on the bank of the river and boarded the boat to float down to the caves, I was filled with such excitement about seeing something that might be very spectacular.

Turns out it wasn't *might*—it *was*!

As a teacher of four- and five-year-olds in Vietnam, I can tell you that I was absolutely blown away. It was magical, it was fantastic, and it was something I would *never* see or experience in any other part of the world. As we took the boat inside this mammoth cave, which was barely lit, adding to the excitement, I was expecting to see Captain Hook, Peter Pan, and Wendy. The guide told us that the caves stretched all the way to Laos, and although we went in only about five kilometers, it was still amazing. I got to touch a stalactite—more than 6,000 years old—and we were allowed to get off the boat and go ashore, where there was a small, private shrine. I wish I had known so that I could have brought a small statue to leave behind, to mark my journey to these wonder-full caves.

Phong Nha Caves

It was not very easy to find information about the Phong Nha Caves in Ho Chi Minh City, where I live, but once in Hue, there were adverts everywhere. For tours, one place to start is the Mandarin Café, recommended by Michael Burr on page 35.

BACH MA NATIONAL PARK

Iris Opdebeeck savors the sunrise from Bach Ma Mountain

On the way to Bach Ma Hotel, on Bach Ma Mountain between Hoi An and Hue, is a nature reserve where the hills are covered in every shade of green imaginable. There are many flowers, including orchids, and birds and insects, yes, lots of them. There is also supposed to be plenty of wildlife, including tigers. Ha! You truly will need a lot of luck to spot one of these creatures.

According to my map, the mountain is 1,444 meters high. The air is *very* humid and cool—cold even, at night. I presume the French must have used the grounds where the hotel now stands as a summer resort, to escape the heat of the low-lying cities. You will see some houses totally abandoned, leftover from colonial times. Others are put to use, like the hotel, which smelled throughout of mold. And the bed sheets were damp, even though we had an electric blanket. Oh well, it was the mountain and not the hotel room that we had come to see.

On the afternoon we arrived, we climbed up to the peak. The view was stunning. We saw the immense jungle on one side and the lagoon and sea on the other. We took a short walk along one of the trails up to a waterfall; although it wasn't that impressive, walking there was peaceful, and we got to experience the jungle inclusive of all its soothing sounds and fresh air. This place really is an escape from the cities—no stink of motorbikes, no horn honky-tonk. And no people at all, except for a couple of tourists who unearthed this little escape in their guidebooks.

Despite its flaws, this area has a notable secret: the sunrise. You need some luck for this, as well. On the day of our first hike, it was just a bit cloudy, but beautiful, and the white, cumulus clouds on an absolute blue sky boded well for the following morning, when we got up at four so that we could again climb to the top of the mountain. When we exited our room, to our astonishment, we found the walls of the hallway covered with insects—literally covered! There were thousands, from caterpillar varieties to huge moths and cicada-looking creatures.

Back at the peak, we arrived at a watchtower with windows peering all the way around, just in time for the sunrise. My God! In a blaze of red and orange, the sun came up over the South China Sea. Some tiny clouds spread over the sky, and the reflection of the early morning light turned the water silver, in contrast to the black of the hills and the flat land beyond with a river flowing into the sea. Amazing. Magical. Then, after twenty minutes, daylight came and the air grew foggy again.

This was an incredible experience, but you need to be there in nice weather, which is not common. All in all, though, I recommend taking your chances—if you do show up on a clear day, this sunrise will be one of the most spectacular sights you'll witness in Vietnam.

Visiting Bach Ma Mountain

Our trip was part of a Hue to Hoi An tour booked through Eco Travel Vietnam. You can also arrange visits through numerous other tour companies in the country.

www.ecotravelvietnam.com

Bach Ma National Park
www.bachma.vnn.vn

NHA TRANG

Alice Driver unwinds in peace outside Nha Trang

The ride began in the middle of the night in the rain, with my husband Isaac and me in the very back of the bus on top of the hot engine. The one good thing about our seats was that we could hardly see the road up front because, as the man beside us pointed out, "You would die of a heart attack if you had to sit up there."

In the playing shadows, with light and dark flickering across his smooth skin, the man appeared wise for his age, which I guessed at around fifty. He was traveling alone throughout Asia, now making his way back to his home in Malaysia. Isaac and I were dead tired, and it turned out that this man was a talker, just looking for a conversation wherever he could find it. I held out hope that he was a guru, who imparts some sort of life-changing advice. However, he turned out to be merely childish as he shouted at passengers with large luggage, "What you got in there, a washing machine?" He repeated this several times, more delighted with himself each time. "Big bag, look, have washing machine ... ha ha." He turned to talk to the Chinese couple on his left. We tried to sleep.

Tried is the operative word for our sixty-kilometer trip from Nha Trang to a drop-off on the side of the highway. It was raining—a mean, fast rain that turned the streets into rivers. The bus driver was barreling head-on into oncoming traffic in the wrong lane. A little game of chicken? No. Here there are no designated lanes, and you pass whenever you want. That means that our mammoth bus, at any moment I happened to look up, was heading directly into the headlights of another bus/group of motorbikes/tiny bicyclers. We passed on curves going speeds that I thought would send us over the edge, out into the gaping night. In addition, the road had turned into a river in various places. However, the bus did not slow down, but just dived in. Huge sprays of water shot out from under the vehicle, running down the roof, leaking into my window, and running down my arm. The holes in the road could not be called potholes: they were monstrous caves waiting to swallow us whole. When we went over them, our bodies took flight, landing hard as we made our way out of the hole.

Luckily, our trip was not a long one,

and soon we were dropped off in the 5 a.m. darkness, an orange peel of color rimming the horizon. I was nervous about the dark, about the deserted roadside—for a moment I felt alone and afraid. But my husband is not the wary type, and he sighted a small store and a bunch of motorbikes on the side of the road. We walked over and found several men who offered to take us to the Jungle Beach Resort, a place recommended by a friend living in Vietnam. My worries dissipated as we packed our backpacks onto the bikes.

We were pelted with bugs as the motorbikes sped along, and we watched the sun come up over a green expanse of fields. Part of the appeal of Jungle Beach is its remoteness—it is far from major cities and other tourist attractions. After thirty minutes we drove through a tiny fishing village and then hit a bumpy dirt road, which took us to the hotel where we were greeted by Sylvio, the friendly Canadian co-owner. No false advertising here, I thought as I looked at the mountainous jungle that rose up behind me and the beach that stretched out in front of the hotel. We were led to our room, a thatched hut facing the sea, with a simple bed surrounded by mosquito netting. Though the property offered indoor rooms, we wanted the alfresco stay. We shared bathroom facilities with other guests, and while the showers were cold, they felt great after a day out on the beach.

We spent one day hiking along the huge boulders of the sea wall to reach a waterfall an hour and a half away. The texture of the sea-worn stones on my feet was delicious, and I hopped happily from one to another as waves crashed below me. Isaac and I arrived at the trail barefoot, but after a few minutes hiking down the muddy trail with its sharp rocks, we realized we would need shoes to reach the waterfall. I decided to try to swim back to the hotel and skirted the edge of the boulders as my husband walked above. The waves felt bigger than they looked, and at moments I felt lost at sea and thought of sharks eating me for dinner. I also underestimated the length of the swim and got tired before reaching the hotel beach. While navigating around the sharp rocks and trying to land safely between crashing waves, I skinned my knees. I lay on a big rock panting and drying in the sun.

Another day we hiked into the mountains hoping to see Douc Langur monkeys, loris, and eagles, though all I managed to see were fire ants—they bit me, at that. We met a wildlife biologist who was there to study and photograph the Douc Langurs, and he often went off hiking for hours in search of the rare animals. For lunch and dinner we enjoyed curries, rice, fresh juice, and fruit at communal meals. However, the one thing I craved was chocolate, and there was none to be found. The meals provided a great way for us to meet other travelers and exchange stories.

The resort has a glorious garden, and three kilometers of deserted private beach. Isaac and I walked up the shore to the village one day at sunset to watch fishermen bringing in their catch. After the busy streets and smog-filled air of Nha Trang, we found Jungle Beach the perfect place to relax, though mosquitoes did manage to get through the netting around our bed and leave us a bit itchy. For those visitors seeking adventure, there are plenty of hiking opportunities and also small kayaks available. Best of all, the Canadian host and his Vietnamese wife are easygoing and helpful, making a stay here all the more relaxing.

Jungle Beach Resort

Rooms cost $15 per person, with meals and snacks included in the price. Be sure to bring your own sweets!

(84-58) 622-384
syl@dng.vnn.vn

Getting there on the cheap

While the hotel can arrange transport for you from Nha Trang, it's much more expensive than hopping the bus north from Nha Trang and getting off at the Doc Let stop. You will be dropped off on the side of the highway. Ask one of the motorbike taxis parked nearby to take you to Jungle Beach. The cost should be around 50,000 VND (about $3) per bike.

DALAT

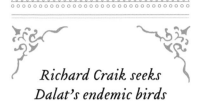

Richard Craik seeks Dalat's endemic birds

Most visitors to Vietnam probably don't come looking for pine forests, twentieth-century European architecture, and kitsch tourist attractions, since all these can most likely be experienced someplace nearer home. However, for the residents of Vietnam's overcrowded and overheated southern metropolis of Ho Chi Minh City, Dalat is the perfect place to escape for a few days. Vietnamese come for the cool mountain air, lakes, pagodas, and quirky attractions, and to dress up in sweaters and scarves, something they never get the chance to do in the sweltering city. Foreign residents, on the other hand, visit to play golf at the Dalat Palace Golf Club, considered by many to be one of the finest courses in Southeast Asia.

But for me and a small, growing number of local and overseas travelers, Dalat's appeal is something completely different—it's for the birds. This may seem a little strange to anybody who has visited Vietnam, since birds, with the exception of domesticated chickens and ducks, are not much in evidence. But a little-known fact is that Vietnam has the highest number of endemic bird species on mainland Southeast Asia, and Vietnam's center of bird endemism is Dalat. If you want to see a Collared or Orange-breasted Laughingthrush, Grey-crowned Crocias, Vietnamese Cutia, or Vietnamese Greenfinch, there is only one place in the world you can find them, and that is on the Dalat Plateau.

The best places to start looking for Dalat's avian attractions are the montane evergreen forests of Langbian Mountain and Tuyen Lam Lake. Langbian Mountain, more than 2,000 meters above sea level, is a twenty-minute drive from Dalat, and its twin peaks can be clearly seen from the center of town. It's a pleasant seven-kilometer walk from the entrance gate at the base to the mountain summit. Arrive at 6 a.m. when the gate opens and walk up in the morning sunshine (for it is usually sunny in the mornings in Dalat) through pine forests full of jays, minivets, nuthatches, and warblers. Listen for the twittering of dainty little Vietnamese Greenfinches in the pines on the way up, and look for the yellow flash of wings as they take flight.

The towering trees, saplings, and scrub that cover the steep slopes around the summit are home to the Vietnamese Cutia and Langbian's most sought-after feathered resident, the Collared Laughingthrush. The Vietnamese Cutia, a plump little bird with a barred white breast and chestnut back, creeps quietly along the moss-covered branches high up in the canopy like an overstuffed nuthatch, and the Collared Laughing-thrush's loud, high-pitched, whistling *weeeeoo* or harsh *arrrrhh* will get birders' pulses racing. But a glimpse of a silver ear patch or a deep orange breast amongst the tangle of the understory is all that many get to see of this little forest skulker.

Tuyen Lam Lake is a man-made reservoir just three kilometers from the center of Dalat. Fortunately, some sizeable areas of remnant evergreen forest still survive among the tourist resorts and market gardens around the lakeshore where the other two Dalat Plateau endemics can be found. If you hear a loud, melodious tune that sounds like your neighbor-hood postman whistling from deep in-side a bush, it is probably an Orange-breasted Laughingthrush. Like most laughingthrushes, the orange and black plumaged Orange-breasted is a shy bird more often heard than seen. The second bird, the strange, shrike-like Grey-crowned Crocias, or *crocias langbianis*, was first discovered on the peaks of Langbian in 1938. It was then not seen again until it was rediscovered on a nearby mountain in 1994: Happily, since then it has been found at several sites around Dalat including the lake. Although it spends much of its time hidden away in the crowns of tall trees, the normally secretive Crocias will sometimes ven-ture boldly out to the forest edge where its strident song can be heard ringing across the treetops.

So even if a boat ride on a moun-tain lake or a round of golf are not really your ideal holiday activities in Vietnam, don't give Dalat a miss—come and spend a few days on the trail of the area's endemic birds.

Escorted birding tours

Contact Richard at Vietnam Birding for tailor-made, escorted birding tours to the Dalat Plateau and other parts of Vietnam.

www.vietnambirding.com

richard@vietnambirding.com

Marc Moynot takes flight over the Dalat Plateau

I made my first paragliding flights in Vietnam on a splendid site near Mui Ne: over the clear seawaters of a large bay with a small island in the middle. My teacher was Mr. Long, a very good Vietnamese paraglider pilot, who is the founder of the first Vietnamese paraglider club, Viet-Wings. It *was* a good spot, with no buildings and a new road that led to the Bau Trang Lakes. I say *was*, be-cause there is now a power line, and it is no longer possible to fly there in safe conditions.

These days, local pilots have to go up the coast to soar on the sea breeze, but this too is often not possi-ble because of strong winds blowing during the dry season. But heading even farther north, 300 kilometers from Ho Chi Minh City, you will find Dalat, at an altitude of 1,500 meters. Just outside Dalat, Langbian Mountain is a tourist site with a road going to the top. Vietnamese people like to go there to enjoy the cool altitude and landscape. They also appreciate watching paragliders taking off and flying over the site, since flying is a fairly new activity in Vietnam.

Four hundred meters below is Tuyen Lam Lake, banked with pine forests on one side, agriculture on the other, and meadows along the meanders of the river that feeds it. During the dry season, the wind comes from the right direction for taking off, and thermals start in the middle or end of the morning. There are some landing zones, though in the countryside these zones are not easy to find, since there are few meadows, many fences, and farms growing coffee and other crops.

Though new to the paragliding world, the site is gaining fame abroad. A few paraglider groups came from the USA and Japan to fly here recently. Some were lucky, flying thermals at twelve meters per second, soaring up to more than 3,000 meters. Others did not fare so well, with a storm off the Vietnamese coast making flight impossible.

Two years ago I brought a hang glider from France (a basic Tecma glider that I liked to use when I would hang glide in France years ago). I had a good flight over the Langbian site with this wing, under a big *cumulus congestus* which lifted me at four to five meters per second up to 2,600

meters. The most pleasant part of the flight was when I was circling at the center of the cloud, and a Peregrine Falcon was using the same thermal on the periphery of it. With the same angular speed, we were watching each other from under the dark bottom of the cloud. Encounters made with birds when flying are unforgettable.

If you would like to experience this region by air, you can contact Mr. Long of Vietwings, in Ho Chi Minh City, who will arrange a tandem flight for you in Dalat, or François Deslauriers, who also flies tandem and is immediately available since he lives in Dalat. If you bring your own wing, you can also get in touch with them for information about soaring from the site. Happy flights!

VietWings

Mr. Pham Duy Long, 090-382-5607 (mobile for in-country), or 84-90-382-5607 (from abroad)

www.vietwings.com (This website is in Vietnamese. Click on *thu viên anh* to look at pictures.)

François Deslauriers

091-978-1696 (mobile phone for in-country), or 84-91-978-1696 (from abroad)

Jibe's Beach Club

While no longer ideal for hang gliding, Mui Ne is a very good spot for kite surfing. If you want to kite surf or windsurf, go to Jibe's, near Full Moon Resort on the road from Phan Thiet to Mui Ne. Run by Pascal, a Frenchman, this was the first operation to set up windsurf and kite surf activities on the Vietnamese coast.

90 Nguyen Dinh Chieu St.
Mui Ne Beach
Phan Thiet
(84-62) 847-405
www.windsurf-vietnam.com

CENTRAL HIGHLANDS

Hal Phillips gets sideways in the Vietnamese highlands

We have been only a day in Phan Thiet, and frankly, I'd like to stay another two at least. The links at the Novotel Ocean Dunes & Golf Resort are superb (good enough to warrant another go-round) and only a fool would beg off one fully flaked-out day on the hotel's quiet stretch of beach. But the itinerary can be a stern taskmaster, so I keep my peace and prepare for our scheduled departure.

Then, on the way to breakfast, I see them—the motorcycles and their attendant sidecars, all neatly lined up in front of the hotel—and my ambivalence melts away. No one in his or her right mind could resist the sheer romance of

a couple hundred kilometers by sidecar from this tropical perch on the South China Sea to the mountain retreat of Dalat. I'm glad to see that my driver, Gilles Poggi, sports a *krama,* that distinctive, all-purpose Cambodian scarf. I want one too. And I'm hoping we can line up behind our respective machines and, at the sound of a gun, begin the journey rally-style.

The reality proves more staid. With the sun now peeking over the hotel façade, we slather on the sunscreen, affix our sunglasses, helmets, and hats, and wait for the last of our group to return from the bathroom. Hardly the stuff of Paris to Dakar, though our three-wheelers do turn over, en masse, with a very satisfying rumble, and we pull out in precise formation, one after another, like starlets from one of those 1930s-era musical follies diving into a pool.

Poggi, a Corsican who wears his *krama* with all the Gallic élan one might expect, is owner and general manager of the posh Princess d'Annam Resort & Spa, located some twenty minutes south of Phan Thiet in Ke Ga. These sidecars and their motorized escorts are his personal obsession, and he leads these trips—along with his friends in Team Camel, their touring club—as a one-of-a-kind amenity for guests seeking 360-degree tours of the south Vietnamese countryside.

"We started adventuring with sidecars more than ten years ago, in Hanoi," Poggi shouts as we travel up the coast, his voice perfectly audible above the four-stroke din. "I had two friends who had hooked up with these sidecars. One of them invited me to go to Sapa, and I've been riding ever since."

Poggi slows down and stops his narrative for the moment to avoid a cavernous pothole. We've turned away from the water now, the roads becoming narrower and dodgier with every passing kilometer. My sidecar, of course, is suspended between three points of a triangle: the two wheels of the motorcycle, to my left, and a third wheel to my right. When Poggi dodges a pothole, my carriage often passes directly over the road blemish. The passenger sees it coming and instinctively braces for a jolt that for some reason never comes. This is a fine metaphor for sidecar travel—all in all, the experience is far more comfortable than one might expect.

"Later, when we moved to Phan Thiet, I decided to get one for myself," Poggi continues. "I met a policeman who was selling one, and when I asked him how much, he quoted me a price— by kilo! So I bought one, for maybe $200. Later, I realized we should have another one, so we could go out as a group. I bought a second, and the policeman told me, 'I'll do you a favor. You buy the second and I'll give you a third for free.' Today, we have eleven."

The ride of choice for Team Camel is the 650cc Ural M-72, a Russian bike based on the vaunted BMW R71, a German army staple during World War II and the very bike Steve McQueen made famous jumping barbedwire fencing in *The Great Escape*. Urals became prevalent in Vietnam only after 1975, and they remain practical, Poggi says, because the Russians did a good job simplifying the design, parts are readily available,

and Vietnamese mechanics know their way around them. They've been fixing them for thirty years, after all.

In our party there are two quite spiffy sidecars bearing the Princess d'Annam emblem; these are the hotel's primary touring vehicles. The others are decorated more flamboyantly, according to the whims of individual club members. Remi Faubel, the resort's celebrated chef, drives a canary yellow Ural featuring the snarling countenance of a large cat-like creature. Poggi and I ride a black model named for the Ramones. It's an odd-but-pleasing juxtaposition, wending my way through a Vietnamese tableau with a Corsican guide, seated in a Russian-made BMW knock-off commemorating the greasers who gave us *Sheena is a Punk Rocker*.

Having passed through a narrow shelf of level ground set aside for rice paddies, we soon set off into the highlands. We are on the back roads where villages are fewer and farther between. The Urals are working hard now, taking on steep inclines and those potholes too large to straddle. The higher we go into the mountains, the less tropical the landscape becomes. But never is it anything less than lush: ten shades of deep green set against still darker greens.

On a treeless plateau set high above a reservoir of sparkling blue-green, we stop for lunch which, thanks to Faubel, qualifies as perhaps the most elegant picnic ever devised by man. Holding a glass of Sauvignon Blanc, Poggi defends his precious Urals from the half-serious charge that they are, well, rather ungainly

CENTRAL VIETNAM

in appearance. "The sidecar is not a very noble piece of transportation, it's true. No matter how we package it. But there is nobility in riding a sidecar, there is nobility in experiencing the highlands in this way, there is nobility in enjoying a lunch of foie gras and perhaps a glass of white wine." There's no arguing this.

After lunch we climb ever higher into the highlands on narrow roads of the switchback variety, each one flanked by precipitous drop-offs lurking just beyond the guardrails—when there are guardrails. It's something of a shock to see that Vietnam can be so legitimately mountainous. Two hours from Dalat we zig-zag our way up through a broad mountain pass and Poggi points to a hillside dotted with cultivated vegetation: "Café," he shouts, lifting an imaginary demitasse to his lips. It was the first of many plantations we would pass in the next half hour.

As we draw closer to our destination, the roads get better and the population less sparse. For several hours, we had passed only through dusty, remote villages where locals met our odd caravan first with surprise, then with smiles and waves. In these more populous areas, our standing as curiosities is more modest. Dalat is a resort mecca that attracts all kinds of tourists, foreign and domestic. A light rain begins to fall. We draw less and less attention as pedestrians veil themselves and we find our place amid the wider flow of traffic.

Though we have been climbing steadily since mid-morning, the final stretch of road is the steepest yet. Halfway up this series of switchbacks, the vegetation turns again; there are

pine trees at the roadside now, and the air sports a startling crispness as we cruise into Dalat. The French influence in Vietnam is hard to miss, even fifty years and three wars removed. But because the French founded Dalat, as opposed to merely occupying it, the city has retained more of its Gallic character than just about any place in Vietnam. Our ultimate destination, the Sofitel Dalat Palace hotel, which opened in 1922 and has been painstakingly restored, evokes a level of French colonial grandeur and indolence unmatched by anything in the country.

Bedecked in shorts and flip-flops, I surely looked a fright as I hoist my dust-covered frame from the Sheena Express. Had I alighted in this state from a mere automobile, I might feel out of place. As it is, I ascend the ornate, white marble steps in the perfect historical idiom, regretting only that I have failed to pack a tuxedo for the evening ahead.

Novotel Ocean Dunes & Golf Resort
1 Ton Duc Thang St.
Phan Thiet City
(84-62) 822-393
www.novotel.com

Princess d'Annam Resort & Spa
Ke Ga Bay
Binh Thuan Province
(84-8) 840-9646
www.princessannam.com

Mui Ne

Adam Bray sleds the serene white dunes of Mui Ne

The area north of the twin villages of Mui Ne and Hon Rom is a vast sea of red, yellow, and snow-white sand dunes where very little grows. When I first arrived in Vietnam, these dunes were approached by nothing more than a dirt road that disintegrated once you reached Hon Rom village. Herds of black and brown goats and solitary cows wandered through town untended. Without a four-wheel-drive jeep, the villages beyond were only reachable by boat or a perilous trek through the desert.

With increased tourism, though, roads were soon paved through the dunes, which extend the length of Binh Thuan Province. Long-isolated communities and blinding white desert landscapes of rolling sand were accessible by standard motor vehicles for the first time. One of the driest places in Southeast Asia, this desert region could now be explored by any traveler up for a little adventure.

Although there are dunes throughout the province, the most impressive I have seen are forty-five minutes north of Mui Ne. The area is referred to by several names, including White Sand Dunes and Bau Trang, or White Lake, because of the large natural reservoir below the dunes. Unfortunately, many popular maps place the lake on the wrong road, leading weary foreigners dozens of kilometers into the arid countryside, where neither water nor petrol is widely available. I fell victim on my first expedition, but as long as you realize the reservoir is found right at the dunes, you'll be fine.

With each visit, I continue to be captivated by the enormous dunes. They are a favorite subject of Vietnamese photographers and painters because of the dramatic contrasts of light and shadow. They are always moving and changing shape—and they are also expanding, according to recent surveys. Clear-cutting and poorly managed agricultural development are the biggest factors leading to the desert's growth, but chemical pollutants and climate change may also be involved. During intense periods of drought, I've witnessed alarming sand storms, and many times I've had to make a choice between taking a bath or watering the fruit trees at my house in Mui Ne. The land is quickly drying out so much that it has caught the attention of UNESCO, which began a program to develop new irrigation systems in order to save the local community.

The lake is the area's only water source, and for more than 1,000 years, its shores have been sparsely settled. According to local legend,

SOUTHERN VIETNAM

a large Cham temple to the goddess Thien Y Ana once stood on the south shore, but the ruins were eventually swallowed up by the marauding dunes. Today, there is a large stand of pine trees on this southern shore, and it's my favorite spot for an afternoon nap while I listen to the wind blowing through the sea of evergreen needles. The area has also become a popular location for shooting Vietnamese music videos and films.

Even in what seems to be the most desolate ecosystem in Vietnam, there is life. My local friends gather eggs laid by sea birds directly on the sand, and hunt enormous lizards in their burrows; these lizards are quite delicious when grilled. The lake is teeming with fish, which you can watch fishermen catching in their small nets. Most inhabitants of this region rely on fishing to survive, but some raise herds of goats, which are sold to local hot pot restaurants. You may catch a glimpse of a covered platform on stilts, hidden within the dunes, where the shepherd boys and their goats sleep at night.

The dunes also offer a unique Vietnamese experience—the best sledding I have had is here. One day when I was out exploring, village kids greeted me with plastic sleds for rent. It's all the fun of the winter sport, without having to worry about any of the typical hazards at the bottom, like trees, rocks, or automobiles. The only part I don't like is the climb back up the hill. Aim for the lake and you can end the ride with a splash. But avoid swimming through the lotus patches. The kids tell stories

of children tangling their feet in the reeds and drowning.

Whether you're looking for some quiet time for reflection, fun physical activity, a light nap, or a bit of adventure in an exotic landscape like nowhere else in the region, the White Sand Dunes are one of Vietnam's top detours off the tourist route.

Transportation

While it is the priciest mode of transport at $20-$25, depending upon the number of people in your group, taking a jeep tour to the dunes is well worth it. Jeeps make half the trip on the beach, allowing you views of the undulating coastline, fishing villages, and a nearby island. It also means you have an experienced driver in case of problems. The trip can also be made by motorbike on the newly paved road. Expect to pay $5-$7 to rent a motorbike for a full day, and up to $10 if you require a driver. The ride is about forty-five minutes each way, not including stops at the Fairy Springs, which is a nice walk but best as a separate trip; the market; the Red Sand Dunes (if you are in a hurry, don't bother); and the Red Canyon.

Getting there

From Mui Ne Beach, travel east to Mui Ne village proper. At the village market, turn left/north. At the next major intersection turn left again, heading past the Red Sand

Dunes on your left, and then the sea on your right. Pass through Hon Rom village and continue north for about thirty minutes on the paved road. Drive along with the sea on your right, and then the road will appear to head out to the countryside. The road will veer right, skirting a small fishing village. Turn left at the next intersection, heading farther into the countryside. You will pass a small mountain with five layers of color on your right. When you come to the next village, turn right on a dirt road that leads you past the lake and into the dunes. Essentially, the entire trip follows the coast, heading northeast.

Provisions

Sunscreen, water, and a full tank of petrol are a *must*. These three things can not be over-emphasized. The last place to buy these is Mui Ne Village, in the market. This is also a good place to pick up some fruit and picnic supplies for lunch. The best times to go are very early in the morning or late in the afternoon because those are the coolest times of the day and provide the most dramatic lighting for photography.

Learning more about the dunes

www.muinebeach.net/white sanddunes.htm

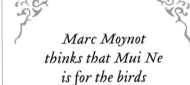

Marc Moynot thinks that Mui Ne is for the birds

As soon as you enter any natural area in Vietnam, you will discover numerous bird species. And for any birder who spends a few days near Phan Thiet-Mui Ne, the dune area encompassing the Bau Trang Lakes must be on the schedule.

The Bau Trang Lakes are a beautiful destination outside Mui Ne, a fishing village up the coast from Phan Thiet. This natural area offers the sight of three lakes lost in a semi-desert area. The biggest has dark waters surrounded by water lilies and lotuses. In the background, large white sand dunes contrast with the lakes' deep blues. Since the lakes are only a few kilometers, as the crow flies, from the sea, strong winds accumulate white sand and reshape the dunes during the dry season.

Arriving to this lake from Mui Ne, the main road turns left. Before you reach this bend, turn right. The road goes just over two kilometers along the lake, then turns left. On the right hand side, there is a small lake that used to be very interesting with the birds species it sheltered, but it is now fenced and its biotope has changed. I used to observe water birds like the Purple Swamphen and Little Grebe that still live on the big lake, as well as the interesting Masked

Finfoot, which probably moved to a quieter place. Still on this smaller lake are four species of herons: Grey Heron, Great-billed Heron, Little Egret, and Great Egret. Another permanent species is the Great Cormorant.

Keep it to yourself, but there is another shallow lake farther on the right, which is not visible from the road. You can find it on foot by following the fence around the previous lake and heading away from the road. Walk about ten minutes, following the fence, and you'll see it. On this lake you can see, early in the morning, the Fulvous Whistling Duck. It is shy and often hidden in the reeds. In the rainy season, there are numerous migrant species like the skilful Little Tern, Small Pratincoles, and the noisy (when disturbed) Red-wattled Lapwing. Go a little farther on the dunes and you'll probably meet the strange Great Thick-knee, a big wader living on the sand.

Everywhere around there are Oriental Skylarks, with their optimistic singing, Kentish Plovers running on the sand, and three species of colorful Bee-eaters. Bee-eaters are probably the most vibrant birds in Vietnam, with blue, green, brown, and yellow coloring. They feed on bees and other insects, caught in flight. They have rather long, pointed wings and fly like swallows.

The most common bird of prey over the lakes is the Osprey, always looking for some fish to catch. Like other predatory birds in the region, including Imperial Eagles and Crested Serpent Eagles, it likes to take advantage of the area's good thermals.

As you're exploring, if you look up, on wires you will see Plain-backed Sparrows, with their yellow breast and belly, gathered to talk about the weather. Other local watch-birds are White-throated Kingfishers and Dollarbirds, in addition to several types of drongos; these are all from the Roller family and look very dark when perched, but display splendid intense blue colors when they fly. The same is true for the Indian Roller, with turquoise colors on wings and crown. Given the dramatic, monochromatic dune landscape of this region, the vibrant contrasts provided by these feathered inhabitants make this one of the most intriguing bird-watching areas of Southeast Asia.

Identifying the birds of Vietnam

Written by Craig Robson, *A Field Guide to the Birds of South-East Asia* is a good source for recognizing Vietnamese birds.

CON DAO ISLANDS

Jon Hoff finds the oddity of the Con Dao Islands appealing

The Con Dao Islands are home to beautiful rocky coves and long deserted sandy beaches, but I'd rather write about some of the stranger things I observed at this remote and unusual destination. I say *remote* because even though it's only a forty-five-minute flight from Ho Chi Minh City, it may as well be ten hours out into the South China Sea. Con Son, the main island, was previously a penal colony used first by the French and then the Americans. These days, only a few Western tourists visit this island, and just 6,000 people live on it; one-third of those are soldiers. Even the main road through Con Son town can be ghostly quiet in the middle of the day.

This wasn't the case when we arrived on Saturday morning, however. During our stay, the town was brimming with groups of ragged-looking men with nowhere to go. They were fishermen who reside on the many boats moored in the harbor, but had disembarked to eat and drink while waiting to go out again. We put the large number down to the fact that the boats were grounded due to rough weather. A storm had hit Danang a few days before our visit, and we were feeling the tail end of it. On Sunday lunchtime I had to weave my bike around these fishermen as they staggered across the street in twos and threes, all of them three sheets to the wind. Dazed by curiosity and also a good lashing of rice wine, some almost walked into lampposts and fell down manholes when they saw us. They gazed at my wife Chi like they'd never seen a woman before.

If I had to pick one adjective to use for Con Son, it would be *rugged*, so

exploring the coast and the island's interior was a priority. But on our first exploratory drive, we became stranded in a torrential downpour. Much to the consternation of Chi, I headed to the nearest beach. We found shelter from the rain among some trees, but I couldn't resist running to the water's edge, which was quite a way as the tide was out. My saturated, beleaguered wife watched in silent astonishment as I sprinted into the distance.

We arrived back at the hotel just as the rain was letting up—of course. My plan for the next few hours was simple. Get clean and dry, then settle somewhere comfy with my book: the verandah outside our bungalow seemed good.

Unlike most seaside bungalows, our resort was separated from the sea by a road. In other words, any passing pedestrian could liberate his intrigue by simply peering through the glass windows into our room—and many did. It's slightly unsettling to be midway through pulling on a pair of jeans and then notice a band of disheveled, gap-toothed men gathered on the sidewalk outside, gawking in with no concern that they are visually trespassing. As the wind swept along the lonely coast road and through our deserted hotel where we were the only guests, the constantly overcast skies and random voyeurs gave the trip something of an edge. I was never comfortable in our room unless the curtains were drawn.

The island is littered with hiking opportunities, and so on the second day we decided to try probably the most arduous trek available. It starts by following the beach of Dong Bac Bay, which is at least two kilometers long, before diving into the forest and eventually finishing at Dam Tre Lagoon. At six kilometers each way, it isn't easy going—the path is rocky and steep in places, and consistent rain showers made the rocks slippery. When we were halfway to the lagoon, a commotion erupted, as if a beast had just emerged from the bushes. I rushed ahead to find an American tourist flailing his arms around like a madman. The track passed a bee's nest. We took a prickly detour around, and thankfully our guide pinpointed the spot on the way back. When we arrived at the lagoon, snorkeling was almost impossible. The tide was well out, exposing around 100 meters of barnacle-encrusted rocks to traverse before reaching water—no good unless you have leather feet. We didn't.

A less strenuous outing was a twenty-minute walk to the rocky cove called Ong Dung. The road up the mountainside to the path turned from sealed, to gravel, to nonexistent, and we had to leave our motorbike unattended. Earlier, at another place, we'd been waved away as ridiculous for asking if it was a wise idea to leave our bike unguarded. I mean, who's going to steal a bike out here! On the way up, we passed two boys who were over the moon to see us; we all waved and smiled, and I thought nothing of it. However, shortly after we retrieved our bike for the return journey, it sputtered and cut out. Luckily we could glide all the way to the road at the

bottom, but then were stranded once again for thirty minutes before help arrived and we realized the problem. Those rascals had flicked the safety valve, which cuts off the flow of petrol to the engine.

Con Son is one of those places in Asia where, despite the natural beauty, something just seems a little off-kilter. To round out the strangeness of our experiences, one evening as we were driving our motorcycle along a badly lit sea road, we saw a big group of guys goading two boys with long, thick staffs. It looked like an organized street fight. Curious, we passed by again, witnessing a lot of shouting and jostling. Even more worrying, the next day we saw two kids, no older than ten, practicing their stick-fighting skills with mini staffs. It was as if they couldn't wait for the opportunity to be in a "real" stick fight of their own one day. As for me, I felt as if I were watching some bizarre BBC special on the stick fighters of the Con Dao Islands. Of course, if there were such a special, it would have to be a series and include episodes on wild bees, peeping Toms, motorcycle vandals, and travelers such as me, who find that such oddities are what give a place its appeal.

Getting There

Vasco Airlines flies to the Con Dao Islands four times a week from Ho Chi Minh City. A return ticket costs around $80. Tickets can be purchased from Saigon Tourist.

49 Le Thanh Ton St.
District 1
Ho Chi Minh City
(84-8) 829-8914
www.saigontourist.net

Getting back to nature

The key to arranging your itinerary on this island is the National Park Headquarters, which is easy to find. In Con Son town simply locate Vo Thi Sau Street, which runs perpendicular from the beach. The Park Center is about one kilometer inland past the market. It is from here that all walking trips should be organized. Because most of the island is a national park, access for visitors is restricted, and often a permit is needed. Also, a guide is recommended for most trips. Guides cost around $6 per day. The Park provides a very useful booklet detailing more than ten ideas for half- and full-day trips. Boat trips to the outlying islands in the bay can also be arranged from the headquarters or your hotel. For diving, check

with Rainbow Divers on Ton Duc Thang Street, near the jetty.

Staying along the seafront

ATC Hotel

A centrally located French villa with four rooms.

16B Ton Duc Thang St.
Con Son Town
(84-64) 830-666

Saigon Con Dao Resort

Also right in town, this property is comprised of old French bungalows.

18 Ton Duc Thanh St.
Con Son Town
(84-64) 830-155

Con Dao Resort

The high-end option, which is a little out of the town center and feels quite isolated at nighttime.

8 Nguyen Duc Thang St.
Con Son Town
(84-64) 830-939

WHEN IN ROME

Lessons on living local and making yourself at home.

E very country has its own traits, sometimes better described as idiosyncrasies. That is what this chapter is all about. And no, I am not referring to the slew of foot massage parlors you cannot avoid in the tourist areas of Hanoi and Ho Chi Minh City. Though they prevail, they are recent imports, inspired no doubt by the popularity of such venues in Thailand. These essays address topics that go beyond trends, topics so ingrained that they brace the very foundation that makes Vietnam distinctly Vietnam—and prove that some clichés, like the dizzying traffic, are not rooted in travelers' apocrypha but in reality.

So, how about that traffic? And why are there five essays here about it? Wouldn't one good one suffice? Absolutely not. An entire book could be written about traffic in Vietnam, and there would still be more left to say. Like the freeways in Los Angeles and the Underground in London, the streets of Vietnam's cities—and even many of its smaller towns—form a subculture, complete with its own language, denizens, and peculiarities. The essays here give you just a taste, beginning with Jan Vail's introduction, which is as frenzied as the traffic itself. Jon Hoff then goes on to describe driving his motorcycle to work every morning, while Marianne Smallwood breaks down the *xe om* experience of hitching a ride on a motorcycle taxi. Focusing on the human aspect are Ed Daniels and Elka Ray, whose personal relationships with their motorcycle drivers are essential to their time in Vietnam.

Another notable quality that sets Vietnam apart is a unique love of country. It is not patriotism or nationalism, but a kind of romance that is conducted between the Vietnamese and their homeland. Traveling through Vietnam with Huong, one of my best girlfriends, I was always amazed by her passion for, and curiosity about, all things Vietnamese, from the tombs of the former emperors to the origins of *bun bo Hue* soup. The attitude can veer into the sentimental at times, but that is part of the charm, as is revealed in Vu Kieu Linh's essay about

the autumnal *hoa sua* flowers of Hanoi, Duong Lam Anh's ruminations on winter in Hue, and Pham Hoi Nam's praise for Ho Chi Minh City's nightlife.

Simone Samuel's descriptions of her alley in Hanoi reminded me of my own lane in Ho Chi Minh City, and Antoine Sirot's portrait of ballroom dancing brought to mind being taken salsa dancing by my students one Saturday at 9 a.m. Describing disco dancing in a public park, rowing a bamboo coracle boat, drinking beer in the Mekong Delta, teaching English to university students, or befriending elderly massage women, each essay touches on something quintessentially Vietnamese, giving you a greater insight into the country's complex character.

HANOI

Vu Kieu Linh savors the fragrance of autumn in Hanoi

I have a bad habit of driving around Hanoi at night without purpose or direction, the weak yellow glow of the streetlights guiding my way. All shops are closed, even my favorites, the street food places. Though a few motorbikes pass me by, and occasional taxis honk at the crossroads, they cannot take away the purity of this city. At midnight, when the streets are empty, Hanoi becomes the familiar hometown of my memory.

With the arrival of autumn, I speed up a little bit in Ba Trieu Street to smell the fragrance of *hoa sua*—milk flower. Numerous songs and poems have been written about Hanoi in the fall, and so many of those are about *hoa sua*, the flower that you can find here only at this time of year. Lining the streets, the tall, rough trees have little white flowers which bloom from the middle of September until the end of October. And then the flower season ends. Hanoians must wait another year for the sweet perfume to return.

When I was young, every year when the fragrance of the *hoa sua* melted in the wind, I knew it was the sign that summer was over and those back-to-school days had come once again. It made me feel excited because I had so many stories to share with my classmates. *Hoa sua* meant I could go to school each day, seeing my friends and my teachers. Now that I am grown up and no longer living in my hometown, each time I return during the autumn months, the fragrant white flowers transport me back to my childhood.

Discovering hoa sua

Starting at the southwest end of Hoan Kiem Lake, begin walking down Ba Trieu Street. At Ly Thuong Kiet Street is the first *hoa sua* tree that you will meet. Continue walking down Ba Trieu for about one kilometer, until you reach Nguyen Du Street. Turn right, and all along this street are *hoa sua* trees—and only *hoa sua* trees—one right after another. You will also see another of Hanoi's beautiful lakes, Thien Quang. Finish your small tour of Hanoi's autumn flower by enjoying the fresh lake breeze. If you do this tour by bike, it will only take fifteen minutes; I recommend that you walk so you can fully enjoy it.

Simone Samuels loses her way in the alleys of Hanoi

In one of the back alleys near my house, a lady in front of a small tea-shop smiles at me. Her kind expression draws me in, so I stroll to her shop, where a young man is smoking tobacco through a large bamboo pipe and sipping green tea from a small egg cup-like vessel. "Where are you going?" she asks me.

"Oh, nowhere really. I'm just taking a walk. I live nearby."

"I have never seen you here before, and I have been living here for a long time." Her English is impeccable as she garners my particulars in a typically Vietnamese manner, which is both casual and inquisitive.

I tell her that this is the first time I've walked this way. Normally I just leave my house and go straight to the main road, but today I feel like wandering.

"Are you going to the temple?" she inquires, pointing at the sticks of incense I have in my hand, which I only bought because the lady selling them in a quiet corner looked so old and frail.

"Not yet, but I think I'll go there next."

This friendly exchange continues for a while, and while I tell her about myself, I also learn about how long she's been living in Hanoi away from her hometown, Sapa, and her life as a tea stand lady. It makes me wonder about the lives of all the people who inhabit the tall, narrow houses along the maze of alleys in the little community where I live. Why have I never meandered through here before?

It's almost as if I have left the Hanoi I know so well and entered a new city. The alleys are quite slender, and as a pedestrian I have to make way for the steady stream of motorbikes and bicycles that are driven through. I don't know where I am going, but it doesn't matter much. I take a left turn and then a right down an alley that entices me. I walk the length of the alley, and then reach a dead end. I stop and listen, and can't believe how quiet it is. I can even hear birds calling from a little garden in front of someone's house.

I turn back the way I came and then take another turn. I'm sure that I'm lost, but I don't mind. I enjoy the almost indecipherable singsong of a lady who rides past on her bicycle as she calls out to the neighborhood that she is selling fresh *banh mi* (sandwiches). I watch as two old women, gray hair pulled back into buns, slowly ride past on rusty, rickety bicycles, chatting away idly as they pedal. There are many bumps and ridges on the ground, but they ride over them expertly, pedals and brakes creaking and screeching all the way.

I keep strolling. A wrinkled and weathered-looking lady in her pajamas sits on a small stool out the front of her small house-front shop, many of which I have seen on this walk. She is casually fanning herself and watching people go by. Two small children giggle as they choose some candy, and their mother barters for a kilogram of rice, which the middle-aged shopkeeper measures out on old-fashioned scales.

I keep walking down the winding, endless alleyways, past modern houses with big, imposing gates and others that look so old I wonder if they even have plumbing. I come to a small vegetable market where the red tomatoes, bright green vegetables, squares of tofu, and vibrantly colored fruits are presented to passersby in large baskets that have been carried there by the conical-hatted ladies who sit and gossip together as I walk by.

At the end of one alley there is a *pho* stand, where steaming bowls of noodle soup are being served to some men for lunch. Dappled spots of sunlight shine onto the ground near the stand. With the alley's walls creating shadows, it looks magical. The two women making the *pho* glance at me curiously as I stroll past.

A small child is learning how to ride his little bike, which his dad is holding onto as he wobbles, trying to gain balance. An old rusty and derelict *cyclo,* which looks like a remnant of the war, is being prodded along with a huge load of furniture piled precariously onto it. A lady pushes a long, heavy-looking clothes rack on wheels. This mobile fashion shop is filled with colorful garments; surely, she makes this trip through the alleys every day. This is real Vietnamese life going on all around me, so different from how I know it out on the main streets.

I definitely don't know where I am now. I hit many dead ends and try to go back the way I came. Instead, I find myself in another new place, where there is a stagnant body of water with a relic of a crashed B-52 bomber aircraft sticking out of it. A small memorial has been erected nearby, and I marvel at how I came across this unfamiliar site, and wonder if I can ever find it again to show others.

I concede defeat at ever finding my way out of the rabbit warren of alleys on my own, so I stop in at a little café set up below someone's house. I walk through the plastic strips hanging down from the doorway, interrupt the young girl who's staring at MTV, and order a *café nau da.* On the way out, as I pay my 7,000 VND for the coffee, I ask the way to Ngo 209, and the girl leaves the café, takes me by the arm, and directs me.

The walls of the alleys are high, and they all look the same. I don't wonder how I missed my turn and got so lost, but I am glad that I did. When I emerge from the alley that I have been directed to walk down, I get my bearings and realize I have done a full circle and am back at the end of the alley where I live. I've returned to Ngo 209, I'm lost no more, and I feel relieved. I make a promise to myself that I will wander some more within my little community. After all, this is where everyday Vietnamese life takes place as it probably always has, and hopefully, always will.

Get lost

Off most main roads in Hanoi, it is possible to walk down the alleys (*ngo*) where people live. This walk began at Ngo 209, Doi Can Street, Ba Dinh District, but could also start at Ngoc Ha Street near the Ho Chi Minh Mausoleum. If coming from Doi Can, walk down Ngo 209 until you have to turn. I took a turn right and then kept walking and exploring. It's possible to emerge at Ngoc Ha Street if you take the correct turns. Pay attention to the direction you walk and note any significant landmarks you see, as these alleys are not marked on any Hanoi maps. If you get lost, just ask a local for the way out.

Renee Friedman gets down with disco dancers in a Hanoi park

Across the street from one of my favorite Hanoi *bia hoi* (beer) joints is where my daughter loves to go for an evening stroll and watch the disco line dancers. With the exception of some ex-pat friends who occasionally join us at my invitation, I am always the only Caucasian in the park, and my Vietnamese child once suggested I dye my hair black.

"Why?" I asked.

"Because it is embarrassing to be seen with a Westerner," she declared.

If you venture into this park, you can see all manner of Vietnamese life. In a country where people often live in tight quarters—ten people to one bedroom—exercise and activity take place outside. Throughout the morning and day in public spaces, you will find older people doing *tai chi*, barefoot boys playing soccer, and women performing aerobics, led by an instructor and a blaring boom box. In the summer, one corner of the park becomes a toddlers' amusement center, complete with erected bumper car rides, merry-go-rounds, and more. There are also concession stands and people hawking wares.

Parks in Hanoi are often situated around the city's many bodies of water, and this one, surrounding Thanh Cong Lake, is no exception.

There is a fountain in the middle of it, which at dusk is turned on and lit up by colored lights. A stroll around the park takes you adjacent to a mini golf course and behind an open-air food and hardware market in the corner of one of the most densely populated areas in middle-working class Hanoi.

Despite all that this park offers, my daughter's favorite spot remains the disco line dancing area right at the main entrance on Lang Ha Street across from the *bia hoi* joint. There, every evening except Sunday, rain or shine, from eight to nine-thirty, a jovial man comes with music and a mike, and calls out instructions while dancing and laughing. On Christmas Eve, he even wore a Santa suit. I learned how to count in Vietnamese from him while everyone danced in unison.

You can join in, and a secret I discovered later, as I marveled at how every Vietnamese person seemed to get the moves without having to learn them first, is that though the dancing starts at eight, people can show up at seven-thirty for more individual instruction. My presence as a spectator was warmly welcomed, and I was often invited to dance, but my daughter who loved to watch, steadfastly and adamantly refused to participate or allow me to leave her side.

Back across the street is the Pink Palace, a multi-story pink restaurant that has an English menu and serves ice cream for dessert. Down the block is the National Cinema, which often hosts international movie festivals that are usually free. If you get a hankering for "home cooking," farther along

is the first Kentucky Fried Chicken in Hanoi, situated on Hoang Ngoc Phac Street, which serves chicken with rice in lieu of fries. As we stroll, or more accurately, navigate through sidewalks that serve primarily as motorcycle parkades, brand new SUVs drive past an old man sitting on a corner with a pump. For pennies, he will pump up the bicycle tire of a working woman coming into town from the countryside, dressed in the standard garb—black loose pants, a long-sleeved, light-colored shirt, conical hat, and plastic slippers.

These streets are literally and figuratively filled with the collision of the modern and traditional, illustrating a country on the cusp of major, irrevocable change that I am quite certain is rapidly occurring even as you read this essay. Construction sites and cars are popping up like mushrooms after a rain, and the daily life of average urban-dwelling Vietnamese throbs around it all. This area is just a thirty-minute public bus ride from the comfort and familiarity of the Old Quarter. Exploration is free and open. You are only limited by the extent of your desire and curiosity. Who knows? You just might turn a corner and come upon an Asian Santa gleefully barking disco directions into a microphone.

Disco dancing in the park
Lang Ha St. and Huynh Thuc Khang St.
Dong Da District
Hanoi

Word to the wise

When walking near the open-air food and hardware market, keep an eye out for used needles on the ground.

HUE

Duong Lam Anh finds beauty in Hue's gray winter days

Winter arrived in Hue rather late this year, but it eventually did, as it always does.

Winter in Hue is wet. This is nothing new to the locals, but those from drier regions find it hard to tolerate. With the humidity up to 90 and sometimes even 100 percent, the whole city suddenly turns into a damp sponge. Rain lingers day and night. Drop by drop it enters your heart. It comes as no surprise to see the rain last even for weeks. People are wet. Vehicles are wet. Buildings are wet. Grass is rotten. Paper soon becomes as soft as tissue. You may wake up to find your computer dead without a word of warning. Telephones and other electrical appliances all at once refuse to function. You are late to work because your motorbike suddenly won't start. That's that.

Winter in Hue is cold. Eighteen Celsius may mean nothing to those from cold lands, but coupled with the humidity, it chills you to the bone. But the streets look festive with people wrapped up in colorful warm clothes and raincoats. They suddenly seem more formal and decent in suit, vest, and jacket; some even don scarves, gloves, and wool caps.

Winter in Hue is hazy, smoky, and gloomy. The sky is gray the entire day. The whole city looks sleepy in a mist of vapor, smoke, and breath. Leaves turn dark green and shiver with cold. There is a lot of talk about the weather, and people on the street seem to be in a hurry because they all want to reach home as quickly as possible. A book, a cup of hot coffee or tea, and some classical music become wise choices.

But despite all sorts of problems and inconveniences that may be caused by the rain and humidity, life must go on. That is what I like best about the winter here. Streets are, as always, crowded with people and vehicles at rush hours. Street stalls serving hot dishes are surrounded by hungry pedestrians. And it seems that tourists do not mind the rain at all. In light casual clothes and with an umbrella or raincoat, they rush around exploring the imperial city.

People who aren't from here and hate the season call it *nasty, horrible, disgusting*. Hue natives living far away from home miss it terribly.

Keeping cozy during winter in Hue

Following are three of my favorite cafés for warming up during the winter months.

Vi Da Xua Café

Located in the Vi Da neighborhood, this café recalls the quiet, rustic atmosphere of the area's once-famous village. For the locals, it is a place to cherish memories of the past. For foreigners, it evokes something very Vietnamese. As a cozy *nha ruong*—a typical, traditional structure of Hue made entirely of wood—it is ideal for cold, rainy days. Not too open or too closed: just perfect.

131 Nguyen Sinh Cung St.

Nam Giao Hoai Co Café

A complex of three *nha ruong* creates this spacious and airy café. Due to its location on the way to the royal tombs, it serves as a pleasant place for visitors to stop by. Though it has open architecture, it doesn't get too cold when it's raining, and you can sip a hot coffee or tea while gazing at the rain outside.

321 Dien Bien Phu St.

Xua Café

Unlike in the West, life in Vietnam is lived in the alleys: they are communities within a community. With its very Vietnamese architecture, this café is small enough to keep you warm on rainy days. Its location in an alley far away from the main streets offers peace, quiet, and privacy.

56/6 Nguyen Cong Tru St.

DANANG

Alice Driver paddles a bamboo coracle at China Beach

The previous two mornings the stars were brilliant and the moon crisp, the light from both turning the ocean a silver-gray, but on this morning the stars were smothered. Despite the early hour, China Beach was populated with people still winding down from a nightlong Young Communist gathering. Music from the police compound where the festivities took place was so loud that it felt as if it were pumping through my veins. Dark figures were scattered across the beach laughing, eating, and swimming in the cottony blackness of early morning.

My husband Isaac and I walked down to the *thung chai* boats at the water's edge, looking for Thanh, a fisherman we had befriended during the month we were spending in the area, learning about traditional boat-making. His wife appeared, her tiny body emerging from the surrounding night, to tell us that he would arrive soon. We sat down in the sand to wait, and I looked out to the horizon trying to divine how the sun would rise. Some days the horizon was aflame with orange, burning into red and pink as the sun rose. Other times the moon held its ground, keeping half the beach in the dark, letting the sun know that day was not to come quickly or easily. The clouds varied—fluffy, hovering, smudged, undefined—the possibilities infinite.

Thanh arrived, his white teeth floating through the night like the grin of the Cheshire Cat. He was half my size, with sinewy legs and a small muscular body. He greeted us as we pushed the coracle into the ocean. Knee deep in the water, we all hopped in, the successive weight causing the circular bamboo boat to tilt wildly. Thanh took the single oar in his calloused hands and moved us toward the horizon.

Sitting cross-legged in the center, I leaned over the edge to catch sight of the oar plying the waters, a trail of emerald phosphorescence following behind. Thanh stood flat-footed, his legs like roots. Then he motioned for Isaac to paddle. The oar is attached to the bobbing boat at its midpoint, which causes it to act as oar or catapult, depending on the rower's skill level. A novice rower could easily be flipped over the side.

Slowly, we moved in the direction of another group of bamboo boats. Thanh indicated that I should take the oar. I stood up, my body feeling huge and awkward next to his tiny one. I took hold of the smooth slab of bamboo, and Isaac simultaneously hooked his fingers through my belt loop to prevent me from being pitched into the water. With much laughing, I rowed in a figure eight, then from side to side, the boat spinning around in circles. Thanh got

up and put his calloused hands over mine, showing me how to grip the oar properly. Then he stirred it in a U-shape, propelling the boat forward.

Isaac took the oar again as Thanh yelled greetings to another fisherman and gestured to Isaac to row over. The dark boats kissed, and Thanh pulled out two cigarettes, giving one to his friend. The lighter changed hands, and after a few words the boats parted, the lighted cigarette floating off into the dark morning.

Thanh rowed in the direction of his squid bait, marked by Styrofoam squares. He took out a spool of fishing line with a weight and a circular spray of fishing hooks. He dropped it over the edge, jerking it sharply as it sank. No luck. We moved to the second Styrofoam block, Thanh repeating his actions. After a minute he excitedly pointed to the line, pulling the translucent body out of the water. The squid spurted water and ink, desperately trying to propel itself away. Thanh held it proudly; the squid's iridescent eye looked out accusingly, its body filled with water that moved up and down with the pumping of its breath. He threw it in a woven basket and started paddling off to the next Styrofoam block. The rest of the morning produced no more squid, making me think that the twenty or so larger boats on the horizon had gobbled everything up.

We moved swiftly toward shore through the clear, unruffled waters. Once near enough, we jumped out and pushed the boat ashore. Isaac and Thanh attached a large bamboo pole to the ropes on the side of the boat and hoisted the pole to their shoulders. Thanh's fifteen-year-old daughter and I grabbed the sides to help lift it off the ground. With the boat sitting in its place on the sand, we shook hands, gave our thanks, and agreed to meet up a little while later to visit a boat builder who lived between China Beach and Hoi An.

We went on motorbikes to visit the boat builder, Anh Lu. After ten minutes on the newly constructed road, we pulled into a sandy driveway and were greeted by a lean old man with a sparse, pointy, black-and-gray beard. He was sitting on a bench under an open shed and was splitting bamboo with his knife.

Isaac pulled out a bamboo weaving Anh Lu had given him the week before, and demonstrated his own efforts to reproduce it. The boat builder smiled, his angular beard pulled up by the corners of his mouth. He took Isaac to the shed and gave him strips of bamboo to work with, allowing him to begin the process of building a bamboo coracle. I sat on a stool in the sand surrounded by a group of curious adults and children. I used my few Vietnamese phrases to begin a conversation underscored with gestures and words in English. They taught me new phrases, offered me fruit, and invited me to lunch.

Meanwhile, Isaac was inside weaving the bamboo and beating the strips into place with a wooden mallet. As he worked, a crowd gathered around him, watching his progress, much as they did every day we were there. It was a pleasant way to spend that month, sharing not only in the work, but also the food, language, and stories of the people who opened their world to us during that time.

Staying at China Beach

China Beach is located just seven kilometers southeast of Danang and can be reached by taxi, motorbike, or bus. For affordable accommodation with personality, Hoa's Place is excellent. Rooms are $7-$12, with the option of air conditioning for a little extra. Hoa cooks up good, simple, local dishes in his restaurant and offers family-style dinners for guests. Hoa's easygoing personality and knowledge of local people and places make this the best place to stay. Visitors should rent a motorbike ($4-$5/day or less if rented for long periods) and spend a day or two exploring the area.

215/14 Huyen Tran Cong Chua St.
Non Nuoc Beach/China Beach
(84-511) 969-216

NHA TRANG

Jessy Needham frolics in the mud outside Nha Trang

Nha Trang is not much fun on a rainy weekend, and one day in

December, when the sky was gray and full of threatening clouds, and the wind was too strong for us to sit on the beach without sand blowing continuously in our faces, my friend and I decided to ride out to the local mud baths. If we couldn't put our bathing suits to good use in the ocean, we figured we could at least go swimming in some hot springs.

"Soaking in mineral mud is very interesting," the billboard on the way to Thap Ba Hot Springs claimed. Imagining the mud baths to be like those spas where Hollywood stars go for elaborate skin treatments, I envisioned myself in a tub of thick, gooey mud in a candlelit room with New Age music playing in the background. In actuality, the atmosphere at the center turned out to be less of a relaxing spa and more like a water park. And to give fair warning: it is not off the beaten track. Carloads of vacationing Vietnamese will travel the few kilometers outside central Nha Trang to spend an afternoon at the baths.

Because budget concerns prevented us from choosing the $145 VIP package, featuring a private room, health check-up, massage, and hot tub adorned with rose petals, my friend and I debated getting our treatments à la carte or purchasing combo specials. While we discussed two-person versus individual tubs, a staff member encouraged us to select the tub for two.

"Are you sure?" I asked. "We're big Americans."

Although he assured us that the tubs were designed for Russians, the two-seater looked like it offered a more intimate experience than we were in the mood for. We big Americans chose individual versions and suited up.

For me, it is sometimes an odd experience to wear a bathing suit in Vietnam. In most places, except swanky bars in the big cities, women tend to stay covered up, either for modesty's sake or to protect their skin from the sun. Up until a few years ago, girls from the countryside rarely wore tank tops in public. Thus it's easy to feel like a Western harlot in your two-piece, especially when you have to unceremoniously strip down to your bathing suit in the middle of a bustling changing area full of curious mud-bath revelers.

The first phase of our experience was a shower, followed by a fifteen-minute soak in mineral mud. The mud, alas, was not thick and gooey, but rather watery and gritty. Still, it was fun to rub-a-dub in a wooden tub, up to our necks in mineral mud, enjoying the bucolic setting of pine trees rustling in the wind. The mud was extremely buoyant, making it difficult to avoid floating around in our tubs. Although we regretted leaving our camera in our locker, we didn't have to worry: a photographer was poised to capture the moment and delivered the photos to our hotel later that evening. We laughingly declined his suggestion that we rub mud on our faces and hair for maximum attractiveness. After the mineral mud, we were invited to sit in the sun for a few minutes. I assume this was to allow the mud to soak into our skin and thereby increase the therapeutic effects, but since there was little sun to be had, we skipped to the rinsing off stage.

Next, after standing in a communal shower with horizontal high-pressure water jets, we relaxed in a heart-shaped hot tub for twenty minutes, our medical ailments being washed away by the therapeutic springs. This is less romantic than it sounds, given the fact that there were quite a few hot tubs, all within a meter of each other, some filled to capacity by Vietnamese teenagers who were perfecting the art of horsing around.

Still, by this point, we definitely felt the experience was entertaining, if not quite as serene as we had expected, and the sight of families hot tubbing together is very charming. The grand finale was a swim in a large, insanely hot pool. The hot spring pool loosened up our muscles so much that all we felt like doing next was wrapping ourselves in our towels, curling up in our chaise lounges, and settling in for a mid-afternoon nap.

Thap Ba Hot Spring

The hot springs are open daily. There are signs all over Nha Trang pointing you to them. They're a little tricky to find, but most taxi drivers and hotel concierges know where they are. If traveling on your own, take the main road out of town to the Po Nagar Cham Towers. A few kilometers past the towers, look for a sign to the left directing you to the springs. For more information, check out the following website.

www.thapbahotspring.com.vn

DALAT

Lorene Strand gets an education at the University of Dalat

"Hello, hello," students shyly call to me as I walk up Phu Dong Thien Vuong Street toward the University of Dalat. The group has just finished lunch at a local *com sinh vien* and is heading back to school. Eager to practice their English, they join me, their musical voices inquiring about where I'm from, my family, my job, my life.

They are eager to share and show me around their university, which is young, founded in 1958 by a group of Catholic bishops. In 1976, following the country's reunification, the school was reorganized and became public, and today it is a multi-field institution, with more than twenty areas of study, including agricultural and botanical research, for which the area is known. Together, the students and I stroll the grounds, among pine and cherry trees, and rhododendron, mimosa, and hydrangea flowers. A sport stadium, outdoor amphitheater, student café, bookstore, library, greenhouse, and assorted buildings dot the hillside setting of what I consider to be the most beautiful university campus in all of Vietnam.

Through Volunteers in Asia, a non-profit organization located at Stanford University, I came to the University of Dalat and settled into a small apartment in a row of housing that lined a hill above the soccer field. I joined a small group of non-native faculty members who taught various English and French classes for the Department of Foreign Languages. The university teaching staff members that I worked with were incredibly gracious, and regularly organized various events to help us "foreigners" feel welcome and at home. I never witnessed any animosity toward any nationality, not Americans, Japanese, French, or Chinese—all past adversaries of Vietnam were warmly welcomed.

The classrooms at the university are basic, with rows of wooden benches facing a chalkboard on an elevated stage where the teacher's desk sits. As for the students, they were awesome: charming, curious, entertaining, and diligent. For example, when learning Business Marketing, the class was doing a focus on magazine advertising, and the students were laughing over a Purina Puppy Chow advertisement.

"Dog food? Really teacher?" questioned Mung.

"Yes, Mung," I replied, and I told him that pet owners can buy food for puppies, adult dogs, and elderly dogs. "There is also special canned dog food for little dogs and large dogs. It's sold at grocery stores and pet stores. Food for cats too."

"Pet stores!" The students laughed, and then later submitted their own advertisement for "Happy Taste," pet food suitable for dogs, cats, chickens, and pigs. The class capstone exercise was to create and promote a new product suitable for their marketplace. The winners were *Forever Love* perfume, *Knock-Out* chocolates, *Macho* sports drink, *Welcome Home* holiday cookies, and *Beautiful You* hair clips. My favorite activities by far, however, were the student performances in Listening and Speaking class, where students acted out plays based on Western culture and entertainment. *The Dating Game, Little Red Riding Hood, A Visit to the Dentist,* and the *Addams Family* were among the most entertaining.

Representing the youth of Vietnam, my students were enthusiastically forward-thinking. They told me, "We look forward to our beautiful future; our past is older than the wars." Indeed, their country's heritage is centuries older than the conflicts for which it is best known, and what impressed me most was their ability to see this, as well as to look ahead. Thus I find myself continually drawn back to the University of Dalat. Since fulfilling my teaching contract in 2003, I have returned almost every year to the hillside campus and its inspirational students.

University of Dalat
The university campus is perched in the hills, just north of Xuan Huong Lake, near the Dalat Golf Course.

01 Phu Dong Thien Vuong St. Dalat

Making new friends
If you'd like to meet up with a group of students, go to Phu Dong Thien

Vuong Street, where you will find dozens of *com sinh vien* restaurants that cater to the university crowd for morning bowls of *pho* soup and afternoon rice dishes. Or bring your badminton racquet and join in an early morning game (around 5 a.m.) or an evening game (around 4 p.m.). After class, soccer games are also common at the sport stadium. The students are happy to practice their English, as well as French and Chinese, with native speakers.

Volunteers in Asia

Teaching English is an excellent and rewarding way to get to know Vietnam. VIA requires a long-term commitment, but many language schools welcome native English speakers to lead single classes.

www.viaprograms.org

Antoine Sirot serenades ballroom dancers in Dalat

Believe it or not, I learned ballet dancing while a teenager in France. The best role I received was the shepherd Aminta in the ballet of *Sylvia*, composed by Leo Delibes. But even that doesn't make me as great a ballroom dancer as the people I enjoy watching at the Golf 3 dancing hall on Sunday nights.

I understand that because of the French influence, ballroom dancing has long been popular in Vietnam, especially in Dalat. In some archives of the Sofitel Dalat Palace hotel, where I am the general manager, we found a 1929 letter from a former manager, begging the colonial government, which was subsidizing the hotel operation, to keep budgeting for the hotel's house band in order to keep the traditional and then-famous ballroom dance parties going.

So, not being such a terrific dancer, I use another talent of mine at Golf 3 and sing famous French melodies with the local band onstage. From up there, I have a great view of the dancing couples, and they seem to enjoy the tunes. One of the songs, *Comme Toi*, has its own Vietnamese version, and I have performed it as a duet with a young local singer from the band. Much appreciated, this song reflects the best of what remains remembered after years of (often painful) colonial history: a blending of cultures. Today, you still hear a lot of French music in the cafés in town, together with American music and of course, pop Vietnamese, but the best place to go for some local musical flavor, and a chance to cha cha, is the Golf 3.

Happy dancing!

Golf 3 Dancing Hall

Local patrons of the dance hall range in age from mid-twenties to sixties. The most popular dances include the tango, cha cha, paso doble, and waltz.

Golf 3 Dalat Hotel
4 Nguyen Thi Minh Khai St.
Dalat
(84-63) 826-042
http://golfhotel.vnn.vn

MUI NE

Adam Bray
remembers those
forgotten in Mui Ne

I lived on the beach in Mui Ne during my first year in Vietnam. It was a very relaxing time but not without unique annoyances. The moment the sun rises between five and five-thirty, it beams into the bungalow and bakes the occupants. Mist from the sea condenses and makes all surfaces sticky. The bed is always full of sand. Whenever you open your door or window, everyone on the beach can—and does—look inside. As well, you get visited by every single peddler of goods and services, whether they are sellers of fresh mangos and pineapples; dried squid, crab, or shrimp cooked right before your eyes; hammocks; bracelets and necklaces; or massages.

I sampled most of the snacks early on and even bought a few souvenirs, but I kept the old massage ladies at bay for a long time. I'm a big guy and a bit shy about taking my shirt off in public and having strangers put their hands all over me.

The old ladies would often sneak up on me in packs of three or four. "You want massage?" they'd ask as they pawed at my arms and shoulders. I ran through a list of excuses, yet day after day they showed up in their big hats, scarves, and gloves, protection from the sun, carrying baskets of lotions, oils, and perfumes. They plopped down around me on the nearest chairs, loosening their scarves and revealing their wrinkled brown faces. They chattered among themselves and lingered so long it seemed like I must be their only anticipated customer of the day.

As the weeks passed, it was obvious that I wasn't moving on like a normal tourist, and they stopped trying to sell massages to me, but I still received my daily social visits. The old ladies befriended me and shared their stories and all the local town gossip. Their temperaments were unpredictable but entertaining. They were often joking, teasing, and even mothering, but at other times they were cantankerous spitfires who swore like sailors. I was perplexed by their English abilities. The colloquialisms and colorful curse words they used were not the sort that locals normally pick up while working around tourists.

One older lady and I became especially close. She told me she liked Americans and that I reminded her of her husband, an American G.I. who was stationed here during the war.

SOUTHERN VIETNAM

She had loved him very much. She said he died in Vietnam, although she never would tell me the circumstances. They had a son who fled to America when he was young, leaving in one of the little boats on the beach, and now he sends her money and calls from time to time. I asked her why she didn't go to America and live with him, but she answered that Vietnam was her home. She had too many good memories with her husband here and felt that leaving would be a betrayal of their life together. She was too old, she said. There was no point now. She stayed despite incredible hardships and persecution after the war, all for marrying an American. Even thirty years later, the police still herd her around from town to town like one of the stray cows on the beach.

Another woman told me she married an American soldier, but he left Vietnam without her when the war ended. Alone and pregnant, she was branded a whore like many of the women who fell in love with foreign servicemen. Her own family disowned her, and she was left to raise her child alone. They were often on the verge of starvation and frequently threatened and harassed by local authorities. Eventually her child died from malaria. She never heard from her husband after he left, and didn't remarry. She carries on alone, but remarkably shows no hint of bitterness.

These women are the forgotten brides, outcasts in their own land. They "aided" the enemy and suffered for it after the war. They have toughened on the outside, but their wounds have never truly healed. A part of each heart is forever locked in the past. They roam beaches selling massages, work in tourist cafés and restaurants, or clean hotel rooms in all the beach towns along the tourism circuits.

When you meet them, ask them about their lives, and you'll hear stories of love, heartache, and incredible determination in the midst of suffering. Not only will you be richly gifted with their friendship and unique life stories, but you will also offer them the opportunity to connect with both a past and present that they long for. Over and over they say, "You don't forget me. I'm afraid you go away to your country and forget me." I hope that in writing about them, they will be known and remembered by many.

Seaview massage

It's normal to tire of the endless stream of peddlers who find you sitting on the beach or at the front of a café. If, however, you view encounters as opportunities, rather than annoyances, you'll begin to value the people of Vietnam even more, and your travels will gain a new richness. By all means, do get a massage. As much as the women will enjoy talking with you, this is their livelihood. Eventually I did and wished I hadn't put it off so long. They're skilled at what they do, and it's much cheaper than what you'll normally pay inside a hotel. Expect a rate of $2-$3 per thirty-minute massage at the beach. Tipping is not normally expected, but is appreciated. In general, if you wait on the beach where there are reclining chairs or tourists congregating, the massage ladies will eventually find you.

HO CHI MINH CITY

Henno Kotze is moons over kids in Ho Chi Minh City

As a teacher living in the intimidating, eye-opening sprawl that is Ho Chi Minh City, I've always found the intricate relationship between parents and children fascinating. Regarding their children's education, parents place such intense pressure upon tiny shoulders, and the response is a sagging, all-consuming disappointment on little faces when they don't live up to these high expectations. Conversely, when it comes to celebrating children and their achievements, these same parents can be as praiseful and as exultant as any I've ever seen.

This doting and recognition comes to the fore on the fifteenth day of the eighth month of the lunar calendar, when the Vietnamese celebrate the Mid-Autumn Festival, or *Tet Trung Thu*. This holiday originated to

welcome the new moon, and adults would provide kids with gifts to make up for the lack of attention they received during the harvest season when their parents were out toiling in the fields all day. But as the tradition evolved, the festival's focus shifted to include children and education, as well as the moon, as I discovered during my first, heady dose of Vietnam's festive culture.

I first noticed the build-up to the Mid-Autumn Festival about six weeks prior to the actual day, as bright, multicolored lantern, toy, and bakery stalls gradually made their appearance along the major roads, vying for the attention of the armies of motorbikes racing past. As time crept closer to the climax on the fifteenth, the electric atmosphere increased as the enticing waft of mooncakes permeated the noise and spinning confusion of Ho Chi Minh City's streets. Filled with rich ingredients such as Chinese sausage, pork, lotus seeds, and durian, each round or square, sweet-savory *banh trung thu* also contains a bright egg yolk that symbolizes the moon. As a teacher I noticed that every classroom was filled with the buzz of chatter and laughter revolving around the festival and the inevitable questions of inquisitive minds: "Teacher, have you ever eaten mooncakes?" or "Teacher, do you have a lantern?"

At dusk on the big day, I headed down to the city center of District One to take part in the celebrations. A light autumn drizzle cooled the air, and an explosion of lanterns and fairy lights greeted me when I turned into the park area in front of Reunification

Palace between Nam Ky Khoi Nghia and Pham Ngoc Thach Streets. Drums resounded through the park as the unicorn dancers with their complex dragon dances entertained excited children on the arms of parents. Outwardly seeming to tolerate the events for the sake of their children, the adults were given away by the glint in their eyes and tap of their feet, which suggested they were secretly enjoying themselves just as much. Stalls selling mooncakes, triangles of waffles on sticks, and round, animal, and star-shaped lanterns in all colors and sizes lined the packed streets as thousands of children, damp hair clinging to their frantic faces, thronged in buoyant moods.

Despite the rain, the fat full moon made an occasional appearance through the clouds, its surface displaying Chu Cuoi, the herder boy, sitting under the leaves of a mythical banyan tree. There are a number of legends about the Mid-Autumn Festival, one being that at full moon in autumn, Chu Cuoi, who was exiled to spend his life on the moon, would be closest to earth where his lover Chi Hang still pined for him. To show him the way down to earth, children would light their lanterns.

It was quite surreal for me to be in the midst of such luminosity and experience the tangent excitement of the festival. Similar celebrations do not take place back in my native South Africa, so I really didn't have a point of comparison. Back home I thought a nice Easter Sunday lunch or Christmas Day dinner was a satisfactory festival

celebration, having never been part of a mass gathering to recognize the power of nature, the moon, and the underrated importance of children and their potential abilities. For a while I just wandered around the park soaking up the sensory overload and, getting caught up in the jovial mood, I even bought a lantern: an intricate, round design with a candle and cut-out paper figures arranged in a circular form inside. The heat from the candle sent figures of children, horses, and fish slowly spinning, casting eerie shadows on the shell of the lantern. The hypnotic spinning caused children, whose chubby cheeks were sticky from the mooncakes and other sweet treats, to break out into euphoric giggles.

As the children's sugar highs, the attention-grabbing stalls, and the lively music finally whittled away the energy of all, what was left was the contentment visible on the faces of the parents, who seemed glad to be able to reward and treat their children for their hard work throughout the year. The culmination of the night's events and the lead-up to it made quite an impression on me. As I made my way home, I finally began to understand the paradoxical relationship between the children and their stern, motivating, and yet adoring parents, who are willing to do so much to ensure the futures—as well as the happiness—of their little ones.

Mid-Autumn Festival

This festival is usually celebrated between the tenth and fifteenth of the eighth lunar month (in

September or October), but mooncakes, lanterns, and toys are sold weeks before and after the actual date from a number of competing bakeries, shops, and vendors on most streets around Ho Chi Minh City.

Where to celebrate

Although some schools offer concerts and lantern-making competitions during this period, and places such as Dam Sen Park (3 Hoa Binh St., District 11, www.damsenpark.com.vn) have lantern boat displays, just trawling through the streets of District One (the area around the Notre Dame Cathedral) should provide enough of a show during the days of the festival.

Mooncakes

Mooncakes have become a major industry in Vietnam with major bakery companies, such as Kinh Do and Dong Khanh, competing against each other. Boxes of four mooncakes can be purchased for as little as 30,000 VND (about $2), but imported Chinese or Korean mooncakes can sell for as much as 500,000 VND or more per set of four. Mooncakes are best within a week of purchase but can last up to a month. They can contain a kaleidoscope of ingredients (and calories), ranging from sugary fruits to meats, eggs, seeds, and traditional medicinal herbs.

Pham Hoai Nam is young at heart in Ho Chi Minh City

I love Ho Chi Minh City because of Saigonese generosity. In my opinion, Saigonese are easy to make friends with, easy to get along with, easy to have fun with, and, most importantly, they are open. If you open yourself up in return, you will be welcomed unconditionally. Saigonese are very hospitable too, and that's the reason why Ho Chi Minh City has become a destination for young people like me from all around Vietnam, who come here to live and work, often long enough to consider the city as their second hometown.

Whenever my wife is away on a business trip, I use it as an excuse to stay out late, because the streets are always animated. This is strange because the Saigonese supposedly have nowhere to go. After all, there is a curfew that orders businesses to close by midnight. But the nature of the city won't allow it: street food kiosks open their doors wide, and no matter the hour, people eat, laugh, talk, and make friends. Take two groups of young people at different tables in a street tavern. After only a few greetings, they are soon sharing a bottle of wine well into the night.

A city can't be a village, and urban dwellers are diverse, made up of all types, including night owls. This is why I believe the Saigonese will always find a way to stay out late. The dark

MEKONG DELTA

streets will continue to be crowded, and the Saigonese will be generous, as usual, no matter what the regulations are. Young-at-heart people like me will get older, but other young people will continue to enjoy Ho Chi Minh City after hours. They will continue to keep the southern metropolis young and active, which is why it seduces everyone who comes here, day and night.

Staying up late

Street food kiosks in Ho Chi Minh City are everywhere. A good selection can be found on Pham Ngu Lao Street (the backpacker area in District One); in Cholon (Chinatown/District Five); and on Phan Dinh Phung Street. I recommend getting a group of people together on Phan Dinh Phung for some draft beer (2,000 VND per mug) and a hot pot (less than 100,000 VND per hot pot). Take Hai Ba Trung Street out of town to where it turns into Phan Dinh Phung, in Phu Nhuan District. Just past Cau Kieu (Kieu Bridge), you will see about ten hot pot shops on both sides of the street. Who knows how many new friends you'll make before the night is over?

Laying down the law

Editor's note: It's difficult to explain to visitors about the curfew in Ho Chi Minh City. While government policies aimed at "social evils" such as drug dealing, prostitution, etc., require food stalls, nightclubs, and other establishments to shut

down by midnight, this rarely happens. Instead, the police keep an eye on the activity, and if you're lucky, you may just witness a raid on a disco or row of street stands during your stay. No need to be alarmed, though. For the locals it's par for the course.

MEKONG DELTA

Tyler Watts raises a toast in the Mekong Delta

On any given evening, as the sun's final gleam cascades across the landscape and transforms buildings and streets with its golden hue, you will find men perched around tables of various sizes and shapes throughout Vietnam. What is this activity they are performing? An ancient ritual? Some may think so. A religious ceremony? To a number it has rites and a sacredness that are the same. Yet at the end of each day as hands heavy from work take a glass to raise a toast, the bond between men takes on a special character. And for a foreigner wishing to move from being an outsider looking in, to a guest of honor in a great family, the flow of beer can often be the key.

Sitting in a pale blue plastic chair—

which looks as though the manufacturing plant where it was made ran out of the materials necessary to complete the legs—I feel a gentle tap on my back. I turn to see a smiling man standing with a beer extended. His hair is wild from the stress of work and the motorbike ride here to Tu Be, one of the local drinking holes I sometimes find myself in with fellow foreign and Vietnamese teachers.

"Excuse me, I'm sorry, where you from?"

This man, like many others, has scraped his memory for any English knowledge he ever received in an attempt to do something beautiful: connect. And though it's not without flaws, the effort is worthwhile. After a brief exchange, he wants to tell us about himself. He stammers out that he is, "Vietnam s'il vous plaît engineer," in a tremendous attempt to recollect his occupation in a foreign tongue. Or in this case, two tongues. The man, a civil engineer (he was so close), smiles shyly and raises his glass again as I nod my head in understanding and in reception of friendship.

Sixty kilometers to the west, on another occasion with thirsty foreign friends, I find myself sitting in My Chi, one of the rare bia hoi locations in the region. These venues, serving homemade draft beer, are popular hangouts in the bigger cities, but not as common in this region. We stand out amongst the small clusters of Vietnamese sitting around us. Two cyclo drivers begin to inch their chairs closer to ours, and it becomes clear they are looking for a way to enter the conversation. Surprisingly, they speak decent English. This probably comes from Chau Doc's growing popularity with tourists. As the night wears on, our chairs scoot together, our tables join, and conversation grows. As one glass after another is emptied, we are drawn deeper into the lives of our new friends.

Wherever bia can be found, I discovered that the opportunity for deep encounters with locals abounded. With glasses raised and inhibitions lowered, there was always an opportunity to strike up a friendship that may only last for the evening, but will be remembered for years to come.

Raising a glass

Beer and wine are certainly not lacking in Vietnam, though beer drinking is primarily a male pursuit. Here are some especially memorable places to share a drink with the locals in the Mekong Delta region.

Tu Be (Quan Binh Dan)

Near the corner of Ly Thai Tho St. and Hung Vuong St.

Long Xuyen City
An Giang Province

Luu Phong

Tran Nhat Duat St.
Long Xuyen City
An Giang Province

Bia Hoi My Chi

For the most accurate directions

RULES FOR THE ROAD

to this place, ask a cyclo driver near the Victoria Hotel at 32 Le Loi Street.

11/C Thu Khoa Huan St.
Chau Doc Town
An Giang Province

GENERAL VIETNAM

Jan Vail finds a land of beauty, culture, mystery ... and TRAFFIC!

For nearly a decade, I have traveled to Vietnam at least four to six times a year and stayed two to three weeks at a time. Solid numbers, and as a result, I feel I have become somewhat of an expert on what to do, what to see, and where to go.

My sojourns have covered much of the country, and I have accompanied businesspeople from various countries; escorted journalists from major and minor publications interested in stories about modern-day Vietnam; palled around with buddies to play golf or have an ice cold 333 beer or two; and generally done business from Hanoi to Ho Chi Minh City on each visit. I have arranged tours of cultural centers, museums, art galleries, temples, and ruins, and usually have a reasonably accurate story

about each destination to relay to the guests during their visits.

Invariably, at the close of each trip, I ask those departing, "What was your impression of Vietnam?"

Everyone, when pressed, is very moved by a number of things they discovered, that were in no way what they expected to find. However, the lasting impression—and also, usually, the first topic of discussion—is TRAFFIC.

There is a virtual sea of vehicles of all sorts and shapes, from the sheer foot-powered, to the occasional Western Harley hog. Two-wheelers, three-wheelers, four-wheelers, not to mention any vehicle that can be pushed, pulled, or conveyed, are on display 24/7. They form a tide washing over each street corner and often overlapping onto the sidewalks, going upstream, downstream, and sideways along every thoroughfare in every city, town, and even village.

The ebb and flow of the TRAFFIC is spellbinding to visitors who are used to orderly vehicle flow regulated by a computerized system of traffic lights and reinforced by traffic officers with the means of chasing down and ticketing offenders—not even remotely possible on the streets of the big cities of Vietnam. Every corner of every block and every straightaway is completely clogged with every type of vehicle going in every possible direction at exactly the same time.

Admittedly, Vietnamese TRAFFIC— *always* deserving of capitalization— is daunting, even to me after all these years. Since I would never advise anyone other than the Vietnamese to drive in Vietnam, passengers like me and all the others with whom I am transported must simply accept the risks of getting into a taxi or car, forge out into the rivers of TRAFFIC, and armed with a sense of adventure, go along for the ride.

Jon Hoff embarks on an everyday journey in Ho Chi Minh City

I climb from my bed bleary-eyed and walk to the kitchen to sip some hot green tea, prepared by my wife. (She's always up earlier than me, no matter how hard I try.) It's one of those days when I'm too lazy to do my morning exercise, so a few stretches have to suffice. I need to get cracking—don the work clothes, pick the least smelly pair of socks, and splash my face with water. Grab the keys, money, and parking ticket. Forgetting any of these things when you live three security locks and sixteen floors up is annoying.

Down the elevator and out into the parking garage. It's cramped here, and the likelihood is that my bike is buried behind three Hondas, each weighing as much as a baby elephant. It's one of the worst things about living in these apartments in Ho Chi Minh City on top of the smelly canal that separates Binh Thanh District and District One.

Sunglasses on. Helmet on. Out onto the street, immediately passing the countless coffee shops smattered at ground level around the huge apartment block. I join the flow on Dinh Tien Hoang Street, straight into the routine: pull the throttle, glide, pull the throttle, glide, weave this way, weave that way. As soon as I manage to get moving, I am stopped, usually on the bridge just outside my residence. Some days, the water on the canal is so still I can see a perfect reflection of the small trees that line the bank. But my drifting thoughts are shattered as the traffic growls forward with a monstrous communal roar. At this time in the morning, cream-clad traffic cops override the signals, commanding red and green with the flick of a switch. Drivers wait on the starting line, suspiciously eyeing imposing compatriots, waiting for the movement toward the magical gray switch box. And we're off again.

In the queue at the junction of Vo Thi Sau and Hai Ba Trung Streets, it feels like I'm part of a Hollywood disaster movie. It's like the whole of the city is using the same road to try to escape a doomsday event behind them. Ugly green buses crammed with people line the street, while noisy motorbikes supporting all manner of goods swarm like an army of ants. Cyclists join the fray and seem completely unaware of the lunacy around them as they wobble their way up onto the pedals. A droning crescendo signifies another gargantuan effort by the masses—the process of inching closer to a final destination is once again underway. The engines spew clouds of nasty chemicals into the air, clearly visible in drifting clouds. I hold my breath through the worst ones, for whatever good it does.

Down Hai Ba Trung and onto Nguyen Dinh Chieu. Not too bad this road, even in rush hour. I swing left onto Nam Khi Khoi Nghia, which will take me out of District Three, through the heart of District One and into District Four. On occasion I share a nod with the boys at the motorcycle garage—sometimes, time permitting, I'll grab an oil change and a bike wash here. Crossing over into District One, I pass Independence Palace. Traffic slows as people take time to gaze in through the gates. Some early morning tourists are wandering around in shorts, cameras hanging from necks. How alien this morning chaos must seem to them; how normal it is now to me. Seeing them often returns that feeling of what it is to experience Vietnam for the first time.

Eventually I break free from the shackles of the city center, passing the construction site of the city's largest engineering project on the way into District Four. At last, turning onto Nguyen Tat Thanh, the Yamaha has a chance to stretch its legs. The sun has risen high and beams down the long stretch of this dangerous thoroughfare, reflecting off the asphalt. Heavy trucks sound their horns as they ruthlessly scream by. I pick up the speed, but not without caution, hunching over the handlebars, keeping the kind of lookout that a circling hawk would be proud of. Around me: twelve-meter juggernauts; 50cc

putt-putters carrying huge baskets of fruit; blue-overalled, yellow-helmeted construction workers on Hondas; and slow-moving laborers with their motorized wheelbarrows. The heat, dust, and noise on this street don't sit well with me—luckily, it's still a little cool in the morning. To try this route in the afternoon, you may as well put yourself inside a washer on hot, having rubbed detergent into your eyes before you climbed in.

I cross the new bridge near the Tan Thuan industrial area and motor along Nguyen Van Linh Parkway. Nearly there. Cruising to a halt at the junction outside FV Hospital, I take the chance to relax on the handlebars. I watch the red light counter tick down from thirty as cars and bikes sail past me regardless. No matter, it's the final leg of the journey—so far it has been like wading through waist-deep water, but now it's like sprinting along a deserted beach, barely leaving a footprint. I take in the remaining green patches of land in this rapidly developing area whilst gulping down clean air, as if I've just emerged from the desert and been handed an ice cold beaker of fresh lemonade. The light glints off the river, which snakes away to the south through a landscape of tropical marshes.

This morning ride to work may only take around thirty minutes, but in that time I travel through the heart of a city's rush hour to its very edges, where the green countryside comes to meet sparkling, still-vacant apartment blocks that now scatter Ho Chi Minh City's first true suburb. It's a journey that takes me through time, from

Vietnam's rural past and toward a cosmopolitan future that has yet to come.

Safety first

To find out where to get a helmet for your own motorbike explorations, check out the fact file in the following essay by Marianne Smallwood.

Marianne Smallwood embraces the fine art of the Honda hug

In Hanoi, a pedestrian will continually encounter one of Hanoi's ever-present sights: a Vietnamese man sitting or lounging on his motorbike and usually reading a paper or quietly surveying the passersby. Depending on whether an eyed passerby is a tourist, Vietnamese, or other qualified rider, a "woo-hoo," "moto-bike?", or "*xe om*!" will issue from the driver. This enterprising individual is known as a *xe om*, and for a quick (literally) cultural dip into Vietnam, or for just getting from point A to point B, a *xe om* can be just the thing.

A *xe om*, translated into "vehicle/motorcycle/or Honda hug," is a motorbike taxi, where would-be passengers hail the nearest driver of their choosing, specify a location, and hop on the back of the motorbike. The *om* (hug) portion of the ride is not usually practiced, though many first-time passengers *om* freely and without hesitation. It's fairly simple to find a *xe om* as they're usually on most Hanoi street corners. Knowing your end location or address in Vietnamese is optimal, though some *xe om* (particularly in the Old Quarter) speak a bit of English as well. Just point to the map or to an address and you're off! A *xe om* ride can be a rush, and the skill at driving, dodging, and carrying multiple persons can be impressive; though I rode my first few times clinging desperately to the sides of the motorbike, I did not fail to notice my driver's blasé and expert maneuvering through Hanoi's crowded intersections.

Professional licenses or certifications are not needed to be a *xe om*, which would explain their large presence. Don't be fooled, though ... it is not a lucrative position, as most drivers earn only a few dollars per day. *Xe om* usually group together with the same circuit of drivers at the same location, and they can be territorial; after once making the mistake of taking another driver who sat ten meters away from my regular group, I was subject to disapproving frowns as we drove off. Loyalty counts here in Vietnam. However, that loyalty can go both ways; once a price is established for a regular location, expect to pay that and no higher for all similar trips. The drivers outside my house never fail to shout a hello and a joke in the morning and have memorized my regular destinations should I ever need a ride. If you like a particular driver, be sure to put his mobile number in your phone. It's convenient for you and a steady source of income for him if he can garner regular customers. One ex-pat I knew used the same *xe om* on his work commute for two years—not a bad gig for the driver who landed it.

There are thousands of *xe om* in Hanoi, not to mention the other cities and towns of Vietnam, a number that includes part-time drivers, students moonlighting for additional income, and educated professionals whose salaries from their regular careers cannot adequately support them or their families. Though there are the horror stories from passengers about paying an overpriced fare, getting lost, and (from a female rider) an overly friendly driver, I've found that the majority of *xe om* I've taken are cheery, polite men (and once, a woman). My last *xe om* ride consisted of the usual introductions, chat about the weather, the details of my job, and even a brief discourse on politics. He dropped me off at my location, I paid him, and off he went with a wave. Sure beats a $10 cab fare or fighting traffic myself. You see, I'm renting my own motorbike these days, but I'm considering giving it back; I'm missing out on a lot of good chats, and my Vietnamese could certainly use the practice.

A few words of advice on xe om riding

Do: Establish a price for the ride before getting on the motorbike, particularly if riding with an unfamiliar *xe om*. Many people,

myself included, have jumped on a bike, been deposited at a location, and then quoted two to four times the typical rate. A ride within the city center of Hanoi should cost no more than 10,000 VND, though rides outside of the city center can be 15,000-30,000, depending on the distance. Inclement weather may ratchet up the price slightly.

Do: Try to find regular *xe om* if you'll be riding to and from familiar places. Not only will this save the hassle of bargaining every time (a price should be set from your first few rides), but the familiarity can be comforting.

Do: Take the mobile number of a favorite *xe om*; he will almost always agree to pick you up or drop you off wherever you need to go, and it's nice to be a regular.

Don't: Ride a *xe om*—or any motorbike—without a helmet. Traffic accidents are common in Vietnam, and, shockingly, most people eschew helmets in the city. One can be bought at Protec, a non-profit manufacturer of high-quality helmets. The price will be about $10.

12B Ngoc Khanh St.
Ba Dinh District
Hanoi

and

18bis/3A Nguyen Thi Minh Khai St.
District 1
Ho Chi Minh City
www.protechelmets.com.vn

Don't: Ride with a *xe om* driver you suspect might have been drinking. In a profession that can often leave a lot of idle time, it isn't unusual for a *xe om* driver to enjoy a few beers during the lunch hour. Take a discreet sniff for alcoholic breath—and check for a usually indicative flushed face—before riding. If you even suspect your driver may have had a drink, opt for another *xe om* or go by taxi.

Don't: Tolerate a *xe om* driver whose attitude or behavior displeases you. If you're unhappy with your driver, have him stop the bike and get off, paying only a few thousand dong, depending on how far you've gone.

Ed Daniels hires an unconventional xe om driver

Nhan approached me as I exited the War Remnants Museum in Ho Chi Minh City. She drove her old motorbike up on the sidewalk and asked if I needed a ride. It is not uncommon to hear this question in the city, but it is rare hearing it from a woman. She was about thirty-five, short, with a slight build, and didn't look like she could handle a seventy-seven-kilo man on the back of a motorbike.

Motorbike drivers are easy enough to find in Vietnam, just look on any street corner, but no one seems interested in anything more than collecting a fee for a single ride somewhere. The thing that bothered me most about that kind of arrangement was the bartering before every ride and the arguing at the destination about the agreed-upon fee, or the added cost since the destination was "difficult to find" or "farther than expected." Because I wanted to find one driver who would consistently take me where I wanted to go without having to go through the bartering/arguing process, I said no, that I was waiting for a driver who had dropped me off earlier and had agreed to come back. The woman drove away.

After about fifteen minutes, she showed back up. "Do you want a ride?" she asked again. I decided the other driver was never going to return, so I asked her if she could take me to the Ho Chi Minh Museum down by the river. She said, "Yeah, yeah," and motioned for me to climb aboard. Little did I know that she didn't have the slightest idea where I wanted to go.

She took me by a museum a few blocks away that I'd been to the previous day. As we passed it, she pointed to it and said something that sounded like "museum." I said, "Yes, I went there yesterday," thinking we were just making conversation. Looking back, I realize the only thing she probably understood was the "yes," because she began to circle the block searching for the entrance. On two sides of the museum were one-way streets, with the traffic going in the opposite direction we were driving. That didn't seem to bother her, as she simply drove up on the sidewalk to avoid the oncoming traffic.

After finding the museum entrance, I realized we weren't making idle chat, but she thought this was where I'd asked her to take me. I decided it was time to pull out the map. Fortunately, the guard at the museum gate spoke a little English and figured out my goal. He gave Nhan directions in Vietnamese, and she smiled and motioned for me to climb back on. I complied, even though I was still not confident that we were going to wind up in the right spot.

We arrived at the museum gate just as it was being closed for the staff's midday nap, so I asked my driver to take me back to my hotel. Knowing the way, I simply had to point in the direction I wanted her to go. As I was paying her for that day, she asked if I needed any more rides in the future. I was planning to leave the next morning for a three-day trip to Vung Tau, so there was no immediate need for Ho Chi Minh City transportation. But I asked if she could meet me at my hotel when I returned. This took a while because of the language barrier, but we managed to reach an agreement on the day and time.

Three days later I walked out of the hotel and saw her waving at me from the other side of the street, since only authorized taxi drivers were allowed to drive to the front of the hotel. I crossed over to meet her and told her I wanted to see a park that contained several large sculptures, which I had passed several days earlier. The problem was that I couldn't remember how to find it. I pointed to one of the parks on the map and she said, "Yeah, yeah." We drove about two blocks before she pulled over and asked a Vietnamese man to direct her. The rest of the morning went like that as we drove around looking for the sculpture park. We never found it, but we did see a lot of places with sculptures, such as graveyards, Buddhist temples, and shops where you could purchase busts of Ho Chi Minh. Fortunately, the park was not high on my list of priorities, and I enjoyed our drive around the city.

As the days passed, Nhan continued to drive me around. Her old motorbike was in pretty bad shape—the taillight didn't work and the rear view mirror was hanging at an awkward angle—but she proved to be as reliable as a fine clock and honest to a tee. A year later, when I returned, she had a new motorbike because her old bike had been "corrupted," but she was still the same good road companion. And by the time my third trip came up, I emailed Nhan with my itinerary and asked if she could also arrange a motorcycle driver for a friend. This time I felt comfortable enough to send her some money through Western Union to help pay the expenses. Everything was arranged when we arrived. She met us at the airport with a taxi and took us to the hotel. Not only did she and another driver friend of hers ferry us around Ho Chi Minh City, but they also took us down to My Tho in the Mekong Delta.

Over the course of three visits to Vietnam, I've come to know and trust Nhan, and I believe she trusts me as well. Aside from the time we've spent on her motorcycle, we've eaten lunch, drank beer, and visited with her friends and family together. While we maintain a business relationship, we consider ourselves friends. As a result, I'm certain I overpay her for the service she provides. However, it doesn't bother me because I know she struggles financially, as do many people in Vietnam. Besides, there is great satisfaction and comfort in knowing she is concerned about my safety and welfare.

Getting around Vietnam on the back of a motorbike is not for everyone. However, I believe the risk is worth it because it is an experience that will not be easily forgotten. Not only is it exciting, but it is a good way to acquire a genuine feeling for the country.

Contacting Nhan

Tran Thi Nhan does not speak English. Still, you can contact her at her friend's email address: toanbj@yahoo.com. In the subject line, write, "Message to Nhan." The friend, Mr. Toan Du, will translate your email. If you are a Vietnamese speaker or have access to one, Nhan's number is 090-251-1291 (in-country) or 84-90-251-1291 (from abroad).

Keep in mind that although I have developed a working relationship with Nhan over the years, you will need to start at the beginning, so negotiate clearly for your rides, and build your own relationship from there.

Battle of the Sexes

At one point during one of my trips, a Vietnamese friend commented that it was very unusual to have a female driver. She said she had never seen a Vietnamese woman in this role. I had not seen other women drivers either, but I considered it a welcome departure from the norm. Nhan is also a nice choice for female travelers who would feel more comfortable with a woman driver.

Local etiquette

One day, while I was waiting to have some laundry done, I suggested that Nhan and I stop for some water. She pulled into the courtyard of a Buddhist temple where there was an outdoor café. She motioned me to a small table with small chairs. As I sat down, she disappeared and came back almost immediately with a bottle of cold water. Then she disappeared again just a quickly. This time she didn't come back. After a while, I looked around and spotted her watching me from a distant chair. I waved to her, indicating I wanted her to sit at a chair by my table, but she shook her head no. After a couple more waves, and a couple more refusals, I figured it must be taboo, so I gave up and continued to drink my water. After a few minutes, an older Vietnamese man who spoke a little English came to the table and asked if he could sit down. I gladly accepted his request. As the older man and I began our conversation, Nhan also appeared at the table and sat down at the chair next to mine. I finally realized the old man's appearance was a setup. The only way for her to sit there in a socially acceptable manner was to have the older man there as well.

Elka Ray makes a loyal friend on the road

I travel to Hanoi from Ho Chi Minh City about once every six weeks, and whenever I arrive, Mr. Duc is the first person I call. Although I have many friends in Hanoi, he's not one of them, or at least not in any conventional sense. In all the years we've known each other, our conversations have been limited to the bare essentials:

"Is Mr. Duc there?"

"Hello, Elka."

"Hello, Mr. Duc. Can you come and get me?"

"Where are you?"

Just as I can pick out the sound of his approaching motorbike before I can see him, I know exactly how our next (and the one after that, and the one after that) conversation will go.

A distinguished-looking man in his forties, Mr. Duc usually wears a baseball hat and khaki slacks. If he appears tired, thinner, or unwell, I worry for him, while he always looks alarmed if I'm the one who's under the weather. But beyond a "How are you?" we don't talk about it, even though I have met Mr. Duc's wife and kids, and he's met most of my friends, ex-boyfriends, and family, accompanying me to just about every place I've gone in Hanoi over the past seven years. He took me to a friend's house when my first marriage disintegrated, to buy my wedding dress, and to the hospital. He's seen me through the deliriously happy months after I met my current husband Thien, the dark days after our daughter's death, and the happily exhausted daze following the birth of our son.

While Mr. Duc doesn't say much, he remembers everything. "Mr. Duc, about three years ago I bought a pink shirt in the Old Quarter. I don't remember whereabouts ... It was a small shop ...."

Mr. Duc doesn't miss a beat. "Hang Hom Street."

I get on the back of his motorbike.

Even after all these years, my Vietnamese remains dodgy at best. "Mr. Duc, there's a tall house on Phan Dinh Phung Street," I might say, referring to an office tower where I sometimes go for meetings.

He nods. And we're off.

Sometimes Mr. Duc is busy, either helping his wife with her soup stand or driving another customer. While many drivers just sit around on street corners waiting for business, regaling passersby with hopeful yells of "*xe om khong*?" or "moto?", being a motorbike taxi driver for him is a full-time job. He transports customers' kids to and from school and drives night owls home from the bars. When it's raining, he dons a plastic poncho and a stoic expression.

I stopped taking random *xe om* many years ago, having had several encounters with drivers who reeked of *ruou* (rice whisky), and one with a man who planted a hand on my thigh, at which point, having momentarily forgotten that we were traveling at high speed, I smacked him in the back of the head. And why would I bother with strangers when I have Mr. Duc?

Invariably, the last person I see before hopping into a cab to Noi Bai Airport is Mr. Duc. After tallying up my fares, he says goodbye.

"See you next month," I say.

"I wish you good health and a happy trip home." Because he doesn't say much, these words sound more sincere than when said by most people.

As Mr. Duc prepares to turn his bike around, there's a moment when I want to say more, to tell him that my trips to Hanoi wouldn't be the same without him. Not wishing to embarrass him, I keep quiet. The day I dial his number and learn that he's retired, Hanoi will change for me. But for now, I know exactly what he'll say the next time I call.

Contacting Mr. Duc

If you would like to hire Mr. Duc, he may be reached at (84-04) 716-0317. He does not speak English, so you will need someone to translate for you.

Hiring a pro

New to Vietnam are companies offering organized *xe om*, much like taxi services. In Hanoi you can choose from the following:

Havina

The receptionist speaks English. The rate is 2,500 VND/kilometer.

(84-04) 562-6262

Cokbi

Founded by two sisters, this company's many goals include providing safe transportation for female riders.

(84-04) 262-6364

PAYING IT FORWARD

Suggestions for giving back while you're on the road.

To give or not to give? This should never be a question, especially when you're traveling in a developing country such as Vietnam, where need is immense and hospitality warm and unconditional. This juxtaposition often amazes travelers I have talked to. How, they want to know, can people who have so little offer so much to visitors and ask for nothing in return?

Of course, sometimes it doesn't feel that way, when you're being bombarded by street kids furiously cursing you for not buying a pack of chewing gum, or harassed by a huckster who is trying to take you—literally and figuratively—for a ride. But remember, these kinds of things happen everywhere, and in Vietnam, those who genuinely welcome you far outweigh those who just want to know how much they can get from you. Also remember with the kids that their attitude is often bred in response to how they have been treated by travelers, and that they are not begging for the fun of it—they are "working," not by choice and usually for an adult, who will punish them if they don't bring money home that night.

So, how do you help these kids and all the others with legitimate needs? Getting started is overwhelming, which is what makes the essays in this chapter so valuable. Personal and compassionate, they are written mainly by people who have worked hands-on with charities, organizations, and programs in Vietnam. When Steve Jackson advises you to eat at Hanoi's KOTO, a restaurant that trains street kids in hospitality industry skills, he isn't just tossing out a random suggestion. He worked with the kids, and he knows how much good the program is doing.

Like KOTO, many charities make it fun for travelers to give back. You might have breakfast or stay the night at Sapa's Baguette & Chocolate (training street kids for the hospitality industry), dine on classic Vietnamese food at Huong Lai (also training street kids), or sip a cup of coffee at Sakura Café (employing intellectually disabled kids). You can also indulge in guilt-free shopping if you pick up fresh flowers, holiday

ornaments, or a purse at Mai Tam Creations (products are made by HIV/AIDS patients) or a hand-stitched blanket from Vietnam Quilts (products are crafted by rural women).

Because choosing where to give is such an individual act, another notable aspect of the charities in Vietnam is their diversity. You can easily find one that suits you. As you read through this chapter, you will discover a Montagnard orphanage in the Central Highlands, a Ho Chi Minh City orphanage for HIV-infected children, a scholarship program for girls in rural communities, and a veterans' foundation rebuilding communities in the former DMZ. You will also find Thin Lei Win Elkin's exceptional list of charity organizations throughout the country.

One of the most moving essays in this chapter is from Michael Brosowski, founder of the Blue Dragon Children's Foundation. In it are some insights and observations from four former shoeshine boys, including, "If somebody does not want to buy from us, they can speak gently and say, 'No, thank you.' They don't need to be harsh. They should think about how we feel. We hope to be treated with respect."

When it comes to giving, this is the bottom line. We are doing more than just donating our time and money. By sharing what we have with those who have less, we are offering our respect to the people we are helping, and are showing our respect to the country that we are visiting.

Hanoi

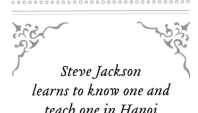

Steve Jackson learns to know one and teach one in Hanoi

I have two families—one with five members in northeast England and another with 300 and growing in Vietnam. In Hanoi, I was accepted into, and proud to be part of, the KOTO family. KOTO is a restaurant run by street kids and disadvantaged youth. If you're a tourist, it's an incredible location to eat at and a great way to give back. If you're a volunteer worker, like I was, it's a place that changes your life as profoundly and absolutely as those of the street kids it teaches.

There are moments experienced there that will stay with me forever. I remember on Christmas Day, when I was feeling a little homesick, I found myself alone with a trainee for a moment. In his previous life he had shined shoes on the street. He smiled, looked me in the eye, and said, "I am very happy."

It nearly broke my heart.

Later, as part of KOTO's outreach program, we visited a residential community of people suffering from the effects of Agent Orange. It is the cruelest affliction. No two symptoms are the same. I have seen sufferers with only one eye, no legs, stumps for bodies, or half their torsos missing. There I approached a KOTO kid, who I saw taking a quiet moment to compose himself after being hit by the sadness he saw around him. He told me through tears, "I am so lucky. I look at myself. Two arms, two legs—I can work."

And I thought the same as any Westerner would think in that position. White, healthy, and middle-class—what does that make me? Born lucky.

Here I was, with a kid who had spent his whole life struggling. His family had tried to grow enough rice to feed itself, and when that proved impossible, he left the countryside for the Hanoi streets with the aim of sending money home. How can hearing that he feels lucky, in those surroundings, not change your life?

There was no spin to KOTO. What you saw was what you got. Its rationale was magical. If you had promise and if you worked hard, you could make it. You could go from working the streets to working in the Sheraton in eighteen months. It is an incredible transformation that 90 percent of each class made and nearly 300 in all have made to date.

It wasn't all hard work though. One week a year we closed up and went on holiday. As a volunteer from a marketing background, suddenly finding myself as travel agent was daunting. With virtually no funding, I had to take staff and kids—close to 100 in all—on a trip.

It was the excursion to Sapa that really stays with me. We had planned a trek for the trainees. Only twelve kilometers, I recall, but we arrived the day before the trek to an absolute downpour, and it had obviously been soaking the place for weeks. Everywhere was muddy. I called the staff together. We were going on the walk no matter what, but I was aware we might have a revolt on our hands. My plan was to out-smile the kids. Not allowing gloom to settle for a second, we'd beam our way round and just hope it was contagious.

So in the morning, we went out and bought 100 pairs of brightly colored rubber boots. For the next few hours we dragged an elongated tail of kids around the mountains and valleys. I recall tap dancing the route at one point. We sang. We chivvied. We made light of wet clothes and boot-induced blisters. And we arrived at our bed for the night in a small ethnic village.

An hour later, the sun was out and the rain had stopped. The kids changed into dry clothes and there was this growing sense of achievement along with genuine, solid contentment and happiness. I could feel us all getting closer as a group. I ducked into the ramshackle kitchen, and there were thirty trainees crammed in there, laughing away, already starting on dinner for us all. Everyone was cutting, peeling, and washing veg, or slicing meat for stir frying.

I was so proud. I was overwhelmed. I smoked a cigarette at the outskirts of the village. Facing away, I cried. Not for the first time, I didn't

know why. I can only explain it as being so humbled by these amazing people and by what we could do to help them and the experiences we could give.

They sang into the night. They danced, played games, and put on shows. Too tired, I barely said a word, but my jaws ached from grinning.

I remain so proud of being part of that family. We looked after each other. And I wasn't the only one moved to tears. A Danish documentary filmmaker missed more moments than she caught because she kept having to leave the room. A big, tough, New York Chef confided in me of the same problem. Was this normal, he asked. I assured him it was.

Eventually, though, like the trainees themselves, my time with KOTO was up. Just as they had to graduate, I knew it was time for me to move on. I dreaded my leaving party. I knew once more that I would be in pieces. I had seen others say goodbye before, and few could manage it without breaking down.

My lasting memory of that final evening is of me, with my arms around a dozen kids and my t-shirt soaked in their tears and mine. KOTO changed my life, just as it has changed the lives of 300 kids.

These days, KOTO has a new restaurant that seats 150 and is regularly full. KOTO provides homes, training, healthcare, an allowance, love, and support for up to eighty trainees at a time. It also provides international standard certificates in kitchen or front-of-house skills. Please, go and eat at KOTO. Tell everyone Steve says hello and that I miss them all so much.

KOTO Restaurant

There are future plans to help more young people with more KOTOs across Vietnam and internationally. The Hanoi restaurant serves up the most fantastic Western and Asian food, as well as great lattes, cakes, juices, and shakes. It is adjacent to the Temple of Literature.

59 Van Mieu St.
Dong Da District
Hanoi
(84-4) 747-0337/0338
www.koto.com.au

Michael Brosowski empowers the street kids of Hanoi

I never expected to be living in Vietnam and running a street children's program. But that's the great thing about travel—you just don't know where you will end up.

I first came to Vietnam in 1999, wanting to find out more about the people and culture. On a journey to Chau Doc in the Mekong Delta, I had a "mountain-bottom" experience that changed my life. Thanks to an episode of food poisoning, I wasn't feeling so great, so when my tour group wanted to climb Sam

Mountain, I declined and sat in the shade on the side of the road. Some local kids, preparing for an English exam, came along to ask for help. Since I was an English teacher back in Australia, I was only too happy to offer assistance.

The kids were earnest and wanted to learn. They and their families asked for nothing else, even though they were clearly very poor. They showered me with sweets, drinks, and fruit, and refused payment. As the tour group came back down the mountain, I realized that I didn't want to leave Vietnam. I felt that I had found what I was looking for in life.

Of course, I did leave. But I kept coming back, and I started planning to move permanently to Vietnam. I stayed in contact with the Sam Mountain families I had met, and returned for some more holidays to see them. After two years of further study in Australia, I packed a bag and moved to live in Ho Chi Minh City.

My life here continued taking twists and turns. I started out as a teacher in the University of Economics, but after moving to Hanoi and meeting the street children, I decided to start Blue Dragon Children's Foundation as a way of helping kids get off the streets and back to school. Today, we have a street children's center in Hanoi, where we meet young people in all sorts of situations and help them with whatever needs they have. For some, that means finding a home; for others, it may mean going to a doctor or hospital. For all of the kids, it means going back to school or get-

NORTHERN VIETNAM

ting training, since a good education is the key to breaking out of poverty.

Outside Hanoi, we sponsor kids who are so poor that their families cannot afford school, and help children who have been trafficked to return home and re-enroll in their classes. These cases are the most touching, as the girls and boys have been through such difficult times.

The first trafficked child I met was a twelve-year-old boy named Ngoc. He had been taken from his family in central Vietnam to sell flowers on the streets of Ho Chi Minh City. His parents thought he was going to school; the traffickers had him working through the night, and they would beat him if he didn't make enough money. He earned nothing. Every cent went to the traffickers.

Ngoc wanted to go home and go to school—he had never been before—and I just couldn't say no. Getting him away from the traffickers was difficult, but finally I succeeded. Ngoc now goes to school and lives just like a regular kid. People who meet him today would never guess what a terrifying life he used to have, trying to survive the streets of the south.

Children like Ngoc are my source of inspiration. Life here is not easy, but it is hugely rewarding. Seeing the children grow from day to day, and leave their lives of poverty behind, is an experience that's impossible to beat.

Blue Dragon Children's Foundation

www.bdcf.org

Blue Dragon Restaurant

The foundation receives support from this privately funded restaurant.

46 Bach Dang St.
Hoi An

From the mouths of babes

Following are some comments from Ky, Chinh, Toan, and Vuong, former shoeshine boys in Hanoi.

- "When we were shining shoes, many people were rude to us. They would look down on us, and treat us like we were stupid. Some people think that because they are rich, they are better than us. But they were rude and sarcastic, and sometimes they threatened to call the police on us."

- "Living and working on the streets was difficult for us. When it rained, or when we were sick, we could not earn any money, so maybe we could not eat. And there are many dangers for us, including people robbing us, or customers who refused to pay."

- "If somebody does not want to buy from us, they can speak gently and say, 'No, thank you.' They don't need to be harsh. They should think about how we feel. We hope to be treated with respect."

SAPA

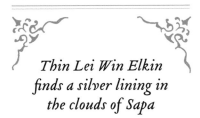

Thin Lei Win Elkin finds a silver lining in the clouds of Sapa

It was only six months into our life in Ho Chi Minh City, and we were itching to do Vietnam's famed Northern Loop, taking in Hanoi, Halong Bay, Ninh Binh, and Sapa. So when my partner's parents came to visit us from half the world away, we decided this was the perfect chance.

In between cautioning us on how to deal with ethnic tribeswomen who follow you around to sell their handcrafted wares, numerous helpful friends gave us tons of tips; and their descriptions of the area's beauty were true enough. On the hour-long coach ride to Sapa from the border town of Lao Cai, where our overnight train from Hanoi had dropped us, the scenery was lush, the air was fresh (when you live in Ho Chi Minh City, you learn to appreciate fresh air), and the hairpin turns offered glimpses of terraced rice plantations that seemed to perch precariously on the sides of sheer mountains. But our friends forgot to mention one of the nicest things about Sapa.

After checking into the Bamboo Sapa Hotel, a clean and spacious place, but with little soul, we flipped through our *Lonely Planet* guide for somewhere to go for breakfast. One name jumped out at my partner, who is partial to everything sweet and bready: Baguette & Chocolate. We decided to pay a visit based on the assumption of delights to come, not realizing that the café is part of the Hoa Sua School in Hanoi, which runs hospitality programs for disadvantaged youths.

The ten-minute or so walk from the hotel in the cold, damp morning wasn't particularly cheerful, but the thought of freshly baked baguettes and mugs of hot chocolate kept us going. It was a haven on that chilly day, at the top of stone steps, glowing with warm light and cheerful staff; it was also where we would end up having our next three breakfasts. The two-story, French-style villa was swathed in white paint, and as soon as we entered the café, we realized it was unique.

The place had a happy vibe. Comfy beanbags, white leather sofas, and low tables were scattered around. And we had to take off our shoes if we wanted to sit inside, thus keeping the parquet floor remarkably clean and shiny, arguably another first in Vietnam for such an unpretentious café. Already, there were numerous patrons—mostly independent travelers in groups of two or four—enjoying their morning drinks before hiking around the ethnic villages near Sapa.

The menu was a delight, offering both Western dishes (including the fresh baguettes, as we'd expected) and local delicacies (the *bun cha* was notable), as well as scrumptious pastries. The breakfast selections, which ranged from a simple baguette and jam, to sandwiches with pâté and ham, were excellent, and included pots of warm tea or hot chocolate—one of the best versions we've tasted. Many others who've been there will testify to this. Even better, there were loads of board games—usual suspects like Snakes and Ladders and Scrabble—encouraging you to just sit and chill.

Sheets of paper explaining the history of Baguette & Chocolate are on every table. The friendly staff members, who speak good English, are former street children who receive free training in hospitality skills that will provide them with a much better future than the one that would have been their fate. Proceeds from the restaurant go toward supporting the Hoa Sua School, which has branches in both Hanoi and Sapa. We also discovered that upstairs from the café are four bedrooms, bright and cheerful like the rest of the place, that come complete with en suite facilities and hot showers.

Knowing the good cause behind the venture somehow made the food more delicious, but by no means was this a two-bit café making money out of sympathetic travelers who only come here out of duty. Baguette & Chocolate is well run and serves some great food. For the next two mornings, we ate there before our daily treks, even though our hotel price included breakfast. We thought it was too good a place to enjoy it only once, and it's one of the lasting impressions we

have of Sapa. After all, as attractive as a landscape is, encounters with locals are what make a place memorable.

Baguette & Chocolate

Rooms here start at $18 a night, and you are taken care of by friendly students being trained in hotel management. The following website is not in English, but you will find a map of Sapa locating the café/hotel.

Thac Bac St. (above the park and craft market)
Sapa
(84-20) 871-766
www.hoasuaschool.com

More ways to help out in Sapa

Craft Link

To support traditional handicrafts, check out Craft Link, with an outlet behind the Sapa District Tourist Information and Promotion Center. This is a not-for-profit fair trade organization supporting the ethnic minorities that make Sapa such a colorful and unforgettable place. Craft Link's quality silk scarves and handbags offer one-of-a-kind designs.

www.craftlink-vietnam.com

Indigo Factory

This organization has an outlet near Bamboo Sapa Hotel and another at the Victoria Sapa Resort. It works on bringing back the traditional method of indigo-dyeing textiles.

DMZ

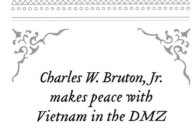

Charles W. Bruton, Jr. makes peace with Vietnam in the DMZ

I am a Vietnam Vet. From June of 1968 to June of 1969, I flew as an FAC in a Bird Dog over South Vietnam in the Northern I Corp region and the Southern part of North Vietnam. After surviving that experience, I swore I would never go back and was fortunate that I was able to avoid a second tour.

Back home, though, I was surprised when I felt perpetually drawn to return to the area where we went hunting for Charlie every day. I fought the thought daily; it was a place I once hated and feared, but the feeling persisted, and it was impossible to ignore.

I finally realized that not only had my soul been won over by Vietnam's natural beauty, it had also been won by the heroic actions of its people in both North and South Vietnam. The stoic nature of the South's ARVN soldier and the discipline and determination of his North Vietnamese counterpart amazed me. Each of us was doing what had to be done at that moment in time, and each was

trying to make the best of a bad situation. I admired and respected them as warriors and hoped they had the same admiration and respect for me.

Emotions run deep when you survive such an experience, and not a day would go by that a sound, a smell, a taste, or some other triggering episode, would bring me back to what we did during that traumatic year of my life. No one but a vet can truly understand how these past events can still play a major role in how you act and react to incidents today. Some vets appear to have adjusted well and are able to seem normal in everyday life. Many others are haunted so much by past events that it affects forever their ability to live at peace with themselves. I was fortunate—I had Vietnam Vet friends who would act as a sounding board and provided tremendous counsel when it was needed.

I was also fortunate to be able to return to Vietnam. When I found an ad for The Veterans Viet Nam Restoration Project, I knew instantly that VVRP was my ticket. Mission #18 was going to Quang Tri Province, the old DMZ area. I knew that area like the back of my hand, but only from the air. Now I would see it from the ground. It was my Area of Operations; Dong Ha was the airport I flew from every day, supporting the Marines of Northern I Corp region and the 109th Artillery Group.

We would be staying in Dong Ha, and VVRP Mission #18 would work on ten homes and an orphanage. This time our mission was not to find the enemy and destroy them, but to work with Vietnamese veterans and non-veterans who had been disabled in the war or had been injured by unspent ordnance left behind after the war. Our mission was to help them build new lives by assisting them in building new homes.

All this was taking place in the same area that I had directed artillery and air strikes, as well as directing the guns of the *Battleship New Jersey*. What I remember leaving behind was nothing but barbed wire, bunkers, bomb craters, scorched earth, and total destruction. Now, thirty-four years later, I would be able to view it again, but this time with a mission plan to build and to mend.

I have to say that the experience was fantastic. My nightmares are gone! My visions now are of a people who have forgiven us, a people who appear extremely happy living their new life of peace. In Vietnam today, progress is everywhere. Wherever we looked, the country was under construction with people actively building homes, offices, factories, schools, and hospitals. The Vietnamese are vibrant, and the streets are packed with motorcycles and bikes: people on the move, full of life, and most of all, they seemed genuinely happy to see us. They sought us out to say hello. We really were welcome in their country, and especially in their homes. I had to remind myself that this was the DMZ, this was Dong Ha. I was working with the same people who had shot at my Bird Dog daily, but now I felt totally safe and

a welcome guest as we helped build ten homes and a computer room for an orphanage.

More work needs to be done, and I plan to assist as much as I can. Seldom have I participated in a project that I felt was doing as much good. The work at times is more symbolic than actual hard labor, with the Vietnamese doing most of the physical work and our team providing the materials, but the results are dramatic. They have new lives in new homes; we gain new lives, at peace with ourselves by helping them accomplish this.

In place of recurring nightmares of guns and planes are images of beautiful countryside, a growing economy, and people who have forgiven us. I needed to forgive them, as well, and by going back I found the way to accomplish that. I also was able to realize that two MIA pilot friends, Don Harrison and Mac Bird, whose bracelets I wear, are not MIAs in my mind any longer. I walked in the area where they were shot down in North Vietnam. During that walk, I realized that although they are lost, and until found, will always be officially MIAs, I now know they are really gone. I now feel they are not alive, and knowing that has lifted a great weight from my shoulders.

The price of this healing is nothing more than a little time and money. The gift of forgiveness I received from the Vietnamese people has healed me from the scars of the past. It has allowed me to rest at night knowing that it is over, and all is well with the people on the DMZ. That gift is priceless.

That year in Vietnam on my tour of duty represented only one sixtieth of my life, but after thirty-four years it still dominates my thoughts, especially when it is quiet and I have time to think. But my quiet time is restful now, and my thoughts of Vietnam are peaceful. That time has been put into perspective, and I can go on enjoying the good things the Lord has provided. Since that weight has been lifted from my shoulders, I appreciate my family and friends, and even more, the experiences of the past are now in proper balance.

The Veterans Viet Nam Restoration Project

VVRP is a grassroots non-profit organization. It sends teams of veterans to Vietnam each year to help them heal from the emotional and spiritual wounds suffered in the war by working alongside the Vietnamese. Teams construct schools, medical clinics, vocational training centers, and disabled veteran housing units. VVRP is sponsored in Vietnam by the Ministry of Labor, Invalids, and Social Affairs (MOLISA), and funds for projects come from donations in the United States. Team membership is open to veterans and their family members. Donations are appreciated. Additional information is available on the organization's website.

www.vvrp.org

KON TUM

Kelly O' Neill finds true love at a Montagnard orphanage

I was born toward the end of the baby boom, so my memories about Vietnam are pretty predictable—anti-war marches, combat footage, and Walter Cronkite, all seen on the pink-hued screen of my grandparents' early-model color television. After the fall of Saigon, Vietnam seemed to descend into a black hole of American ennui. I had lost no one personally, so it was something I rarely thought about, usually only if the TV was running a "what did the sixties really mean?"-type special.

You might understand, then, that I'm more than a tad surprised to find myself one of a group of ten circling Ho Chi Minh City's Tan Son Nhat Airport. My husband, a big, hairy Viking of a man, and I, an average, round, beige, American woman with a mediocre perm, are here to pursue our dream of a family. We've been chasing parenthood for years now, but when the effort goes from "Hey baby, wanna give it another try?" to "We need to schedule a date with the doctor and a lab tech," the mys-

CENTRAL VIETNAM

tery and romance are definitely gone. For us, adoption means putting magic back into our lives, and we're traveling to St. Vincent's Orphanage in Kontum in the Central Highlands to meet our toddler son and infant daughter.

The vast majority of the children in this orphanage, one of three in this small community, are Montagnard, a French word meaning "hill people." Montagnards include the descendants of the Polynesians who originally settled the coast of Vietnam. With huge, round, dark eyes and masses of thick, curly hair, they are considered unattractive by the Vietnamese children they go to school with, but in every one of the pictures that we have received of our children, they look like models on a poster for an exotic vacation.

Because of their allegiance with the United States during the war, the Montagnards are considered traitors by many Vietnamese. They are trapped in grinding poverty, and slowly their tribes, cultures, and communities are disappearing from the face of the earth. This is the legacy we are facing as we deplane from the fourth flight and seventieth hour of our trip at the airport in Pleiku.

Every time we exit a controlled atmosphere, like the cabin of this old Soviet airliner, the heat and humidity, (which are rapidly becoming one word: *heamidity*), confront us like a brick wall, making it impossible to inhale. When I do get my breath back, the air is saturated with the smell of coffee drying on the landing strip next to ours. The sight is as sensual as the smell: mounds of oily, dark

beans, glossy in the sun. If it were cooler, I'd want to roll in them.

We stagger, drunk on fatigue and foreignness, toward the tiny shack that is the terminal. Small men wrangle our suitcases out of the belly of the plane and onto a rickety cart. Our hosts from the justice department arrive with bouquets of tuberoses and giant smiles. After lots of gesturing, we're loaded into vans. We weave and bob our way down the two-lane blacktop, the driver nonchalantly dodging the crops of rice and coffee drying on the road. The conversation is frenetically happy, the dads calming their nerves by videotaping anything they can see out of the small van windows, as we head to Kontum, one step closer to meeting our children.

After checking into our hotel, we pile back into the vans, one kilometer left out of the many thousands already traveled. The orphanage is nicely out of sight behind an old Catholic church, whose walls are vertical planks, which have shrunk and bowed over the seasons and are the color of the now familiar coffee beans. You can see between the boards, and lacy light shows walls hand-painted with Montagnard saints and Madonnas. The wood smells of decades of incense. The pews are plank benches with no backs. We walk to the back of the church and find that we have arrived.

We are met by the elderly Sister Sang. She is less than 150 centimeters (five feet) tall and looks like she could be Buddha's grandma. God help her, in this heat, she's wearing a navy blue, polyester Mao suit and matching veil. She grins, yells over her shoulder, grabs my hand, and pulls me into the shade of the doorway. We walk down the hall past the inside porta-potty and a class-room containing only narrow desks and benches, and a scruffy old chalkboard. Then we're out in the cement and stucco courtyard.

Nuns' voices echo back and forth as they call our children's names from one end of the compound to another. Gradually a trickle of kids forms, some leading littler ones, some carrying the babies, some com-ing out of curiosity, and a few others watching with a sad mixture of hope and relief, wanting and not wanting at the same time to go to that world of foreign families.

The older children place Hai Anh (named after the men who found her by the road and brought her to the sisters), reluctantly into my arms. A translator is not necessary to read their faces. Clearly, a round, soft thing such as myself is not strong enough to firmly hold a baby. They hover and touch, frequently taking her back, or clapping their hands in front of her little face, poverty's ver-sion of a rattle.

The nuns have gathered en masse. They are so proud of the children. "Look! Healthy baby! Healthy baby!" they chirp at us. They pull on our sleeves to make sure we're really seeing how wonderful our children are; they don't understand Western in-fertility, and they're not quite sure why we want these children so badly. They seem to feel that they must convince

us that the miracles we are about to receive are really worthwhile.

At long last, I hold my beautiful daughter, Hai Anh. Fifteen months old, five kilograms (eleven pounds). A bony baby doll. Pretty face and thin, Brillo pad wisps of hair. She has pus running out of her right ear and open wounds on her head from boils that have ruptured. Her skin is rashy and inflamed. She has scabies and lice, intestinal parasites, pneumonia, and diarrhea. She takes one look into my bizarre blue eyes and starts a two-hour scream. The sisters can't afford diapers, so the old shirt that is wrapped around her little bum is immediately wet. You can't believe how much I've longed for this.

Our son, Thak, was named by his father who surrendered him after his mother was killed by a land mine while plowing a rice paddy. It means "waterfall," although we joke that it might mean "constantly moving." He's a small, cocoa-colored, fireplug of a boy. Thick-boned, but muscles wasted. Large, round, distended belly. He's thirty months old and weighs eight kilograms (eighteen pounds). He has Giardia, a diarrhea causing parasite, which prevents him from gaining weight.

He reeks, a smell made of rancid body oil that has rarely seen soap, and he has black stumps for teeth, as well as ear fungus. He has pneu-monia, infected ears with ruptured drums, intestinal parasites, and tuberculosis. He also has a great awareness of the fun available in the world, and the attitude that ensures he's gonna get his share, starting

CENTRAL VIETNAM

with his infatuated new daddy! The sisters are right. By their standards, at least, our kids are very healthy. And they've been fattened up in anticipation of our arrival. Their adopted status lowers their risk of death, thereby justifying the extra calories that have been invested in them.

Sadly, not all the children who enter this haven walk away, even though malaria medicine costs only ten cents a day. The nuns usually forego theirs, instead spending the money on rice. When purchasing life, they must decide. Short term or long? No wimpy, ruler-wielding nuns of American folk myth are these. They are miniature brown Valkyries carrying the souls of the world's unwanted infants into the afterlife.

Trying to soften the transition from the familiar to the bizarre, we take our babies back and forth to the orphanage every day. They visit the comforting faces of the sisters, toddle around the homey open courtyard, and eat a little lunch. Then we go back to that hotel room of cold air, soapy smells, terrifying toilet, and exotic bathtub. Thak and Hai Anh sleep like the dead each night on their little mattress on the floor. In reality, they're in blue-eyed, pink-skinned shock. Life is simply too overwhelmingly weird to stay conscious all the time. We think they're just *fabulous* children.

On our last day, out of the watchful eyes of the police observers, in a small windowless room, we slip the sisters $500. They try to return it. They explain that we've already done so much for our children just by taking them. Out of the thousands of dollars it

has taken us to get here, we have only $500 left to give. About one-fortieth of what this adventure in familyhood has cost us. So much to them, so little to us, especially considering our reward.

Epilogue

After nine months of four times daily medication, Thak's tuberculosis was considered cured. At the age of thirty-two months, he had four teeth pulled, five crowned, and seven filled. His ear infections were so severe that he lost some hearing in his right ear and the majority of hearing in his left. He wears a bone anchored, surgically implanted hearing aid. None of that prevents him from being a soccer demon. Hai Anh's health problems were much less severe, as she was younger when she was adopted. Thak and Hai Anh have grown into their promise, and are the loving, lovable children of our hearts. They have also been joined by a younger brother and sister from India.

Since our visit, Sister Sang has died of breast cancer. There are so many cancer deaths and life-destroying birth defects in the Highlands, and I suspect the Agent Orange that lingers in so much of the groundwater. In addition, adoptions of Montagnard children have been stopped by the Vietnamese government. As an alternative, Janey Coyle, who once facilitated adoptions, has started an aid agency to help children in the Central Highlands of Vietnam. Through her non-profit organization, the Vietnam Fund for Education, Music & Infrastructure (VFEMI), she travels twice a year to Kontum to bring funds, aid, supplies, and support.

VFEMI

If you would like to change a life or save a child while enjoying the beauty that is Vietnam, it is simple to do. You can begin with a donation—$20 can bring about a world of change. In addition to money, always a much appreciated gift, there are many other ways to help. If you plan to visit the orphanage, some airlines will now allow you to take an extra suitcase for charity on your travels, or you can pack light and leave a corner of your bag for the kids. We recommend taking antibiotic and anti-fungal creams, baby acetaminophen, aspirin, or ibuprofen, soaps, shampoos, vitamins, toothbrushes, combs, pencils, school supplies, and/or toys. All are small and light and more appreciated than you can ever know. You may also purchase such products once you're in Vietnam. With medicinal gifts, make sure to give them to a person in charge who understands how they are administered.

www.vietnamemifund.org

HO CHI MINH CITY

Linh Do adopts a giving attitude in Ho Chi Minh City

When my friends or even local taxi drivers first see Tam Binh 2 Orphanage in Ho Chi Minh City, they are quite surprised at how nice it looks and how healthy the children seem, even though a large percentage of them are infected with HIV/AIDS, as they were born to HIV-positive mothers. The children are adorable. They happily cling to you so you will pick them up as you make your way around their cribs. But if you put them down, they are sure to cry, and some convulse for want of human connection.

Visiting an orphanage can bring a tossed salad of emotions, but working in one takes it to a whole other level. As Vietnam's Country Director for Worldwide Orphans Foundation, I get to see many of the children grow up because rarely is an HIV-positive child adopted. We make plans for them not only to go to public school, but also to university and become a part of the community beyond the orphanage's gated walls.

The orphanage opened in November 2001 and was built primar-

SOUTHERN VIETNAM

ily with funding from the People's Committee of Ho Chi Minh City and three international NGOs (Germany's International Child's Care Organization and the United States' Children of Peace, and Maine Aid and Protection) to provide shelter for children born to HIV-infected mothers. In the beginning, many of the children were very sick, and HIV medicines were not available to help keep some of them alive, but now WWO works with the orphanage to bring the first pediatrics HIV/AIDS training for physicians in Vietnam and to provide expertise to build the competency of those caring for the children. In collaboration with a government staff, WWO provides pediatric medical and psychosocial care focused on the special developmental needs of institutionalized children, especially those living with HIV/AIDS.

Through this work, I get to see how anti-retroviral drugs, individual attention, and focused early intervention through activities such as WWO's HeaRT volunteer program have helped these children develop like those in more "normal" circumstances. We are also expanding our work into the community to support families to care for their children, and to help prevent the abandonment of children.

As in many places around the world, there is fear and lack of understanding, and as a result, there are stigmas and discrimination against people living with HIV/AIDS, even children. The Hieu Roi Thuong (HeaRT = "Understanding Brings Compassion") program builds

awareness in the local community about the facts of HIV/AIDS and child developmental needs, and enables volunteers to show by example how it's safe, and rewarding, to work with the children. WWO also provides training for caretakers in child development and psychology so that they can increase their knowledge in caring for the children.

Since September 2005, the programs supported by WWO have been partially funded by WWO's individual and corporate donors and USAID's PEPFAR program, and anti-retroviral drugs for the children are from PEPFAR and the Clinton Foundation, as part of the government of Vietnam's program on HIV/AIDS. But more help is always welcome. The staff takes on a lot of work, caring for so many children under the challenging circumstances of limited resources and a low caretaker-to-child ratio. Come spend time with the children, joke with them, play with them. They will make an indelible impression on you, and you will have a chance to bring some fun and attention into their lives.

Contacting Tam Binh 2 Orphanage

Trung Tam Nuoi Duong Bao Tro Tre em Tam Binh 2 (Tam Binh 2 Center for Child Nourishment and Protection)

30/3 Ba Giang St.
Linh Xuan Ward
Thu Duc District
Ho Chi Minh City
(84-08) 724-1445

Visiting the orphanage

It takes about ninety minutes by the #612 bus to reach the orphanage from Ben Thanh Market in District One in the center of Ho Chi Minh City. Stop at the Cao Dai Temple in Thu Duc, cross the street, and walk for about five minutes down the smaller Ba Giang Street. The orphanage will be on your left; keep an eye out for turquoise and beige paint. For non-Vietnamese citizens, you should call the orphanage in advance for permission to enter; unless you speak Vietnamese, you will need someone to place the call for you. Alternatively, you can contact WWO at least a couple weeks in advance, and we might be able to help you file visitation papers with DOLISA (Department of Labor, Invalids, and Social Affairs).

www.wwo.org
Vietnam@wwo.org

How you can help

Let the kids practice their English and climb and tug on you, and they'll give you a dose of happiness and hope. If you would like, you can bring healthy snacks or small gifts, such as clothing, nice books, and stickers for the children, who range from newborns to teens. Please refrain from bringing candy and junk food, as they get too much of this. We also need help to succeed with

a new comprehensive dental program, generously donated by volunteers from Journey for Children and Maple Healthcare Dental Center. If you plan on staying in Ho Chi Minh City a while, please check with WWO for possible longer-term volunteer opportunities.

Opportunities in the north

There is also an orphanage for HIV-positive children that WWO works with in Ba Vi, an hour and a half west of Hanoi. Please email WWO if you would like further information about visiting and volunteering.

Joe Springer-Miller perks up over coffee in Ho Chi Minh City

Vietnam is coffee-rich in so many ways. It's the number two producer of coffee in the world after Brazil, and the overpowering aroma of java throughout the cities lures just about every visitor into its ubiquitous café culture. One of the surprising pleasures for newcomers here is the chocolaty *ca phe sua da*, a thick drip coffee with sweet condensed milk and ice. And, of course, all the Western-style, cream-topped, and flavored varieties are available too.

In Ho Chi Minh City, I have a particular favorite place for coffee near my house. Although it's on the corner of busy, centrally located Ton Duc Thanh and Le Thanh Ton Streets, and although it fills up a whole corner of a college for preschool teachers, you wouldn't notice it when you passed it by. There is no sign. You must walk through a discreet gap in the wall to find Sakura Café (Hoa Anh Dao Café), the brainchild of Chisato Esaki.

The first time I wandered in, I enjoyed the cool, pleasant atmosphere, good coffee and juice, and super-friendly staff. Then I saw the bill. Prices at most cafés in this part of town are going through the roof, the equivalent of $3-$4 a cup. Here they were on par with the street stalls, 6,000-9,000 VND, about fifty cents a cup! It turns out that Chisato started this café not to bilk caffeine junkies, but as a project to involve young people with mild intellectual disabilities and Down Syndrome in their community. I'm now a regular at Sakura, and last week I sat down with Chisato to hear a bit more about her intentions.

As we talked, Chisato drank tea while I worked on, you guessed it, *ca phe sua da*. She explained that she started the café with private funds, and a part of the success is the repayment of all her debts. By undertaking this privately, without money from NGOs or a government, Chisato hopes to inspire Vietnamese to follow the example and create other similar venues. Why? Because this kind of thing is not common in Vietnam. In fact, involving such young, intellectually challenged people in jobs that

deal with the public is not done at all.

Eloquently describing the kindness of the Vietnamese toward those with disabilities, Chisato explained that in contrast, the physically handicapped are accepted in society and working life in Vietnam. Visitors will notice older wheelchair "cowboys" around town in their push cars—going to work or selling lottery tickets from a kind of combination tricycle/wheelchair that is used even in traffic. There are also three-wheeled motorcycles or rather precarious-looking motorcycles with side wheels. Whether these people are older and injured during the war or young and were injured in motorcycle accidents, they are a regular part of daily life.

In Chisato's experience, many are willing to help people in wheelchairs without even being asked. And though most places in Vietnam are not handicap-accessible, she told me that when she arrives for shopping with her friend who is in a wheelchair, people don't wait to be asked to help, or even ask if they can help, for that matter ... they just pick her friend up, chair and all, and carry him up the stairs. In these situations, "the feeling of Vietnamese people is barrier-free," she said, adding her hope that Sukura will help to usher in the same sense of openness toward the intellectually handicapped.

Education, of course, is also a factor. A child that is intellectually disabled can go to school in the big city, but in rural areas like the Mekong, there are no schools for these kids. They don't exist. And even for those who do go to school, they still must face the place—or rather, lack of—that society has for them once they are through with their education. Most return to help their mothers or fathers, if their parents work out of the home. But if parents work outside, these young men and women have nothing to do but watch TV and sit around, growing old without fulfilling their potential.

Chisato smiled with pride as she explained that because members of the serving staff have the greatest interaction with the public, it is important for young, intellectually challenged people to hold these positions. By doing so, they have the chance to work and interact in their own communities. The café is also intended to create a place for the staff's family members to gather in a relaxed atmosphere. Additional goals include helping Vietnam's young population understand how capable the disabled are, and therefore making a direct impact on the discriminatory thinking of Vietnamese society.

Chisato should have also included brewing a great cup of joe in her ambitions, for that achievement was clear, as she smiled broadly and said, "The café is a success! It's 3 p.m. now, so lots of students are at school and people have to work, but in the evening the place is packed. We know it's a success because people don't just come once or twice; they come again and again and tell their friends. And the staff, by working here, they progress. Before they behaved immaturely. Now they behave like friends and siblings."

As we talked, our server came over to check on us. He had a giant smile on his face. It was full of appreciation for life and work, and clearly for Chisato too. I asked him what he liked about the job, and he said he just loved to serve people coffee. Chisato beamed. "See? I don't just help them, they help me."

Sakura Café
(Café Hoa Anh Dao)

Opened on April 18, 2004, Vietnam's annual "Day for Disabled People," the café was founded and is run by its chief volunteer, Chisato Esaki, who teaches social welfare at the Ho Chi Minh City Open University and in Sendai, Japan, for a joint program with Tohoku Fukushi University. The café is located on the corner of Ton Duc Thanh and Le Thanh Ton Streets across from The Sushi Bar. It is in a corner of the College of Primary School Education building, which supports the venture through favorable terms.

4 Ton Duc Thang St.
District 1
Ho Chi Minh City

Samantha Coomber nibbles on feel good food in Ho Chi Minh City

Luckily for those of us living in Vietnam, dining out is a pleasure we can afford to enjoy every night. Throw in

SOUTHERN VIETNAM

contributing to a good cause while you feast, and you have a feel-good-factor times two.

In Hanoi, Hoa Sua and KOTO restaurants help disadvantaged children enter the hospitality business. Now, I discover, there is Huong Lai in Ho Chi Minh City. Founded in 2001 by Jin Shirai, a resident Japanese businessman who you're likely to find floating around the restaurant most nights, Huong Lai dedicates part of its operation to teaching life skills, English, and hospitality training, plus offering opportunities to attend school. At this privately run restaurant, young people—including orphans and street children—receive ongoing, on-the-job training as in-house chefs, wait staff, and assistant managers. In short, preparation for new lives filled with potential.

The Huong Lai philosophy is simple: offer delicious Vietnamese cuisine without pretence or high prices, served by friendly and caring staff. The delightful restaurant is hidden away upstairs in a large renovated block of old colonial buildings on Ly Tu Trong Street in the center of Ho Chi Minh City. With simple décor of bare brickwork and earthy tones, as well as ethnic wall hangings and adornments, the intimate, understated dining room sets the scene for authentic Vietnamese home cooking.

The à la carte menu offers a range of popular Vietnamese dishes, great to share communally with friends. These include grilled eggplant with minced pork, sautéed chicken with lemongrass and chili, braised fish

in clay pots, and fried rice with tofu and vegetables. The Huong Lai Plate Sampler, featuring fried and fresh spring rolls and lotus salad, is an ideal starter. There are also set lunch and set dinner menus; prices are very reasonable, though dishes come in small portions.

Huong Lai is a breath of fresh air for tourists looking for a "real deal" Vietnamese dining experience, or jaded ex-pats who may need to get back to their Vietnamese roots. But whatever, most of all it's a fun way to contribute to a worthy cause.

Huong Lai

Open for lunch and dinner, Huong Lai also supports a privately run orphanage.

38 Ly Tu Trong St.
District 1
Ho Chi Minh City
(84-8) 822-6814

Tenley Mogk shops for a good cause in Ho Chi Minh City

In early 2007, Father John Toai of the Archdiocese of Ho Chi Minh City invited me to visit the space that would become the storefront for Mai Tam Creations. Did I think green walls would work? Should the purses be hung up or placed on shelves? Although the nuns were in charge, really, Father John enjoyed the exercise of imagining what was to come.

Today, nestled into a cozy space in District One, the shop for Mai Tam Creations now sells fresh cut and silk flowers, purses, and ornaments, with proceeds going directly to the health needs and employment of women infected with HIV/AIDS. The program is run by the Archdiocese's Pastoral Care Committee; under Father John, the committee is a leader in HIV/AIDS care and treatment in Ho Chi Minh City, which has Vietnam's highest number of people living with the virus/syndrome.

Savvy when it comes to business, the shop meets Vietnam's countless floral needs, providing flowers for church services and traditional family ceremonies, nearby office buildings, and holidays such as Women's and Teachers' Days, as well as for passersby on the street—you can walk right in and buy a bouquet, if you'd like to offer a sure-to-be-appreciated thank you to a helpful hotel desk clerk or tour guide. The flowers are brought in from Dalat, the country's famed garden city in the highlands, a six-hour drive away. Along with the flowers are beaded purses—I am often asked where I bought my little retro bags when I'm back in San Francisco—and holiday ornaments, all made by hand by HIV/AIDS patients and their families.

With an overwhelming stigma in Vietnam against people living with HIV/AIDS, jobs are near impossible to find. Any purchase at Mai Tam will directly benefit employment and/or health care. As for what you get

in return, aside from knowing that you're making a difference, you will be delighted by what an adorable Santa ornament the nuns can design.

Mai Tam Creations

30 Dinh Tien Hoang St.
District 1
Ho Chi Minh City
(84-08) 822-9997
http://maitamcreations.com

Margaret Scott makes room for reading in southern Vietnam

As our driver navigates the hectic streets of Ho Chi Minh City, my Room to Read guide, Linh, explains the obstacles to education in Vietnam. Although it is highly prized in Vietnamese culture, and the government officially sponsors universal education, financial resources are not available to rural schools, and poverty often drives families to pull their children out of school for work or caring for younger siblings.

Thirty years ago, as a university student at Berkeley, I demonstrated against the war in a divided Vietnam. Today I am visiting a different, unified country, and my focus is on our destination: Phuoc Lai Primary School in Long An Province. An educator myself, I am convinced that increased literacy is the path by which world change can occur. True equity will come one school, one library, one child at a time, and programs such as San Francisco-based Room to Read are a means of achieving this goal.

Room to Read not only partners with villages to build schools; publish new children's books; and establish libraries, computer labs, and language labs; but also provides long-term scholarships for girls in eight countries in Asia and Southern Africa. The organization was founded in 1999 with a mission to help eradicate the illiteracy that deprives 750 million people around the world of their basic human rights. It accomplishes this end by empowering local teams to make programmatic decisions that will be most fitting for their communities.

An hour into our drive, we cross a bridge barely two meters wide and land on a dirt road that we share with mopeds, bicyclists, pedestrians of the two-legged (people, chickens) and four-legged (dogs, cats, cows) kind, as well as the ever-present honking horns. At the school, the principal greets us warmly. He guides us through Phuoc Lai, which has none of the amenities I have come to expect in an elementary school: no playgrounds, bathrooms, or cafeteria. Before the partnership with Room to Read, there were no computers or library either.

The Room to Read library is a magical island of bold, joyous color. It offers visual relief from the plain mud walls and asphalt floors of the rest of the school. Cheerful letters, numbers, and pictures decorate the room, and the floor is covered with a bright, com-

fortable alphabet rug that beckons a sit with a good book. This rug is the only floor covering that exists in the school. Vietnamese writers and illustrators have collaborated to produce many of the books in the library, some of which are based on Vietnamese legends and folk tales. Perusing the enchanting book covers, I imagine how joyful this space is when filled with children whose imaginations hunger for stories ... stories that they will find here. We move on to the Room to Read computer lab, with its carefully arranged rows of monitors, offering access to the world.

The next stage of the visit is to the home of one of the Room to Read scholarship recipients. To each scholar, Room to Read makes a long-term commitment. Depending on the needs of the individual girl, the scholarship may supply tuition, tutoring, medical check-ups, a bicycle for transportation, and lunch money. Linh offers me a conical straw hat as protection from the tropical sun, and we climb on mopeds. As I hold onto my hat with one hand and grip a tiny metal handle with the other, we fly down alleys, over rice paddies, and through backyards filled with chickens. Although the slightest movement on my part requires a skillful correction by my driver, we make it safely to our first stop, the home of nine-year-old Thanh.

Thanh has been a Room to Read scholar for three years. She lives with her mother, father, and three sisters in a two-room hut made of mud and board and covered with a metal roof. Situated in a rice paddy, their home has no plumbing and no electricity, except for a generator to power the one fluorescent light. The front room holds only a plastic table, chairs, and an altar. Thanh's mother tells us that they just installed tile because their dirt floor would turn to mud for much of the rainy season.

Thanh's family supports itself by cutting palm fronds and weaving them together for roofing material, providing a meager subsistence. With Linh interpreting, I ask Thanh's mother about her hopes for the future of her daughter. She stares off and then responds, "I want Thanh to have a better life than mine ... to go to school so that she will be able to make decisions about her life ... to move to the city where there is more opportunity ... to be happy." She does not have this hope for her two older daughters, who are past school age and will most likely continue in a life just like her own. She tells us that she had never been beyond this village until the summer before, when Room to Read provided transportation for her to attend a parent workshop.

As we talk, the room fills with women and children. They are fascinated by the visitors and especially by the strange-looking Westerner. They touch the bridge of my nose, giggling at its prominence. Thanh's father serves us drinks from coconuts that he has chopped from the tree outside.

We return to the school for a lunch of *pho* and fried shrimp in the welcome coolness of the library. The principal and I share humorous stories of

school life: universal tales. What is not universal, however, is a well-rounded education for everyone. There are more than 650 girls on Room to Read scholarships in Vietnam, but millions of children could benefit from such support. That Room to Read does not have the funds to provide a scholarship for every deserving child is tragic, considering what a difference such a scholarship can make. In American currency, the commitment amounts to a mere $250 a year. For the children of Vietnam, that commitment means a life of promise beyond mud floors.

Room to Read

This organization provides educational support in India, Cambodia, Laos, Nepal, Sri Lanka, and Southern Africa, as well as Vietnam. It offers site visits on a quarterly basis in each of the countries in which it has operations. In order to sign up for a visit, please go to the website for the annual calendar and instructions on how to participate.

www.roomtoread.org

Sue Wise finds beauty in the quilt of rural Vietnamese life

To me, Vietnam is made up of many individual pieces of fabric that represent the stories of the lives of women

SOUTHERN VIETNAM

in poor, rural communities. Deeply hued tangerine pieces symbolize the women who travel far afield to secure work, enabling their children to attend school. Rich earth-brown pieces are the women who work in brick or cashew nut factories to earn two dollars a day, while olive-green pieces are women who have to lock their children in their homes all day while they tend the rice paddy fields. All of these pieces also represent one need—to earn a regular income.

I am extremely lucky to be assigned by Australian Volunteers International to a non-profit, community development project called Vietnam Quilts. Started in 2001, this organization is like a quilt itself, whose center is one piece of material in the shape of an enormous heart. This heart is a compassionate woman who wanted to thread all the other pieces together and give them a steady income in a secure and safe environment. Many times the pieces have been pulled apart and redone. The initial result was a small, crib-size quilt—in the form of a shop—in Ho Chi Minh City. Word spread about how and why this tiny shop was created. However, this happened too slowly. Some pieces abandoned the project, as there was not enough regular income to meet their needs. But the shop and all that it represented was attractive, the heart was still pumping, and eventually forty-five pieces from around the country came together.

In order for this little project to continue, it had to borrow money to purchase more batting and thread. Then, from a land far away, an ocean-blue piece traveled to Ho Chi Minh City, to assist. The task for this blue piece was easy: promote Vietnam Quilts. When the public was shown how this simple, small organization benefit the women of Vietnam, they liked what they saw, and they bought.

Over the next two years, another ninety-five multi-colored pieces joined. These pieces have laughed together, eaten together, and played together at the seaside, believing in the reason they are united—to enable them to send their children to school and feed their families. For most of these pieces, their incomes doubled during this period of time. They were the lucky ones.

Their success can now be shared, and the project now gives back. Five hundred children from less fortunate families are able to attend school; women have participated in health education programs; latrines have been built in poor families' homes; and more than 1,000 mosquito nets have been distributed. This is all because Vietnam Quilts is well-designed and has been made with love by many very special pieces of material.

There are always other pieces of fabric, with their own stories to tell, who want to be stitched into the quilt to make it—figuratively and literally— a queen-sized organization: the deep-burgundy piece with six children to feed, the saffron piece who raises rabbits for an income, and the dazzling pink piece whose husband left her to feed three children by herself. To make this happen, the ocean-blue piece has been traveling to the north, to continue her role in spreading the news about this Vietnamese quilt.

I have loved every minute of working in this project. It has been a privilege watching Vietnam Quilts grow over this time. The handmade blankets are beautiful, and I often think about how the many I have collected will give me such comfort and fond memories when I finally return home.

Vietnam Quilts

For more information on Vietnam Quilts' philosophy, quilters, and shops in Ho Chi Minh City (in the process of moving at the time of publication) and Hanoi (opposite Highway 4 restaurant—yum!), check out the organization's website.

www.vietnam-quilts.org

Purchasing a quilt

It is a fulfilling feeling to buy a good quality product that makes a difference to the lives of women in rural Vietnam. The women are paid a daily salary for their work, even if the quilt is not sold, and any profits made are given to our NGO, for community development, or are put back into the business to employ more women. The quilts range in price from $25 for a cot/twin to $145 for a king-size. As well, you are able to design your own quilt with available fabrics. All the quilts are handmade, and shipping can be arranged to any part of the world. Other accessories are also offered.

GENERAL VIETNAM

Thin Lei Win Elkin reflects on ways to give in Vietnam

What can you get in Vietnam with 100,000 VND?

A glass of good wine? A dish of foie gras? Perhaps a round of beer?

For the twenty-eight boys at **Green Bamboo Shelter** in Ho Chi Minh City, it provides a month's worth of survival. Most are either orphaned or from families who are unable to look after them, and this amount (less than $10) keeps a boy in school and his family afloat.

Given the booming economy, it's easy to forget that Ho Chi Minh City and its surrounding provinces have their fair share of poverty. As in any developing country, the government's resources are limited, which leaves charities, non-government organizations (NGOs), and individuals like Elizabeth Copley and her colleague, Tram Ho, to help out as much as they can.

By day, Liz and Tram work for ILA Vietnam—an education and training organization—and they raise funds for Green Bamboo and **Ho Chi Minh City Cancer Centre** during their free time. Liz began volunteering after a New Year's resolution, and she says,

251

GENERAL VIETNAM

"Only 25 percent of the children at the hospital have a chance of survival, so although it's very difficult to choose, we sponsor treatments for the ones that have the highest chance." She and Tram organized their first bring-and-buy sale in Pham Ngu Lao Street, raising 8.5 million VND to pay for school fees, bicycles for the boys to travel to school, and expensive chemotherapy treatments, among other things.

Not every one of us is blessed with similar fundraising skills. However, if you would like to help in your own way, there are many other worthy organizations that need volunteers and donations.

The three-story building of the **Christina Noble Children's Foundation (CNCF)** is a school, medical center, and shelter all rolled into one. The Sunshine School provides primary education and food, as well as music, art, and sports programs to 300 children from underprivileged families. Meanwhile, 700 poor families come through the doors of the adjoining medical center every month for free healthcare. CNCF has also established residential shelters—according to the organization, there an estimated 15,000 street children in Saigon; 5,000 are female.

Started as a government school twenty years ago, **15 May School** has evolved, with the help of foreign and local volunteers, to provide vocational training and much-needed shelter for kids in Ho Chi Minh City's District One. This doesn't mean it turns away kids from other areas,

though. Jessica Perrin, former PR and fund-raising manager, recounts the story of a boy whose parents left him on the roadside on a trip to the city. He's now the youngest member of the 15 May School family.

While the school provides the national curriculum from grade one to nine, the vocational part concentrates on hair and beauty, performing arts, baking, sewing, and computing. The school's current project is a halfway house. Jessica explains that students who are getting older but not fluent enough in their vocational skills, will stay there. The house will also make the transition of returning to the outside world smoother.

According to **Operation Smile Vietnam**, one in 500 children in Vietnam is born with a cleft palate (around 3,000 cases a year). Despite its busy schedule—twelve to seventeen local missions are planned annually—it can only treat 2,000 patients each year. Couple that shortfall with an original backlog of around 15,000 cases and you have thousands of patients waiting to get rid of their deformities.

Julie Atkinson, Operation Smile's go-to person in Vietnam, says, "We have to turn away two out of three children. This is not just a cosmetic surgery—babies with cleft palates can't suck properly, which means they are malnourished. Their teeth grow in strange places, which can lead to blindness if the teeth get infected. Our goal is to raise awareness to an extent where [the Vietnamese] see a need to help the victims instead of ostracizing them."

East Meets West Foundation is also active in healthcare. Its diverse activities include large infrastructure projects, community development, health and well being, and programs for disadvantaged families. However, it is passionate about two programs in particular, according to Robin King Austin, the director of development. Operation Healthy Heart provides medical care for children with heart defects; the foundation says more than 20,000 children in Vietnam need surgery. In addition, the Dental Program has treated 30,000 patients in ten years, and it is now expanding nationwide to reach remote villages.

Catalyst Foundation, meanwhile, focuses on "Preventing girls from being trafficked through scholarships, micro loans, and community education." Bao Nguyen, the project's in-country director, says operations have expanded beyond Ho Chi Minh City, starting with Dong Thap Province near the border with Cambodia. Catalyst is building a school in Ken Giang town to help more than 300 children living and working in a garbage dumpsite who previously couldn't go to school because of distance and long labor hours.

For those interested in fair trade and empowering women, check out **Mai Handicrafts**. This organization has been around since 1990, but it was only in 1994 that the founders, former Vietnamese social workers, saw the opportunity of opening a handicraft shop. What started out as a small project to prevent school dropouts in Ho Chi Minh City's Phu Nhuan District from becoming street children, has become an income-generating and educational program for hundreds of poor and disadvantaged women throughout Vietnam.

Charity ignites an age-old debate. Detractors say money with no strings attached creates reliance, while supporters say society's poorest and most vulnerable need unconditional help. Mark Estes says, "We work in a way so that victims become part of the process instead of passive recipients. So there's pride, ownership, finance, and dignity involved." Mark is the country director of **Habitat for Humanity**, an international NGO that focuses on providing shelter to those who can't afford it. It started its operations in Vietnam in 2001, focusing on Danang, and finally moved south in 2003, where it has branched out into sanitation and access to clean water.

Habitat works with Vietnam's local people's committees to offer technical support and advice on loans to poor families. And despite its religious foundation, Mark says Habitat is non-discriminatory. "Everything is decided based on need. Do they live in sub-standard housing? Do they have an ability to pay back? Do they have an ability not just to help themselves but also others?" He adds, "Rural poverty is different from urban poverty. It's more overt and reasons go deeper. We do micro-finance because the poor can't handle a long-term mortgage. It's about giving them hope."

Whether you are cash poor and time rich or vice versa, there are many ways you can contribute. Most NGOs are always looking out for volunteers, whether to raise general awareness or provide specific skills, such as product design, marketing, etc. For example, Operation Smile uses groups of volunteer surgeons, nurses, and orderlies who eschew payment and donate their skills for one week.

One caveat, though—most groups prefer volunteers to commit to at least three months or the length of a project. Being a volunteer can be a rewarding job, knowing that your efforts will improve lives, but it also requires patience and commitment. Another way is to help spread the message, whether to stop consuming exotic animal products or to contribute to a charity that helps disadvantaged kids lead normal lives.

Money, of course, is a big factor. It is needed to implement projects and for administrative costs. For most of these organizations, it is a constant uphill struggle to keep the donations flowing. The thing to keep in mind is that you don't have to be a millionaire to make a difference.

According to East Meets West, $10 provides a year's worth of dental care to an impoverished child, while $20 ensures a lifetime of clean drinking water for one person. Fifty dollars will keep a disadvantaged kid in school for a year, and it costs just $85 for a forty-five-minute cleft palate surgery that will bring about change for a lifetime. So instead of splurging on the next glass of wine, save that 100,000 VND for a child who needs education.

Buy products from Mai Handicrafts for the next birthday/wedding/holiday gift. Purchase some Sozo cookies, which are made by disadvantaged families. Or have a cup of coffee at Bobby Brewer's on Tuesdays, as proceeds support local orphanages.

How you can help

15 May School

The school would like to refurbish the children's living quarters. It also needs donations for scholarships, furniture for the halfway house, help fulfilling the children's wish lists, and general volunteers.

www.15mayschool.org

Bobby Brewers

Buy coffee on Tuesdays; proceeds help children affected by Agent Orange.

45 Bui Vien St.
District 1
Ho Chi Minh City
www.bobbybrewers.com

Catalyst Foundation

The foundation needs volunteers for projects and events, as well as donations.

www.catalystfoundation.org

Christina Noble Children's Foundation

The foundation needs volunteers and sponsors for projects. It is also looking for help with fulfilling the annual Christmas wish list for 1,800 kids.

www.cncf.org

East Meets West Foundation

Long-term volunteers are required for projects. Donations are also needed.

www.eastmeetswest.org

Green Bamboo Shelter and HCMC Cancer Centre

You can provide general donations or sponsorships for schooling (100,000 VND/month) and chemotherapy treatments. Volunteers are also needed to teach English and other specific subjects. On the website below, click "Community Network" for more information.

www.ilavietnam.com

Habitat for Humanity

Donations for projects are needed. As well, volunteers are needed for administration, marketing, and project work.

www.habitatvietnam.com

Mai Handicrafts

Purchase products from Mai— this means more work and more income for the producers. Mai also needs suggestions on product design and development.

298 Nguyen Trong Tuyen St.
Tan Binh District
Ho Chi Minh City

Operation Smile Vietnam

Provide general donations or sponsor a child. Volunteers are needed for fundraising events.

www.operationsmilevietnam.org

Sozo

Buy a cookie to help street kids earn a living.

176 Bui Vien St.
District 1
Ho Chi Minh City
www.myspace.com/sozostudents

RESOURCES FOR THE ROAD

Practical advice to help you prepare for your travels.

With so many ways to plan a trip and a variety of great resources to choose from, it's difficult to know where to begin. First, since *To Vietnam With Love* is not a typical guidebook, you should choose at least one: Lonely Planet, Rough Guide, Frommer's, etc. Having been a bookseller, avid traveler, and travel writer—sometimes all three at once—for nearly twenty years, I feel confident in saying that the big name publications are reliable ... or at least as reliable as a guidebook can be for a country like Vietnam, which is changing at such a rapid pace. Picking one over the other depends on what you want from your trip. I recommend that you give yourself a few hours—at least—to visit a bookshop. Pick some destinations and attractions, and read how each book covers them. Then choose the book that best suits your personality and interests.

Keep in mind that no guidebook will ever take you to an undiscovered place. That is the Catch-22 of a remote village or hidden pagoda showing up on a blog, *Travel Channel* program, or the pages of Lonely Planet. The fact is that the planet just isn't all that lonely anymore. That's why I'm such a believer in doing alternative research, beginning with fiction. Novels and short stories may not introduce you to something that no one has seen before, but they can give you new insights into what you are seeing. Although I read the story "The Traffic Policeman at a Crossroads" more than ten years ago, I still think of its main character, a disillusioned, disappointed former soldier turned traffic cop, every time I see a traffic policeman whistling and waving at the anarchy that is traffic in Vietnam. Traffic policemen are people who tourists often find slapstick, futile, and/or annoying, but after I read the story, they fascinated me.

I also think a trip is lacking without knowledge of a country's history. I occasionally cruise around the web reading travel forums, and I'm always saddened when I read comments about

how "cool" and "distant" the people of northern Vietnam are. These comments are written, I assume, by people who do not understand how a history of struggle and suffering, particularly in the north, still casts a shadow over the collective memory. It is this background that I believe fuels the reserve travelers sometimes mistake for rudeness in certain areas. As for choosing from the countless non-fiction books available, I find that the best understanding comes from a balanced combination of historical and personal accounts.

Along with books, there are numerous websites that can also help lay the groundwork for your trip. One of the best things the web has done for the world is to allow small publications and specialized groups to share their information with anyone who is interested. Of course, much on the web must be taken discriminately, since fact checking is not a number one priority in cyberspace.

In this chapter I have included my personal recommendations for books, websites, and movies, along with a few contributor suggestions for reading and language learning. As well, there are some picks for cooking classes, which are popular in Vietnam. This chapter is not exhaustive. Nor is it meant to be exclusive. I am sure in the next few years I will read a dozen more books, see a few more movies, and discover some more interesting websites that I would urge you to investigate—not to mention take a few more cooking classes. In the meantime, the suggestions here provide a place to begin planning your trip and gaining a deeper understanding of Vietnam.

Book Recommendations

FICTION

Annam
by Christophe Bataille

This slender novel examines Vietnam through the lives of French missionaries during and just after the reign of Louis XVI in the 1700s. Stark but lyrical language adds to the potency of the already charged story about the reinvention of ideology in a far-off land.

Paradise of the Blind
by Duong Thu Huong

Controversial writer Duong gained international attention with this book, and deservingly so. The story is moving in its simplicity, following a young girl through the years after the American War. It is worth reading solely for the descriptions of food, which bring home the reality of how hard life was in post-1975 Vietnam. This novel is a must for anyone who wants to understand the country's recent past. Duong has written other novels, which are quite good, but this is my favorite.

The Quiet American
by Graham Greene

It doesn't matter that this novel is a traveler's joke—photocopied versions are as common as *pho* on the streets of Vietnam. The bottom line is that this is an exceptional book, one of the best in showing—ideologically and emotionally—how America got involved so inextricably in Vietnam. I have read it more than a dozen times, and I am amazed by Greene's perceptivity every time.

The Sea Wall
by Marguerite Duras

Forget *The Lover*. Well, you don't need to forget it, but if you must choose only one of Duras' novels set in Vietnam, choose this one. In the way that Greene sheds light on America's rise to power in Vietnam, Duras illuminates France's fall, using the encroaching sea and a crumbling wall on a family's property as a metaphor for the disintegration of colonization.

Tale of Kieu
by Nguyen Du

Available in most bookshops selling English language publications in Vietnam, this is the country's premier novel in translation. Adapted from an ancient Chinese story, this Vietnamese prose poem was written in the early 1800s. Its flowery, often euphemistic language—"To avoid any transgression of the rules of decency," according to the forward to my edition—describes the travails of Kieu, a genteel young woman exposed to numerous misfortunes before being reunited with her one true love.

NON-FICTION

A Bright, Shining Lie: John Paul Vann and America in Vietnam
by Neil Sheehan

This is both a biography and a commentary on the war. It tells the story of America's involvement in Vietnam through the eyes of Lieutenant Colonel John Paul Vann, whose early support for the conflict splintered beneath the weight of his disillusionment. Vann's most notable trait was his unwillingness to keep his mouth shut, dishing out his often prescient opinions on corruption, political lies, and ineptitude to reporters, including Sheehan, one of the era's best.

Dispatches
by Michael Herr

Raw. If I had to choose only one word to describe this book, that would be it. A from-the-gut telling of the Vietnam War, written by a man who was in the thick of it, reporting on it for *Esquire* and *Rolling Stone*, this is a must read for anyone who wants a better understanding of war's darkest of dark sides ... body bags and all. It's as relevant today as it was when it was published in 1977.

Fire in the Lake: The Vietnamese and the Americans in Vietnam
by Frances FitzGerald

This multi-award-winning book competes with Stanley Karnow's *Vietnam: A History* for best historical overview, with a focus on the American War. Neither is a light read; both are essential if you're serious

about understanding the complexities of Vietnam's history. Originally published in 1972, (as opposed to Karnow's book, which was published after the war in 1983), FitzGerald's analyses are sometimes eerie to read, since you know how the story is eventually going to turn out.

Hell in a Very Small Place: The Siege of Dien Bien Phu
by Bernard Fall

Dien Bien Phu, one of Vietnam's most significant battles, split the country in so many ways in 1954. It ousted the French and led to the geographical halving that served as the justification for America's involvement in the country. Fall is an old-school war journalist whose examination of the fifty-six-day siege by Viet Minh guerilla forces against the French military gives you everything you need to know about why America did not later win its own war in Vietnam.

The House on Dream Street: Memoir of an American Woman in Vietnam
by Dana Sachs

I do not usually recommend travel narratives about Vietnam because, to be frank, I haven't liked many that I've read. I don't think they are bad (for the most part), but I do think they are skin deep. Sach's book is different. First, she lived in Vietnam for a year in the early 1990s. Second, she cares so much about the people she is writing about. Her book is incredibly domestic, and this is what makes it valuable, because Vietnam is a domestic country. To be invited inside a home is to be invited inside Vietnam. This book invites you not only into the house of the family Sachs lived with, but also into the relationships in that house and neighborhood, including Sachs' own poignant love affair with a local motorcycle mechanic.

Once Upon a Distant War
by William Prochnau

Although there are certainly more comprehensive books about the Vietnam War, this macro lens view of the conflict during the early 1960s— through the lives of journalists David Halberstam, Peter Arnett, and Neil Sheehan—gave me my best understanding of how and why the war was doomed. It follows the men during such events as Kennedy's secret escalation of troops, the disastrous Strategic Hamlets Program, and the assassination of South Vietnamese President Ngo Dinh Diem. Part adventure story, part political history, and filled with tales of great parties and bad-boy behavior, this book held me captive during the four days it took me to devour its 500+ pages.

Over the Moat: Love Among the Ruins of Imperial Vietnam
by James Sullivan

In so many travel books I've read by Westerners, the author spends three weeks scooting around the country, makes some clever observations and numerous definitive pronouncements about the Vietnamese, and then goes home, leaving his readers to think that he *knows* Vietnam. He doesn't. To know Vietnam, you need to spend *a lot* of time there. James Sullivan did just that, although he wasn't expecting to when he hopped on his bike in 1992 for a top-to-tip tour. In the former imperial city of Hue, when he falls for a young woman, he decides to stay, vying with local suitors to win her heart. His insights into local customs, particularly when it comes to love, are as simple and elegant as Hue itself. And ... this isn't a plot spoiler, especially if you've read his contributions in these pages here ... he gets the girl.

The Sacred Willow: Four Generations in the Life of a Vietnamese Family
by Duong Van Mai Elliott

The subtitle of this book says it all. Elliott has written a biography of her family, dating back to the 1800s, which included mandarins, French-affiliated government officials, and Viet Minh soldiers. There does not seem to be a single aspect of Vietnam's history from the past 150 years that is not represented among her relatives. If you want to understand what it means for a country, culture, and families to be torn apart, this is the place to begin.

Shadows and Wind:
A View of Modern Vietnam
by Robert Templer

This book provides an important, and accessible, look at numerous aspects of contemporary Vietnam. Although

BOOK RECOMMENDATIONS

a pell-mell-into-the-future decade has passed since its publication, this book has a timelessness about it. I was fascinated by a pair of chapters that compare how Vietnam is remembered versus how it is imagined. And I felt I had a greater understanding of my Vietnamese friends' parents after reading the chapter entitled "Famine." From youth culture to the role China plays in Vietnam's progress, Templer explores issues that will continue to dominate the Vietnamese landscape for years to come.

Vietnam: The Valor and the Sorrow
by Thomas D. Boettcher

I found this heavy (literally) book in a thrift shop and consider it one of my great treasures. Along with telling a fairly straightforward history, it is filled with archival photographs and sidebars containing obscure quotes, trivia, and anecdotes.

RECOMMENDED SOURCES

ABE Books
www.abebooks.com

I have often used this website to track down out-of-print books about Vietnam. One of my most prized purchases is a dignified hardcover copy of Norman Lewis' *A Dragon Apparent*, which came with the foldout maps still in it, from a helpful bookseller in England. You can correspond directly with a shop's owners and clerks to ask questions about a book. The site represents more than 10,000 bookshops around the globe, making it a good way to support the used book business.

Curbstone Press
www.curbstone.org

This small press is a gem. Along with publishing modern Vietnamese poetry, it offers *Voices from Vietnam*, a highly regarded contemporary fiction series. Any one of the volumes will enrich your trip, but I especially like the short story anthologies for on-the-road reading: *Behind the Red Mist, The Cemetery of Chua Village, Crossing the River, Love after War, The Other Side of Heaven*, and *The Stars, The Earth, The River*.

Dalley Book Service
www.dalleybookservice.com

Although this website's specialty is the Vietnam War, I once ordered an interesting cookbook from it: *Vietnamese Dishes*, by Duong Thi Thanh Lien, a spiral bound, English language volume published in Saigon in 1973. (It lists the all-purpose "coolie hat" in the essential kitchenware section and states that MSG is an exciting new ingredient in Vietnamese cooking.) Because the catalog on this website is difficult to navigate, I suggest emailing the company to ask for the book you are seeking. The owner is very helpful.

Dana Sachs
www.danasachs.com

Author of *The House on Dream Street* and *If You Lived Here*, a memoir and novel, respectively, Sachs writes books that reflect the way she sees Vietnam: like a lover, with passion and a tender, forgiving acceptance of flaws. She has co-written *Two Cakes Fit for a King* (a collection of Vietnamese folk tales), and translated Curbstone Press' *Crossing the River*. In the Vietnam section of her website, you will find an annotated list of recommended reading.

University of Washington Library
www.lib.washington.edu/Southeast Asia/vietlit.html

Although divided by categories such as "Modern Fiction in Translation" and "Francophone Vietnamese Literature," this comprehensive list can be intimidating. But if you're serious about exploring nearly all there is to offer, this is the place to start your research. You will find titles from *The Gioi* (The World) Publishers in Hanoi (formerly the Foreign Languages Publishing House), a number of university presses, and more. Unfortunately, the list is just that: a list. As for getting your hands on some of the more obscure titles, try checking the recommended sources in this section.

White Lotus Press
www.whitelotusbooks.com

I am madly in love with this press, which reprints some unusual and excellent books. Among my favorites is *Three Years in Vietnam (1907-1910)* by Gabrielle M. Vassal. The memoir of a French doctor's wife in Nha Trang, this beats any contemporary travelogue I've read about the region. The best part of White Lotus is its eclecticism. Where else can you find volumes of *People and Wildlife in*

and Around Saigon (1872-1873) and *Saigon 1975*, Tiziano Terzani's invaluable account of the fall of Saigon and—because he stuck around—the three months that followed?

Viet Nam Literature Project
www.vietnamlit.org

Through the home page of this website, which promotes Vietnamese literature in English translation, you can reach WikiVietLit, a superb resource for information on Vietnamese writers, past and present. You will find sections for a variety of categories, including fiction, poetry, plays, essays, and performance art. One of the fun things about this site is that following the biography of each writer is a list of links to online materials, such as excerpts, literary criticism, and interviews.

Vietnam Art Books
www.vietnamartbooks.com

Vietnam has a very groovy art world where you might find everything from an original, avant-garde lacquer work to an exceptional reproduction of Monet's *Water Lilies*. Although Vietnamese art was heavily influenced by the opening of the Ecole des Beaux-Arts d'Indochine in Hanoi in 1925, it has been finding its own way in recent years. On this website, you can find books about Bui Xuan Phai, one of the twentieth-century's most respected painters; contemporary art as analyzed by an independent Russian curator; and ethnic minority artists. It's fun just to browse the site and look at samples of artwork from the books.

Dan Duffy encourages you to read Vietnam

Like most nations, Vietnam is ruled by one government and dominated by one ethnic group. It has a national style of architecture and decoration, unique language, and distinctive way of raising children, eating, and so forth. When you travel to Vietnam, you will learn more of these national traits than any anthropologist can teach you. But you might not know how to talk about them.

Fortunately, you can learn. Even assuming you don't speak Vietnamese, or the Chinese, French, and Russian languages that have dominated Vietnam's modern history, or any of the dozens of minority languages that play their subordinate role, you can listen in on the conversations that make up life in this country.

That is, you can read Vietnamese literature.

To get started, as you travel through Vietnam, stop at the office of World Publishers in Hanoi, where you will find a bookstore that sells English language books. The publishing house started during the American War, and one of its great accomplishments in that time of desperate struggle was to publish a series of translations of Vietnamese literature: novels, volumes of short stories and poems, and a series of massive anthologies.

Most of these are out of print. The subsidies that supported them passed with the coming of the new economy. You have to buy them from used booksellers, or the people who sell photocopies in the stalls and alleys of Trang Tien Street. There is one big book still in print, though, by one of the founders of the publishing house.

When I was working for the company in the 1990s, Huu Ngoc still had an office behind the bookstore, off the courtyard of the company's villa. Half blind since birth, he nonetheless had served the revolution as a soldier, re-educating African prisoners of war and returning them through the lines to their units. He spent his life thereafter as an "importer and exporter of culture," publishing in foreign languages, writing his own books about France and the United States, mentoring foreigners like me, and writing a weekly column for Hanoi's English-language newspaper.

Huu's *Sketches for a Portrait of Vietnamese Culture,* available at the bookstore, draws from his career of translation and original work to present his country to the world. Ask for a copy, and maybe ask if Ngoc still comes to the office and might sign it for you ... this passport to the culture of Vietnam.

The Gioi (The World) Publishers

Formerly the Foreign Languages Publishing House, this state-run company offers a selection of books about Vietnamese culture, history, and politics. Among the best is *The Cuisine of Viet Nam: Nourishing a Culture*, an anthology that contains essays, written mostly by locals, about dishes, traditions, and regional distinctions.

46 Tran Hung Dao St.
Hoan Kiem District
Hanoi
http://thegioipublishers.com.vn

Viet Nam Literature Project

Another avenue for reading Vietnamese work is Viet Nam Literature Project, launched in the United States. Free of supervision by any government, the project's website is home to numerous works by Vietnamese writers. It includes works from the Vietnamese diaspora and from the former nation of South Vietnam.

www.vietnamlit.org

Online shopping

Sketches for a Portrait of Vietnamese Culture, as well as other books by Huu Ngoc, may also be ordered from ThingsAsian.

http://store.thingsasian.com

Preyanka Clark Prakash pays tribute to a passion for Vietnam

I like to say that my love affair with Vietnam began long before I was born, with a mother dangerously attracted to war zones. It wasn't, though, the war that drew her there in the early 1970s, a time of escalating violence and chaos. It was the far simpler desire to bring home the children she was in the process of adopting. Her book, *After Sorrow Comes Joy,* is, in essence, the story of why she ended up staying and the person she became because of it. It is the story of her transformation from an Indiana farm girl to an international figure of courage and compassion. Documenting her rescue of sick, abandoned, and orphaned children, the book is a testament to her humanitarian efforts.

In a sense, Cherie Clark was forged in the violence, terror, and desolation that was war-torn Vietnam. But what emerged was not something ugly. It was pure, with a singularity of purpose: she became a visionary who saw the power of hope and its refusal to perish amidst the gravest of human suffering. When she was forced to leave Vietnam in the panicked exodus before the fall of Saigon, she carried that hope with her, along with a determination to keep it alive in others.

My mother has yet to write the sequel to her book, about her journey to Calcutta where she was invited to work with Mother Teresa. While in India, she met my father, had my sister and me, and founded the International Mission of Hope (IMH), an organization that boasted one of the finest neonatal care facilities in the country, and which in its twenty-five years of operation, saved countless lives and found loving homes for more than 5,000 orphans. She also has yet to write the story of her emotional and healing return to Vietnam in 1988 and her subsequent decision to move to Hanoi in 1992 with her two youngest children, my sister Shauna and me. She continues to live in Hanoi and dedicate her life to humanitarian causes.

While I wasn't forced out of Vietnam amidst exploding rockets, clutching dying babies in my arms, I did leave after finishing high school with a great deal of sadness and uncertainty as to when I would return. I know that I will, like my mother, find my way back to the country that may not have given birth to me but certainly raised me *and* taught me how to love, to dream, and, most of all, to hope.

WEBSITE RECOMMENDATIONS

Active Travel Vietnam
www.activetravelvietnam.com

While I have never used this company, so I cannot vouch for it, I love its website for the listing of Vietnam's national parks. Divided by region, the list includes links to a page for each park, with complete descriptions of flora, fauna, and unique topography—sand dunes, caves, karsts, and all. If you are a nature lover and want to spend time exploring Vietnam's diverse wilderness areas, this site is a great place to start researching your trip.

Duong Lam Anh
http://duonglamanh.typepad.com

There are loads of blogs out there about Vietnam, many of them good. In this one, Duong, a university professor in Hue, riffs on a range of topics, including his travels, which take him around the imperial city, throughout his country, and—occasionally—beyond. Don't be intimidated when you open the site and see Vietnamese text. Scroll down the main page and you will see an index of entries in English. Pick a link, and you may find yourself guided on a tour of Hue-area churches or to a quiet pagoda with a famous, 100-year-old star fruit tree. Along with offering snapshots of the country Duong loves, entries also include cultural musings—a true insider's view.

Mui Ne Beach
www.muinebeach.net

This website publishes every bit of information you could possibly want about Mui Ne, one of the most popular beach destinations in Vietnam. Along with providing up-to-date regional news, it offers loads of practical information, from pharmacy locations to descriptions of the area's unique dune ecosystem. You will also appreciate insider tips: *don't* purchase coral products (this encourages the destruction of reefs), and *do* attend the Festival at the Magician's Temple.

WEBSITE RECOMMENDATIONS

ThingsAsian

www.thingsasian.com

ThingsAsian is the granddaddy of Asia travelogue websites, and I'm not saying that just because this book is affiliated with it. With its origins in the art-heavy print magazine, *Destination: Vietnam*, this site has hundreds of articles—many commissioned, many freely contributed—about Vietnam and the surrounding countries. The articles, most of which describe personal travel experiences, date back more than a decade. This is a good place to publish your own writing and photographs once you return from your trip.

Viet Nam News

http://vietnamnews.vnanet.vn

Government-run, this daily newspaper has a large culture section where you can delve into the country's book, film, photography, music, and theater scenes. If there's a noteworthy art exhibit or festival taking place while you're in the country, chances are you'll find details here. There are also restaurant reviews, articles on "hidden gem" destinations in the travel section, and short stories on Sundays.

Vietnam Investment Review

www.vir.com.vn

A state-run news weekly with a focus on business and the economy, *VIR* publishes *Time Out*, a small magazine supplement covering what's happening in the big cities. Pick up a copy in-country to read reviews of new restaurants, as well as articles about lesser known attractions and destinations that may only get a couple lines—if that—in your guidebook. Tip: search for "Forestry Guesthouse" in the *Time Out* section online; this place (complete with spa baths using ethnic herbs) looks terrific.

Vietnam Tourism

www.vietnamtourism.com

Usually, official government tourism websites feel like Madison Avenue campaigns gone awry: too slick, and with not enough substance. Not so this one. There is something down-to-earth about it that suits the country it represents, and it's filled with pleasant surprises. If you're patient enough to click around and see where you might go, you will find cool bits of information—about the festival ritual of statue washing, perhaps, or a garden where you can pick fresh fruit. Every time I go on this site, I can't find my way back to where I was before. But while trying, I always find something new and interesting.

VietnamNetBridge

http://english.vietnamnet.vn

There are two sections on this website worth exploring. In *Life in Vietnam*, check out *What's On* (weekly exhibition and performance listings), *Fare Fest* (restaurant reviews and current food events), and *Get-away* (travel destinations). Also interesting is *The Good Life*, with a few odd articles on Vietnam's counter-culture. Aside from *What's On*, many articles are a little dated, but they provide interesting travel suggestions, such as the Pu Luong Nature Reserve outside Hanoi or the stone garden in the hamlet of Loc Nga.

CITY TOURISM SITES

Dalat
www.dalattourist.com.vn

Haiphong
www.haiphong.gov.vn

Halong City and Halong Bay
www.halong.org.vn

Hanoi
www.hanoi.gov.vn

Ho Chi Minh City
http://tourism.hochiminhcity.gov.vn/english/home.php

Nha Trang
www.nhatrang-travel.com

MOVIE RECOMMENDATIONS

Daughter from Danang
www.daughterfromdanang.com

Absolutely heartbreaking, this Academy Award-nominated documentary takes on the life of Heidi, the daughter of a Vietnamese woman and U.S. serviceman. As the war neared its end, there were rumors that the Communists were killing Amerasian children, and fearing for Heidi's safety, her mother gave her up for adoption. Heidi was raised as an all-American kid in Tennessee, and this documentary traces her return as an adult to Vietnam, to reunite with her family. What happened when she arrived in Vietnam caught me completely by surprise, and brought home just one more way in which the war destroyed lives.

In the Year of the Pig
Because this Academy Award-nominated documentary was made in 1968, it is anchored in the middle of the Vietnam War. This film, controversial at the time of its release, is no retrospective, gazing back in judgment on past events. Using interviews and footage that feel both prescient and conclusive, filmmaker Emile de Antonio creates an eloquently critical portrait of madness and the madmen responsible for it. He also gives the war its foundation in the French conflict that preceded it.

The Vertical Ray of the Sun
Whenever I miss Vietnam, I watch this movie about three sisters in Hanoi. Spying on contemporary family life, it captures those intimate relationships that develop among women—one of the loveliest things about Vietnam. This movie is also memorable for its surprising use of Lou Reed songs and gorgeous, saturated colors, which underscore the mood of each scene. Filmmaker Tran Anh Hung also made the well-worth-watching movies *The Scent of Green Papaya* and *Cyclo*.

Vietnam: A Television History

www.pbs.org/wgbh/amex/vietnam

Originally a thirteen-part series when it came out on PBS in 1983, *Vietnam* was later honed down to a manageable eleven hours. It focuses on an unceasingly volatile thirty-year period, from 1945 to 1975, and includes solid background information (the fall of French Indochina and Ho Chi Minh's original petitions for independence), an episode on the byproduct devastation of Cambodia and Laos, and a look at the war's effect inside America. The series is an investment of time—and emotion—but it will give you a greater understanding of and appreciation for the people who welcome you so warmly during your travels.

Vietnam War: Movie Listing

www.illyria.com/vnbooks.html

Although this website is titled *Books About Vietnam*, it has a massive movie section, as well. The focus is war, and you will find everything imaginable, from the standard *Apocalypse Now* and *Platoon* to little known films like *Battle's Poison Cloud*, a documentary about Agent Orange. There is also a link to a Tim O'Brien section, which is filled with information about the author who defined the Vietnam War novel with his essential *The Things They Carried*.

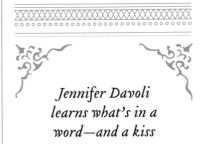

LEARNING VIETNAMESE

Jennifer Davoli learns what's in a word—and a kiss

For those who appreciate the profound relationship between language and culture, studying a foreign tongue prior to travel is simply a part of standard preparation, like buying plane tickets or a guidebook. In order to truly permeate the depth of another culture, we must communicate, at some point, and in some form, in "their" terms. Learning the language of a land, even a mere few words, opens doors that otherwise go unnoticed, and can result in unpredictable, unforgettable experiences.

Naturally, upon my arrival in Hanoi, where I planned to live for a year, gaining a solid grasp of Vietnamese was of utmost importance. Fortunately, Vietnamese offers one advantage over other Asian languages, in that it uses Romanized letters instead of characters, despite having strong roots in Chinese. In the seventeenth century, with the arrival of European traders and missionaries, the language was transformed. A Romanized script was developed, and starting in 1919, under French colonization, all official documents had to be produced in the Latin alphabet. This edict overflowed into daily life, and Chinese characters were left behind for the scholars of history alone.

While this is a bonus for Western learners, who don't have to grapple with seeming hieroglyphics, there is still the matter of tones. Tonally, Vietnamese dwarfs all other Asian languages with up to six distinctive tones for each of its twenty-nine letters. This means that some letters can be pronounced as many as six different ways—and words spelled the same, but with different tonal marks, carry entirely different meaning. For example, depending on the tone they are given, *ma, má, mà,* and *mã,* do not sound the same, and definitely do not mean the same. After my first week of lessons in-country, this led me to learn to say one thing clearly: *toi met.* That is, "I'm tired."

But though worn out, I was not ready to give up, despite the obstacles that cluttered my path. One day it was a young boy at my hotel who insisted on greeting me with "*Nao halo,*" driving me crazy trying to figure out the phrase until I realized he was cheekily, and a bit meanly, saying, "No hello." Another time I sat through breakfast with my bilingual hotel staff understanding almost nothing, despite my many lessons. And on the last day of the course, at a local café, came a stinging blow. The waitress set my dish down, and in Vietnamese, I said, "Thanks." I pronounced it loudly and clearly, with the confidence of a native—after all, it's the first phrase everyone learns, and I was sure I had it mastered. She smiled ... and two

minutes later handed me a large glass of orange juice.

To the English-listening ear, the Vietnamese thank you—*cam on*— sounds like "calm uhhn." Orange juice is pronounced "nuoc cam." Quite different, though my waitress didn't think so when I said it. After only a few weeks in the country, I truly needed a vacation.

But the following evening, in my local Internet café, one of the hundreds of run-down, teenage-boy-PlayStation-ridden spots found all over the city, I finally found something to grab onto—some hope, a reason to carry on with my mission.

When I arrived, it was late, ten or so, and I was planning to make a computer call to the United States. The skinny young Vietnamese boy set me up, as he always did. He greeted me with a classic, "*Chao chi*"— "Hello, older sister"—and helped me with a headphone and a microphone. He let me use my Vietnamese and smiled all the while, understanding correctly, which was just what my ego needed.

When I completed my call, I gathered my bag and attempted to apologize for staying so late. The young boy assured me, "*Khong co gi*"—"No problem," and I actually got it. I responded, "*Hen gap lai*"—"See you later"—and he understood me. Successful communication. A peaceful night of sleep was surely in store.

Boosted by our exchange, I confidently retorted, "Sweet dreams," a common saying that boys, girls, friends, and family use freely and regularly.

Literally, it means, "Wish you delicious sleep." He understood again. And he responded, "*Chut chut*," stopping me in my tracks, as the words were familiar, but not in this circumstance.

Chut chut means "kiss-kiss," literally, and as I processed his comment it occurred to me, this young man was flirting—he was using a phrase only my Vietnamese "sister" and "mother" had shared with me, late at night, before bed, quite intimately.

Finally, I was communicating on "their" terms.

Too bad he was only fifteen.

Inside tip

Pick up a copy of the locally published *Tieng Viet*. I got my copy of this workbook at one of the bookstores near Hanoi's Trang Tien Plaza in Hoan Kiem District. You should also be able to find it in most large bookstores in cities throughout the country. I also recommend the Pimsleur audio lessons, which are described in the following essay.

Adam Bray helps you get the hang of speaking Vietnamese

Learning even just a few greetings, numbers, and phrases in Vietnamese can alter the course of your travels. Locals are often surprised when a foreigner speaks Vietnamese and seem to greatly appreciate the effort. It can open doors to new friendships, make travel easier, help you avoid mishaps, and even save you some money in the market.

Vietnamese is generally considered to have three dialects (northern, central, and southern), though there can be minor differences in accents and colloquialisms from village to village. Although I have my own philosophical objections to the following claim, as I'm a resident of the south, the Hanoi accent, representative of the northern dialect, is generally considered the standard, and is most often used for audio CDs. Practically speaking, it matters very little which dialect or accent you learn.

Most language books and CDs stress one or more aspects of language (reading, writing, speaking, or listening), but rarely all of them. For this reason, it's often helpful to supplement your basic resource with secondary material. Because Vietnamese is a tonal language, access to listening examples is essential for learning. Some free audio resources are available on the Internet. For example, World Nomads (www.worldnomads.com) offers a free, albeit irreverent, fifteen-minute, iTune podcast that teaches introductory phrases (with corresponding text online); as well, a number of Vietnamese-only podcasts are free on iTunes.

LEARNING VIETNAMESE

Phrasebooks

Phrasebooks, supplemented with some audio, are the best places to start for beginners. Rough Guide and Lonely Planet both provide popular, pocket-sized books, although each is organized in a very different way. While it does contain short sections on "How the Language Works," "Scenarios," and "Basic Phrases," The Rough Guide phrasebook is primarily a travel-friendly dictionary with useful related phrases for many entries. One of the strongest points of the guide is that nearly thirty minutes of free MP3 downloads are available at www.roughguides.com, covering all sixteen scenario topics from the book. No purchase is required to download the audio.

Lonely Planet's phrasebook excels as a color-coded, topical language guide. Like its Rough Guide counterpart, the Lonely Planet edition contains a section on grammar, as well as a much smaller general dictionary and separate culinary dictionary. It surpasses Rough Guide, however, by offering numerous cultural notes and diagrams, and a separate Vietnamese index, (for times when you need to hand the book to someone who can't speak English), along with an essential phrases and numbers quick chart on the inside cover. Previous editions have also been packaged with *Travel Talk* (Penton Overseas) audio cassettes, although the audio does not directly correlate with the phrasebook. (This set had not come out on CD at the time of this book's publication). I enjoyed using the Lonely Planet 2000 edition as my first informal textbook while living in Vietnam. With the addition of phonetic examples for each entry, the 2006 edition has become a bit cluttered, but this publisher is still my personal favorite.

Vietnamese: Start Speaking Today! (Educational Services Corporation/ Language 30, www.lang30.com) describes itself as an audio CD course, but it's really an audio phrasebook with a helpful forty-eight-page booklet. The two CDs cover nearly thirty topics—really everything the average traveler needs to know. They include examples of both male and female speakers. This set makes a great supplement when using one of the other phrasebooks.

Mini Self-Study Courses

Rosetta Stone and Pimsleur are perhaps the two most well-known language course providers, and although expensive in their full forms, both now offer introductory packages suitable for beginners with short-term needs. Neither relies on memorizing long lists of vocabulary or grammatical rules, and both take a more natural approach to language learning.

Pimsleur's *Basic Vietnamese* is an audio-only course of ten half-hour lessons. Simon & Schuster offers the first lesson free on its website (www.simonsays.com), as well as a $50 credit if you upgrade to the comprehensive program. Loaded onto an MP3 player, this package is perfect if you spend a lot of time driving, exercising, or doing other activities that leave you free to listen.

Rosetta Stone's system is software-based, and the only self-study program I've found to actively engage reading, writing, listening, and speaking. A subscription-based online version of the program is available for three months ($109.95) and six months ($159.95), allowing you to later change to one of thirty other languages by contacting customer service. A free demo with multiple lessons is available at www.rosettastone.com.

Teach Yourself Vietnamese (McGraw Hill) is an excellent textbook-based course with two audio CDs. This is a thorough program, covering vocabulary (a dictionary is included), grammar, and cultural items. There are numerous writing exercises and complete answer keys for each of the units. Lessons contain multiple conversations and reading excerpts in Vietnamese, with translations. The CDs contain mostly the conversations of four male and female actors. I enjoyed working through the entire course. My only complaint is that later units include less audio than earlier ones.

Keep in mind that some readily available items are perhaps inappropriately marketed to beginners. *VocabuLearn* (Penton Overseas) is an audio-only series. Each volume contains four CDs of vocabulary drills for nouns, adverbs and adjectives, verbs, and expressions, respectively. The drills on each CD are randomized, which makes it impossible to use the CDs in conjunction with any kind of topical or structured lessons.

Supplemental Material

Most phrasebooks and textbooks include a basic dictionary, so it's unlikely that you'll need to purchase one separately. Once in Vietnam, you can also find dictionaries and thesauruses at any bookstore for a fraction of the US cost. Also available once you have arrived are children's books and classroom-style charts of animals, fruit, vehicles, and other objects. All are designed to teach kids English, and they work equally well to teach you Vietnamese.

Your First 100 Words in Vietnamese (McGraw Hill) is an excellent workbook designed to teach you ten words (mostly nouns) at a time, by taking you through a series of puzzles. It emphasizes reading and writing skills, and makes excellent supplemental material for any study. I wish the publishers would produce a sequel.

Making Out in Vietnamese (Tuttle Publishing) is a popular booklet that appears to be a guide to colloquial Vietnamese. However, due to inappropriate selections of pronouns and offensive slang, use of the booklet by beginners could lead to a lot of problems and embarrassment. The book is probably only suitable for intermediate speakers to round out their vocabulary or for entertainment purposes.

Most travelers will only want to learn the dominant Vietnamese language for their trip, but it is worth noting that in remote (usually mountainous) areas, many ethnic minorities do speak their own languages. *Hill Tribes Phrasebook* (Lonely Planet, 1999) is one of the

LEARNING VIETNAMESE

only readily available phrasebooks for minority languages, which include Hmong and Dao.

In-country lessons

A note from contributor Alice Driver: A personal language teacher is an excellent and affordable way to enrich your Vietnam experience. In Hanoi, a private language teacher for two people costs $6-$7/hour. The Department of Applied Linguistics at the Institute of Linguistics of Vietnam offers knowledgeable teachers who will help you learn a few basic phrases, or as much as you are willing to take on. They will either come to your hotel or invite you to have class in their homes. If you attend class two hours a day for seven days and study like your life depends on it, you can learn enough basic Vietnamese to get around (or to get in trouble).

38 Hang Chuoi St.
Hai Ba Trung District
Hanoi
(84-4) 971-0630

Vnstudy88@yahoo.com (contact Ms. Huong or Ms. Chi)

COOKING IN VIETNAM

"Although I spent five weeks determinedly eating and cooking my way through Vietnam researching a food book, I cannot say that I am an expert on preparing Vietnamese cuisine. But the thirteen lessons I took did give me a decent foundation. Along with attending popular cooking schools for tourists, I took private classes with chefs and even the mother of a dear friend. While I cannot vouch for all of the many classes offered in Vietnam, the following are my top picks from my trip for a fun holiday experience.

HOI AN

It feels like Hoi An has nearly as many cooking schools as it does tailor shops, making it the perfect place to park yourself for a few days and get into a kitchen. Most schools have followed in the wake of a few originals, which are still going strong today. I sampled both the fly-by-night and tried-and-true varieties. No surprise: stick with the tried and true.

Morning Glory Cooking School
www.hoianhospitality.com

Run by the charming Miss Vy, the classes at this school are arguably the most in-depth you'll find on the tourist circuit. Miss Vy takes the cultural and social history of

Vietnamese food seriously, and she shares her knowledge as a prelude to hands-on cooking. Some travelers may find her lecture too much, but I think it's a prize for anyone interested in Vietnamese food. As for the food you will make, it's exceptional. You will come away from your session with unique family recipes that you can easily make back home, such as an incredible turmeric fish in banana leaves and the worth-making-again-and-again caramelized eggplant.

Red Bridge Cooking School
www.visithoian.com

I recommend this school foremost for its entertainment value. From the moment your class begins at Hai Scout Café, you will feel as if you're at a comedy show. Sure, it's a bit of a shtick, but it's lots of fun, as you walk through the market and then are taken by boat to the lovely, open-air classroom outside town. I can't say I was fond of most of the dishes we made, but everyone in the class seemed to be satisfied, and it was interesting —and challenging—to prepare traditional rice paper. An enjoyable way to spend a sunny day.

DALAT

In the highlands of Vietnam, Dalat is home to most of the country's vegetable gardens. The climate is cool and crisp, and the misty, pine-shrouded setting makes it appealing to spend an afternoon in a cozy kitchen.

Sofitel Dalat Palace
www.sofitel.com

While not home to an official school, the hotel offers individual classes led by Chef Huong, who is one of the most charming men I've ever met. Upon request, you will receive a choice of recipes, and before you prepare them in the kitchen of the private villa inhabited by the hotel's general manager, Chef Huong will take you to the market to purchase the ingredients. Although this class is mainly demonstration, I still highly recommend it, as I do trying one of the hotel's excellently priced prix fixe meals and the Lang Bian Barbecue at Y Nhu Y behind the hotel—Chef Huong presides over both kitchens.

12 Tran Phu St.
(84-63) 825-444

HO CHI MINH CITY

Both Hanoi and Ho Chi Minh City offer numerous cooking classes, particularly in the big hotels and popular restaurants. I did not take any in Hanoi that I would like to recommend, which doesn't mean there aren't any good ones; it just means the ones I selected didn't appeal to me. In Ho Chi Minh City, of the handful I took, two stand out.

Dzoan Cam Van

With a popular television cooking show, Mrs. Cam Van is hailed as the Julia Child of Vietnam. Though the dishes she teaches are basic, the classes are in her home, which gives you the chance to cook in an authentic Vietnamese kitchen—the same one she uses to prepare family meals

COOKING IN VIETNAM

and some dishes for her eponymous restaurant. One of the most appealing aspects of her classes is her gentle demeanor. Make sure to ask her about her cooking background, which is fascinating. Mrs. Cam Van may be contacted through her restaurant.

34 Nguyen Thi Dieu St.
District 3
(84-8) 930-6120
dzoan34ntd@yahoo.com

The Vietnam Cookery Centre
www.expat-services.com

Despite the mediocre market tour that jump-started the class I took (it may have been an off day), I was very impressed. The classroom setting is attractive, and the entertaining, well-presented lecture that preceded the hands-on cooking contained just the right balance of kitchen lore and ingredient information. As with all the lessons on this list, cooking is followed by a pleasant meal consisting of the dishes you have prepared.

Stocking your library

If you're serious about preparing Vietnamese food at home, it's nice to have a staple set of cookbooks for researching techniques and all those strange herbs you sampled during your travels. They can also inspire to you try more than just the dishes you learned in class. I've enjoyed using all of the following during my trials and tribulations with fish sauce, rice noodles, and other quintessentially Vietnamese ingredients.

Café Vietnam
by Annabel Jackson

Although out of print, this book is well worth tracking down. It includes many favorites, such as Crab and Asparagus Soup and Southern Vietnamese Chicken Curry. In addition, the recipes are simple and gently adapted for Western kitchens, making it great for a beginner.

Into the Vietnamese Kitchen
by Andrea Nguyen

As you become more practiced at Vietnamese cookery, you can upgrade to this glossy book, whose thorough collection of recipes are not for the faint of heart. You'll find the real deal here; and while some of the recipes are intimidating, with their long list of ingredients and directions, you will be satisfied with the results. Nguyen also runs an excellent website, which offers a monthly newsletter: www.vietworldkitchen.com.

The Little Saigon Cookbook
by Ann Le

Sure, this is a shameless plug for my dear friend Ann, but that doesn't mean this isn't a good book. Along with plenty of classic recipes, and dishe s from her grandmother's kitchen, it contains stories about the Little Saigon community in Southern California in the United States. The recipes are divided into categories ranging from salads and seafood to comfort foods and celebration feasts.

Lonely Planet's World Food Vietnam
by Richard Sterling

While it has a few recipes in

it, this is not a cookbook. It's a primer on Vietnamese food. Its handy size means you can take it with you and read about regional distinctions and culinary traditions during your travels. There are also useful food-related phrase and dictionary sections.

Mui Ne fishing boat

COOKING IN VIETNAM

Epilogue

One writer learns that happiness isn't everything when she brings her family to Vietnam.

DANA SACHS TEACHES HER FAMILY
TO LIVE AND LOVE IN VIETNAM

My husband Todd Berliner and I always planned to move to another country for a year. Todd is a tenured professor of film studies at the University of North Carolina at Wilmington, and sabbaticals are among the perks of his profession. As a film scholar, he could do his research almost anywhere, as long as he could bring some boxes of books and DVDs. About eighteen months before his first sabbatical was to start, we began discussing our options. Vietnam was a possibility, of course. I had lived there before we got married, I adored the place, and my writing focused on it. But we considered other possibilities as well. As much as I yearned to live once again in Vietnam, I hesitated to drag Todd and our boys—Jesse, who would be eight, and Sam, who would be five—to a country where I wasn't sure they'd be happy.

But over the past fourteen years, I had come to know the country intimately, especially Hanoi. The cramped tables of my favorite *bun bo nam bo* restaurant were as much a part of my life as the red-checked tablecloths of our local pizza joint back home. I could picture the dark recesses of tiny Ba Da Temple on Nha Tho Street as easily as I could the sanctuary of my synagogue in North Carolina. I had absorbed a lot of local knowledge, like the shortcut through tiny alleyways between Hang Bong Street and the Hang Da Market, a route that passed three or four popular little shops that sold moonshine, including my favorite, a sweet apple-flavored variety. In any other country, we would begin as strangers. In Vietnam, we had friends already, and my familiarity with the place would ease the transition for my husband and my kids.

And so, in August of 2005, our family flew to Hanoi. It's hard for a child to fathom what it means to move to a foreign country, and Sam and Jesse's pre-trip excitement centered not so much on living *in* Vietnam as it did on traveling *to* Vietnam—on an airplane that

The kitchen of Hanoi's historic Cha Ca La Vong

featured nonstop movies *on demand*. About Vietnam itself, they really had no preconceptions, and, to our surprise, they didn't have any obvious culture shock when we arrived. Doing our best to make the transition as smooth as possible, we frequented Al Fresco's, a kid-friendly, Australian-owned establishment similar to Chili's back home. We picked up Chinese-made Power Rangers at the toy shops on Luong Van Can Street, and, after we found cheap roller skates on Trinh Hoai Duc Street, the boys raced around the outdoor rink near the Botanical Gardens.

Other foreign children may have suffered terribly from the humid August weather, but my kids had flown here from North Carolina, and in their opinions, summer heat is summer heat. They liked Vietnamese food too—or at least, they liked most of it. The first time Jesse tried *bun bo nam bo*, he insisted we order an extra bowl so he could have seconds. And Sam, our super-carnivore who turns up his nose at rice, could eat a grown-up's portion of *bun cha* all by himself. They didn't seem terribly bothered by the strangeness of their surroundings, either. After we moved into our rented house, a French-style villa on the northern edge of the Old Quarter, the boys were delighted to discover two or three famous dog meat restaurants located just up the road. They continually urged their less adventurous parents to relent and to let them try this local specialty. When we refused, they came up with a prank, slyly asking visiting relatives, "Hey, Uncle Mark! Aunt Lynne! Want to have HOT DOGS for lunch?"

Not that our entire year was perfect, however. Because we come from a culture that values privacy and personal space, Vietnam can feel oppressive. For example, Vietnamese love children, but when smitten old ladies grabbed Sam on the street, pulled him into their laps, and pinched his cheeks, those attentions left him so rattled and discouraged that I had to use my body as a shield. Loneliness could be a problem, too. Although Sam and Jesse both made friends in their classrooms at the United Nations International School, they also pined for their buddies back home. And during our travels in the countryside and right there on the streets of the city, they witnessed a level of poverty they had never seen at home, and those observations led to questions about "haves" and "have nots" that the world's wisest philosophers could never adequately answer.

So, in the year that we lived in Hanoi, did my husband and children fall in love with the country as I had? No, they didn't. There's a kind of chemistry that develops between a person and a place. It can evolve into something life-changing and passionate, but in most cases, it won't. However, we can experience many different kinds of emotion when we travel, and what I saw in my husband and kids strikes me as beautiful enough. As the months passed, they developed a warm, though somewhat variable, affection for Vietnam, and that affection seemed to increase steadily as they came to feel more at home there. I could see it, for example, in the expression of pride that swept across Todd's face after he successfully used his rudimentary Vietnamese to communicate to a gas station attendant his desire to fill his motorbike tank with gas. Not knowing the proper verb for "fill up," he substituted a phrase he did know, saying, "*Tram phan tram*!"—"100 percent!"—a term Vietnamese use while drinking as they challenge each other to down their shots. Happily, the gas station attendant got the message.

In Vietnam, Jesse became expert at *nem lon*, an urban street game in which children toss rubber sandals in order to knock down an empty bottle, and his facility with chopsticks is now, alas, much better than my own. Sam loved kicking the soccer ball around with the teenage boys who ran the car wash on our street, and he became so intrigued by the legend of the giant turtle in Hoan Kiem Lake that he kept one eye on the water whenever we walked by. Perhaps most touching, Jesse and Sam both developed a warm friendship with Duc, the twelve-year-old son of my dear friends and former landlords. Jesse and Duc, in particular, spent whole weekends together playing Monopoly,

and it was sweet and often hilarious to hear the racket of real estate deals negotiated between two children who shared a common vocabulary of maybe twenty words.

Now that we've returned to the States, Vietnam has seeped its way into the consciousness of our entire family. I'm not the only one who will spin a globe on its axis to search for Hanoi, although I am still the only one who does so avidly. When a Vietnamese-American friend brought over a traditional *banh tet* cake for us to eat during the Lunar New Year celebration this year, Jesse reacted in the way that many Vietnamese children react to the heavy pork and pork-fat laden concoction: "Never liked it, never will." And though Sam can't remember many words of Vietnamese, he continues to say *"xin loi"*—"sorry"— when he wants his apology to completely disarm me. He still takes off his shoes before going upstairs too.

Before making the decision to spend our year in Vietnam, I had worried that my family could not be happy there. It turned out that we could. Not *just* happy, however. We could be sad, annoyed, indulged, challenged, amused, perplexed, discouraged, and charmed, as well. Vietnam brought out every emotion, and isn't that what we want most out of our travels?

A few of Dana's favorites in and around Hanoi

Best yogurt and crème caramel

Okay, this assertion is (very) debatable, but Hanoians, who have enjoyed these French-inspired delights since the colonial period, line up here in droves, despite the fact that the "establishment" is only a window onto a busy street, and you have to sit on stools on the sidewalk to eat. A single glass of yogurt will set you back only a few thousand VND, but be careful! The stuff is addictive.

29 Hang Than St.
Ba Dinh District
Hanoi

Bun Bo Nam Bo

This succulent dish of grilled beef served over a bed of rice noodles and fresh greens is, as they say in guidebooks, "worth the trip." There are two very famous establishments, nearly side-by-side, easy to find on short Hang Dieu Street near the Hang Da Market in the Old Quarter. The ambience is loud and the floors are covered with the discarded banana-leaf wrappers of snack sausages, but the food is fresh and unforgettable.

Chua Thầy

The Red River Delta region surrounds Hanoi; you can drive out of the city in almost any direction and find traditional villages, pagodas, and temples. In Ha Tay Province, Chua Thay, the Teacher's Pagoda, dates back to the eleventh century and sits at the base of dramatic Thay Hill. Although it's famous for its serene architecture and setting, you're unlikely to meet any other tourists when you visit. Make a day of it by visiting the pagoda and climbing the hill.

Knives

They're not pretty, and they'll get rusty when you get them home—don't worry about it, just wash them off, and keep the blades oiled—but you'll never use another knife to slice a tomato again. Vietnam's handmade knives have simple wooden handles and blades like

something out of a ninja movie. At less than a dollar apiece, you should buy a dozen and bring them home as gifts. You may get lucky and spot roving vendors with baskets of knives, scissors, and other hardware wandering through the Old Quarter. If not, you can buy them from the hardware vendors behind the Dong Xuan Market, in the building at the southeast corner of Cau Dong and Nguyen Thien Thuat Streets.

Thien Son–Suoi Nga Resort

This lovely eco-friendly resort is just a few hours' drive from Hanoi on Ba Vi Mountain and caters to a Vietnamese, rather than foreign, clientele. Short landscaped trails take you to the base of a waterfall, and if you bring your bathing suit, you can take a refreshing dip in the stream below.

Van Hoa Commune
Ha Tay Province
(84-34) 881-411

Contributor Biographies, Credits and Index

Mark Barnett
(Pg. 134)

Born in the United States, Mark Barnett has lived in Vietnam since 1994. He is the director of Pacific Basin Partnership, Inc., a company that grows and exports spices in Vietnam and China, and the owner and host of Cassia Cottage, a vacation retreat with garden dining on Phu Quoc Island. He and his wife Thuy have two children, Sarabecca in California and Hoang Lawrence in Hanoi.

www.pbpspice.com
www.cassiacottage.com

Todd Berliner
(Pg. 102)

Todd Berliner is Associate Professor of Film Studies at the University of North Carolina Wilmington. His articles have appeared in *Film Quarterly, Cinema Journal, Journal of Film and Video, Style, Film International,* and the *Cambridge Film Handbook: Martin Scorsese's Raging Bull.* He spent the 2005-6 academic year as a Fulbright Scholar in Vietnam teaching American film at the Hanoi University of Theater and Cinema.

Joanna Blundell
(Pg. 153)

Joanna Blundell is a journalist from London. She works for the BBC and *The Daily Telegraph* newspaper and website, among other media. Her favorite memory of Asia is buzzing around the Angkor temples in Cambodia on a hair dryer motorbike.

She's always looking for the next adventure—at home or abroad.

Adam Bray
(Pg. 39, 77, 187, 209, 271)

Adam Bray is an American citizen and has lived in Phan Thiet, Vietnam, for more than two years. Formerly a primatologist working with chimps, bonobos, and orangutans, he is now a freelance web developer and writer. As well, he is a composer and has informal ties to the Vietnamese music scene.

www.muinebeach.net

Michael Brosowski
(Pg. 231)

Michael Brosowski is the founder and director of Vietnam's Blue Dragon Children's Foundation. He grew up in Australia, spending some years in Sydney and the rural northwest, before becoming an English teacher and gifted education coordinator. He lives in Hanoi with his extended family of street kids and two dogs.

www.bdcf.org

Charles W. Bruton, Jr.
(Pg. 235)

All his life, Bud Bruton has stepped forward to serve and to lead. After graduating from Washington & Jefferson College with an ROTC commission, he flew in Vietnam as a Forward Air Controller and was awarded the Distinguished Flying Cross, Air Medal with nineteen Oak Leaf Clusters, and a Bronze Star. He has been a trusted advisor to businesses and individuals

Selling vegetables on the steps of the Dalat Market

in Pennsylvania's Brandywine Valley for more than thirty years.

Michael Burr
(Pg. 35, 84, 156)

A native of New York with a BA in Art History, Michael Burr enlisted in the US Air Force in 1969 and was sent to Vietnam as an English language instructor to the Republic of Viet Nam Air Force. In December of 2003, he returned for the first time, and he now travels regularly to the region. He is a professional photographer and lives in Long Beach, California.

www.mburrphoto.com
www.printroom.compro/mburrphotos

Tom Chard
(Pg. 121, 124)

Tom Chard is a travel writer, novelist, tour guide, motorbike enthusiast, and general misfit. He funds these hobbies by working as a hospitality and customer service training consultant for five-star hotels worldwide. He has been based in Southeast Asia for six years and has no intention of leaving.

Samantha Coomber
(Pg. 68, 88, 91, 103, 245)

English freelance travel writer Samantha Coomber came to Vietnam in 1998 for a one-month backpacking trip, which turned into more than six years of living, working, and traveling in Vietnam. She is now based in Ho Chi Minh City, and her published credits include updating and researching *The Rough Guide*

to Vietnam and LUXE City Guides; co-founding, co-editing, and writing a governmental tourist magazine based in Hanoi; and writing the first edition *Insight Pocket Guide: Hanoi & Northern Vietnam.*

www.travelwriters.comsaigonsam

Richard Craik
(Pg. 181)

Born in Chester, UK, Richard Craik worked as a truck driver, graphic designer, bar manager, and English teacher, amongst other things, before settling in Vietnam, where he has worked in tourism since 1992. A keen birder, he recently combined this interest with his years of tourism experience to set up Vietnam Birding, which offers escorted birding tours. He lives in Ho Chi Minh City with his wife Lan and daughter Carmen.

www.vietnambirding.com

Ed Daniels
(Pg. 221)

A retired university administrator, Ed Daniels is also a Vietnam veteran who served in the US Army from 1967-68. Since 1993, he has visited Vietnam numerous times. He serves on the Board of Directors for the Veterans Viet Nam Restoration Project, an NGO program for Vietnam veterans wishing to heal from the emotional effects of the war. Making his home in Chico, California, he is married with two daughters.

Jennifer Davoli
(Pg. 23, 31, 144, 269)

Currently teaching world history and literature in Sao Paulo, Brazil, Jennifer Davoli worked with youth in poverty in New York's South Bronx for ten years and in Hanoi for a year. She was a Peace Corps volunteer in Uruguay and pursued her MA in Bilingual/Bicultural Education at Columbia University.

Linh Do
(Pg. 241)

Born in Vietnam, Linh Do immigrated to St. Louis, Missouri. She attended Stanford University and worked in management consulting, startups, and nonprofits in San Francisco. She pursued an MBA at Berkeley with the intention to do development work, and is grateful to now be involved in the work she loves *and* get to kitesurf at Mui Ne. Now living back in Vietnam, she encourages others to consider a profession in development work.

Alice Driver
(Pg. 36, 118, 178, 202)

Alice Driver spent a year working and traveling with her husband Isaac Bingham as he studied indigenous boat building in Vietnam, Thailand, Malaysia, New Zealand (Tokelau), Peru, Bolivia, and Ecuador. Next year she will finish her master's degree in Hispanic Studies at the University of Kentucky. Her first academic article appeared in the winter 2007 issue of *Romance Quarterly*.

www.savantsofthesea.com

Dan Duffy
(Pg. 264)

Dan Duffy is an anthropologist who works with Vietnamese authors. He helped start Harold Bloom's Chelsea House Library of Literary Criticism; assisted Kali Tal with Viet Nam Generation, Inc.; ran Yale's Viet Nam Forum series; worked in Hanoi as a consultant to *The Gioi* publishers; and mapped the Vietnamese bookstores of Paris. He now runs Viet Nam Literature Project.

www.vietnamlit.org

Duong Lam Anh
(Pg. 33, 115, 152, 201)

Duong Lam Anh was born and raised in the city of Hue in central Vietnam. He graduated from the College of Education at Hue University and pursued his graduate studies in Boston, Massachusetts. He likes traveling to explore new cultures and writing for magazines. Proud to be a Hue native, he enjoys writing about his hometown. Presently, he is a lecturer at Hue University's College of Foreign Languages.

http://duonglamanh.typepad.com

Thin Lei Win Elkin
(Pg. 41, 233, 251)

Yangon-born, Saigon-based Thin Lei Win Elkin is a food and travel enthusiast—with a particular interest in sustainable travel—who delights in sharing her latest finds, whether they be shopping tips or NGO adventure trips.

www.thin-ink.com

CONTRIBUTOR BIOGRAPHIES

Stephen Engle
(Pg. 27)

Seattle native Stephen Engle first went to China in 1990 to "fall off the face of the earth for a while." He's still tumbling. The charming rust belt of Manchuria was his dumping off spot. He has since lived in Japan, Taiwan, Guam, Singapore, Hong Kong, and Beijing, which he now calls home with his wife Jessica and daughter Yvette.

Lillian Forsyth
(Pg. 86, 133)

Lillian Forsyth grew up in St. Louis, Missouri, and received her BA in East Asian Languages and Cultures from Barnard College in New York City. She has been interested in Vietnam for several years and conducted thesis research about street children there. For the past year, she has been teaching English in An Giang through an American organization called Volunteers in Asia.

Renee Friedman
(Pg. 21, 28, 141, 199)

Born and bred in Brooklyn, New York, Renee Friedman finally followed her thumb out to an island on the west coast of Canada, where she presently resides and always returns after pursuing her first love—travel. She now teaches and enjoys gardening, reading, hiking, kayaking, and the spectacular view. Most of her time is spent mothering and smothering her daughter. She also occasionally indulges in her fantasy of being a writer, to which the essays in this book can attest.

Dominic Hong Duc Golding
(Pg. 54, 63, 126)

An adoptee from Vietnam, Dominic Golding is a playwright and performing artist based in Melbourne. While he makes his home in Australia, his soul and life's inspiration are rooted in his birth country. He has worked with the Vietnamese-Australian community in Melbourne on numerous productions. *Shrimp,* his play, was produced in 2005 for the Big West Festival and again in 2007, for the theatre touring program of Regional Arts Victoria. His poetry/photo blog documents his experiences in Vietnam.

http://dmztour.blogspot.com

Jeff Greenwald
(Pg. 161)

Oakland, California-based Jeff Greenwald is the author of five books, including *Shopping for Buddhas, The Size of the World,* and a recent anthology called *Scratching the Surface.* His work appears in *Wired, Tricycle,* and *Salon.com.* He is also the Executive Director of Ethical Traveler, a global alliance of travelers dedicated to social and environmental change. Jeff recently launched his stage career with a one-man show, "Strange Travel Suggestions."

www.ethicaltraveler.org
www.jeffgreenwald.com

Nicole Hankins
(Pg. 44)

Born in Vietnam, Nicole Hankins left in 1969 when she was six years old. Along with her family, she lived in Paris for ten years before settling in Southern California. She started traveling back to Vietnam in 1998 for work, and she grew keen to start a business in her birthplace. So she packed her bags, took all of her savings, and moved to Ho Chi Minh City in 2003 to launch Nutrifort, the country's first health and fitness company.

www.nutrifort.com

Jon Hoff
(Pg. 190, 217)

Jonathan Hoff was born in Bournemouth, England, in 1980. After graduating in 2001, he discovered the joys of travel and has lived and worked in Asia ever since. He now finds himself based in Ho Chi Minh City, where he somehow managed to pick up a wife.

http://itsthefinalword.blogspot.com

Emily Huckson
(Pg. 43, 176)

After spending far too many winters in her hometown in northern Ontario, Canada, Emily Huckson moved to Ho Chi Minh City in 1995 and has put all her underwear in one drawer. Apart from giving advice to numerous travelers in her "host" city, she is also involved in raising money for disabled children via "treading the boards" in theatrical productions. She has two cats, a fridge, and a hammock, so one can assume she is there for the duration.

Steve Jackson
(Pg. 229)

Steve Jackson spent two and a half years in Vietnam, where he worked as

a full-time volunteer for KOTO, a hospitality training center for street and disadvantaged youth. During his time there, he documented his experiences on the website *Our Man in Hanoi.*

www.ourmaninhanoi.com

Henno Kotze
(Pg. 211)

Henno Kotze grew up and went to school in Stellenbosch, South Africa. After graduating with honors in journalism from the University of Stellenbosch and a brief sojourn at a golf magazine in Cape Town, he made the leap to Vietnam in 2006, where he has been plying his trade ever since.

http://backwaterviews.blogspot.com

Chris Mitchell
(Pg. 142)

Chris Mitchell is a British travel writer based in Bangkok, Thailand. He edits the Asian travel site *Travel Happy* and the Asian scuba diving site *Dive Happy.*

http://travelhappy.info
http://divehappy.com

Tenley Mogk
(Pg. 19, 246)

Tenley Mogk is named after Olympic ice skater Tenley Albright. Tenley (Mogk) does not skate well, despite having grown up in freezing Michigan. She can, however, soar through the streets of Hanoi—her home for seven years—on a bicycle. Vocation: public health. Fascination: aging. Favorite food: avocadoes. She now lives in California, studying anatomy and selling ornaments made by recovering addicts in Vietnam.

www.littlebeadpeople.com

Marc Moynot
(Pg. 182, 189)

Business studies: big mistake. Crash helmet lessons: much better. Marc Moynot considers his best training was as a trekking guide and ski patroller in the French Alps for fifteen years. He moved to Vietnam in 1995 to work as a French teacher, and has been a chocolatier for the past six years. When he finds a little spare time, he goes hang gliding in Dalat.

www.chocolatsdefrance.com

Jessy Needham
(Pg. 56, 109, 125, 163, 204)

Jessy Needham has lived in Vietnam since 2003. For two years, she worked as a volunteer with Volunteers in Asia, teaching English in rural Bac Giang Province. After her teaching stint was through, she became a program officer at the Institute of International Education, administering scholarships for the Fulbright Program in Vietnam.

Nguyen Qui Duc
(Pg. 13)

Nguyen Qui Duc has more than twenty years of experience in international media. The author, translator, and editor of several books relating to Vietnam, he has lived and worked in the USA, Indonesia, the UK, and Morocco. He

now lives in Hanoi, where he is the Asia editor for KQED's *Pacific Time*, a national public radio program focusing on Asian affairs.

Kathrine Hee Nielsen
(Pg. 150)

Kathrine Hee Nielsen is a political science major from Denmark. She spends her spare time and money traveling in Asia ... or dreaming of it. She has enjoyed the expatriate life in Hanoi, but is currently based in the lovely Danish capital, Copenhagen.

Kelly O'Neil
(Pg. 237)

Kelly O'Neil lives with her husband and four adopted children in the hills outside of Portland, Oregon. Their household also contains four dogs, two guinea pigs, two gerbils, three hens, one rooster, and a species-identification-confused duck. In her copious free time, she loves to read and sleep.

Iris Opdebeeck
(Pg. 66, 168, 177)

Iris Opdebeeck was born in Mechelen, Belgium, where she worked and lived until the age of thirty-five. In April 2004, her husband Jan took an assignment for Procter & Gamble in Ho Chi Minh City, where they stayed for two and a half years. They then extended their adventures and moved to Chandigarh, India. Sharing a passion for travel and new cultures, she and Jan are now back in Belgium.

Pham Hoai Nam
(Pg. 213)

Pham Hoai Nam was born in Hanoi in the late 1960s and moved with his family to southern Vietnam almost thirty years ago. After working as a Russian language interpreter for twelve years, he tried his hand at pantomime, theater, music composition, painting, dancing, literature, and DJing. His most recent interest is photography. He lives in Ho Chi Minh City with his wife and daughter.

Hal Phillips
(Pg. 184)

Hal Phillips directs his media firm which serves clients in North America, Europe, and Southeast Asia. Hal reckons his barn, from whence he writes on sporting and travel matters, is the most cosmopolitan out-building in the Great State of Maine. Raised a Boston suburbanite, he never dreamed he'd own a barn, much less make his living in one, often dressed in nothing but a pair of Bermuda shorts. Said barn sits at the terminus of a long dirt road, where he resides with his wife Sharon and their two children, Silas and Clara.

www.mandarinmedia.net

Jan Polatschek
(Pg. 93)

Jan Polatschek was married before the Vietnam War began in earnest, so he received a deferment from the Selective Service System. In addition, his mother persuaded him to be a teacher, and she may have saved his life. Teachers were also exempt from the draft. He was apprehensive about his trip to Vietnam in 2003, but to his surprise, he was greeted with warmth and hospitality. From his new home in Bangkok, he plans his travels and edits his letters and photographs.

www.travelwithjan.com

Preyanka Clark Prakash
(Pg. 148, 265)

Preyanka Clark Prakash is a high school English teacher and graduate student living in Colorado. She is of American and Indian heritage, has lived in Thailand and India, and attended the United Nations International School of Hanoi for eight years until her graduation in 2000. She blogs about her experiences at *Dreaming of Hanoi.*

www.preyanka.com

Nick Pulley
(Pg. 96)

Nick Pulley's love affair with Southeast Asia began while traveling in the region during the early 1990s. Now suited and booted in his London office, he's almost unrecognizable from the Thai-dye days when he launched the first half moon parties on Koh Phan Ngan and went round saying "man" a lot. His passion for travel has taken him from the deserts of Namibia to the frozen tundra of the Canadian Arctic, but his heart has always remained firmly in Asia. In 2005, he founded Selective Asia, which offers privately guided, customized holidays.

www.selectiveasia.com

CONTRIBUTOR BIOGRAPHIES

CONTRIBUTOR BIOGRAPHIES

Elka Ray
(Pg. 22, 128, 224)

Born in England and raised in Canada, Elka Ray has spent the past eleven years in Vietnam, working as a free-lance writer and editor. Elka now lives in Ho Chi Minh City with her husband, baby son, and two cats—both of which have fallen six stories and survived.

Graham Roemmele
(Pg. 173)

Fuelled by a trip through Southeast Asia, Graham Roemmele left the blighted shores of Wales and moved to Thailand in 2002, searching for new adventures and experiences. Currently working as an English teacher in Bangkok, Graham often escapes the city to photograph and write about his travels throughout the region.

http://gromily.blogspot.com
www.lightstalkers.org/graham_roem
mele

Dana Sachs
(Pg. 279)

Dana Sachs is the author of *The House on Dream Street: Memoir of an American Woman in Vietnam* and the novel *If You Lived Here*. Her articles have appeared in many publications, including *National Geographic*, *Travel + Leisure Family*, and *The International Herald Tribune*. In 2006, as a Fulbright Scholar in Hanoi, she conducted research for a book on Operation Babylift, the US-sponsored evacuation of displaced children at the end of the war in Vietnam.

www.danasachs.com

Simone Samuels
(Pg. 58, 101, 107, 146, 166, 197)

Simone Samuels has journeyed and lived abroad in many places, but no place has captured her heart as much as Vietnam. Originally from Brisbane, Australia, she now makes her home away from home in Hanoi, where she and her partner regularly update their blog, *Vagabonding*. Simone has a journalism background and became a dedicated English teacher and teacher trainer as a way to fund her even greater passions for traveling, writing, photography, and studying languages.

www.getjealous.com/sim.mal

Margaret Scott
(Pg. 247)

Margaret Scott attended UC Berkeley during the height of the war in Vietnam. That experience led to her life-long interest in cultures and a commitment to seeking a just and equitable world. She spends her time reading, writing, hiking California trails, and planning her next adventure.

Antoine Sirot
(Pg. 74, 208)

Since 1993, Antoine Sirot has managed hotels for the Accor Group in Indonesia, Thailand, and as of 2002, Vietnam at the Sofitel Dalat Palace. The history of former colonies is not well taught in France and is even still a taboo. Having to answer many inquiries on the history of Dalat, Antoine has undertaken in-depth research, mostly through French writings from various historical works, but also by gathering testimonies of elderly hotel guests who lived in Dalat in the old days.

Marianne Smallwood
(Pg. 105, 219)

An American raised by a Vietnamese father and Filipina mother, Marianne Smallwood left the corporate world in 2006 and moved to Vietnam to reconnect with her paternal roots. Currently working at an NGO in Hanoi, she plans to continue her career within Southeast Asian economic development. Marianne can be regularly seen at Café Mai.

Joe Springer-Miller
(Pg. 30, 117, 120, 243)

A native of Vermont, Joe Springer-Miller moved to Japan in 1993 to teach for the federal government there. In the same year he made his first visit to Vietnam, and he moved to Ho Chi Minh City in 2002 to start and coordinate a bilingual program for the Korean consular school. He also worked for International SOS; has been involved with the local arts, business, and consular communities; and is a founding member of Saigon Players, a local theater group

Lorene Strand
(Pg. 82, 130, 206)

As the stepdaughter of a Vietnam veteran, Lorene Strand has always been captivated by Vietnam; she first toured the country in 1998. In 2001 she moved to Vietnam, first living in Dalat and later Ho Chi Minh City. Returning "home" to the States in 2006, she is currently on a quest to find the best Vietnamese restaurant in America. She welcomes your suggestions.

lorene_strand@hotmail.com

James Sullivan
(Pg. 72, 79, 113)

James Sullivan is the author of *Over The Moat*, a memoir of courtship in Vietnam that *The Boston Globe* celebrated as "near-perfect" and the *Washington Post* hailed as "an essential entry in the canon of expatriate literature." After graduating from the Iowa Writer's Workshop with a James Michener Fellowship in 1992, he bicycled without escort up National Highway 1 from Ho Chi Minh City to Hanoi. He has written travel features for *National Geographic Traveler*, *The New York Times,* and other leading publications.

To Hanh Trinh
(Pg. 17)

Born in Hanoi, To Hanh Trinh earned a BA in teaching English at the secondary school level. From 1985-1999, she worked for the Department of Mining and Geology, PetroVietnam, and British Petroleum. In 2002, she opened Wild Rice restaurant with two longtime friends and partners. This venture was followed by Moon River Retreat in 2003 and Wild Lotus restaurant in 2005. Painting, photography, and decorating are among her hobbies. Married with two daughters, she lives in Hanoi.

Jan Vail
(Pg. 216)

An international bon vivant, raconteur, and man of mystery, Jan Vail has traveled the world in first and business class, stayed in five-star hotels, and wined and dined in the finest restaurants on the globe ... all under the guise of work. As the old saying goes, "Someone has to do it." Whilst pursuing these worldly pleasures, he has managed to have sufficient success in enough endeavors to convince others to perpetuate his lifestyle with a succession of consulting projects around the world.

Vu Kieu Linh
(Pg. 196)

Born in Hanoi, Vu Kieu Linh left for Europe when she was eleven. She moved back to Vietnam in 1996 to undertake her BA and then went to Singapore for her MBA from 2003-05. She is currently working as a Public Relations Manager for a multinational corporation in Vietnam. She admits that she didn't realize her love for her hometown until recently, when she returned for a business trip. She writes her own blog, and some of her entries are published in Vietnam's well-known magazines.

Christine Thuy-Anh Vu
(Pg. 15, 51)

Christine Thuy-Anh Vu writes and edits work about the arts, culture, and science. Serving as art advisor to several international collections, she has also been an executive director to a Vietnam-based international arts organization. A Fulbright Fellow in Contemporary Vietnamese Art, she has received other honors and fellowships for her research in Europe and the USA in psychology, gastronomy, and contemporary art.

Ray Waddington
(Pg. 61)

Ray Waddington is the president of The Peoples of the World Foundation, a secular, apolitical, non-profit organization based in the USA. He established the foundation to fund educational scholarships for indigenous people after witnessing their lack of educational opportunities and the negative impact this has on political representation. He recently celebrated his one-millionth kilometer of international travel and is preparing a travel/humor book based on his experiences.

www.peoplesoftheworld.org

Tyler Watts
(Pg. 131, 214)

Tyler Watts is currently participating in his third year with the California-based organization Volunteers in Asia. He lived in the Mekong Delta region for two years, teaching English language and literature courses at An Giang University. He now resides in Hue, but his heart remains in the south of Vietnam.

Sue Wise
(Pg. 250)

After working for a company for fifteen years, making profits for the owners, Sue Wise decided it was time to give back and is now working as a volunteer for the non-profit organization Vietnam Quilts. She has recently moved to Hanoi to set up the organization's second retail outlet. After realizing that a little help goes a long way in less developed countries, she will find it hard to return to Australia and resume working for someone else's benefit.

Paul Young
(Pg. 170)

Paul Young has spent the past few years living and teaching ESL in South Korea. When on holiday, he can be found either back home in his native Canada or exploring Southeast Asia looking for some fun in the sun on the beach with a bottle of sunscreen. He currently maintains *Oriental Tales*, an online travel magazine featuring stories of travel and adventure in Asia.

www.orientaltales.com

CREDITS

"Alice Driver paddles a bamboo coracle at China Beach" reprinted in an edited form from "Reflections on the Vietnamese Bamboo Coracle: China Beach, Vietnam," originally published at *Free World Group* (www.freeworldgroup.com). Reprinted by permission of the author. Copyright © 2007 by Alice Driver.

"Charles W. Bruton, Jr. makes peace with Vietnam in the DMZ" reprinted in an edited form from "Letter to VVRP," originally published at Veterans Viet Nam Restoration Project (www.vvrp.org). Reprinted by permission of the author. Copyright © by Charles W. Bruton, Jr.

"Duong Lam Anh finds beauty in Hue's gray winter days" reprinted in an edited form from "Winter in Hue," originally published at *Duong Lam Anh: My Outlook on Life* (http://duonglamanh.typepad.com). Reprinted by permission of the author. Copyright © 2007 by Duong Lam Anh.

"Duong Lam Anh gets more than he bargained for in Hue" reprinted in an edited form from "Bargaining," originally published at *Duong Lam Anh: My Outlook on Life* (http://duonglamanh.typepad.com). Reprinted by permission of the author. Copyright © 2006 by Duong Lam Anh.

"Elka Ray finds a strange new world in Ho Chi Minh City" reprinted in an edited form from "Phu My Hung: A Strange New World," originally published in *Heritage Fashion*. Reprinted by permission of the author. Copyright © 2007 by Elka Ray.

"Graham Roemmele motors full throttle in northern Vietnam" excerpted in an edited form from "Full Throttle," originally published in *Untamed Travel*. Reprinted by permission of the author. Copyright © by Graham Roemmele.

"James Sullivan travels back to Dalat's gracious beginnings" excerpted in an edited form from "French Twist," originally published in *DestinAsian*. Reprinted by permission of the author. Copyright © 2007 by James Sullivan.

"Jan Polatschek discovers love and the American war" excerpted in an edited form from "In Country: Love and the American War," originally published at *Travel with Jan* (www.travelwithjan.com). Reprinted by permission of the author. Copyright © 2003 by Jan Polatschek.

"Jeff Greenwald stalks the elusive langur of Cat Ba Island" excerpted from "Valley of the Langurs," originally published at *Seacology* (www.seacology.com). Reprinted by permission of the author. Copyright © 2006 by Jeff Greenwald.

"Joanna Blundell falls into a shopping frenzy in Hoi An" excerpted in an edited form from "Shopping for Exotica in Vietnam," originally published at *Student Traveler* (www.studenttraveler.com). Reprinted by permission of the author. Copyright © 2006 by Joanna Blundell.

"Jon Hoff embarks on an everyday journey in Ho Chi Minh City" reprinted in an edited form from "An Everyday Journey," originally published at *The Final Word ... in Saigon* (http://itsthefinalword.blogspot.com). Reprinted by permission of the author. Copyright © 2007 by Jon Hoff.

"Lillian Forsyth interprets "crowded is happy" in Tra Vinh" reprinted in an edited form from "The beach, and everything is vui," originally published at *Hang Ngay* (http://li11ian11.wordpress.com). Reprinted by permission of the author. Copyright © 2007 by Lillian Forsyth.

"Nguyen Qui Duc obsesses about *bun cha* in Hanoi" excerpted in an edited form from "The *Bun Cha* Obsession," originally published at *ThingsAsian* (www.thingsasian.com). Reprinted by permission of the author. Copyright © 1995 by Nguyen Qui Duc.

"Paul Young climbs to Vietnam's highest point" excerpted in an edited form from "Climbing Fansipan," originally published at *Oriental Tales* (www.orientaltales.com). Reprinted by permission of the author. Copyright © by Paul Young.

"Samantha Coomber reflects on life and death in Ba Chuc" reprinted in an edited form from "Across the River and Into Hell," originally published in *Vietnam Adventures* (www.vietnamadventures.com). Reprinted by permission of the author. Copyright © by Samantha Coomber.

INDEX *(side tab: INDEX)*

INDEX

EDITOR AND PHOTOGRAPHER PROFILES

Kim Fay

Julie Fay Ashborn

Pacific Northwest native Kim Fay first traveled to Southeast Asia in 1991. Since then, she spent four years living in Vietnam and has traveled back frequently, writing about the region. She is the creator and series editor of the *To Asia With Love* guidebooks, and the author of *Communion: A Culinary Journey Through Vietnam*. She resides in Los Angeles. www.kimfay.net

Julie Fay Ashborn's travels through Southeast Asia inspired her photography in *To Asia With Love*, *The Little Saigon Cookbook*, and *Communion: A Culinary Journey through Vietnam*. Other favorite subjects include architecture and retro motel signs. As well as being a photographer, she works in the film industry. She was raised in the Pacific Northwest and now splits her time between Los Angeles and London with her husband Clive and daughter Charlie. To view more of her photography, go to www.juleprints.com.